Dance and Politics

DANCE AND POLITICS

Alexandra Kolb (ed.)

PETER LANG

Oxford · Bern · Berlin · Bruxelles · Frankfurt am Main · New York · Wien

Bibliographic information published by Die Deutsche Nationalbibliothek
Die Deutsche Nationalbibliothek lists this publication in the Deutsche Nationalbibliografie;
detailed bibliographic data is available on the Internet at http://dnb.d-nb.de.

A catalogue record for this book is available from the British Library.

Library of Congress Cataloging-in-Publication Data:

Dance and politics / [compiled by] Alexandra Kolb.
    p. cm.
  Includes bibliographical references and index.
  ISBN 978-3-03911-848-9 (alk. paper)
  1. Dance--Political aspects. 2. Dance--Social aspects. I. Kolb,
Alexandra.
  GV1588.45.D36 2010
  306.4'846--dc22
                            2010032377

ISBN 978-3-03911-848-9

Cover photograph: *Underground* (2006) by David Dorfman. David Dorfman Dance.
Photograph: Gary Noel. Courtesy of the photographer.

© Peter Lang AG, International Academic Publishers, Bern 2011
Hochfeldstrasse 32, CH-3012 Bern, Switzerland
info@peterlang.com, www.peterlang.com, www.peterlang.net

Contents

List of Figures

Acknowledgements

I should foremost like to express my thanks to the contributors to this book. The invaluable expertise, enthusiasm and patience they brought to this project have been instrumental in shaping this, in my view, much-needed collection on the relationship between dance and politics.

For financial support I offer thanks to the University of Otago whose research grant made this project possible in the first place. The School of Physical Education, the Dean Douglas Booth and my colleagues in the Dance Studies Programme have been very supportive.

For his advice and unwavering support at all stages of the work I thank Luke Purshouse. My appreciation also goes to Shanon O'Sullivan who has been my research assistant; her efforts to research, administer and facilitate parts of the project were marvellous. Thanks must also go to August Obermayer who provided the translations of the German texts and whose expert advice on matters German has been much appreciated. I should not forget to mention my colleague Glenn Braid's gracious general and editorial assistance.

I would also like to express gratitude to the artists who have allowed me to interview them: notably David Dorfman, Johann Kresnik and Steve Paxton. Thanks also to the various scholars who have offered comments or advice on earlier drafts of contributions and who are named in individual chapters. I am grateful to Graham Speake from Peter Lang for his very professional help in bringing the book together.

Finally, I thank those who have not been directly implicated in the book project *per se* but who have sustained me with their intellectual discussions, affection and hospitality: my friends in Dunedin and various locations around the world. They definitely made the time working on this book more enjoyable. Without them, it would have been completed sooner.

About this Book

Dance and Politics is the first collection to investigate the intricate relation-ships between dance and politics across a range of topics. It examines crises such as wars and revolutions as choreographic subject matter, and explores artistic activism and the portrayal of nationalism and class. It addresses the compatibility of, and choreographic perspectives on, dance and terrorism, and looks at the ramifications of cultural policy on dance production. The multi-layered crosscurrents of dance and politics raise further questions: Are civil and human rights fostered or denied through dance? How are ideologies at both ends of the political spectrum expressed in and through dance, for instance fascism and communism? How do choreographers express their protest against such ideologies? Is a dance which does not make explicit political statements consequently apolitical? These are just some elements of a rich kaleidoscope that illuminate the mutuality of dance and dance studies on one hand, and political thought and action, on the other.

Having researched, taught and published on topics related to dance and politics for several years, I was aware that a book addressing the various facets of these connections was much needed. This book fills an obvious gap in existing literature, and working on it has been an exciting process for all involved. The articles in this volume are original, previously unpublished texts in the English language.

Obvious choices had to be made concerning what to include. Clearly, there are other political implications of dance well worth exploring, such as gender, race and disability. Many of them constitute significant fields of enquiry in their own right and have recently been well researched. As is obvious from the above list, this book concerns the implications of dance in the explicitly political realm (though admittedly, it is difficult to attempt a definition of 'politics' given its fluid boundaries, as I address in my introductory Chapter 1 below). The collection centres predominantly on twentieth- and early twenty-first-century Western stage dance, although some articles allude to developments outside and beyond it. Maintaining this primary focus for the anthology has, I believe, helped make it a meaningful and coherent entity.

This book is structured as follows. The individual contributions are preceded by an introduction which gives an overview of current thinking about dance and politics and an outline of attempts by choreographers to tackle a wide range of political subject matters. I initially agonised over whether to merge the synthesis of the research chapters and the introduction, but ultimately decided to keep them as separate sections so that each could be read independently. The remainder of the book is divided into four sections, each comprising three contributions linked by overlapping themes.

Part I – *Choreographing the Revolution* – is broadly focused on the capacity of dance, and dance analysis, to communicate political ideas of a left-wing or anti-establishment character.

Roger Copeland's controversial 'state-of-the-art' critique of recent developments in dance studies draws heavily on both literary theory and twentieth-century ideological developments. He takes issue with current tendencies in dance research to promote works created through collective endeavour – often in community contexts – at the expense of individually choreographed pieces and to view notions of artistic or authorial 'genius' with suspicion. As Copeland argues, these trends are the products of a misguided association of individual authorship with the economic individualism of post-industrial Western societies and even with the values of new-right conservatism. Defending the capacity of modernist sole-authored choreography to deliver social criticism of a progressive or anti-establishment nature, Copeland demonstrates how some folk and traditional dance styles can be employed to reactionary ends, casting further doubt on their privileged status in recent dance theory. He combines these arguments with a more general broadside against the alleged 'academicising' of politics by a liberal intelligentsia which has, on Copeland's account, supplanted genuine activism and protest with introspection, symbolism and gesture.

In 2008 I interviewed the Marxist Austrian choreographer Johann Kresnik, who in this discussion details his involvement in the left-wing activist circles of 1960s West Germany, and explains how this background helped shape his development as a creative artist. He comments on a range of political issues addressed in his choreographies, from American global dominance to the former communist regime in East Germany; and discusses the personalities his works have depicted, such as the anarchist Red Army Faction campaigner Ulrike Meinhof and the conservative German Chancellor Helmut Kohl. Touching on the controversy aroused by some of his more incendiary pieces, Kresnik's remarks articulate his view that dance – and art in general – is duty-bound to engage with real-world issues and address matters of social relevance, rather than retreating into a formalism which over-emphasises surface appearance and technique. He concludes with an outlook on prospects for the European dance scene, speculating on possible themes for future choreographic treatment.

My own article uses one of Kresnik's most famous pieces – *Ulrike Meinhof* (1990) – alongside the American artist David Dorfman's *Underground* (2006) to examine how these choreographers tackle the highly contentious subject of anti-state terrorism. Taking recourse to Frankfurt-school theorists who question the boundaries between the aesthetic and political, I suggest that just as terrorist acts may have theatrical properties, so certain theatre dance works aim to shock and frighten their audiences into greater awareness of social and political reality. While Kresnik openly sympathises with the aims of his protagonist and offers a grotesque and harrowing depiction of the capitalist society that Meinhof sought to undermine, Dorfman's portrayal of historical events is more opaque – although his discourse against political apathy is clearly expressed through speech as well as bodily movement and other visual media. Moreover, while both works are ostensibly about the far-left movements of the 1960s and 1970s – the German RAF and US Weathermen respectively – both artists allude to more recent developments in their countries, namely, German re-unification and American neo-conservatism under George W. Bush.

Part II of the book – *Dance of Enemies* – comprises three articles which relate dance to the major conflict of twentieth-century ideologies which culminated in World War II. Two of them concern dance developments in Weimar and Nazi Germany; the third in wartime America.

Marion Kant's contribution offers a political perspective on the leading German Modern Dance exponent, Mary Wigman. She shows how Wigman eschewed any explicit political references in her writings or choreography, often holding her status as an artist to be 'beyond' the political realm and preferring to engage with questions of a spiritual or meta-personal nature. However, Kant also demonstrates how we might detect definite right-wing or indeed fascist sympathies in her approach to group dynamics, which espoused a collective 'choric' identity bound together under strong leadership; and even more so in her nationalist yearning for a renewal of German culture, to which end she used dance as a medium. During the period of the Third Reich, moreover, Wigman willingly collaborated with the Nazi regime, even sympathising to some extent with its anti-semitic principles. Kant argues that despite her profession of an apolitical artistic œuvre, Wigman in fact adhered to 'an ideology based on Nietzschean categories and ideas' in a life 'permeated' by political influences.

Gunhild Oberzaucher-Schüller has pieced together a detailed account, based on little-known primary sources, of National Socialist (i.e. Nazi) policies towards dance, in particular its stage varieties. She outlines the efforts of the Hitler regime to co-ordinate the diverse range of pre-existing dance practices under a single administrative and ideological framework. Viewing dance as 'a manifestation of a healthy expression of the people' with potential to express the German character, the Nazis condemned both the individualism of many expressive choreographers and the international flavour of traditional ballet. Schüller explains how a new genre known as 'German ballet' emerged under fascist rule, focusing on easy accessibility and the incorporation of folk or popular cultural elements. Strict stipulations were imposed regarding plot, music and movement vocabulary, aimed at ensuring conformity with the party's ideological precepts, for instance with respect to leadership, nationalism and the division of gender roles. Collating an array of reviews and commentaries on relevant works, Schüller concludes by noting a marked continuity between the repertoires performed during the Nazi period and thereafter, particularly in eastern Germany.

Turning to the Allied side of World War II, Stacey Prickett presents a politically based analysis of dance developments in early 1940s America. Her principal theme is the tendency among left-wing US artists, who in other contexts might have criticised their government or followed anti-war agendas, to lend active support to the country's fight against fascism. The examples Prickett discusses include social dance activities organised for soldiers and civilians and the socially affirmative and patriotic wartime choreographies of the Dudley-Maslow-Bales Trio and José Limón, who when conscripted by the army arranged dance shows for and involving military personnel. These dancers' celebrations of American values of freedom and democracy at a time of national crisis – driven largely, no doubt, by their overriding antipathy to the Nazi enemy – contrasts notably with the socially critical deployment of dance during other periods in the US and elsewhere (as addressed by other contributors to this book).

Part III – *Dancers, Rights and Wrongs* – addresses recent political concerns around notions of human rights and more specifically the 'war on terror' prosecuted by the US after 9/11. These topics are conceptually linked insofar as the latter raised questions about the legitimacy of state-sponsored violence, the (mis)treatment of 'enemy' combatants and the trade-off between national security and the protection of civil liberties.

Naomi M. Jackson's paper theorises and illustrates a wide range of connections between dance and human rights. She begins with the right to dance itself, analysing ethical and legal grounds for its protection and considering several instances of its restriction by national governments. Notwithstanding that dance is often associated with the free expression of the individual self, Jackson notes how its potential has been exploited by autocratic regimes seeking to strengthen their grip on power. Subsequent discussions focus on the use of dance as therapy for those suffering from the impact of human rights abuses and its more explicitly political function of protesting against oppressive policies and regimes. Jackson's conclusion that dance has an ambivalent status in respect to rights – figuring in different contexts as either their advocate or their opponent – is backed by a plethora of examples rooted in diverse cultures and periods of history: from nineteenth-century Canada, via twentieth-century Chile and Zaire, to present-day Iran.

In the book's second contribution by a contemporary choreographer, Victoria Marks presents a personal literary angle on her own work *Not About Iraq* (2007). Interweaving criticism of the Bush government with reminiscences of the piece's creative process and broader reflections about the functions of dance, Marks refuses to give a definitive interpretation of her choreography but insists that it can convey different messages – political or otherwise – depending on the viewer's perspective. Not 'directly' meant as a comment on the Iraq war, it might nonetheless be seen to raise closely related issues such as race, power and the (ab)use of information by those in office.

Suzanne Little's paper likewise centres on a specific dance work: *Black Milk* (2006), by the New Zealand choreographer Douglas Wright. Little provides a comprehensive analysis and critique of Wright's treatment of issues of torture and sexual abuse, focusing on his extended dance sequence inspired by the much-publicised atrocities committed and photographed by US guards in Abu Graibh prison in 2004. A major public-relations blow for supporters of the Iraq invasion at the time, Little questions the overall effectiveness of representing these distressing events in a performing arts context. She argues that notwithstanding Wright's worthy intentions to expose and condemn the horrors perpetrated in America's name, his piece runs the risk of reinscribing the original actions and their widely disseminated imagery, while possibly desensitising audiences to this 'traumatic real' event through a version of catharsis.

The final trio of articles in Part IV – *Dancing to Market Forces* – refer in diverse ways to the development and impact of neo-liberal economics since the latter half of the twentieth century.

The first, by Ramsay Burt, marks an overlap with the preceding section in that it observes two (arguably) related political issues – the Iraq war and the rise of global capitalism – through lenses moulded by contemporary dance makers Anne Teresa de Keersmaeker and Tino Sehgal. Burt shows how de Keersmaeker's solo *Once* (2002) draws on the 1960s protest music of Joan Baez and Bob Dylan to deliver a discomforting choreographic warning over the then-ongoing preparations for war in the Middle East. Sehgal's installation-work *Instead of allowing something to rise…* (2000) captures feelings of alienation and social exclusion which are by-products of modern consumerist culture. Both pieces, according to Burt, express affective states of vulnerability and powerlessness, employing dance to articulate passions and perspectives which the Western socio-political climate has tended to suppress.

Soo Hee Lee and Tatjana E. Byrne give a comparative analysis of the socio-economic implications of recent government policies towards the dance sectors in the UK and Germany respectively. The more market-driven British model, they argue, has led to a flourishing of commercialism and sponsorship at the price of endangering dance's status as a serious creative art form. Moreover, a focus on purely instrumental benefits of dance – for instance as an didactic or therapeutic tool – allied to a managerial discourse emphasising efficiency and target-setting, has undermined artistic elitism but also compromised innovation and aesthetic values. In Germany, greater commitments to the integrity of the arts and to public funding have helped maintain creative standards within a relatively autonomous 'art dance' sector, although historically the power of the regions (Länder) has hindered a unified approach and recent years have seen significant cuts to budgets. While Lee and Byrne conclude that both systems could learn from each other's strengths, they evince concern over what they see as the UK's current 'policy vacuum' and hint at a need for more Europe-wide collaboration in this sphere.

The book concludes with Luke Purshouse's discussion of the popular film and stage-musical *Billy Elliot*, with its presentation of a story of classical ballet set against the backdrop of a working-class community during the 1984 British coalminers' strike. Purshouse examines how the author, Lee Hall, approaches the vexed questions of ballet's perceived elitism and class associations and delivers a poignant critique of Margaret Thatcher's radical market-based reforms of the UK economy and society during the 1980s. While *Billy Elliot* carries a strong message of support for personal ambition and self-expression, delivered through the title-character's successful – albeit unconventional – pursuit of a career in dance, Hall's sympathies clearly lie with the lives and communities left behind in Thatcherism's fiercely competitive and arguably atomistic social model. Purshouse's reading of the screenplay outlines different conceptions of the relationship between the individual and community which are explored in the work and their reverberations in the political discourse of the period.

ALEXANDRA KOLB

1 Cross-Currents of Dance and Politics: An Introduction

After all, dancing has no other purpose but to display beautiful bodies in
graceful poses and develop lines that are pleasing to the eye.
— THÉOPHILE GAUTIER 1837

It's remarkable how prevalent is the assumption that dance draws up its
skirts in panicked withdrawal from anything resembling real life.
— JUDITH MACKRELL 2004

If we believe the cultural theorist Jean Baudrillard, in contemporary society
everything has become political and therefore nothing is political.[1] When
categories such as the political or the aesthetic are generalised to the greatest
possible extent, they lose their specificities and become utterly interchange-
able (1999: 9). Baudrillard complains that the political sphere has become
'increasingly transparent: the more it distends, the more it virtually ceases
to exist. When everything is political, that is the end of politics as destiny:
it is the beginning of politics as culture and the immediate poverty of that
cultural politics' (1997).

This notion of the 'political' (as a category) becoming vacuous due to
its excessive proliferation can also be observed in the field of dance studies.
Here, the ubiquity of the buzzword 'politics' is evident in titles which refer
to the politics of the 'body', 'identity' or 'preservation'. For sure, the axis of

---

1   I am particularly indebted to Roger Copeland who provided valuable advice on a
     previous draft of this paper, and gratefully acknowledge further comments from
     Stacey Prickett and Jonathan Marshall.

gender politics, race and nation has justifiably attracted a lot of academic attention in the last thirty years, and it should be noted that alongside publications which incorporate the word 'politics' in their title without being, strictly speaking, about Politics with a capital 'P', there are various scholarly texts addressing political issues in a more familiar sense. Their topics range from street demonstrations and Cold War dance politics, to protest culture and human rights.[2]

It is noteworthy, however, that the emphasis on political agendas extends even to the analysis of expressly or intentionally non-political dance works. Roger Copeland has written in his article 'In Defence of Formalism' that the interpretation of abstract, formalist choreographies in ideological terms has become strikingly fashionable since the 1980s. He attributes

---

2   In his recent book chapter on 'Dance and the Political', Mark Franko writes that dance 'does not operate directly in the political sphere, and thus is not strictly speaking political'. Franko argues that it is 'ideological', carrying 'inevitable political effects for this reason' (2007: 14). This raises several intriguing questions. First, as Baudrillard suggests, it is next-to-impossible to define the 'political sphere'. We can no longer work on the assumption that politics is tightly defined, but especially since the 1960s and the assertion that the private is the political (which challenged assumptions that the private sphere is not implicated in networks of power), the notion of politics has become much more fluid and open-ended. In fact, it has moved closer to the category of 'ideological' which Franko prefers in application to dance. Secondly, perhaps Franko is saying that true political engagement is limited to the sphere of 'real' politics – that of government, legislation, elections and so on – rather than merely 'represented' politics in a theatrical context. Of course, no-one would claim that the only way dance could operate 'directly in the political sphere' was by dancers actually pirouetting in, say, a house of parliament or congress. However, dance's operation in, and productive interaction with, the political arena is illustrated by numerous examples: for instance through politically-informed choreographies which express similar stances to more traditional forms of political opinion-voicing. The mere fact that numerous communities, states, or other administrative entities have chosen either to promote, or clamp down on, specific dance forms suggests that they take dance seriously as a medium of political utterance and rhetoric. And dancers have sometimes intervened directly in politics as a unified group outside of theatres, for instance in strikes and demonstrations; for example, the *Dancers for Disarmament*, founded in 1981, voiced their anti-nuclear concerns in major protest marches in New York.

the view that all art is necessarily ideological to post-structuralism and the utilitarianism of that decade. However, he sounds a note of caution:

> To say that all art is in some sense political [...] is not at all the same as concluding that art is nothing but political. Indeed, to reduce works of art to their content (political or otherwise) is to lose sight of what makes them works of art, rather than some other form of expression. (1990: 7)

Hence, such approaches to art works neglect their intrinsic and unique qualities: those which make an art work an art work, such as (among others) qualities of form, structure and line.

While Copeland is concerned about the loss of art works' unique aesthetic qualities (where art is completely absorbed into the political, a view not dissimilar to Baudrillard's), another performance theorist, Baz Kershaw, argues that the collapse of the traditional binary opposition of aesthetics and politics means it has become virtually impossible to evaluate the political importance or substance of individual performances. In other words, if *all* art is regarded as political in some broad sense of the word, then we lose any meaningful measure by which to deem certain works 'more' political than others. As Kershaw himself puts it, the 'democratisation' of the political has resulted in:

> an increasing sensitivity to the ways in which – *pace* Foucault – power relations are embedded in all cultural practices, including those of theatre and performance. What is lost is a stable set of concepts that would enable us to identify once and for all the ideological or political significance of any particular performance text or practice in any context. A performance that could be considered radical or revolutionary or progressive in one place or perspective might be seen as quite the opposite in another. This profound destabilisation of tradition threatens to cast theatre adrift in a constantly shifting sea of 'political' perspectives on performance. (1999: 68–69)[3]

The prominence of the political in research on dance (and even more so in theatre studies) seems astounding given that theatres in our pluralistic society have arguably lost their politicised, clearly defined target

---

3   Kershaw attributes this phenomenon to globalisation and the 'explosion of theory' (1999: 67).

audiences, such as the revolutionary proletariat, which was key to the 1930s workers' dance groups as well as Bertolt Brecht's and Erwin Piscator's politically motivated theatre; and perhaps the revolutionary youth in the 1960s, when performances were explicitly directed against capitalism, imperialism and the bourgeoisie. The later part of the twentieth century, as Baudrillard lamented in a *Le Monde* article (2001), was characterised by great *ennui*, deplete with historical and political energy, 'stagnant' and banal (a situation only eventually but all the more forcefully ruptured by 9/11). Moreover, the emphasis on the political in dance studies appears at odds with the oft-cited public disillusionment with politics in recent years. A number of publications – both coffee-table books and scholarly texts – on phenomena such as political apathy and the dearth of alternative social ideals following the collapse of Soviet-style communism and the fall of the Berlin Wall testify to this lack of interest.

While we may now argue about whether dance, like other art forms, necessarily has a political or ideological message, historically speaking the main debate was over whether dance *should* be political. The tension between dance's potential or actual socio-political uses and *l'art pour l'art*, which (in outline) is the view that art is an autonomous entity free of any extrinsic functions, has been discussed in various academic and artistic circles and remains an important factor in dance scholarship and practice, as we shall see below. The view that art should serve practical purposes dates back to Plato, who indeed appears to contend, in *The Laws*, that it is *only* valuable insofar as it serves a political, educational or moral function. Dance can help human beings to acquire virtue, i.e. represent them as, and turn them into, good citizens or useful soldiers. If the concept of 'goodness' is grasped in singing and dancing, 'we have also a sound criterion for distinguishing the educated man from the uneducated' (54d). War dances, 'which portray fine physiques and noble characters, reflect military virtues' (815a).

On the other hand, the philosopher Immanuel Kant's view is inextricably linked with the perception of art in autonomous terms. The concept of the autonomy of art, in a strict sense, holds that the evaluation of an art work *as* an art work must be on the basis of its intrinsic value alone. Such an assessment presupposes a spectator's contemplation of the work's artistic or aesthetic properties as the only relevant standpoint, excluding other criteria for judgement – in particular instrumental values such as morality or the production of knowledge. An aesthetic response is based on what Kant (in his *Critique of Judgment*) terms 'disinterested interest', which means that the pleasure one derives from it is contemplative and must not satisfy subjective desires or appetites. Beauty engenders pleasurable feelings that are distinct from other forms of pleasure (such as the appreciation of good food, or moral approval of someone's actions) because they do not involve taking an egoistic or practical view of the object's qualities. Kant's views on art resonate in the influential French writer and dance critic Théophile Gautier: opposing, like Kant, the idea of art serving extrinsic social ends, he writes in the preface to his 1835 work *Mademoiselle de Maupin*: 'Nothing is truly beautiful except that which can serve for nothing: whatever is useful is ugly' (Gautier 1979: 57).

We find variations on this in the twentieth century. Arlene Croce's dictum against 'victim art' in her 1994 article 'Discussing the Undiscussable', which was a refusal to attend and review Bill T. Jones's piece *Still/Here* about terminal illnesses such as AIDS, is perhaps the best known example. Croce, a long-serving critic for *The New Yorker* magazine, maligned the choreography's use of audio and video tapes of real people, as opposed to actors, suffering from such illnesses as 'intolerably voyeuristic' and attacked this art as 'utilitarian' and 'socially useful' (2000: 711). Her article provoked hostile tirades with accusations ranging from political incorrectness to homophobia, and kicked off a wide-reaching public debate which actually vindicated the political relevance of dance, or more specifically dance criticism. The article also, however, earned Croce an Aristos[4] award for 'exemplary human achievement'; the praise published on the Internet asserts that she 'rightly chides Jones for "cross[ing] the line between theater and reality" and thereby ignoring the fundamental distinction between the two' (Aristos awards, undated). In more recent interviews, Croce has defended her view on the incompatibility of dance and politics:

4   Aristos is an online review organ for the arts which describes itself as 'advocating objective standards in arts scholarship and criticism' and as being in opposition to the 'seemingly endless concoctions of postmodernism' (Aristos, undated).

Choreographers mix dance with politics because it is the only way to get attention. And get grants too [...]. I've stopped attending dance attractions because the last thing I want to see is dancers wasting their time on some high-minded godawful piece of choreography. I don't want to be told about Iraq or Bush or Katrina by someone younger and dumber than I am. (quoted in O'Mahony 2006)

It is ultimately difficult to ascertain whether Croce's view is guided by aesthetic considerations alone, or perhaps by conservative politics masquerading as a theory of art. (In a nutshell, her unease might be indicative of her fear that if dance becomes 'political' it may propagate social change which, one might conjecture, she is eager to avoid. Such leanings are also suggested by her prior involvement with the conservative journal *National Review*). But even leaving aside Croce's rather extreme views, the dance critic Judith Mackrell has collated a number of choreographic voices offering reservations about the ability, or suitability, of dance to convey political messages, including the British artist Siobhan Davies, the Israeli Ohad Naharin and indeed Merce Cunningham (Mackrell 2004). She further claims that while dance may be more emotionally powerful than text, it 'can present only the most generalised of facts, the most obvious of symbols, the most stereotypical of narratives. It can't analyse, it can't argue, it can't contextualise' (ibid.).

The fact is that opinion is divided: one view holds that dance should capture the *zeitgeist* rather than senselessly 'fiddling about' with abstract themes, to cite Valeska Gert (quoted in Hildenbrandt 1928: 36). Some go even further by seeking justifications 'why no art form better captures the horrors and hypocrisies of conflict [than dance]' (O'Mahony 2006). Others, by contrast, are adamant that dance should remain unpolluted by politics because as a non-verbal art form it does not lend itself to, or perhaps occupies a high-ground beyond, political engagement. And, one wonders, can or should we deny audiences compensatory aesthetic experiences within the artistic realm, or sweepingly pigeonhole such works as escapist?

When we speak of political theatre, we typically refer to forms which challenge the status quo, usually from a left-wing perspective such as those supporting the communist or socialist cause in the 1930s, or forms of agit-prop which often aimed at rallying the proletariat. It may also encompass recent choreographic protests against the Bush government, the Iraq war or Western capitalism by choreographers such as Johann Kresnik or perhaps William Forsythe in *Three Atmospheric Studies* (2005). Arguably, however, Western theatre dance[5] (which is the focus of this book) has more often than not sought to accommodate or even perpetuate the status quo. This not only includes forms of ballet which represented and strengthened notions of aristocratic identities, but extends to much more contemporary productions such as several West End or Broadway shows which may be seen as socially affirmative and conservative.[6] Examples include *Chicago*, which appears to vindicate capitalist 'greed', *Miss Saigon* which seems to be pro-American intervention in Vietnam, and *The Phantom of the Opera* in which the eponymous villain is physically disabled and the hero a handsome viscount. Such theatre is not normally politically motivated, i.e. it is not intentional political practice and indeed may present itself as apolitical.

However, according to Augusto Boal, political agendas are frequently hidden and therefore not easy to recognise as such. For instance, Boal claims that Aristotelian *catharsis*, the purging of the audience's 'bad' traits, is an effective and 'extremely powerful poetic-political system for intimidation of the spectator' (1979: xxvi). The audience, which recreate the tragic protagonist's mistakes, character flaws or errors of judgment[7] during the performance by way of empathy (i.e. identification with another's feelings) resolve not to make such mistakes and thereby lead a more virtuous life. Thus the tragedy 'modifies any of their actions which are socially unacceptable'

---

5   By 'theatre dance' I mean dance specifically choreographed for the stage or a spectacle.

6   According to a textbook definition, 'conservatism is based on a desire to defend the existing social order'. Conservatives generally 'celebrate the "accumulated wisdom of the past" and claim to be opposed to radical change and social upheaval, believing these to be detrimental to the continuity and stability of state and society. [...] Political conservatives may defend conventional or traditional ways of thinking and being, but conservative political ideologies are based on more explicit criteria, such as defence of private property, support for organised authority, faith in the institutions of the free market and opposition to permissive social values' (Woodley 2006: 5).

7   One example of a protagonist's mistake is Othello's misguided trust in Iago, whose conduct is based on deceit.

(Aristotle, quoted in ibid.: xix) – which according to Boal means those intolerable to the ruling classes. If we accept this view, then we have to concede that audience members for this type of performance might be brought into line with a dominant ideology without even perceiving it.

Kinetic empathy, a concept applied to modern dance by John Martin in a 1946 publication, and emotional introspection might be seen as twentieth-century dance-world equivalents of the Aristotelian concept of empathy. Kinetic empathy is defined as 'the inherent contagion of bodily movement, which makes the onlooker feel sympathetically in his own musculature the exertion he sees in somebody else's musculature' (Martin 1983: 22). The audience are hereby deemed to experience an instantaneous, corresponding sensory perception in their own bodies while watching a dance. Modern dance furthermore conveys 'emotional experience – intuitive perceptions, elusive truths – which cannot be communicated in reasoned terms or reduced to mere statements of fact' (ibid.). Spectators, it is claimed, can recollect and consequently identify the different emotional states associated with certain bodily movements, and thereupon respond to what they see on stage by actually undergoing the relevant emotions. Thus their identification with the performer(s) takes place on a passionate as well as physiological level. The potential of dance to 'capture' its audience in these ways makes it potentially subject to (mis)appropriation for a range of different political agendas, whether emancipatory, conservative or fascist – the Third Reich being a case in point.

By contrast, playwrights such as Bertolt Brecht have sought to undermine the empathy which is central to Aristotelian *catharsis*. The *Verfremdungseffekt* (alienation effect), a theatrical device introduced by Brecht, entails a double distancing: the actor no longer identifies (i.e. 'becomes one') with the character he portrays but can 'step outside' and conflict with it. Secondly, the V-effect distances the audience from the on-stage character by discouraging passive identification and instead engaging their capacities for critical judgement and action. A number of choreographies play on their audience's ability to make judgments and utilise techniques similar to alienation; examples include many of Johann Kresnik's pieces, which are didactic and/or seek to provoke reflection on political matters.

In the following sections, I shall engage with various facets of the dance-politics relationship. In order to give structure to this wide and often disorganised terrain, I shall offer notes and illustrations of four major ways in which the two can interact: (I) dance content, (II) dance genre and form, (III) the impact of dance on external (political) reality, and (IV) the effect of state and governmental politics on dance. Of course these four sections partially overlap and by no means constitute closed entities of academic enquiry. I hope that these reflections will stimulate further thought on the subject.

I Content

Dance works with political content mostly derive themes and significance from political events which are chronologically or logically prior to the work, and usually located outside of art. Political upheavals often provide choreographic subject-matter, and a significant number of works have been created in response to war(s): Kurt Jooss's *The Green Table* (1932) and Anna Sokolow's *Anti-War Trilogy* (1933) were reminders of World War I, foreshadowing future events. There is a plethora of material revolving around World War II. Sokolow's *The Exile* (1939) scorned the Nazi regime, and Antony Tudor's *Echoing of Trumpets* (1963) is said to have been inspired by the Nazi massacre in the village of Lidice, Czechoslovakia, in 1942. Other artists created pieces based on the first nuclear bombing of Japan, notably *Hiroshima* (1947) by the New Dance Group in Wellington (New Zealand), a namesake of the better-known American organisation, and another *Hiroshima* (1962) by the Hungarian choreographer Imre Eck. Among the most notable works are perhaps those depicting Jewish themes, such as *The Village I Knew* (1949) by the American Sophie Maslow whose last section portrays a pogrom, and John Cranko's *Ami Yam Ami Ya'ar* (1971) centering on the Holocaust. Other wars too have incited the choreographic imagination: for instance the Vietnam conflict with pieces by Steve Paxton (*Collaboration with Winter Soldier*, 1971) and Anna Halprin (*Blank Placard Dance*, 1968); the conflict in Yugoslavia treated by Darshan Singh Bhuller (*Planted Seeds*, 1998) and Jiří Kylián (*Arcimboldo*, 1995); and more recently the Iraq War tackled by artists such as William Forsythe (*Three Atmospheric Studies*, 2005) and Victoria Marks (*Not about Iraq*, 2007).

Choreographers have also made statements about dictatorships, such as Christopher Bruce in *Ghost Dances* (1981) and *Silence is the End of our Song* (1983); racism, for instance in *Last Supper at Uncle Tom's Cabin/The Promised Land* (1990) by Bill T. Jones, *Soweto* (1977) by Mats Ek and *Bars* (late 1970s) by New Zealand artist Shona Dunlop MacTavish, both of which tackle apartheid in South Africa; and various facets of gender and queer issues by a wide range of artists, for example Lloyd Newson's *Enter Achilles* (1995). There are also a relatively small number of environmentally themed pieces, such as *Still Life at the Penguin Café* (1988) by David Bintley (Artistic Director of the Birmingham Royal Ballet) and *Endangered Species* (2006) by Siobhan Davies. However, choreographies and scholarly literature in dance studies on ecological topics do not (yet) match the topic's vivid presence in contemporary political debate. And this list is obviously not exhaustive.[8]

Some choreographers' express aim has been to commit their works to political or other socially relevant themes. Lloyd Newson, artistic director of DV8 Physical Theatre in Britain, has complained that dance 'excluded all the life concerns I was interested in: religion, politics, sexuality, psychology, class' (quoted in O'Mahoney 2006). He has further commented that:

> One of the things about DV8's work is it is about subject matter, for a lot of people who go and see dance it is not about anything and DV8 is about something. [...] I've been so tired over the years of watching so much dance on one level, it may be very pretty, but it just goes on and on, it's pretty nice, pretty much the same and pretty dull really, a lot of it. So my big concern is to try and present images through movement and to talk about the whole range of social and psychological situations. (quoted in Boden 2003)

8   See Susan Reed (1998) for a survey of ethnographic and historical studies of dance from an anthropological perspective. She also reviews past and current research concerning the interrelation of dance, power and political structures.

Other artists such as William Forsythe, while creating works of socio-political relevance, have been keen not to become pigeonholed as 'political' choreographers.[9] And whereas the political content of some works is clear and unmistakable, other pieces contain double-coded messages, require knowledge of local specifics, or carry heavy symbolism, forcing the viewer to conjecture their meaning through interviews, programme notes and other clues outside of the actual performance. For instance, while Christopher Bruce's *Ghost Dances* self-evidently harks back to pre-existing musical and kinetic folk discourses from South America, not all spectators will easily comprehend the piece's attack on the human rights violations under Chile's dictator Augusto Pinochet without the aid of secondary material. Other works can be read metaphorically either as a whole or in parts, such as Meredith Monk's *Quarry* (1976) in which 'the central role of the sick child [...] may be a metaphor for Europe in the troubled years before the Second World War' (Au 1997: 202).

Historically speaking, Western theatre dance has had strong political connotations through ballet's genesis at aristocratic courts. Most researchers concur in the view that court ballet celebrated royalty: Barbara Ravelhofer sees the honouring of kings as an act of *realpolitik* in that 'the monarch enjoyed a satisfying display of control which could be projected to third observers' (2006: 105). Themes of court ballets ranged from mythological tales to love stories and historical dramas. Ravelhofer argues that the bodily configuration of early ballet also reflected 'discourses of power':

> The many rules of *danse noble* 'alienated' the dancing subject, making it subservient to the ruler's will, for whom it performed. The particularization of the body into distinct parts which had to perform different movements disturbed the dancer's sense of wholeness and weakened the performing body's resilience against absolutist appropriation. (Ravelhofer 2006: 97)

9   In an email communication with myself in June 2008, Forsythe's dramaturg Freya Vass-Rhee wrote that he 'points out that not all of his current or past works overtly address political themes and, as such, he does not wish to be presented solely as a "political" choreographer or as a choreographer who has "turned" political'.

While this species of ballet might be seen as innately conservative, other dance forms, in particular from the twentieth century, are radical in content; and often the radicalisation of dance has gone hand in hand with that of society. Much research has been invested into the 1930s American workers' dance movement and other left-leaning dance artistry, for instance in early 1930s Germany with practitioners such as the 'red dancer' Jean Weidt, which gained momentum in a time of struggle during the difficult years of economic downturn and depression.[10] The workers' dance movement in the US is a good example to illustrate how political topics can shape dance. Here, dance both reflected and advanced a radically left-wing school of thought (often with Marxist-Leninist leanings) and was used as a 'revolutionary weapon' (Douglas 1935: 140) to depict the struggle of the working classes against bourgeois and capitalist society. It sought to initiate fundamental social change for the better, and many dance artists involved in the movement (a number of whom hailed from immigrant and working-class families) were engaged in political as well as artistic activism.

Content was the essence of (what was then called) revolutionary dance. Even the most cursory glance through lists of titles by relevant artists confirms the choice of working-class themes, in particular 'choreographic depictions of hunger, oppression, charity, hypocrisy, uprising, strike, collectivism, racial fraternity' (Eisenberg 1935: 130). The well-researched New Dance Group in New York City, a member organisation of the Workers Dance League, performed pieces such as *Strike* (1933), *Hunger* (1933) and *Survival of the Fittest* (1940). German equivalents by Weidt include *Tanz mit der roten Fahne* (Dance with the Red Flag, between 1925 and 1928), and *Arbeiter* (Worker, 1925).

Thanks to Jane Dudley, we have a highly detailed description of how Marxist ideology was supposed to be translated into movement images and qualities in a dance called *Strike*, which depicts a group of pickets attempting to call factory workers to join a strike despite a militia's efforts to hold them back. It becomes evident from Dudley's description that the

10   See for instance Graff (1997), Geduld (2007) and (2008), Prickett (1990) and (1994), Franko (1995) and (2002), and Rosen (2000) for the American context; and Ropa (1988) and Yvonne Hardt (2004) with respect to Germany.

dance had a somewhat simplistic storyline in accordance with orthodox Marxist schools of thought, and allowed for the technical limitations of the 'lay' dancers employed – their use being significant from a political perspective. The ensemble was divided into three different groups, with the workers/pickets and militia representing opposing ideological camps; predictably the latter were depicted in starkly negative terms and ultimately 'lost' the battle:

> As the pickets prepare to attack, the workers raise their arms to break through the militia. As the pickets move towards the militia the workers, their group wedge shaped, lunge forward. The line of the militia splits in the center. Through the opening surge the workers to join the pickets. From the center the workers and pickets together press the militia back to each side. Here the dance ends. (Dudley 1934: 122)

Revolutionary dance was conceived in opposition both to ballet's 'sterile formalism' (Gold 1929, quoted in Franko 1995: 109) and the modern dance of the likes of Martha Graham and Mary Wigman which was perceived to be too individualist and purportedly apolitical. Their allegedly 'bourgeois' repertoire was said to be the expression of an 'ego-cult, which rhapsodized "art for art's sake"' (Douglas 1935: 138) and was criticised for shying away from contemporary issues. By contrast, radical dance prided itself on creating a proletarian art form which promoted inclusivity by offering classes to amateur working-class dancers, and applied collaborative methods of choreography and performance. Its collectivist thinking even extended to the chosen themes which, as the dancer Edith Segal maintained, were not subject to the authorial control of the 'genius' creator: 'The theme or subject matter of the group dance is therefore not the private property of the director, or even of the group, but that of the audience, of society' (Segal 1935: 23).[11]

Works by such dance groups – especially those in which workers formed part of the performing ensemble – were occasionally criticised for a lack of aesthetic sophistication in terms of execution and style (see Graff

---

11   Roger Copeland's article in this collection addresses the theme of 'collective' dance making and its relation to politics in a more critical light.

1997: 9), highlighting the conflict which arises when content takes priority over form. This conflict has led some critics to admonish the incongruity between (novel) working-class themes and the use of an existing movement vocabulary based largely on modern dance, which despite its young age was already seen as an established technique and associated with the bourgeoisie:

> The inseparability of form and content is forgotten by those who in their eagerness to use the dance as a revolutionary weapon seize upon forms which have been perfected for the projection of ideas totally different and sometimes completely at odds with progressive thought and material. (Douglas 1935: 141)[12]

However, revolutionary dancers were obliged to content themselves with modern dance techniques, while retaining the hope that a dance form might be invented in future which more adequately expressed 'revolutionary' content (see Freedman 1934: 123).

II Genre and Form

As in the above case, there seems an underlying (but not always outspoken) assumption that dance genres, regardless of the choreographies' actual content, are not only implicitly or explicitly political but allied to particular positions on the political spectrum. Given its genesis, with roots at aristocratic courts, ballet is often associated with the upper or upper-middle classes, and hence with a form of government and values linked to the (mostly 'right-wing') socio-political establishment.[13] In some countries,

---

12   See also Franko's discussion (1995: esp. 27–29).

13   Lincoln Kirstein furthermore adds that ballet embraces conservative ideology because, despite its physiological and psychological limitations, it has essentially been preserved in the same state for many centuries – throughout upheavals such as wars and revolutions (1985: 17).

the suffix 'royal' still indicates a close connection between ballet and the aristocracy, for instance the 'Royal Ballet' in London or the 'Royal Danish Ballet'. In both the UK and New Zealand, two countries I have lived in for several years, ballet has continually had to defend itself against allegations of elitism. This critique extends to audience composition, student intakes, ticket prices, and occasionally even the ideological messages that classical ballet works convey in terms of their narratives.

Upon closer inspection, however, ballet is neither quite so straight-forwardly elitist, nor is it necessarily linked with right-wing values. At the turn of the nineteenth century, the Viennese Court Opera Ballet, among others, employed girls hailing from working class backgrounds. Their parents needed the income derived from the children's performance nights, while wealthier families often sought to protect their children from the machinations and the ill-repute of ballet companies (see Kolb 2009: 108–109). Similarly, the erotic entertainment of rich patrons by working-class corps members of the Paris Opera Ballet is well known and has been immortalised in Degas's paintings. In the British music hall in the late nineteenth century, ballet interludes were programmed next to juggling acts for audiences that were a far cry from the wealthy spectatorship usu-ally associated with ballet. The form has also been widely employed both as an ideological tool and as entertainment by communist countries,[14] and indeed under the opposite ideological extreme of fascism, notably in Germany.[15] In both cases, ballet figures as a representative cultural organ for state forms not remotely similar to those which originally spawned it, albeit with alterations of content and kinetic repertory.

In the same vein, the forms of modern dance which might broadly be associated with values of liberalism, emancipation and freedom have been turned to both communist and fascist purposes. Isadora Duncan was invited to open a school in Moscow in 1921 because her style was deemed to capture

14   Examples include the Soviet Union – for instance during the Cold War, as I shall specify below, and Maoist China (see Li Cunxin's wide-selling biography).
15   See Gunhild Oberzaucher-Schüller's discussion in this book. Though opposites in many respects, both of these systems are in some sense collectivist and have totalitar-ian leanings.

contemporary (anti-monarchist) Soviet ideology. Other styles, however, were suppressed and all other dance schools, except for the Bolshoi, forcibly closed down (see Geduld 2008: 44).[16] Rudolf von Laban and Mary Wigman adapted the style and content of their works to reflect the Nazi ethos in their 1930s choreographies, thus aligning modern dance with political thought at the opposite end of the political spectrum. Wigman created dances, including *Frauentänze* in 1934, which celebrated traditional female roles such as maternity and were at odds with the portrayal of strong, independent women in her pre-Third Reich choreographies. Moreover, protagonists of German expressive dance which (actually) had a strongly individualistic flair and was seen by Nazi officials as a manifestation of democracy,[17] produced choreographic reflections of the Nazi 'Führer principle' which demanded from the masses uniformity, conformity, and unconditional trust in the leader.[18] The homogenous mass dance displays in German stadiums at sporting events and other large-scale public gatherings are apt examples of this 'massification' of the population in and through modern dance, at the expense of individual expression. The performance of *Olympische Jugend* with massed ranks of young people at the 1936 Olympic Games in Berlin, choreographed by among others Gret Palucca, Dorothee Günther and Maja Lex, is a particularly well-known spectacle of this kind.

Postmodern dance provides a good illustration of how certain dance forms are often subject to political interpretation: given the politicised, revolutionary 1960s environment in which it was born, with student uprisings, the Vietnam War, black and female liberation movements and so on, it is regarded by many as intrinsically political in nature. However, Ramsay Burt in his 2006 book on the Judson Dance Theater acutely observes that a number of choreographers of this era did *not* seek to express a political

16   Regarding the impact of the October revolution on dance developments in Russia, see also Pouillade (2003: 23–24).

17   Joseph Goebbels wrote about Weimar artistry in 1933 that 'parliamentarianism was the political spawn of this boundless liberal individualism and dictated the creative activities of the past decades' (1933: 50).

18   Whether they did so forcibly or from choice remains a matter of debate.

message through their works. Citing Yvonne Rainer,[19] Burt grapples with this apparent contradiction between the artists' alleged distance from political matters on one hand, and their embeddedness in the politicised 1960s atmosphere and active participation in protest movements on the other (see also Banes 1980: 15). Steve Paxton concurs with Rainer in claiming that many dance scholars unjustifiably impose political meanings on choreographies which in fact had no political intent. He confided to me in an email from October 2006:

> I never bought the line that my work, in general the quotidian movement work, was ever about democratization of stage dance [...]. Arguably critics were bereft of their favorite moments of spotting the virtuosos, or appreciating how the dance and music marry. They were perhaps left to grasp for some way to provide a possible positive impression of walking bodies as dance, and I suppose I am grateful for their efforts. But it seems to me that in that period they were shocked mostly by the collapse of traditional hierarchies in dance and choreography extant for 200 years or more, and they reacted by choosing a word the opposite of hierarchical, thus displacing the issues of the works from the physiological to the political.

But, we might contend, are these choreographers simply in denial regarding the 'actual' political nature of their own works? The answer perhaps lies elsewhere. A key shift in postmodern theatre has been the increasing attempt to emphasise formal innovations such as the undermining of previous artistic conventions, together with a growing tendency to charge (and interpret) form politically. Thus, the 'political' aspect is located in the work's radical form – as a new way of producing, disrupting, or interrogating the definition of meaning – rather than its thematisation of a political concern external to the work itself.

The performer-audience relation is one example. Augusto Boal and Richard Schechner politicised this relationship in their 1970s writings on, and practice of, experimental political theatre. Both favoured audience participation and interaction over the traditional theatrical model which

19   Rainer writes: 'Just as ideological issues have no bearing on the nature of the work [The Mind is a Muscle], neither does the tenor of current political and social conditions have any bearing on its execution' (Rainer 1974: 71, cited in Burt 2006: 116).

requires a strict separation of the audience from the stage, as exemplified by
the concept of fourth-wall naturalism which demands passive and sedate
behaviour by audience members. Boal's and Schechner's construal of audiences as active participants was meant as a pedagogical tool and form of
artistic activism by which they sought to gear impoverished and oppressed
sections of the population into action. Schechner also regarded the conventional proscenium arch as an architectural reflection of capitalism,[20]
arguing that the strict division between the backstage area of the theatre
(occupied by workers) and the front of house (lavishly decorated and
frequented by the higher classes) is comparable to the divide between the
factory site where items are produced and the shop where they are sold
(1988: 161).

There is a plethora of parallel examples in the dance world of challenges
to theatrical conventions, including a range of Yvonne Rainer's works,
such as *Yellow Belly* (1969) in which the audience was asked to heckle the
performer, and the outdoor site-specific *Roofpiece* (1971) which featured
performers on the rooftops of lower Manhattan. Meredith Monk's *Portable*
(1966) reversed the positioning of audience and spectators in its closing
scenes. A number of these pieces are interactive, subvert preconceived ways
of performing and viewing, or blur the boundaries between performance
and the commonplace – for instance by placing the work in street contexts
or through the use of everyday movement material. The changes to the form
of theatrical works relate to what might more broadly be understood as
'political' concepts: for instance, a less 'authoritarian' relationship between
audience and performer seems inextricably linked to notions of democracy, equality, liberalism and so on. Hence, where dance has experimented
with greater flexibility in this relationship, and in cases where works are
performed outside of traditional 'establishment' venues, they can be seen
as making political statements of sorts.

20   Similar reservations have been voiced by a number of dancers and critics, such as
     Lincoln Kirstein who in a note on Balanchine lauded his 'destruction of the pro-
     scenium arch as an obstructive fallacy' (Kirstein 1985: 219).

A well-known theorist of postmodern theatre is Jürgen Lehmann, whose book on the topic has had a wide-reaching impact since its 2006 translation into English. Lehmann diagnoses a general crisis of theatre in the wake of an explosion of image-based media in a globalised (and less 'manageable') world, and the genesis of a civilisation dominated by the 'passive consumption of images and data' (2006: 16). He identifies a particular and oft-cited problem for political theatre as being the breakdown of the opposition between the cultural and economic spheres, resulting from a commodification of art in highly developed, multinational capitalism. This appears to foreclose theatre's potential to act against the system as an external political counterforce. However, Lehmann maintains that postdramatic theatre (a concept widely resonant with postmodern theatre) is an adequate form to address the challenges of our society, and posits its political potential in the *interruption* of the law or dominant mode.

This new theatre is contrasted with the pre-1960s paradigm of dramatic theatre, which Lehmann identifies as being based on a fictional dramatic world, narrative and character. Dramatic theatre is determined by the representation of action and speeches ('the making present', ibid.: 21) and hence the *imitation* of a fictive pre-existent universe, as for instance in narrative ballets which have a coherent plot. Postdramatic theatre, on the other hand, not only privileges discontinuity and reliance on modern media, but also foregrounds the audience as active participants who help shape the production (rather than remaining a passive tacit entity). Among its key elements is an accentuation of the materiality of performance, prioritising presence ('the doing in the real', Lehmann, 2006: 104) over representation. Trisha Brown's *Man Walking Down the Side of a Building* (1970) or 'happening-like' theatre such as *Theatre Piece No. 1* (1952), a cooperation between among others Cage, Rauschenberg and Cunningham, provide apt examples of performances which no longer make claims to a fictional totality, closed off by a fourth wall. In dance, Lehmann argues, 'we find most radically expressed what is true for postdramatic theatre in general: it articulates not meaning but energy, it represents not illustrations but actions' (ibid.: 163).

Echoing some of the theorists mentioned earlier, Lehmann contends that theatre no longer generates or accelerates a revolution in social relations, and hence has lost the function of a political countermovement in a traditional (e.g. Marxist or utopian) sense: 'That politically oppressed people are shown on stage does not make theatre political' (ibid.: 178). Rather, Lehmann suggests that 'theatre becomes political [...] through the implicit substance and critical value of its *mode of representation*' (ibid.). In other words, the radical *form* of postmodern theatre, which disrupts authoritarian and logocentric structures, renders it an adequate response to current political challenges:

> We can clearly see here that theatre does not attain its political, ethical reality by way of information, theses and messages; in short: by way of its content in the traditional sense. On the contrary: it is part of the constitution to hurt feelings, to produce shock and disorientation, which point the spectators to their own presence precisely through 'amoral', 'asocial' and seemingly 'cynical' events. (ibid.: 187)

Whether dramatic theatre, and its dance world equivalent, may be deemed outdated and hence discounted as modes of political expression (a conceivable inference which might be drawn from Lehmann's account of the two theatre paradigms) is debatable. In critical response to Lehmann, theatre scholar Denise Varney challenges 'the opposition of dramatic and postdramatic theatre where the former is cast as an antiquated form incapable of dealing with the complex issues of late capitalism and globalisation' (2008: 8). She claims that despite their discrepancy in terms of aesthetic form, both can nonetheless transmit politically valid messages.

III The Impact of Dance on External Politics

The question here is whether dance which *is* politically motivated can actually have an impact on external reality or manage to inaugurate societal change. I will draw upon models proposed in the realm of theatre studies, where this matter has been more widely discussed than with respect to dance in particular. Some performance undeniably seeks to challenge the socio-political status quo. Take, for example, the renowned proponent of political theatre Erwin Piscator, or the 1930s radical left-wing artistic workers' movement which sought to replace capitalism with a classless society. Late twentieth-century theorists have been cautious, however, in their evaluation of the bearing that performance may have on the outside (political) world.

The notion of 'efficacy' has been used to measure the effectiveness, i.e. perceptible impact of a performance on external events. In his 1992 book on *The Politics of Performance*, Kershaw specifies 'performance efficacy' (adapting a term first used by Richard Schechner, 1988) as 'the potential that theatre may have to make the immediate effects of performance influence, however minutely, the general historical evolution of wider social and political realities' (Kershaw 1992: 1). Although he concedes that measuring efficacy is tricky, it is plausible to argue that theatrical practices achieve it insofar as they influence their audiences and change their minds regarding political ideas or state-of-affairs, rather than (necessarily) directly affecting governmental or legislative processes. So, for instance, while Steve Paxton's *Collaboration with Wintersoldier* (1971), which attacked US-American war crimes during the Vietnam War, might possibly be said to have had the war's ending as its ultimate 'aim', this would have been a somewhat unrealistic target. On Kershaw's account, however, Paxton's performance could be seen to have had *some* degree of efficacy provided he managed to influence some spectators' views about the wisdom of the war. Performances can be said to promote certain ideologies such as egalitarianism or libertarianism (ibid.: 18), but a work's efficacy will be to some extent contingent on its relevance to the audience/community in which it is performed. Impact can be maximised, for instance, by ensuring identification with the audience by speaking their language or using non-professionals from the community in the production and performance process (ibid.: in particular 246–248).

Clearly, not all performance which opposes the status quo necessarily seeks to instantiate dogmatic social reform. Kershaw proposed the term 'radical performance' instead of 'political theatre' in an attempt to broaden the scope of the function and impact such works might have. He refers back to Raymond Williams's use of the term 'radical' as 'a way of avoiding factional association while reasserting the need for vigorous and fundamental change' (Williams 1976: 210, quoted in Kershaw 1999: 18). The advantage of this term is that it circumvents the tendentiousness of the phrase 'political theatre', which is invariably associated with left-wing ideologies, whereas right-wing theatre does not, by these lights, qualify as 'political'. 'Radical performance', by contrast, may be associated with either right or left-wing political thought, and challenges the status quo without necessarily requiring dogmatic political change – i.e. it does not necessarily try to enforce a new doctrine or impose new laws. It evokes freedoms not just *from* oppression, repression, exploitation [...] but also freedom *to reach beyond* existing systems of formalised power' (ibid.); thus, it might transcend ideology itself.

If I understand Kershaw's line of thought correctly, he is arguing that radical performance is not inevitably socially interventionist, but creates spaces – *within* performance – that are not controlled by the logic of hegemony, juridical authorities, the state or other forms of political power. In other words, radical performance offers alternative models of freedom by which the audience may experience a (temporary) escape from certain forms of domination, thus planting in them the seeds of previously unimaginable thought, action or experience which subvert conventional ideologies and gesture towards new socio-political possibilities. For instance, ecstasy, which involves the transgression of the ego in states of heightened affectivity, is an important factor in many dance forms and may provide someone with a kind of otherwise unobtainable freedom – a freedom that it is next-to-impossible to experience in conventional life scenarios (and whose use, of course, may or may not be politically motivated). Thus, performance can be critical of existing social arrangements without specifying what exactly should take their place.

The trouble is that under such conditions, efficacy becomes even harder to measure. The possibility of political art in postmodern society, where every certainty has been eroded, is subject to fierce debate.[21] Kershaw (1999:

---

21   Other theorists who have raised the issue of how art can be political under the conditions of postmodernism, but who cannot be dealt with here for reasons of space,

16–17) claims that the theories of the likes of Foucault, who locates power in everything; Butler, who has shown that even gender is culturally constructed; and Baudrillard, who has banished the real, lead to the conclusion that everything 'drowns' in a sea of relativity and individual perspectives. While one person might view a performance as having enormous political impact, another may see it as ideologically insignificant. Consequently, 'any conclusion about the potential ideological efficacy of any particular approach to performance practice inevitably will be constrained in their scope' (ibid.: 17). As pointed out at the beginning of this essay, we might lose the means of evaluating the effects of theatre and performance on politics.

Shifting from theory to practice, how do dance artists themselves view the possible impact of their performances on reality? Choreographers have often proved sceptical about the perceptible impact of their political works. While Kurt Jooss's *The Green Table* (1932) is commonly regarded as one of the first dance works with an explicitly political (in this case, pacifist) message, the choreographer seemed adamant in a 1976 interview that dance was not able to promote political change directly: 'One should not try, in a piece of art, to improve life or mankind or politics [...]. That is not for the arts to do. The task for the arts altogether, I think, is to confess inner things, to bring out emotions [...] but not to bring solutions' (Jooss in Omnibus, 1976). And there is indeed much anecdotal evidence of dance's powerlessness to stem the tide of political history. The hopes of the 1930s American workers' dance movement were dashed by 1950s McCarthyism, while Johann Kresnik's socialist choreographic theatre did little to arrest what some (mostly left-wing) commentators regarded as the capitalist takeover of the East German state by West Germany following the 1990 reunification.

And yet, perhaps it is wrong to despair altogether of dance's efficacy. To mention just a few more 'encouraging' examples: Valeska Gert's very first performance during the war in 1916, *Tanz in orange* – a grotesque

---

include Philip Auslander (1992) and Frederic Jameson (1985). See also Lehmann's discussion above.

parody of ballet steps performed in an orange dress – prompted police officers to come and check on the theatre after reports of indecency and turmoil on stage (Gert 1968: 38). While Gert's little choreography did not even strive for political impact, the authorities became suspicious on the grounds of its being too unconventional and a threat to the social order in the conservative and authoritarian milieu of the German Reich. (Here, admittedly, the efficacy was limited to raising questions of what is socially acceptable within the theatrical environment itself.)

Johann Kresnik, on the other hand, received a bomb threat after it became known that his piece *Ulrike Meinhof* vindicated the actions of its terrorist protagonist, even before the first showing of the piece in February 1990. The threat was taken seriously by police and resulted in Kresnik's children receiving an escort, the postponement of the premiere, and a search of the theatre premises (see interview with Kresnik, in Kretz-Mangold 2006). Kresnik is certainly not one to shy away from scandals. His 2004 work *Hannelore Kohl*, about the former German Chancellor's wife who committed suicide after suffering for years from an incurable illness, attacked Helmut Kohl through some vicious choreographic imagery. The work caused heated discussions among CDU (Christian Democratic Union)[22] officials and supporters, prompting newspaper articles, commentaries from local politicians, complaints about the CDU mayor who originally signed off the piece, semi-public readings from Kohl biographies in protest against the allegations, and apparently a fax sent by Kohl himself to one of his party colleagues in which he lamented the work's 'pathetic abuse of artistic freedom' (Wassermann, 2005). CDU supporters have since occasionally called for boycotts of Kresnik's pieces, proving both their radical, disruptive potential and their efficacy as political media, bearing as they do a wide-reaching resonance with communal, national and indeed international politics.

Shona Dunlop MacTavish, a former Bodenwieser dancer and choreographer in her own right, informs me of another incident dating from her time as a dance lecturer at Silliman University in the Negros Oriental province of the Philippines. Ferdinand Marcos, then President of the

22 The CDU is the German centre-right 'conservative' party.

Philippines, was contemplating the installation of a nuclear arsenal on the island of Negros, and Dunlop MacTavish choreographed an anti-nuclear modern dance piece entitled *Requiem for the Living* (1982). After the performance, all her dancers, members of the faculty at which it was produced, and island representatives were invited to meet together and engage in a detailed discussion of the work's message and the consequences of constructing a nuclear base on the island. The meeting's attendees, including the dancers, were encouraged to sign a document to send to General Marcos opposing the move; so this would seem a good example of dance resulting in concrete political action. (It should be noted that the planned arsenal was eventually abandoned, though how much the dance-based petition actually contributed to this is hard to establish.)

The AIDS pandemic of the mid-1980s to 1990s which shook the world is one of the better-known occurrences leading to an increased politicisation of choreographers and dancers in the later twentieth century. AIDS led to the stigmatisation of the body, and especially of the homosexual body as the disease was widely associated with the practice of gay sex. David Gere's 2004 book traces the impact of AIDS on the dance scene in the US, arguing that analogies were drawn in the public mind between homosexuality, AIDS and male dance. The anxieties surrounding HIV and AIDS and the stigmatisation of gay men had particular implications for dance which, by its very nature, foregrounds physicality and the emission of bodily fluids (sweat), and whose male artists were (and often still are) suspected of being homosexual. He writes that the American government, in an inadequate strategic response to the outbreak and social marginalisation of AIDS, turned a blind eye to the deaths caused by the disease (ibid.: 146). Consequently, choreographers set out to protest against the 'heterosexist, patriarchal, and homophobic U.S. society' (ibid.: 147) they perceived, making art that was both aesthetic and decidedly political in the attempt to destabilise and protest against the forces of homophobic oppression and resist civil authority.

Ultimately, it remains tricky to assess the extent to which performance can influence society. The answer ultimately depends on how narrowly or widely we define 'politics' on one hand, and political 'impact' on the other. It also stands to question what possible means or tools could be used to measure efficacy – other than gathering statistical information from audiences, which as Kershaw notes is often inconclusive (1992: 3). Certainly, the relationship between dance and the social order conceivably extends far beyond the duration of an individual performance, and it is plausible that many (or most) effects may be long-term or roundabout, making it difficult to gather reliable data. While choreographies seem unlikely to change or influence a government's policies directly, they might contribute to a social movement campaigning for a specific political cause, and it makes sense to say that if they even induce *someone* in the audience to go out and vote, boycott a product, or change their mind about an issue, they are efficacious to some degree. While the tools for measuring the extent of efficacy are beyond the scope of this discussion, suffice it to say that certain historical examples suggest *prima facie* that a political impact for dance is possible.

IV The Impact of State and Governmental Politics on Dance

It is particularly intriguing to analyse how political structures can become determinants of dance production and/or audience reception of works. State or governmental agencies impact on dance through cultural policy and other administrative organisations. This is most obviously so where dance's potential is used to embody a particular set of national political values or to assert the primacy of an ideology, for instance during the cultural Cold War between the communist East and liberal democratic West: 'The ambiguity of the arts makes them a powerful weapon in cultural diplomacy. They are capable of double coding, as both innocent of politics and heavily implicated in it' (Nicholas 2001: 97). In such cases, dance is effectively turned into a forum for state politics. Its implication in the diplomatic tug-of-war between the imperial ideologies has been examined in some detail (Prevots 1998, Nicholas 2001, Caute 2003). Excellence and achievements in dance were used as publicity tools: companies, their works and staff symbolised and represented their respective political models, furthering international prestige in an era of mass media.

On the East side of the iron curtain, socialism was heavily promoted through the Soviet Union's flagship companies, notably the Bolshoi and Kirov. Historian David Caute highlights a paradox in the appropriation of classical ballet within the Marxist framework of the USSR, pointing out 'how unlikely an art form it is for cultivation by a proletarian revolution in a land of thumping peasant dances' (2003: 469). However, ballets such as Lashchilin's and Tikhomirov's *The Red Poppy* (first performed in 1927), Belsky's *Coast of Hope* (1959) and *Spartacus* (of which several versions exist; premiered in 1956) clearly embraced Soviet ideology through their content – notably the glorification of workers' revolution – and their form, by using concrete narratives and dramatic plots. Modernist dance trends such as formalism, abstraction and intuitivism, associated as they were with the 'decadent' West, were rejected as incompatible with the aims of Socialist Realism.

Soviet teachers and dance philosophy had a vital influence on developments in Maoist China, and Cuba following the rise of Fidel Castro. The Cuban leader sought to transform ballet in the Soviet style into a socialist realist propaganda tool, manifesting his desire to showcase Cuba as a force to be reckoned with. Several dance teachers from the Soviet Union, for instance the Bolshoi's Viktor Zaplin, were invited to offer courses in the country. Vice versa, Cuban artists were sent to the Soviet Union: Alberto Alonso, for instance, created *Carmen* for the Bolshoi in 1967, the first foreign artist ever to choreograph for this company. The war of cultures between West and East was also fiercely fought beyond the theatres' actual performance spaces. Caute details some of the Cold War feuds, mutual recriminations and mishaps of cultural diplomacy, many of which revolved around the exchange visits by dance companies. The defection of several high-calibre ballet dancers from the Soviet Union, such as Rudolf Nureyev and Mikhail Baryshnikov, was a particular propaganda disaster for the Soviets.

It would of course be wrong to assume that today, twenty years after the collapse of the communist bloc, dance has become a sphere untainted by state politics. The socio-political, economic and institutional contexts within which art works are situated are still important factors in dance making and perception, even without a clearly delineated internal or external state 'enemy' as in the case of the Cold War. While cultural policy and

funding decisions attract far less public notice, they continue to be significant frameworks for dance artistry, and I shall conclude this introduction
by outlining several pertinent issues.

Europe, with its multitude of countries in close proximity, is an interesting case in point. Despite certain pan-European cultural policies,[23] the
countries boast distinct national administrative systems, of which Béla-
Rásky and Perez offer the following typology:

> Italy or France are regarded as the centralist state-oriented systems, Ireland or the
> United Kingdom with their independent Arts Councils are seen as the classic exam-
> ples of the Anglo-Saxon arm's length principle, the Nordic model found in Scandina-
> via and Finland shows a corporate approach to culture with a strong socio-political
> leaning, while Germany, Austria and Switzerland count as the significant federalist
> systems of cultural administration in Europe. (Béla-Rásky & Perez 1996: 4)

The types of cultural administration and political structures have concrete
implications for dance. Funding is one: the UK, for instance, with its strong
emphasis on the separation of state and art, offers less public subsidy to
dance companies than Germany where state intervention has traditionally
been more significant. Jennifer Delaney noted in a 1997 article that the
Royal Ballet (which traditionally receives the lion's share of the English
Arts Council's dance budget) only covered approximately a third of its
costs from government subsidy, compared to the 65% that a comparable
German company would have received. This led the author to raise concerns about dance standards in Britain; for while trusts, foundations and
private sector funding can make up the difference,

> private companies do not fund the arts for the good of their health. They seek some
> kind of benefit in return, whether it be the public relations prestige of being per-
> ceived as a patron of the arts, their logo prominently displayed to all visitors to an
> exhibition/performance, or access to an 'exclusive' environment ideal for corporate
> entertainment. (Delaney 1997)

23   See, for instance, Europe's Cultural Convention of May 1955. This was designed
     'between members of the Council [of Europe] [...] to pursue a policy of common
     action designed to safeguard and encourage the development of European culture'.
     The full text is available on the Internet at <http://www.bologna-bergen2005.no/
     EN/MAIN_DOC/Cultural1.HTM>.

The need to attract private patrons or rely on ticket sales may force company directors to arrange programmes so as to meet their sponsors' or the
audiences' expectations, e.g. to give preference to showcase pieces such as
Swan Lake and *Sleeping Beauty* at the expense of experimental, critical,
or otherwise 'inconvenient' works, thus effectively pursuing conservative programming policies. However, governmental funding for the arts
has equally come under strong attack. Criticism has often been fuelled
by concerns about artistic elitism, supported by the politically motivated
argument that where taxation or lottery money is used to fund expensive
ballet tickets, poorer sections of the population effectively subsidise the
leisure activities of the rich.[24] Moreover, state support does not necessarily
prevent interference in the content of cultural production and programmes:
centre-right parties, for instance, are sometimes deemed to be suspicious of
experimental, provocative or left-leaning art; and when in power at local
governmental levels may prefer appointments of more traditionalist theatre or ballet directors. Although this was not the official line taken by the
party's establishment, Haywood (et al.) note that some British Conservative Party arts commentators in the cash-strapped late 1970s and 1980s,
such as the Selsdon Group, challenged state subsidy and embraced a radical free market agenda:

> The argument was that public money tends to be wasted in purchasing and promoting
> experimental art forms, since art administrators strive to demonstrate their commit-
> ment to the 'avant garde' by making purchases at inflated prices of items which would
> fetch little in the unsubsidised, private market place. (Haywood et al. 1995: 196)

24   Internet discussion of this issue is intriguing to follow. Consider the following blog
     by an American opponent of governmental subsidies: 'Why is there a National
     Endowment for the Arts as opposed to a National Endowment for Plumbers? Art is
     a profession like any other. Artists who depend on the government dole are express-
     ing nothing so much as their inability to succeed in the real world where they would
     have to satisfy the same standards of free-market competence imposed upon the rest
     of us'. She further continues: 'In short, the NEA [the independent federal agency in
     the US which supports excellence in the arts] is a discriminatory and elitist organi-
     zation that is proud to be out-of-touch with the "common" people who fund it'
     (McElroy 1999).

The British Conservatives' grassroots have thus been said to 'cling to Thatcher's pro-free-market stance' (McDowell, 2008). But low state subsidy, or cuts in public funding, might mean that theatres and other comparable venues resort to a more traditional, popular repertoire, as experimental pieces do not tend to attract large audiences and may not be financially viable.

Beyond party allegiances, politics play a crucial role in dance administration, in particular when one considers the politically related factors which often underpin cultural policy and funding decisions. These include diversity (offering a spread of different dance forms), the initiation of positive social change, audience sizes and accessibility. Accessibility issues in turn include pricing policies – for instance the demand that the cheapest tickets should correspond to the price of a cinema visit[25] – and the geographical distribution of dance works. Burns and Harrison, in an official English Arts Council document, write that:

> Like theatre, dance needs to develop new approaches to touring to ensure that audiences countrywide have access to high quality work, touring companies and venues are able to plan ahead strategically and the Arts Council's investment is applied where it has most impact. (2009: 5)

Diversity and accessibility issues may provide 'justifications' for why certain companies or productions receive funding while others miss out. And the impact of cultural administration may extend to works' content and form. In her article on 'The Aesthetics and Politics of Daniel Larrieu's Mobile ou le Miroir du Château', Anna Pakes uses the French choreographer's piece as a case study to demonstrate 'how the political and economic imperatives of its surrounding environment help to shape the work's aesthetic fabric and audience experience of the dance' (2004: 41). In short, Pakes explains how the French Ministry of Culture expected that Larrieu's choreography, which was devised and initially performed in the Tours area of France, should reflect the region's specificities and cultural interests – thus constructing and proliferating a particular (preferably marketable) image of the locality in which it was produced. Such state-imposed obligations can, as Pakes suggests, conflict with a choreographer's own artistic agenda.

---

25   See the guidelines of the French Ministry of Culture in 1991 (La Musique 1991).

Lastly, amongst the arts, funding, audiences and recognition are objects of competition: ballet, contemporary dance companies and independent artists not only compete with each other, but also with other art forms and (where funding is concerned) with institutions outside art, such as sport. Consequently, dance has repeatedly had to defend its value and function, both as art, physical exercise and in economic terms. An editorial in the British newspaper *The Guardian* caught my attention: its unnamed author, in a brief comment on the TV series *Strictly Come Dancing*, wrote that 'dancing is affirmative, optimistic and democratic' (In praise, 2008), a catchphrase which was later quoted in large lettering in the *2004–8 Dance Mapping: Executive Summary Report* published by the English Arts Council. The author, like the Arts Council, obviously felt the need to acknowledge the value of dance within a certain political culture (namely democracy) and its associated values such as social equality, as well as its connection with positively connoted mental states.

But does this imply that dance forms which are *not* optimistic and socially affirmative, or which have a sombre or critical vision of reality, are not worthy of similar funding? If we subscribe to the notion that dance needs to be positive and uplifting to justify state support, we risk depriving it of its disruptive, risk-taking or 'disenchanting' potentials. And if we believe some contemporary theorists, it is exactly the latter functions – the 'basic disrespect for tenability or positive affirmation' and the 'transgression of taboos' (Lehmann 2006: 186) – that constitute the essence of political theatre under postmodernism. We thus imperil a significant medium which can provide a plausible counter-construct to the political status quo.

Works Cited

Aristos. An Online Review of the Arts. Undated. Available: <http://www.aristos.org/aristos2.htm> [2 January 2010].
The Aristos Awards (Annotated List of Winners). Available: <http://www.aristos.org/aris-award-3.htm> [26 January 2010].

Au, S. 1988. *Ballet and Modern Dance*. Introduction by Selma Jeanne Cohen. London: Thames and Hudson.

Auslander, P. 1992. *Presence and Resistance: Postmodernism and Cultural Politics in Contemporary American Performance*. Ann Arbor: University of Michigan Press.

Banes, S. 1980. *Terpsichore in Sneakers: Post-Modern Dance*. Boston, MA: Houghton Mifflin.

Baudrillard, J. 1997. Paroxysm: The End of the Millennium or the Countdown. *Economy and Society* 26/4: 447–455. [Online]. Available: <http://www.egs.edu/faculty/jean-baudrillard/articles/paroxysm-the-end-of-the-millennium-or-the-countdown> [6 November 2009].

Baudrillard, J. 1999. *The Transparency of Evil: Essays in Extreme Phenomena*. Translated by James Benedict. London: Verso.

Baudrillard, Jean. 2001. L'esprit du Terrorisme. *Le Monde*, 2 November. English translation available at <http://www.egs.edu/faculty/baudrillard-the-spirit-of-terrorism.html> [2 February 2009].

Béla-Rásky & Wolf Perez, E. 1996. Introduction, in *Cultural Policy and Cultural Administration in Europe: 42 Outlines*. Vienna: Österreichische Kulturdokumentation: 4–6.

Boal, A. 1979. *Theater of the Oppressed*. London: Pluto Press.

Boden, Zoe. 2003. *Article 19*. Interview with Lloyd Newson. 22 July. Available: <http://www.article19.co.uk/06/interview/lloyd_newson.php> [4 December 2009].

Burns, S. & Harrison, S. 2009. *Dance Mapping. A window on dance 2004–2008. Executive summary*. Published by the Arts Council England. Available: <http://www.artscouncil.org.uk/media/uploads/dance_mapping_executive_summary.pdf> [5 January 2010].

Burt, R. 2006. *Judson Dance Theater. Performative Traces*. London/New York: Routledge.

Caute, D. 2003. *The Dancer Defects. The Struggle for Cultural Supremacy During the Cold War*. Oxford: Oxford University Press.

Copeland, R. 1990. In Defence of Formalism. The Politics of Disinterestedness. *Dance Theatre Journal* 7/4: 4–7 & 37–39.

Croce, A. 2000. Discussing the Undiscussable, in Arlene Croce: *Writing in the Dark, Dancing in the 'New Yorker'*. Gainesville: University Press of Florida.

Cunxin, L. 2003. *Mao's Last Dancer*. Camberwell, Victoria: Viking/Penguin Press.

Delaney, J. 1997. An Introduction to Arts Council Dance Funding. *Ballet Magazine*. October. [Online]. Available: <http://www.ballet.co.uk/oct97/arts_council_dance_funding.htm> [14 December 2009].

Douglas, P. 1935. Modern Dance Forms, *New Theater*, 26–27 November, in Mark Franko 1995: *Dancing Modernism/Performing Politics*. Bloomington and Indianapolis: Indiana University Press: 137–142.

Dudley, J. 1934. The Mass Dance. *New Theatre*, 17–18 December, in Mark Franko, 1995: *Dancing Modernism/Performing Politics*. Bloomington and Indianapolis: Indiana University Press: 119–122.

Eisenberg, E. 1935. Ladies of the Revolutionary Dance Movement. *New Theatre*, 10–11 February, in Mark Franko, 1995: *Dancing Modernism/Performing Politics*. Bloomington and Indianapolis: Indiana University Press: 129–133.

Franko, M. 1995. *Dancing Modernism/Performing Politics*. Bloomington and Indianapolis: Indiana University Press.

Franko, M. 2002. *The Work of Dance: Labor, Movement and Identity in the 1930s*. Middletown, CT: Wesleyan University Press.

Franko, M. 2007. Dance and the Political. States of Exception, in *Dance Discourses. Keywords in Dance Research*. Edited by Susanne Franco and Marina Nordera. In conjunction with the Centre national de la danse. London/New York: Routledge: 11–28.

Freedman, E. 1934. Dance: Which Technique? *New Theatre*, 17–18 May, in Mark Franko, 1995: *Dancing Modernism/Performing Politics*. Bloomington and Indianapolis: Indiana University Press: 122–124.

Gautier, T. 1986. Opera: Return of Fanny Elssler in La Tempête (1837), in Théophile Gautier: *Gautier on Dance*. Selected, translated and annotated by Ivor Guest. London: Dance Books.

Gautier, T. 1979. *Mademoiselle de Maupin*. Texte présenté et commenté par Jacques Robichez. Paris: Imprimerie nationale.

Gere, D. 2004. *How to Make Dances in an Epidemic. Tracking Choreography in the Age of AIDS*. Madison, WI: The University of Wisconsin Press.

Gert, V. 1968. *Ich bin eine Hexe. Kaleidoscop meines Lebens*. Munich: Schneekluth.

Goebbels, J. 1933. Du holde Kunst, ich danke Dir, in *Theater-Tageblatt*, Festnummer. 10 June.

Gold, M. 1929. The Loves of Isadora. New Masses 4, 20–21 March, in Mark Franko, 1995: *Dancing Modernism/Performing Politics*. Bloomington and Indianapolis: Indiana University Press: 109–113.

Graff, E. 1997. *Stepping Left. Dance and Politics in New York City, 1928–1942*. Durham, NC: Duke University Press.

Geduld, V. 2007. *Dance is a Weapon 1932–1955*. Pantin: Centre national de la danse.

Geduld, V. 2008. Performing Communism in the American Dance: Culture, Politics and the New Dance Group. *American Communist History* 7/1: 39–65.

Hardt, Y. 2004. *Politische Körper. Ausdruckstanz, Choreographien des Protests und die Arbeiter-Kulturbewegung in der Weimarer Republik*. Münster: LIT Verlag.

Haywood, L., Kew, F. Brahmham, P. et al. 2002. *Understanding Leisure*. Cheltenham: Nelson Thornes.

Hildenbrandt, F. 1928. *Die Tänzerin Valeska Gert. Mit 27 ganzseitigen Bildern*. Stuttgart: Hädecke.

In praise of dancing. Editorial. 2008. *The Guardian*, 20 December <http://www.
guardian.co.uk/commentisfree/2008/dec/20/strictly-come-dancing-bbc> [15
December 2010].

Jameson, F. 1985. Postmodernism and Consumer Society, in *Postmodern Culture*.
Edited by Hal Foster. London/Sydney: Pluto Press.

Kant, I. 1952. *The Critique of Judgement*. Translated by J. C. Meredith. Oxford: Oxford
University Press.

Kershaw, B. 1992. *Politics of Performance: Radical Theatre as Cultural Intervention*.
London/New York: Routledge.

Kershaw, B. 1999. *Radical in Performance: Between Brecht and Baudrillard*. London/
New York: Routledge.

Kirstein, L. 1985. Revolutionary Ballet Forms, in *New Theatre and Film 1934–1937.
An Anthology*. Edited by Herbert Kline. San Diego, CA: Harcourt Brace
Jovanovich.

Kolb, A. 2009. *Performing Femininity. Dance and Literature in German Modernism*.
Oxford: Peter Lang.

Kretz-Mangold, M. 2006. *Grelle Szenen eines Lebens*. Interview with Johann Kresnik. 12
February. Available: <http://www.wdr.de/themen/kultur/theater/ulrike_mein-
hof/interview_kresnik.jhtml> [31 October 2007].

Lehmann, H.-T. 2006. *Postdramatic Theatre*. Translated and with an introduction by
Karen Jürs-Munby. London and New York: Routledge.

Mackrell, J. 2004. The Power to Provoke. *The Guardian*, June 5. [Online]. Available:
<http://guardian.c.uk/sage/2004/jun/05/dance.music> [1 November 2009].

Martin, J. 1983. From 'The Dance'. Dance as a Means of Communication, in *What is
Dance? Readings in Theory and Criticism*. Edited by Roger Copeland and Marshall
Cohen. Oxford/New York/Toronto: Oxford University Press: 22–23.

McDowell, A. 2008. Politics has no place in arts funding, say UK Tories. *National
Post*, 19 August. [Online]. Available: <http://www.cimamusic.ca/Page.asp?Pag
eID=122&ContentID=1329&SiteNodeID=66> [4 February 2010].

McElroy, W. 1999. *Art and State: The Case for Separation* (originally posted on <http://
www.mises.org>, September 28). Available: <http://www.wendymcelroy.com/
mises/artandstate.html> [2 March 2010].

La Musique et la danse. La politique culturelle 1981–1991. 1991. Published by the Min-
istère de la culture, de la communication et des grands travaux.

Nicholas, L. 2001. Fellow Travellers: Dance and British Cold War Politics in the Early
1950s. *Dance Research* 19/2: 83–105.

O'Mahony, J. 2006. Baghdad Ballet. *Guardian*, 28 September. [Online]. <http://www. guardian.co.uk/stage/2006/sep28/dance.iraq> [28 November 2009].

Omnibus. 1976. BBC1. Television programme about Kurt Jooss and *The Green Table*.

Pakes, A. 2004. Stepping Though the Looking Glass? The Aesthetics and Politics of Daniel Larrieu's Mobile ou le Miroir du Château. *Dance Research* 22/1: 22–44.

Plato. *The Laws*. London: Penguin.

Pouillaude, F. 2003. *Danse et Politique. Démarche artistique et contexte historique*. Centre national de la danse, Pantin, France: Centre national de la danse.

Prickett, S. 1990. Dance and the Workers' Struggle. *Dance Research*, 8/1: 47–61.

Prickett, S. 1994. The People: Issues of Identity Within the Revolutionary Dance, in *Of, By and For the People: Dancing on the Left in the 1930s*. Edited by Lynn Garafola. Studies in Dance History, Vol. 1. Madison, WI: Society of Dance History Scholars.

Prevots, N. 1998. *Dance for Export: Cultural Diplomacy and the Cold War*. Hanover, NH: University Press of New England.

Rainer, Y. 1974. *Work 1961–73*. Halifax, NS: The Press of Nova Scotia College of Art and Design.

Ravelhofer, B. 2006. *The Early Stuart Masque. Dance, Costume and Music*. Oxford University Press.

Reed, S. 1998. The Politics and Poetics of Dance. *Annual Review of Anthropology* 27: 503–532.

Ropa, Eugenia Casini. 1988. *La Danza et l'agitprop. I teatri non-teatrali nella cultura tedesca del primo novecento*. Bologna: Il Mulino.

Rosen, B. 2000. *The New Dance Group: Movement for a Change*. London and New York: Routledge.

Schechner, R. 1988. *Performance Theory*. New York: Routledge.

Segal, E. 1935. Directing the New Dance, *New Theatre* (May): 23.

Varney, D. 2008. Being Political in German Theatre and Performance: Anna Langhoff and Christoph Schlingensief, in *Proceedings of the 2006 Annual Conference of the Australasian Association for Drama, Theatre and Performance Studies*. Edited by Ian Maxwell. University of Sydney: 1–9.

Wassermann, A. 2005. Hannelore Kohls unwillkommene Wiederkehr. *Spiegel online*, 18 January. Available: <http://www.spiegel.de/kultur/gesellschaft/0,1518,336800,00. html> [5 February 2010].

Woodley, D. 2006. *Conservatism*. Deddington: Philip Allan Updates.

PART I

Choreographing the Revolution

ROGER COPELAND

2 The Death of the Choreographer

The Paradigm Shifts

The summer of 2009 marked a melancholy milestone in the history of dance as an art form. Two of the great living choreographers, Pina Bausch and Merce Cunningham, died within a depressingly brief span of thirty days. The pantheon of 'world class' choreographers who had dominated Western theatrical dance in the second half of the twentieth century was left greatly impoverished. But from the perspective of academic dance studies, the era that Bausch and Cunningham represented – that of 'The Great Western Individual Choreographer' – had already come and gone.

Alas, even the most superficial survey of the subjects now approved for doctoral dissertations (or for presentations at academic conferences) reveals a drastic swing of the pendulum away from dances created by 'individual' Western choreographers such as Nijinsky, Ashton, Tudor, Graham, Balanchine, Cunningham, Tharp, Morris (et al.) and toward traditional, culture-specific and/or collectivist movement-forms such as salsa, flamenco, kapa haka, break dancing, capoeira, contra-dance, belly dancing, Bharata Natyam and contact improvisation.

Of course, to some extent, this paradigm shift is merely an inevitable (and wholly welcome) consequence of globalization and its curricular corollaries: multiculturalism and cultural diversity. To wit: would any reputable dance scholar (no matter how 'Western' his or her areas of specialization) deny that Indian Kathakali or Japanese Noh or the Javanese Bedoyo belong in the choreographic canon alongside Petipa's *Swan Lake*, Balanchine's *Concerto Barocco* or Martha Graham's *Primitive Mysteries*? I hope not. But to my mind, this radical revision of the curriculum has less to do with the self-evident beauty and complexity of much non-western dance and more to do with ideology: a misguided belief that 'collectively created' works are superior (at least in some theoretically 'political' sense) to dances whose 'authorship' can be attributed to unique, Western individuals.

Consider, for example, a recent essay by Susan Foster titled 'Choreographies and Choreographers' published in June of 2008. Foster is highly critical of the 'special place' that twentieth-century Western dance scholarship has traditionally afforded to 'dances authored by a single artist as distinct from forms of dance practiced world-wide that could not be traced to a single creator' (Foster 2008: 12). Granted, the phrase 'world-wide' might lead one to assume that Foster is merely reasserting the value of studying dance in a global, rather than Eurocentric or Western context. But I do not believe that her eagerness to de-emphasize the individual choreographic 'author' can be explained quite so simply. Note for example that even when discussing Euro-American trends in contemporary dance (e.g. contact improvisation), Foster champions an alternative choreographic model which conceives of the dancemaker as 'laborer and collaborator' rather than 'inspired genius' (2008: 15). She even argues (unconvincingly) that the linguistic practice of bestowing the honorific label of 'choreography' on some forms of dance – but not others – is part and parcel of the early twentieth-century tradition of heroic modernism and its attendant cult of individual artistic genius:

> Beginning in the late 1920s and early 1930s [...] the term 'choreography' came into widespread and new usage, especially in the United States. It was used regularly in concert programs, newspaper reviews, and significantly, in the curriculum of the Bennington Summer Dance Festival. (ibid.: 9)

During the 1930s, Bennington was often the summer home of the principal pioneers of American modern dance: Martha Graham and Doris Humphrey. Indeed, for Foster, the very concept of the individual choreographer as 'inspired genius' is intimately linked to the ascendance of early modern dance:

> The inspired genius of the individual took on a new luster in comparison with the role of social dance teachers and arrangers of dances, such as those who were setting pieces for reviews, night club entertainments, or other Broadway attractions. (ibid.: 11–12)

But the real problem for Foster is that this hierarchical distinction between choreographic art and popular, commercially viable dance

accomplished one further exclusion: it secured a special place for dances authored by a single artist [...] while excluding group authored or anonymously authored work. (ibid.: 12)

It's true (of course!) that choreographers of Broadway musicals – at least before the advent of Jerome Robbins – rarely exercised as much authorial control over their work as they might have wished. But why would Foster – herself a choreographer as well as a dance historian – choose to criticize rather than applaud Graham and Humphrey for placing a higher value on their 'labor' as modern dance choreographers than on the commercial and artistically unsatisfying work-for-hire they had churned out for Shubert Alley and The Greenwich Village Follies? (Not so very long ago, we used to refer to this sort of authorial control as artistic freedom.) More to the point, why has it become politically problematic flatly to assert, without conditions or apologies, that Graham's and Humphrey's most important contribution to dance history consists of the choreography they created for the concert stage – which is to say, the dances over which they achieved the greatest degree of authorial control?

From Modern to Post-Modern Politics

Today of course, political agendas invariably take precedence over more 'purely' aesthetic concerns such as sensory beauty, formal complexity, or emotional expressiveness. But even if the only allowable criterion for arriving at choreographic value-judgments has been wholly politicized, it should still be relatively easy to express a clear preference for, say, Graham's *Lamentation* over and above the 'ballet ballads' she devised for The Greenwich Village Follies in 1923.

To be sure, the privileged genre of early modern dance was the solo. One and the same 'inspired genius' often served as both choreographer *and* performer (thereby placing a double emphasis on the uniqueness of her movement 'signature'). Then again, the principal reason the choreographer was devising dances on her own body often had as much or more to do with budgetary limitations than with an aesthetics of self-expression (or some egomaniacal obsession with the singular self).

A political critique of early modern dance which proceeds without reference to economics is naïve enough. But that naïveté is compounded many times over if it fails to factor the sexual politics of early twentieth-century feminism into the mix. Surely Foster has not forgotten that the female pioneers of early modern dance were rejecting the two dominant genres of theatrical dance in the US at the turn of the twentieth century: ballet and 'show dancing'? And would she deny that the early years of American modern dance were inspired as much by a progressive sexual politics as by an aesthetic of modernist individualism? Little more than a generation ago – back in the halcyon days of Modernism (broadly construed) – Foster would, no doubt, have hailed Duncan, St. Denis, Graham, and Humphrey as feminist pioneers who fearlessly discarded the impersonal movement vocabulary of ballet in favor of their own uniquely personal styles of movement. She would also, I presume, have been just as quick to congratulate these 'founding mothers' for helping to steer young female dancers away from the degradations of vaudevillian spectacle (where geometric formations of leggy, scantily clad chorus girls titillated rowdy male voyeurs).

In Irving Berlin's Hollywood musical *White Christmas* (1954), Danny Kaye plays an unpretentious hoofer who archly satirizes the monochromatic starkness, flexed foot angularity, and 'deep seriousness' of an all-female Martha Graham-style modern dance ensemble. The song Kaye sings (aptly titled *Choreography*) waxes nostalgic for an earlier era when stage dancing wasn't quite so 'highfalutin': 'The the'ter, the the'ter, what's happened to the the'ter?/ Especially where dancing is concerned [...]/ Chicks who did kicks aren't kicking anymore/ They're doing choreography' (Berlin 1954). Would Foster prefer that we revert to the era of chicks doing kicks? Is the sexual politics at the heart of early modern dance no longer considered progressive? Or, has a trendier (and dare I say, more certifiably post-modern) politics come to the fore, one that now regards modern dance as just another vestige of a discredited artistic modernism?

And if so, does this post-modern politics rest on a re-evaluation of 'Western individualism' more generally and the way in which its more extreme manifestations have been embodied historically in stereotypes of the 'romantic genius' and the 'visionary modernist'? Certainly, there is something in the air today – a set of factors both generational and technological that seem to promote collectivism of one sort or another: online social networking, viral videos, MP3s and other modes of file sharing, the burgeoning aesthetic of the re-mix and the mash-up, the 'open source' and 'creative commons' movements, Lawrence Lessig's campaign against copyright laws, etc. (Lessig: 2008). Certainly, the World Wide Web itself – so central to any definition of the Zeitgeist – is all but bursting with examples of what Foster refers to as 'group authored or anonymously authored work' (most prominently perhaps, Wikipedia).

But this essay will deal primarily with dance; and in that regard Foster is simply giving us the dance world equivalent of an argument that Fredric Jameson has been making since the early 1980s. His classic essay 'Postmodernism and the Consumer Society' is an excellent example of the now familiar practice of using artistic modernism as a barometer for measuring the rise of extreme individualism in Western societies. Jameson begins by asking 'why classical modernism is a thing of the past and why post-modernism should have taken its place' (1983: 114). The answer derives from his belief that 'the great modernisms' were 'organically linked to the conception of a unique self and private identity' (ibid.). Jameson makes no mention of dance, modern or otherwise; but he does cite, as examples of these 'great modernisms': 'Abstract Expressionism, the great modernist poetry of Pound, Eliot or Wallace Stevens, the International Style (Le Corbusier, Frank Lloyd Wright, Mies); Stravinsky, Joyce, Proust and Mann...' (ibid.: 111–112). Each of these modernisms, according to Jameson, is 'predicated on the invention of a personal, private style, as unmistakable as your fingerprint, as incomparable as your own body' (ibid.: 114).

Demonizing the Auteur

If our analysis of Jameson's argument were to end here, he might be accused of merely rehashing the tired, old Marxist diatribe against idiosyncratic, personal styles which stray too far from a 'realistic' depiction of the material world that is readily recognizable to the average person. In the early 1930s for example, the British Marxist Christopher Caudwell vilified surrealism as 'the ultimate bourgeois revolution' – solely because of its preoccupation with the unconscious (which Caudwell equated with the most interior and private realm of the individual 'self'; quoted by Poggioli 1968: 98). But Jameson is drawing on the work of French post-structuralists like Barthes, Derrida and Foucault whose critique of the concept of 'authorship' can be traced back to the 1960s.

Even earlier, Jacques Lacan had challenged the central underlying assumption of American 'ego psychology': the idea that the ego masters the id, thereby integrating and synthesizing separate elements of the psyche into a unified whole. According to this argument, as long as the ego remains 'in control' of the otherwise unruly id, even the most competitive and rugged individuals will then be guided by rational self-interest (thereby alleviating any need for governmental regulation of the capitalist free market.) That at least is the argument in defense of laissez-faire capitalism which Lacan attributes to the American ego psychologists (Mehlman 1972: 19). Needless to say, Lacan proceeds to completely demolish this argument, along with any claim for a stable, unified 'I' or 'self'.

But the essay that did the most to bring this critique of the individual author and the 'unitary ego' to bear upon the arts was undoubtedly Roland Barthes' 'The Death of the Author'. (Barthes' essay enjoyed the added cachet of having been published in 1968 – a year that has been mythologized in ways that make it virtually synonymous with radical collectivism of all kinds.) In that seminal essay, Barthes wrote:

> The author is a modern figure, a product of our society insofar as, emerging from the Middle Ages and the personal faith of the Reformation, it discovered the prestige of the individual [...] the epitome and culmination of capitalist ideology, which has attached the greatest importance to the 'person' of the author. (1977a: 142–143)

(Note that Barthes is already proposing a connection between authorship, individualism, and capitalist ideology.)

The conclusion to Barthes' essay has become one of the most frequently quoted sentences in the academic literature of the past forty years: 'The birth of the reader must be at the cost of the death of the author' (ibid.: 148). 'Classic criticism', he maintains, 'has never paid any attention to the reader: for it, the writer is the only person in literature...' (ibid.). But in Barthes' view, 'A text's unity lies not in its origin, but in its destination' (ibid.). That destination is, of course, the newly radicalized reader.

So merely by proclaiming 'death' to the author, Barthes would have us believe that the reader has been greatly empowered – that he or she is no longer a passive 'consumer' of the author's intended meaning, but rather an active 'co-producer' of that meaning (indeed a co-creator of the literary work in question.) As a result, the poor beleaguered author was now consigned to a fate even *worse* than death. He (and I choose that pronoun advisedly because the author's gender was invariably presumed to be male) was now cast in the role of dictatorial villain determined to impose his own signature – his own vision of the world – on the poor, passive, victimized reader. Worse still: individual authorship came to signify the totalitarian – or theocratic – practice of insisting on a single 'official' meaning (or interpretation) for every text. Authorship thus came to be pejoratively associated with the arbitrary exercise of *authority*.

Barthes would soon go on to distinguish between 'readerly' texts and 'writerly' texts. Only in the writerly variety is the reader (or, in the case of the performing arts, the audience) a co-producer of the work's meaning. I mention Barthes' distinction between the readerly and the writerly because Susan Foster had already begun to utilize this aspect of his argument in her very first book, *Reading Dancing* (1986). In fact, the root of Foster's eventual critique of Martha Graham as 'inspired genius' is evident in the following passage from *Reading Dancing*:

> According to Barthes, the readerly work, the equivalent of Graham's choreography, suffocates the reader with its single intended message, whereas the writerly text offers the reader the opportunity to participate in the creation of its meaning. (1986: 240)

(Note that for Foster, Martha Graham is the quintessential example of a choreographic 'author' who imposes her intended 'meanings' on the viewer in a dictatorial fashion.)

In his subsequent writings, Barthes will re-conceive of literary criticism as a project whose primary goal is to 'de-originate the utterance', thereby highlighting the collective, or in his words 'polyvocal' (rather than 'univocal') nature of authorship (1974: 21). Here Barthes is also harking back to some of his earliest writing about Brecht in the mid-1950s. In a revealing 1974 interview Barthes admitted 'I would be so happy if these words of Brecht could be applied to me: "He thought in the heads of others; and in his own, others than he were thinking"' (1985: 195).

Building on Lacan's deconstruction of the 'unified ego', Barthes will, in effect, argue that the singular 'authorial' consciousness from which the idiosyncratic styles of high modernism were thought to originate is at best an ideological construction of Western capitalist individualism. In fact, the difficulty of tracing such seemingly unique styles back to a single point of origin will lead Barthes and his followers to question the very existence of absolute 'originality'. In *S/Z* (1970), he describes more precisely what he means by the 'polyvocal' nature of authorship: '… in their interweaving, these voices, (whose origin is "lost" in the vast perspective of the already-written) de-originate the utterance' (1974: 21).

By 1971, in *From Work to Text* Barthes had begun to associate the ideology of individual authorship not only with capitalist ownership (i.e. the birth of copyright laws) but also with patriarchal authority:

> The author is reputed the father and owner of his work: literary science therefore teaches *respect* (his emphasis) for the manuscript and the author's declared intentions, while society asserts the legality of the relation of author to work (the 'droit d'auteur' or copyright)... (1977b: 160–161)

This is the theoretical foundation Jameson is building on when – little more than a decade later – he argues that in the post-modern era, highly individualized styles are neither possible nor desirable:

> … today, from any number of distinct perspectives, the social theorists, the psychoanalysts, even the linguists [...] are all exploring the notion that *that* kind of individualism

and personal identity is a thing of the past [...] and that one might even describe the concept of the unique individual and the theoretical basis of individualism as ideological. (1983: 114–115)

Similarly, just a few years later, Susan Foster adopts this same approach to the 'unique individual' in *Reading Dancing*:

> Throughout the book, I have used the term *subject* to refer to the 'I' or the 'self' of the person dancing. I have chosen to speak of the dancer's subject rather than the more commonly used 'dancer's self' to signify a theoretical position that holds that the self is not a natural or fixed entity but rather a process constituted by various cultural and historical circumstances. Barthes summarizes a wealth of recent anthropological, historical, and philosophical research on this matter when he says, 'The "I" which approaches the text is already a plurality of other texts...' (1986: 236)

No wonder Foster finds fault with the highly individuated conception of 'self' at the heart of early modern dance! Is there another variety of modernist art more fiercely committed to the discovery of a 'personal, private style [...] as incomparable as your own body' (1983: 114)? Consider, for example, the deep subjectivity and interiority embodied in Doris Humphrey's insistence on 'moving from *the inside* out' or Martha Graham's declared intention to 'make visible the *interior* landscape' (both quoted in Cohen, 1974: 122).

Here then is the key to Foster's and Jameson's post-modern update of Marxist aesthetics: rather than attacking idiosyncratic, modernist styles in the outmoded manner of a 1930s socialist realist, they can achieve the same result in a more intellectually nuanced way. Individualism *itself* will now come under attack as a peculiarly Western 'ideological construction': a historical and cultural convention rather than a biological given. Or, in Jameson's own words, '... not only is the bourgeois individual subject a thing of the past, it is also a myth; it never really existed in the first place; there have never been autonomous subjects of that type' (1983: 115).

From Theory to Practice

So much for the theory. Time for a reality check. Is there any evidence to
suggest that 'individual' Western modernists (e.g. choreographers who
set out to devise uniquely original and deeply personal vocabularies of
movement) are either consciously or unconsciously promoting bourgeois
values of competitive individualism in a capitalist free market? To cite only
the most obvious counter-examples, the dances that Graham and Humphrey choreographed during the 1930s are not exactly tributes to social
Darwinism, robber-baron mercantilism, or for that matter, even rugged
individualism. In fact, Humphrey's *New Dance* (1935) is a profound medi-
tation on the importance of *balancing* the needs of the individual with the
equally compelling claims of the group. In her notes for this dance, she
writes, 'Solo dances flow out of the group and back into it again without
break and the most important part is the group. Except for an occasional
brilliant individual, the day of the solo dance is over' (quoted in Cohen,
1974: 148). Even the overtly patriotic tributes to American 'frontier spirit'
that Graham choreographed during World War II (*Appalachian Spring* in
1944, for example) emphasize the values of communal interdependence as
much as individual accomplishment.

Conversely, are we to assume that the group-oriented 'movement
choirs' Rudolph von Laban organized in Hitler's Germany between 1934
and 1936 were exercises in progressive collectivism simply because they
de-emphasized the individual and were designed to accommodate – in a
seemingly egalitarian fashion – participants with widely varying degrees of
technical training? Would these movement choirs have been sponsored so
enthusiastically by Joseph Goebbels if they were thought to have promoted
a left-leaning politics of 'the people' rather than a right-wing politics of 'the
masses' (a fascistically politicized conception of the 'Volk' which would
eventually culminate in the orgiastic group choreography of the Nuremberg
Rallies as documented by Leni Riefenstahl in *Triumph of the Will*)?

By contrast, was it not Martha Graham who quite publically rejected
an invitation to perform at the 1936 Summer Olympics in Berlin, precisely

because she wanted to protest against the politics of fascism? Similarly, it was Graham, not Laban, who created *Chronicle* in 1936 as well as *Deep Song* and *Immediate Tragedy* a year later – all three conceived at least in part for the purpose of lending emotional support to the Republican struggle against Francisco Franco and his forces during the Spanish Civil War. And what is true of Graham and Humphrey is as true or truer of many of the modernists in other art forms whom Fredric Jameson singles out for the uniqueness of their styles. Picasso is a prime example.

The violent dislocations in both analytic and synthetic cubism might initially appear to typify what Malraux had in mind when he wrote that 'The modern artist's supreme aim is to subdue all things to his style' (1953: 119). But does this aesthetic strategy translate into a fascistic desire on Picasso's part to subdue his fellow Spaniards in real life? If so, wouldn't he have been a supporter, rather than an outspoken opponent, of Generalissimo Franco?

Similarly, many of these same high modernists viewed the singular 'self' as more of a burden than a boon, an obstacle to be transcended or otherwise submerged into neo-classical traditions. Stravinsky, Schoenberg, Joyce, and Pound would all have subscribed to T. S. Eliot's belief that 'The progress of an artist is a continual self-sacrifice, a continual extinction of personality' (1963: 143). The very title of Eliot's luminous essay of 1919 ('Tradition and the Individual Talent') refutes the simpleminded idea that high modernism uncritically celebrates 'individual' talent at the expense of time-honored traditions.

Eliot's conception of modernism finds its closest choreographic parallel in many of the Balanchine ballets (e.g. *Apollo*) which typify this choreographer's paradoxical commitment to modern neo-classicism. Or, as Balanchine himself phrased it (much more aphoristically): 'Foreward to Petipa' (1984: 26). Similarly, Balanchine's sleek, minimalist, high *modernist* ballets (*Agon, Stravinsky Violin Concerto*) constitute an important reminder that high modernism in dance connotes much more than modern dance *per se*. Balanchine (and Cunningham as well) were both – in their own ways – exemplary modernists. But neither were proponents of unbridled romantic individualism or the cult of inspired genius. Balanchine for example considered it blasphemous to refer to choreographers as the 'creators' of dances. 'God creates, I assemble', he once quipped (1984: 32). Another of his famously self-deprecating aphorisms was: 'My muse must come to me on union time' (ibid.: 7). (So much for 'inspiration'.) Analogously, Merce Cunningham's use of 'chance procedures' as a choreographic tool was expressly designed to circumvent his own uniquely personal habits of movement invention.

The arguments of Barthes, Jameson, and Foster notwithstanding, there is no meaningful correlation between an art work's style of authorship and its politics. There are of course examples of successful artist/activist collectives such as The Guerrilla Girls, Gran Fury or Wu Ming for whom the collaborative – and often anonymous – nature of authorship is an essential component of the artistic enterprise. Anonymity also plays a practical role for 'guerilla' artists whose work may involve illegal activities such as trespassing or the defacement of property.

But all too often, the decision to create art *collectively* leads to muddled and artistically compromised results. Would anyone possessing the slightest degree of aesthetic sophistication argue that The Living Theatre's 'collective creations' (e.g. *Paradise Now* 1968) were artistically superior to their work of the late 50s and early 60s (e.g. their productions of Jack Gelber's *The Connection* or Kenneth Brown's *The Brig*: theater pieces that continued to employ a hierarchical division of labor among author, director and performer)? Granted, the rehearsal process which led to *Paradise Now* was undeniably more egalitarian and collectivist. But the product that resulted from this process was excruciatingly naïve (*politically* as well as aesthetically).

Clearly, the uniquely personal vision of an 'auteur' is just as likely to promote a progressive as a conservative politics – or, for that matter, no discernable politics at all. Conversely, group or anonymously authored work does not automatically yield a populist, egalitarian or progressive result (let alone a satisfying *artistic* result). In this regard, it might be worth noting that Jimmy Wales, who conceived of Wikipedia, is a libertarian not a democratic socialist or a political progressive; and the same is true of many proponents of the hacker/cyberpunk credo: 'information wants to be free'.

Modernism and Individualism

Of course, only a fool would deny the existence of any connection whatsoever between modernism and individualism. And by modernism, I mean both a specific period of Western history and a specific era in Western art. Whether or not it constitutes the official beginning of the modernist era, the posthumous publication of Rousseau's *Confessions* in 1782 marks a momentous break with the eighteenth-century Enlightenment belief that human dignity derives principally from what we hold in common with others. The opening paragraph of Rousseau's memoir contains the following declaration of difference: 'I am made unlike anyone I have ever met. I will venture to say, I am like no one in the whole world. I may be no better, but at least I am different' (1953: 17). And from that proud assertion of originality and uniqueness, it is a relatively short leap to Rimbaud's defiant assertion of otherness ('Je est un autre') a century later in 1871.

Now, it is probably true that a *poète maudit* like Rimbaud will be difficult to enlist in a communal enterprise. As Wallace Stevens once quipped, 'A community of originals is not a community' (quoted by Young-blood, 1970: 605). But on the other hand, the deracinated avant-gardist is unlikely to be mistaken for a middle class merchant. And when it comes to the art works created by these unique individuals, even the most insular, abstract, and self-referential modernist styles issue their own quiet protest against the 'utilitarian' character of middle class life: the idea that everything of value serves some practical end 'beyond itself' in society at large. Similarly, Johan Huizinga contrasts the non-utilitarian (and thus anti-economic) nature of 'homo ludens' (man at play) with the behavior of 'homo economicus' (Huizinga 1950: 1938). Thus, the modernist who prides himself on the singular originality of his work (even if that originality manifests itself in hermetic insularity) has more in common with the former than the latter.

But these counter-arguments appear to be lost on the post-modernists for whom the outsider status of the prototypical modern artist invariably comes to symbolize a social order which celebrates individualism at the expense of nearly everything else. Suzi Gablik for example in *Has Modernism Failed?* (1984) argues that

> For better or worse, modern consciousness is solitary, consequent to the disestablish-ing of communal reality. It is the most intense form of individualism the world has ever known. [...] The most fundamental assumption of modernity [...] is that the social unit of society is not the group, guild, tribe, or city, but the person. That the contemporary bourgeois artist, as a result of these historical processes, sees his rela-tion to art as an individual, and not as a social relation, is inevitable. (1984: 31)

To her credit, Gablik acknowledges that the modernist 'auteur' or 'individual genius' is not necessarily a proponent of – or even indirectly complicit with – the ideology of laissez-faire capitalism: 'Modern capitalist society [...] has been largely an object of dislike by its artists. Our great art has almost never been socially celebrative; it has been overtly hostile or coldly indifferent to the social order...' (ibid.: 30).

Gablik movingly laments the 'social and psychological facts [that] have dislocated artists from their embeddedness in the real world' (ibid.). But the alternative she offers is both regressive and unrealistic: the sug-gestion that we in the West emulate 'traditional' societies and non-West-ern cultures which have not yet been infected by the virus of modernist individualism:

> In traditional societies, the individual lives submerged in tradition which is, for him, immutable reality, transmitted from a venerable past; the individual does nothing on his own account, apart from the social group. Indeed, nothing is more terrible than to be cast out of the collective and to remain alone. (ibid.: 30)

In fact, so eager is Gablik to re-integrate the artist into society-at-large, that even the Middle Ages appear to hold more appeal for her than modernity does: 'Medieval society, to cite another instance, placed art at the service of religion. The artist exalted the dominant values of his society. [...] Reli-gion, ritual, and art existed primarily to support the social order' (ibid.). So what exactly are post-modernists like Gablik advocating? A return to the Middle Ages? Do they really want contemporary artists to 'exalt the dominant values of society'? Why are they so reluctant to acknowledge the potentially *constructive* role the artist might play as a social 'outsider'?

Still, if nothing else, Gablik's celebration of traditional and non-Western societies helps illuminate another essential dimension of the sea-change in dance studies we discussed at the beginning of this essay: the current swing of the curricular pendulum away from dances 'authored by a single artist' and toward works that are created collectively or anonymously. When Gablik praises the art of traditional societies, arguing that 'Primitive art [...] is never personal. It doesn't reflect a private point of view' (ibid.), she is giving us yet another variation on Barthes' critique of individual authorship. In fact, Barthes himself took a tentative step in this direction when he wrote in 'The Death of the Author':

> In ethnographic societies, the responsibility for a narrative is never assumed by a person but by a mediator, shaman or relator, whose 'performance' – the mastery of the narrative code – may possibly be admired, but never his genius. The author is a modern figure, a product of our society... (1977a: 142)

Culture in the Age of Cultural Studies

Today, of course, Barthes' use of the term 'ethnographic' would strike most academics as both quaint and politically incorrect. In the twenty-first century, the anthropologically approved terminology would be 'indigenous' and/or 'traditional' cultures. But in any event, these are the cultures in which group or anonymously authored work is still common. In Western post-industrial societies, by contrast, the genie of individualism escaped from the bottle more than four centuries ago. At least since the Renaissance, the arts which Matthew Arnold included in his definition of 'high culture' have been created principally by unique individuals. And in the modernist period, these individuals have often adopted what Lionel Trilling called an 'adversary relationship' toward mainstream culture (1968: 105). They are no longer the vessels through which the dominant cultural mythologies – Barthes' 'narrative codes' – are communicated. Quite the contrary. Art for them is a means of resisting (if not completely escaping) the very societal conditioning which produces 'normative' culture. As the contemporary visual artist Carl Andre once put it 'Culture is something that is done to us. Art is something that we do to culture' (quoted in Dirda 1998: Section X: 4).

Note that Andre (unlike Matthew Arnold) is using the word 'culture' in its broad, anthropological sense to connote impersonal systems of inherited belief, standardized social characteristics, and customary rules of behavior. Culture of this kind is always a collective creation; and in the age of Cultural Studies *this* is the concept of culture which now matters most in academia. That, of course, has always been the case for the social sciences like anthropology and sociology. But it is only since the rise of Cultural Studies over the past generation that this has been equally true in the Arts and Humanities.

At a minimum, Cultural Studies has expanded the parameters of 'culture' well beyond the domain of classical and modernist art, neither of which was deeply 'embedded' – to use Gablik's term – in the daily lives of common people. Hence the new prominence of the phrase 'cultural production' – a verbal umbrella which can open wide enough to cover everything from mechanically reproducible, globally disseminated forms of popular culture (television programs like *Dancing With The Stars*) to the most localized, indigenous, and site-specific forms of ritual performed by traditional, non-Western peoples. Certainly this helps explain Susan Foster's determination to ensure that Graham's *Lamentation* will be given no special pride of place over the 'ballet ballads' she devised for the Greenwich Village Follies.

The most visible consequence of this more inclusive conception of culture is that the sheer range of worldwide dance activity deemed worthy of academic study has expanded exponentially to embrace leisure-time activity (social dance), religious and ritual dance as well as countless varieties of public festival such as Mardi Gras and other manifestations of carnival. Note that the emphasis in many of these examples is on dan*cing* – not choreography or even dancemaking – *per se*. In fact, in this expanded, global context, dance as an activity people 'do' begins to take precedence over dance as an activity some people (merely) watch. Thus, choreography that is conceived of as an art form requiring the validation of an audience becomes just one more mode of cultural production.

Thus, to a considerable extent (at least in the academy) both Susan Foster and Suzi Gablik have been granted their wish: 'culture specific' dances that are deeply embedded into the foundation of the social order – and which in many cases have been 'authored' collectively or anonymously – are now the academic *flavor de jour*. By contrast, dances which do not function as an anthropological mirror of a specific culture, which are (merely!) the idiosyncratic creation of a single individual (and which are of interest only to an elite minority of dancegoers) are deemed less worthy of sustained academic attention. Now we see why a doctoral candidate in dance studies who wants to write about a Balinese possession ritual such as the Sang Hyang Dedari (one of several sources for the classical Legong) will often have less trouble finding approval for his or her dissertation than a student who wants to write about Balanchine; unless, of course, the latter chooses to focus on Balanchine's work for Broadway, Hollywood, or the circus.

Now, there are of course many compelling reasons for wanting to enlarge the scope of dance studies beyond the realm of strictly 'aesthetic' experiences. But anthropological and sociological inclusiveness should not, in and of itself, be regarded as inherently progressive. In fact, if the growing emphasis on traditional and popular culture evolves into a zero-sum game that is played at the *expense* of individual Western choreographic 'authors', the real beneficiaries of this curricular re-orientation will be cultural conservatives.

This has already happened in the realm of public funding for the arts in America. During the so-called culture wars of the 1990s, America's National Endowment for the Arts was attacked by right wing politicians and cultural conservatives for having funded sexually 'transgressive' performances by Karen Finley and Tim Miller (among others) – not to mention the agency's indirect support for exhibitions of allegedly 'blasphemous' and/or 'obscene' photographs such as Andres Serrano's *Piss Christ* or the sado-masochistic, homoerotic images contained in Robert Mapplethorpe's *X Portfolio*. In 1990, the arts endowment was saddled by the US Congress with a statutory provision (the so-called 'decency clause') requiring the agency to factor 'standards of decency and respect for the diverse beliefs and values of the American public' into the grant-awarding process (quoted by Bauerlein 2009: 128). Then, in the US general elections of 1994, the

Republican Party gained control of both houses of Congress for the first time in forty years. Newt Gingrich, the mastermind of this 'Republican Revolution', was installed as Speaker of the House in 1995; and he quickly announced his intention to 'zero out' (i.e. eliminate all funding for) the NEA by 1997. Gingrich and his conservative cronies may not have succeeded in totally abolishing the arts endowment, but they did manage to enfeeble it. In addition to slashing its budget by 40%, they demanded that the NEA be radically re-structured in ways that would effectively prevent it from funding controversial work. Significantly, the specific program they were most eager to de-fund was the one that provided fellowships for individual artists.

Why did cultural conservatives like Gingrich single out funding for work created by individuals rather than, say, funding for folk and traditional art forms where authorship was more likely to be collective or anonymous? The answer is simple: the troublemakers who had used taxpayer dollars to create work which offended significant portions of 'the public' were all *individual* artists. Furthermore, it is no coincidence that in 1997 – Gingrich's original target date for the complete abolition of the NEA – President Clinton agreed to appoint as the endowment's new chair William Ivey, a businessman who had worked most recently as director of The Country Music Foundation in Nashville, Tennessee. A longtime partisan of folk and traditional art, Ivey was greeted warmly by cultural conservatives who viewed him as a welcome antidote to the East Coast 'elitists' who had traditionally headed the arts agency.

Ivey's populist agenda was immediately evident in a radically revised mission statement he devised for the NEA titled *An Investment in America's Living Cultural Heritage* (note the emphasis on 'heritage'). In his accompanying chairman's statement, he added:

> Today, art is no longer confined to paintings in museums – or dances, plays and symphonies in concert halls and theaters [...]. (T)he arts give communities a sense of identity, shared pride [...] and a way to communicate across cultural boundaries [...]. It is vital to democracy to honor and preserve its multi-cultural artistic heritage as well as support new ideas. (quoted by Bauerlein 2009: 132)

Of course, in actual practice the newly reconstituted NEA was considerably less committed to supporting (potentially controversial) 'new ideas' than it was to promoting family-friendly examples of culturally diverse folk and traditional art. So rather than daring to defend its (at best occasional) support for culturally combative individual artists such as Finley and Serrano, the endowment fell back on what might be dubbed 'the multi-cultural alibi': the idea, promulgated by post-modernists like Suzi Gablik, that a shift of focus away from difficult, adversarial artworks (created by avant-garde individuals) and toward traditional and culture-specific forms is part and parcel of a broad, politically progressive agenda; one consistent, moreover, with the aspirations of a culturally diverse nation. Thus, endowment employees who might have otherwise felt guilty about having caved in to censorious pressures from paleo-conservatives like Jesse Helms could now salve their troubled consciences simply by flaunting their 'multi-cultural' funding credentials.

But this is sheer self-delusion. The fact of the matter is that individual avant-garde artists who define themselves in opposition to the conformist, anti-intellectual, and consumerist tendencies of contemporary American culture are often behaving in ways that are incomparably more progressive than 'traditional' artists who perpetuate the prevailing values of the social order in which their work is so deeply embedded. In fact, the anthropological conception of culture so central to Cultural Studies is inherently conservative. In the words of anthropologist Richard Shweder: 'The genius of culture is to create an ontological system so compelling that what is inside and outside of a person are viewed as of a piece, no seams and patches noticeable' (1990: 3).

Ironically, this unifying conception of culture and individual self promotes the very concept of organic unity that Lacan and the post-structualists set out to deconstruct. When Suzi Gablik laments the 'social and psychological facts (that) have dislocated artists from their embeddedness in the real world' (1984: 30), she is waxing nostalgic for the sort of anthropological system Shweder describes – one in which the artist, no less than any other individual, is stitched so tightly and woven so deeply into the fabric of culture that it becomes impossible for him or her to ever stand fully *outside* that system in order to criticize it. Lionel Trilling, in his landmark essay 'Freud: Within and Beyond Culture' wrote:

> [Freud] made it apparent to us how entirely implicated in culture we all are [...]
> he made plain how the culture suffuses the remotest parts of the individual mind,
> being taken in almost literally with the mother's milk [...]. But he also sees the self
> as set against the culture, struggling against it, having been from the first reluctant
> to enter it... (1968: 105)

So when Carl Andre (in the quip cited earlier) states that 'Culture is something that is done to us. Art is something that we do to culture', he is aphoristically summarizing Trilling's idea that the adversarial modern artist will 'see the self as set against the culture'.

Needless to say, the social practices of some traditional cultures can also function as a radical critique of the economic inequalities that plague free market societies. For example, aboriginal communities such as the Nuxwalk and the Tlingit in the Pacific Northwest have traditionally relied on a ceremony called the Potlatch which promotes stability by ritually redistributing tribal wealth. But the inherently conservative function of 'culture' within those societies will continue to prevent their own members from criticizing other social practices that post-modernists do *not* regard as progressive (certain gender role assumptions, hunting practices, etc.).

Privatization in the 1980s

It is easy, though, to understand why the post-modern critique of personal, 'private' styles and other visionary aspects of high modernist art came to fruition when it did: in the 1980s. If ever a period of political history cried out for a serious critique of individualism-run-rampant, it was surely the eighties. This, after all, was the decade in which Margaret Thatcher attempted to dismantle the British welfare state, while her partner in privatization Ronald Reagan set out to repeal the progressive accomplishments of FDR's New Deal and of LBJ's Great Society. The Iron Lady's political philosophy is probably best summed up by her notorious proclamation that 'There is no such thing as society. There are individual men and women...' (Thatcher, 1987).

But in what sense is Jameson's or Foster's or Gablik's re-examination of the uniquely personal styles of high modernists like Proust, Pound, or Martha Graham in any way commensurate with an analysis of Thatcher's and Reagan's vision of society as little more than a competitive conglomeration of atomized individuals? A 'private' style in art – no matter how insular or hermetic – is not synonymous with a desire to dismantle (i.e. privatize) the public sector.

A serious reconsideration of individualism makes sense in a political context only if it is brought to bear on the many ways in which 'privatization' undermines the common good. For example, one could (indeed, one *should*) argue that the American infatuation with private automobiles precludes good public transportation. Similarly, the deeply ingrained American fear of socialized medicine – and its accompanying belief that health is an essentially private matter – militates against the establishment of universal health care in the US. (Note that Barack Obama never even proposed a 'single payer' plan like the United Kingdom's. In fact, the insurance reform he eventually passed does not even contain a 'public option'.) Likewise, a widespread conviction that the Second Amendment to the US Constitution protects a pre-existing individual right to own firearms stands in the way of effective gun control legislation. And – precisely because US elections are not publically financed – lobbying groups like the National Rifle Association exercise disproportionate influence over both the electoral and the legislative process.

But were the great visionary modernists either consciously or unconsciously complicit with those right wing politicians and libertarian political theorists who refuse to acknowledge that even the most fundamental social services (i.e. health care, transportation, energy, education, the prison system, et al.) should remain entirely public and wholly immune to the privatizing incentives of the profit motive? Obviously not. But ironically, their critics (e.g. writers like Gablik and Foster) often championed an identity-based politics which perversely – if inadvertently – perpetuated Reagan's and Thatcher's attack on the very idea of society as a 'totality' which transcends both the self-interest of individuals and the particularized agendas of special interest groups.

Indeed, in the age of Cultural Studies, the most unforgiveable sin of all is to 'totalize'. Any attempt to identify social or cultural universals is now dismissed as a disguised (and despised) 'centrism' of one sort or another (euro-, logo-, phallogo-, etc.). Thus, for all practical purposes, identity politics re-enforced Margaret Thatcher's agenda by assuring that there will be 'no such thing as (a single, cohesive) society'. A politics based on multiple group identities balkanizes and re-tribalizes individuals into mutually exclusive constituencies that are unlikely to forge the sort of broad alliances that might resist – in a progressive way – the anti-social 'reforms' Thatcher and Reagan enacted.

Conclusion: The Academicizing of Politics

Barthes' immensely influential 'The Death of the Author' was written in 1968, the year of the short-lived worker-student alliance in Paris. Susan Foster's essay 'Choreographies and Choreographers' was published exactly 40 years later, in 2008: an anniversary which inevitably sparked a great deal of reflection about the decline of the international political left over the course of the intervening four decades.

In fact, on April 24th 2008, the official fortieth anniversary of the alliance that fizzled, *Challenge: The Revolutionary Communist Newspaper of the PLP*, a quaint vestige of the Old Left, offered this analysis of why the marriage between workers and students ended so quickly in divorce. Their conclusion: factory workers and academics mix about as well as oil and water:

> The revolt occurred at a time when the concept of the working class's role in society and the revolutionary process had come under assault from a gaggle of fake-left 'theorists,' led by a professor named Herbert Marcuse. The millions who struck France's factories exposed the shallowness of this viewpoint and dramatically showed that the working class alone, which builds and runs everything, has the potential to revolutionize society and bring about meaningful change. This principle is just as valid today. (*How 10 Million*, 2008)

Now, if those who purport to speak for the working class regard Herbert Marcuse as a 'fake-left theorist', what pray tell would they think of Roland Barthes, Fredric Jameson, Suzi Gablik or Susan Foster? Marcuse, after all, was a genuine activist who believed that academic analysis and theory are meaningless unless they exercise some measurable influence on society-at-large. But viewed in historical context, it makes perfect sense that Barthes' seminal study of 'authorship' was born of the confusion and despair that followed in the wake (literally and figuratively) of the 1968 worker/student alliance. Needless to say, the actual workers in Paris did not become owners of the actual means of production (the factories); even if – in Barthes' compensatory scenario – the reader acquires part ownership of the means of *literary* production. But isn't there a fundamental difference between the production and consumption of literary meanings and the production and consumption of material goods? What Barthes' essay inaugurated is not so much the birth of the reader as the birth of a massive confusion between real politics and a purely symbolic politics that has no existence beyond the ivory tower.

The very title of Barthes' next major essay 'From Work to Text' gives the game away: a shell game of linguistic bait and switch, whereby something tangible ('the Work') morphs into something intangible, indeed infinitely malleable ('Le Texte'). As Barthes himself puts it 'The work can be held in the hand, the text is held in language' (1977b: 157). Barthes will subsequently define all cultural experiences – whether verbal or non-verbal – as 'texts to be read'. Even an art form as bodily as dance can become grist for this textual mill. (Hence the title of Susan Foster's first book: *Reading Dancing*.) In this utopian cloud-cuckoo-land – where the world is *constructed* of words rather than merely described by them – anything is possible. Real politics, by contrast, is usually defined in a less utopian way, as the art of the *possible*.

Conservative cultural commentators like Hilton Kramer and Roger Kimball (co-editors of *The New Criterion*) are forever complaining about the politicizing of academia, by which they mean the infiltration and subsequent domination of college and university faculties by 'leftist professors' and 'tenured radicals' (2005: 1). Unsurprisingly, they often trace this development back to 1968, the *annis miribilis* of the decade that both cultural and political conservatives demonize as the root of all evil. But the irony is that Kramer and his culturally conservative brethren should actually be rejoicing. Why? Because the supposed politicizing of academia which they deplore has actually resulted in the academicizing of politics, which might be defined as the sublimation of genuine political action into a purely imaginary – and at best, symbolic or 'textual' – substitute. Let's face it: a vision of choreographic authorship which conceives of the dancemaker as 'laborer and collaborator' is a pretty poor substitute for a genuinely progressive tax code or an increase in the minimum wage.

Ironically, the proliferation of new academic disciplines based on 'identity' (gender studies, queer studies, diaspora studies, etc.) was perhaps the most notable development in higher education during the Reagan/ Thatcher era. Given what was happening in the real world outside the academy, one can almost forgive the members of these separate subcultures for taking refuge in their academic bunkers and seeking out the parochial comfort and security of their own kind. But take refuge they did. And nothing provides a more complete refuge from political reality than the doctrine of 'textuality'. As the post-structuralists like to say 'il n'y a pas de hors texte' ('there is nothing outside the text') (Derrida 1992: 918). Who but a professor of gender studies could convince herself that academic seminars should be gynocentrically re-titled 'ovulars' in order to avoid inadvertently perpetuating the politics of phallogocentrism? (Oh, pity the poor 'hard' sciences.) Furthermore, a politics conducted in a language this insular is destined to remain confined within the rarified echo-chamber of elite academic self-enclosure.

If Susan Foster really believes that by de-emphasizing the curricular importance of dances choreographed by unique Western individuals like Merce Cunningham, George Balanchine, and Twyla Tharp, she is somehow striking a blow against the excesses of capitalist individualism, she is practicing a peculiarly academic form of self-delusion. The depth of this delusion takes on an added poignancy if one considers what was happening in the real world during the summer of 2008 when Foster's re-assessment of individual authorship and ownership in dance was published. The sub-prime mortgage crisis and the intra-bank credit crunch were about to unleash the most serious worldwide economic meltdown since the Great Depression.

George W. Bush's vision of America as an 'ownership society' – with its implicit assumption that individuals are incapable of caring for things (aka domiciles) that they do not privately own – played a (prime) role in precipitating the sub-prime lending crisis. A similar philosophy led Margaret Thatcher to privatize public housing in the UK during the 1980s. But what does the academic left's knee-jerk equating of artistic 'authorship' and 'ownership' have to do with this very real crisis – the housing bubble – that resulted in part from the Bush administration's ideological commitment to an ownership society? This was no time for pseudo-Marxist posturing (i.e. the fake proletariat vocabulary of 'cultural production'). In place of these ineffectual, essentially symbolic nods to populism and collectivism, perhaps the time had come to reread Marx: not as an ideal alternative to the present economic system, but as a countervailing force, a much needed brake on the engines of raw capitalism and market fundamentalism.

Or, if Marx remains too unfashionable, how about Thorsten Veblen's witty parody of conspicuous consumption in late nineteenth-century America, *Theory of the Leisure Class* (1899)? Veblen was arguably the first economist to describe the sort of Wall Street wizard who produces neither goods nor services, but who generates wealth through complex financial transactions. The abstract universe in which money is made by money has more than a little in common with the academic hall of mirrors where objective political reality is obscured by utopian textuality. (The transition Barthes traces from old-fashioned 'work' to post-modern 'text' may turn out to be the academic equivalent of Richard Nixon's decision to untether the US dollar from the fixity of the gold standard). If Veblen were alive today, he might be tempted to toss off an amusing treatise on the similarities between investment bankers who dream up exotic financial jargon like 'credit default swaps' or 'collateralized debt obligations' and the post-modern academics who produce papers with titles like 'Postcolonial Phallogocentrism and the Challenge of Radical Alterity' (Netto, 2004). This sort of obfuscating jargon is proof positive that theory has become the leisure of the post-modern class.

D. H. Lawrence loved to complain about people whose erotic lives are limited to 'sex in the head' (1956: 84). The academicizing of politics amounts to 'revolution in the head'. But unfortunately, nowhere else. As Irving Howe trenchantly predicted, 'they (the academic left) don't want to take over the government; they just want to take over the English department' (quoted by Hirsch, 2007).

Works Cited

1968: How Ten Million Workers Shut Down France. 2008. Internet blog, posted April 24, in *Challenge: The Revolutionary Communist Newspaper of PLP*. [Online]. Available: <http://challengenewspaper.wordpress.com/2008/04/24/1968-how-10-million-workers-shut-down-france/> [March 2009].

Arnold, M. 1869. *Culture and Anarchy*. London: Smith, Elder.

Balanchine, G. 1984. *By George Balanchine*. New York: San Marco Press.

Barthes, R. 1974. *S/Z*. Translated by Richard Miller. New York: Hill and Wang.

Barthes, R. 1977a. The Death of the Author, in *Image-Music-Text*. Edited and translated by Stephen Heath. New York: Hill and Wang: 142–148.

Barthes, R. 1977b. From Work To Text, in *Image-Music-Text*. Edited and translated Stephen Heath. New York: Hill and Wang: 155–164.

Barthes, R. 1985. *The Grain of The Voice*. Translated by Linda Coverdale. New York: Hill and Wang.

Bauerlein, M. with Grantham, E. (eds.). 2009. National Endowment for the Arts: A History, 1965–2008. Published online by the NEA at <http://www.arts.gov> [May 2009].

Berlin, I. [1954]. *lyrics.time* [online]. Available: <http://www.lyricstime.com/irving-berlin-choreography-lyrics.html> [December 2009].

Cohen, S. J. 1974. *Dance As A Theatre Art*. New York: Dodd, Mead, and Co.

Derrida, J. 1992. Of Grammatology, in *Art in Theory*. Edited by Charles Harrison and Paul Wood. Oxford and Cambridge: Blackwell: 918–928.

Dirda, M. 1998. Something Up His Sleeve. *The Washington Post*, February 8: 4 (Section X).

Eliot, T. S. 1963. Tradition and the Individual Talent, in *Modern Criticism*. Edited by Walter Sutton and Richard Foster. New York: Odyssey Press: 140–145.

Foster, S. L. 1986. *Reading Dancing: Bodies and Subjects in Contemporary American Dance*. Berkeley and Los Angeles: University of California Press.

Foster, S. L. 2008. Choreographies and Choreographers: Four Definitions of the Terms, in *Modern Dance: Multifaceted Dimension*. Edited by Scruti Bandopadhay. Kolkata, India: Eminent Printing Works: 5–33.

Gablik, S. 1984. *Has Modernism Failed?* London: Thames and Hudson.

Hirsch. E. D. 2007. E. D. Hirsch Comments on *ToughLiberal*. Education Sector Author Talk, 20 September. [Online]. Available: <http://www.educationsector.org/supplementary/supplementary_show.htm?doc_id=529397> [December 2008].

Huizinga, J. 1950. *Homo Ludens: A Study of the Play Element in Culture*. Boston: Beacon Press.

Ivey, W. 2009. Quotation in: National Endowment for the Arts: A History, 1965–2008. [Online]. Edited by Mark Bauerlein with Ellen Grantham. Published online by the NEA at <http://www.arts.gov> [May 2009].

Jameson, F. 1983. Post-Modernism and Consumer Society, in *Postmodern Culture*. Edited by Hal Foster. London and Sydney: Pluto Press, 1983: 111–125.

Kramer, H., and Kimball, R. 2005. Notes and Comments: Faculty Follies. *The New Criterion*, 23 (10).

Lawrence, D. H. 1956. *Selected Literary Criticism*. Edited by Anthony Beal. New York: Viking.

Lessig, L. 2008 *Remix: Making Art and Commerce Thrive in the Hybrid Economy*. New York: Penguin Press.

Malraux, A. 1953. *The Voices of Silence*, Translated by Stuart Gilbert. Garden City, NY: Doubleday: 119.

Mehlman, J. 1972. The Floating Signifier: From Levi-Strauss to Lacan, in French Freud: Structural Studies in Psychoanalysis. Special issue of *Yale French Studies* 48: 10–37.

Netto, P. 2004. *Postcolonial Phallogocentrism and The Challenge Of Radical Alterity*, paper presented at the annual meeting of the International Studies Association, Le Centre Sheraton Hotel, Montreal, Quebec, Canada, 17 March.

Poggioli, R. 1971. *The Theory of the Avant-Garde*. Translated by Gerald Fitzgerald. New York: Icon Editions Harper and Row.

Rousseau, J. J. 1953. *The Confessions of Jean-Jacques Rousseau* (1782). Translated by John Michael Cohen. London: Penguin Books Ltd.

Shweder, R. A. 1990. Cultural Psychology – What Is It?, in *Cultural Psychology: Essays on Comparative Human Development*. Edited by James Stigler, Richard Shweder, and Gilbert Herdt. Cambridge: Cambridge University Press: 1–43.

Thatcher, M. 1987. *Epitaph for the Eighties? 'There is no such thing as society'*. Prime Minister Margaret Thatcher, Talking To Women's Own Magazine. *Briandeer. com* [Online]. 31 October. Available: <http://briandeer.com/social/thatcher-society.htm> [September 2009].

Trilling, L. 1968. Freud: Within and Beyond Culture, in *Beyond Culture: Essays on Literature and Learning*. New York: Viking Press: 89–118.

Veblen, T. 1915. *Theory of the Leisure Class* [1899]. New York: MacMillan.

Youngblood, G. 1974. Art, Entertainment, Entropy, in *Film Theory and Criticism*. Edited by Gerald Mast and Marshall Cohen. New York: Oxford University Press: 605–611.

3 'Theatre has to become political again...' Interview by Alexandra Kolb

Born in 1939 in St. Margarethen, Austria, Johann Kresnik established his career in neighbouring Germany. He has been a most prolific dance and theatre director, having choreographed and directed around one hundred full-length works. Kresnik is also perhaps the most politically outspoken – and belligerently criticised – representative of German dance theatre. His often extreme choreographic images have earned him epithets such as the *enfant terrible* and *Berserker* of the German dance scene. I met the choreographer, together with dramaturg and author Christoph Klimke, in Erfurt in April 2008, where Kresnik was directing a production of *Maskenball* (*A Masked Ball*). (See Figure 1.)

Kolb: How did your career in dance take off?[1]

Kresnik: It started totally by accident, as a walk-on at the Graz opera house. We had a meter-reader who frequently visited the opera and one time he said to me 'Don't you want to come with me?' and I said 'OK'. I was then about fifteen or sixteen. We saw *Aida* and I was totally amazed that something like that existed. From TV I knew the Prisoners' Chorus and the Triumphal March and things like that. It all fascinated me. And then I heard that they were looking for walk-ons for a production of *Sommer-nachtstraum* (*A Midsummer Night's Dream*) at the Schlossberg in Graz, so I went along. There the manager and the Russian ballet-master saw me, and the ballet-master said 'You come to me and we will do *Jäger* [sic:

---

1   This text is an abridged version of the interview, translated by August Obermayer.

he probably means Peter] *und der Wolf* (*Peter and the Wolf*)'. But before that we did *Zirkusprinzessin* (*Circus Princess*), because I was very good at somersaults and flips. This is how I started, but straight away I danced principal parts in *Der heilige Sebastian* (*St. Sebastian*), which was telecast, and *Pulcinella*. Then the choreographer left – he was Russian – and Jean Deroc came from Switzerland and although I was a beginner, he gave me a contract and I danced all these things. Then I was due to do my military service in Austria and I said to myself 'No, I won't even touch a gun for this country' and I decamped. I went to Germany with Jean Duroc. I was already a member of the Austrian Communist Party and since then I have remained in Germany.

Kolb: But you did have dance lessons?

Kresnik: Never ever.

Kolb: But later on you did ballet?

Kresnik: Yes, but I already had a contract with the *corps de ballet* in Cologne. And there was the famous teacher Leon Wojcikowski, who was actually a successor of Nijinsky from the Ballets Russes. And there was also Aurel von Miloss. He said to me, 'You train with me and work with me and in two or three years you will be a soloist'. And so it happened and I worked with Cranko and Béjart and with Balanchine. My technique then was purely classical. But after a while I got fed up with all the classical stuff.

Kolb: But how and when did you learn to dance?

Kresnik: I have never learned to dance. I would start classical training with Wojzikowski at 8 o'clock in the morning. At 10 o'clock was the next training, then there were rehearsals, in the afternoon there was training again for me and some others who received private tuition from him, and in the evenings there were performances or rehearsals.

Kolb: So you were naturally gifted?

Kresnik: I had an incredibly good body for all those things, incredible power, because I have always done all sorts of exercises and gymnastics. Because of my very stable body I can jump extremely well, like a devil. After all, I have danced with the Balanchine people and others. They all had decades of training – I was able to keep up with them.

Kolb: One very rarely hears a story like that, especially in the ballet scene.

Kresnik: At the time, this required a lot of willpower and energy. When my mother heard that I was going to join the theatre she said 'Oh my god, now my boy doesn't want to work any more!' She could never imagine what it involved. And then I was lucky that I could work directly with people like Cranko, Béjart and Balanchine. Balanchine was a neo-classicist. All that was of course OK. I asked Balanchine why he did Mozart and such things, all pieces without a plot. As a twenty-five year old I had to drag a woman across the stage and then just hang around. He said he would extend the music. I replied that Mozart would turn in his grave if he knew this. Cranko said: 'Hans, you have to do your own things'. As I was in the Marxist Movement, I was more interested in street demonstrations and in my acquaintance with Bloch[2] than in the stupid theatre.

Kolb: How well did you actually know Ernst Bloch?

Kresnik: I got to know him playing chess. In the chess club in Cologne there was a grey-haired man and I thought he looked somewhat familiar. And then I said to him, 'Are you Ernst Bloch?' 'Yes, yes, I like playing chess.' That is how it happened. Then I visited him frequently in Tübingen. He also came often to Cologne, took part in demonstrations, like the one

---

2   Ernst Bloch, German Marxist philosopher known in particular for his monumental work *The Principle of Hope* (written between 1938 and 1947).

against the Emergency Acts[3] where I was arrested in Bonn for the first time because I was a foreigner and politically active and a member of the KPÖ (Austrian Communist Party) and Marxist Movement in Cologne. It was already obvious that police agents were present. That was sometime between 1966 and 1968. Suddenly there were a lot of strange types about, behaving exactly as we did. But then they said 'If you need weapons, no problem, if you need dollars, no problem, if you need drugs...'. All this had been recorded by the police. All those who were tricked by that had to go underground quickly and from that moment on they were on the police search list.

Kolb: Really, as soon as you went underground?

Klimke: The most famous example is Ulrike Meinhof.

Kresnik: And when you got caught, it meant fifteen years. So naturally you would remain well-hidden. Thank god I got out of this rather quickly.

Kolb: But you were underground for a while?

Kresnik: Yes, we were in the Marxist Movement and I had the feeling that something was wrong, something was very strange. There were such strange types at the evening meetings. They had infiltrated us with their agents.

Kolb: But surely the real members knew each other?

Kresnik: Yes, yes, but suddenly there were strangers.

---

3   Passed in 1968, these laws effected a change in the German constitution in the attempt to ensure the government's ability to act efficiently in situations of crisis, such as natural catastrophes, war or uprisings. They extended the power of the *Bund*, in particular the executive branch, in cases of emergency and placed limitations on the privacy of correspondence and confidentiality of post and telecommunication. The legislation was heavily criticised, in particular by the APO (see note 4), as it was seen as an assault on democratic rights and as parallel to the laws of the Weimar Republic which had enabled Hitler's ascent to power.

Kolb: Couldn't they have been thrown out?

Kresnik: We were keen to get new members. In those days we weren't just 20 or 30, we were about 160. It was already moving towards the APO[4] movement, and then the RAF [Red Army Faction]. [...] And the scene grew ever more radical. I kept away from the RAF, because one cannot kill innocent people in order to change a political situation. We demonstrated in front of the Deutsche Oper [in Berlin]; first the Persian soldiers used truncheons and then it all kicked off. Then the police came...

Kolb: What were you mainly demonstrating against in those days?

Kresnik: It was about liberation from the national-socialist parents, teachers and institutions.[5] The Americans themselves had installed these old Nazis into their positions. And then it was of course an anti-American Vietnam demonstration. Then there were the flower children, Woodstock *et cetera*. I was one of the first to run up to the director's office, ignore the secretary and open the door. For a dancer it used to be quite impossible to get an appointment with the director. I said that I would like to be part of the discussions about next season's programme. What would be in there for us? Couldn't we be part of the deliberations? The ballet masters didn't want to have anything to do with this because they would have been slaughtered. I was already a better-known soloist and I said, 'No, not me, I will not have any part in this shit'. But I would never have boycotted someone like Balanchine because I appreciated him as an artist.

4   Abbreviation for Außerparlamentarische Opposition (Opposition outside Parliament). The APO in the late 1960s and early 1970s consisted primarily of students who voiced their dissatisfaction with several burning political issues of the time, such as the Vietnam War, the structure of tertiary education institutions, and remnants of National Socialism. Extra-parliamentary protest was mounted partly because the grand coalition between the two major German political parties (CDU and SPD) in 1966 meant there was no real opposition in parliament apart from the smaller liberal FDP (Freie Demokratische Partei), which had about forty seats. The APO was also opposed to the Notstandsgesetzgebung (German Emergency Acts) – see note 3.

5   Many youths campaigned, for instance, for the expulsion of academic staff who had been active during the Nazi era.

Kolb: Were you not initially trained in a trade?

Kresnik: Yes, I was trained to be a toolmaker. But I already knew after one year that this was not for me. I found it totally stupid to go every day at six or seven to the idiotic workshop.

Kolb: Did this influence your political outlook?

Kresnik: No, that was my stepfather. He was a member of the Austrian Communist Party. In the dance company they all thought I was stupid: 'What are you doing in the Marxist Movement?' I then tried to enlighten the dancers, but they didn't grasp it at all. None of the dancers has ever had anything to do with politics.

Kolb: Why is it, in your opinion, that only a few dancers and choreographers are interested in politics?

Kresnik: It starts at the ballet school. They are not allowed any opinions, they have to shut up and move their muscles.

Kolb: But even the number of contemporary dancers who tackle political topics is limited?

Kresnik: They don't give a damn. They are only interested in their bodies, their injuries, their problems and so on. I know only a very few dancers who are interested in politics. I don't know why. Perhaps there are a few more in the free/alternative dance scene. The politicians control the theatres. That means the theatres have to be filled. But on the other hand, new forms have to be discovered. But the subscribers are not interested in this and stay away. This is the reason why young people don't go to the theatre.

Kolb: Which ideologies or political thinkers were you influenced by?

Kresnik: My stepfather, certainly Karl Marx, the Austrian communist Ernst Fischer; they held meetings at the Styrian branch in Graz, and this was how I got into it. And it remained that way. Initially, of course, I had a tendency towards Lenin although Trotsky was perhaps most interesting.

Kolb: Apart from politics, were you influenced by anything else?

Kresnik: I was very interested in painting. I met a lot of painters and graphic artists.

Kolb (to Klimke): Were you influenced by similar thinkers?

Klimke: I belong to a different generation. I am a quite a bit younger and therefore have a different life story. At the time of the '68 revolution I was ten years old. But I had the same experiences privately. I had a very old father who experienced the Hitler regime. Through discussions with my father I ended up in this scene. My passion for [Pier Paolo] Pasolini can be explained by the fact that his orientation was left-wing. He was not a member of any political party, but of course he was a political artist.

Kresnik: He was a visionary.

Klimke: He invented a word, back in the sixties, for what we are bringing on stage today in *Maskenball* (*A Masked Ball*): consumption-fascism. Capitalism was going to turn into consumption-fascism. And he was right. Since 1989 this has been the only model because there is no alternative. In the sixties there was the GDR – whatever one might think of it – but now there is only consumption and nothing else.

Kresnik: He did say the new fascism is the terror of consumption and he is totally right.

Kolb: What was your position on the then-GDR? In your work *Wendewut* you were somewhat critical.

Kresnik: Heiner Müller[6] was a good friend of mine and I was frequently in the GDR. Then my view was naturally a bit rosy. Between 1968 and 1975 we collected medicines and got them into the GDR to ship them to war

---

6   Important twentieth-century German (formerly East German) dramatist and theatre
     director, 1929–1995.

zones. But after a while I managed to see what types of people Ulbricht, Honecker and Mielke[7] really were. Just think that Mielke himself was a murderer, shot two policemen and then got such a position. And there were also a lot of old Nazis protected in the GDR. Soon things took their course. For me and others the German reunification was a disappointment, because the aim of many was not to disestablish the GDR but to create a different GDR.

Kolb: And you would have supported that? You were against the reunification?

Kresnik: Yes, I was against the reunification – at least the reunification the way it happened. But the GDR would not have been able to stabilise its economy; that was not possible any more. The Cold War almost impoverished the Russians and the Americans. And then Gorbachev said 'Actually we can't carry on like this'. And then the Americans said, 'Let's stop it'.

Klimke: The disappointing thing in 1989 was that there was hardly any resistance from East Germany. Not that they didn't want their freedom, clearly they wanted it; but that they allowed themselves to be taken over and had to take on the old model of the Federal Republic without any criticism – that is disappointing. It is a falsification of history when they talk about a peaceful revolution today. There was no revolution at all. The GDR was bankrupt, that was it; the Soviet Union was bankrupt, that was the reason.

Kolb: But back then when the GDR still existed, you considered it an alternative to the Federal Republic?

---

7   Erich Honecker, Walter Ulbricht and Erich Mielke were leading communist politicians of the German Democratic Republic. Both Ulbricht and Honecker were General Secretaries of the Socialist Unity Party (Ulbricht from 1950–1971, and Honecker, who succeeded Ulbricht as the leader of East Germany, from 1971–1989). Mielke was Minister of State Security from 1957 to 1989.

Kresnik: Yes, but I had been thinking for years how changes could be implemented. It is impossible to lock people into a country, quite impossible. Why should somebody living in the GDR not to be able to see Olympia, or Greece or Rome?

Klimke: Then there was also a very severe censorship imposed on critical artists. The Stasi[8] prisons were full.

Kresnik: All this played a role for my new themes. People always asked 'How will you get all this onto the stage?' – for example, *PigAsUs*, the election propaganda between Nixon and Johnson, the murder of Meredith Hunter and so on. I said: 'Of course one can get all this onto the stage, but in a different way. It is going to be different, without language.' Or *Kriegsanleitung für jedermann* (*War Instructions for Everybody*) or *Schwanensee-AG* (*Swan Lake Inc.*): I was the first to destroy the content of the classical repertory. In my production the swans were factory workers. The critics slaughtered me, even though the practice of radically reinterpreting Shakespeare and others was already known from the theatre. It took a very long time until a choreographer came along and tried to reinterpret the classical dance repertory, to give it a new meaning.

Kolb: What do you see as the main themes of your choreography?

Kresnik: Society and politics. Outsiders, people living at the edge of society, people who are exiled by society. I also work a lot with drama. I think I am the only choreographer who also does a lot of drama and directs opera.

Kolb: You used to refuse to go to America. Have you now changed your stance?

---

8   Abbreviation of Ministerium für Staatssicherheit, the infamous Ministry for State Security in East Germany.

Kresnik: I have been invited several times. Once I had declined immediately but then I went to do *Rosenkavalier* (*The Knight of the Rose*) because Gottfried Hellwein and Maximilian Schell[9] were working there, and I know them very well. Then I declined to do Wagner; I didn't want to because I didn't want to work in this country. When I was contracted to Heidelberg the Americans came and wanted to get me and the whole troupe to America. Stolzenberg said 'There's no way I will let you break your contract'. They wanted me. But I didn't go because my aversion to America is quite strong. And when you see what they do to their soldiers in Afghanistan and Iraq – they don't give a damn about them. But then they turn them into heroes.

Klimke: There is a very funny anecdote: we did a play about Picasso, and at the time they went into Iraq, Bush had to give a speech at the UN. He went in front of a microphone but insisted that the picture behind him be covered up. This was a copy of Picasso's *Guernica*. He did not want to argue for the war in front of this picture. This just goes to show that art does have some influence after all.

Kolb: Do you think that your work influences the political views and perceptions of your audiences?

Kresnik: I have had considerable political success with the audience, especially in Latin and South America, much more so than here in Germany. It is my task to get the audience to discuss things. I don't want to instruct them. I can show things and everyone can form an opinion. But it is a pity that there will be no successor to do the things I am doing – at least I don't think so. It's over.

Kolb: But you surely did influence people, choreographers with whose work you can identify?

9   Gottfried Hellwein, born in 1948, is an Austrian fine and performance artist; Maximilian Schell, born in 1930, a Swiss actor and film director.

Kresnik: Yes, but they didn't make it – they did not become choreographers as such. Some did try, but it was not possible. Nothing came of it.

Klimke: But there are a number of theatre directors who steal from Hans, steal images. When one looks closely, one can see, oh... they were used several times in Kresnik productions.

Kolb: So you did influence people after all, if only people from the playhouses?

Kresnik: I got all the opera and theatre directors to go to the dance theatre, because there were totally different images, without text, without singing. So they saw that you can do it that way too.

Kolb: Who had the greatest influence on you?

Klimke: As a supporter, [Kurt] Hübner.

Kresnik: He brought me from Cologne to Bremen, where Peter Zadek, Peter Stein, Bruno Ganz, Fassbinder, Wilfried Minks and people like that worked. Tabori came later. These people still exist. I don't know what would have become of me had I gone to Osnabrück.

Klimke: Hübner was a director like Wüstenhöfer with Pina Bausch, who would say that even if there are not many people at the first few nights, you should still carry on.

Kolb: What about choreographers working before you, like Kurt Jooss – did they influence you?

Kresnik: I was very interested in *Der Grüne Tisch* (*The Green Table*) from a content point of view, not from the point of view of movement. It was too much 1920s or 30s. But I was impressed that someone did something with such content. I talked a lot about that with Kurt Jooss. I knew him, met him at a summer academy in Cologne. Kurt Jooss and I talked a lot about politics, but he had to bugger off in 1937 when this *Green Table* came out, because he was a Jew[10] and he went, I think, to England. He had encouraged me a lot. He said to me 'You really have to get on'. Then I went to Bremen to Hübner and saw Zadek and Stein, and such strong images. Shit, what do I do, I can't really do a pretty little ballet here. I immediately felt an attack of humility, then I did *Kriegsanleitung* (*War Instructions for Everybody*), *Schwanensee AG* (*Swan Lake Inc.*) *PigAsUs* and so on. Fassbaender shook his head and said: 'I would really like to go on tour with you'. All the critics clobbered me as hard as they could. But for the first time they found someone who didn't take it lying down.

Kolb: And that was you?

Kresnik: Yes, of course, I didn't only talk back – I also threatened violence: 'The next time I'll clobber you'. The critics did partly tell lies. They wrote that the house was half empty, that there was no acceptance by the audience, no applause: all lies. They wrote, for instance, 'He has only thirteen performances a year'. We had sixty-five performances. It was all lies. And Jochen Schmidt seemed to be a friend, Mr. Wendland seemed to be a friend, Mr. Regitz also;[11] they were all left-wing when we were in Cologne together, and now? Mr. Schmidt today is where he belongs – he writes for the *Welt*, the *Frankfurter* has sacked him – totally deluded. These people have ruined German dance theatre.

Kolb: Why? Is it because these days they belong to the establishment?

Kresnik: No, suddenly the minimal dance came here from America. Schmidt wrote, 'It's the greatest thing!' The poor dancer with his foot, his muscles and his sweat; but they didn't give a damn about the content. They only went for these stupid in-things, which lasted two years at most.

---

10   This claim is factually incorrect. Jooss was not Jewish himself but refused to dismiss his Jewish collaborators. In danger of being arrested, he left Germany in 1933.
11   Jochen Schmidt, Hartmut Regitz and Jens Wendland are well-known dance critics and authors.

Kolb: What do you think about formalist dance?

Kresnik: I have no problem with it, only I miss the content. I can see marvel-lous bodies on stage and they can do fifty pirouettes standing on their heads or on their arses and do thirty somersaults. And I have to say that's fantastic. Fantastic body. But for me it is important to see some content. It is possible to communicate content with the body. Pina Bausch (†) has found her way, she doesn't need to do any more as she has become an icon, which is quite alright. Pina Bausch and I differ a lot as far as content is concerned.

Kolb: It requires some preparation or background knowledge to grasp the full content and meaning of your choreographies, and deciphering the symbolism takes time.

Kresnik: The problems I had with *Ulrike Meinhof*! They said one cannot show that, it is rubbish, no one is interested in it. It has almost become a didactic play for young people. They ask: 'Ulrike Meinhof – who was that?'

Kolb: Normally Ulrike Meinhof is portrayed in a negative light, often as a murderer. Your portrayal, on the other hand, is much more positive.

Kresnik: She was never a murderer, never touched a pistol, never shot anyone. She was one of the best and greatest journalists who in the sixties went into factories where women worked and wrote about the problems of these women. She was the one who said of the child-murderer Jürgen Bartsch that it is not enough just to condemn; one also has to understand what his background was. And it turned out that he was a very difficult child and had to overcome lots and lots of problems. She really was fantastic. And the fact that Meinhof joined the RAF – the politicians almost forced her into that situation! Today some members of the RAF are still in prison.[12] Not even mass murderers are imprisoned for fifteen years today.

---

12   Kresnik is most likely referring to prisoners such as Christin Klar, the second-gen-eration RAF terrorist who at the time of the interview had been incarcerated for 26 years. He was released, though still on probation, in late 2008.

Kolb: Back then, before the premiere of *Ulrike Meinhof* (1990), there were threats of bomb attacks?

Kresnik: Yes, there were threats. They came with German shepherd dogs and searched the whole house. My two little children were accompanied by police to the kindergarten. They wanted to guard me, but I said rubbish. Also when we did the *Zehn Gebote* (*Ten Commandments*) in a church in Bremen there were threats of bomb attacks, police guards and all that. They set fire to the house of the female priest of the church. Two children were almost burned to death.

Kolb: And when did you receive the threat of the bomb attack when you did *Ulrike Meinhof*?

Kresnik: Two days before the premiere. Also when we did *Macbeth* in Heidelberg, with the death of Uwe Barschel in the bath tub,[13] there were threats of bomb attacks.

Kolb: But this shows that your choreographies stir things up. And don't you want to achieve this provocation?

Kresnik: It is all the same to me. Provocation, well – provocation is easy to achieve. I would only need to put a girl in underpants on stage with Koran written on her bottom. That would be quite enough!

Kolb: Would you not be afraid if you went that far?

---

13   Well-known German conservative politician and Minister President of the State of
      Schleswig Holstein from 1982 to '87. In 1987, two German journalists found his dead
      body in a bathtub filled with water in a Geneva hotel room. The cause of his death
      was widely discussed in the media but has remained controversial: speculations range
      from suicide to murder by an Israeli killer commando.

Kresnik: I wanted to do the *Satanische Verse* (*Satanic Verses*) but then we decided against it. But the choreography about Hannelore Kohl – dear god, what a sensation that created! Helmut Kohl[14] is just a swine, a human pig. A huge uproar: demonstrations by members of the CDU. There were letters from Mr Kohl. On the first night, readings from his biography in pubs by members of the CDU and things like that.

Kolb: Do you think he really treated Hannelore [his wife] that badly?

Kresnik: When an old woman is locked up in her flat, curtains drawn and the son gets married in Turkey and she finds out by telephone and things like that – she was just written off. The sons ignored her too. Of course she was not all that tame: she had a boyfriend from the Bundestag, when that finished she committed suicide. I made an icon of her. I have shown what a victim of Kohl's political career looks like. He is still sitting with his broad arse over Germany.

Kolb: And there were actual protests from the CDU?

Kresnik: Quite so. At the time we had a guest appearance in Ludwigshafen, and the house was totally sold out. Kohl of course comes from Ludwigshafen. It was a great success. A political success – it was not important for them what I did on stage. The papers wrote 'All of Germany's communists must have gathered together'. Rubbish. That Kohl play was done very aesthetically. I had a walk-on who looked exactly like him: the belly, the face – just like him, incredible!

Kolb: Do your dancers actually share your political views, more or less, and if not is there trouble?

14   Helmut Kohl was Chancellor of Germany from 1982–98 (of West Germany until 1990 and of the united country between 1990 and 1998). Hannelore Kohl, his wife of forty years, committed suicide after suffering from photodermatitis for some time, a sunlight allergy which forced her to stay indoors without any daylight.

Kresnik: Some do, but if not there is no problem. I run a different system from other ballet companies. In my company everyone has a say.

Klimke: They are also all paid the same.

Kresnik: I already introduced it in 1968 with Hübner that everyone gets the same salary.

Kolb: But if someone was an enthusiastic CDU fan, wouldn't this create problems?

Klimke: Such a person wouldn't come to Hans.

Kresnik: There are many foreigners in my company. We discuss the work. They get material about the pieces. We also engage in a lot of improvisations, and when people do something and it is better than what I did, then I say 'We'll do it that way'. I do take note of each body. I cannot expect that everybody will move like I do. We do not work with a repertoire of studied steps. If someone has a funny soft body, then I mould the character into a soft one with soft movements.

Kolb: What do you consider to be the main themes of your style?

Kresnik: The images which I compose are dominant. Not forms of movement, I was never one to worry about steps. I have never tried to think for weeks about a step, which is what the others do – think about lifts. Most lifts one sees, in whatever style, classical or modern, have already been done by Cranko or Balanchine. No one can tell me otherwise.

Kolb: But you use more theatrical means?

Kresnik: I can only do that with older dancers. I have nothing against young dancers, only I can't have twenty young dancers in my company – where would this leave the older man and the older woman? My oldest dancer was 67. Susanne, an Argentine woman, was 65, but she had to stop because she had a hernia and couldn't dance any more.

Kolb: Did you name your style choreographic theatre because of your use of theatrical means?

Kresnik: I invented that back in Cologne. The phrase 'dance theatre' was not yet in use. Pina Bausch was not yet on the scene, she came four years after me. Choreographic theatre also contains text. When I used text for the first time with dancers on stage, I was heavily criticised. They said, 'Now he has no new ideas any more, now he has dancers speak on stage'. That was a text about Jürgen Bartsch, *Die Kindermörder* (*The Child Murderers*). We had the premiere at the Academy of the Arts, the piece was *Jaromir* based on Grillparzer, in which we included text. The critics were beside themselves, Mr Kögler and Mr Wendtland and Mr Schneider and Regitz: 'Now he has dancers speak!'

Kolb: Is it still dance?

Kresnik: No actor can perform it. I can do a lot with actors. I can work with actors the same way I work with dancers, but the actors will not be able to do what the dancers can with their bodies. And dancers cannot speak or sing the way actors can. They speak as they are able and if someone has an American or Argentine accent, so what? I don't mind. I can't expect a dancer to speak High German like Kinski.[15]

Kolb: You would, then, define your style as dance, rather than playacting?

Kresnik: Yes, absolutely it is dance. I can do a piece with top athletes, that is no problem. I did *Prinz Igor* in Straßburg, the *Polowetzer Tänze* (*Polovtsian Dances*) with break-dancers. This was a great success, people were jumping onto their chairs. One dancer did a hundred and fifty pirouettes on his head. People were enthralled.

---

15   Klaus Kinski was a famous German actor and collaborator of Werner Herzog. He featured in numerous films, including *Doctor Zhivago* and *Fitzcarraldo*.

Kolb: You have already mentioned that your dancers were either trained in a classical or a modern/contemporary way. Do they still have ballet or contemporary dance classes each morning?

Kresnik: They choose a training each day, either ballet or modern. Maybe twice or three times a week they have classical training, then twice or three times modern and once a week, either Saturday or Monday, Pilates. Interestingly, our office people take part in the Pilates training.

Kolb: Would you be interested in doing another choreography about a politician or political events?

Kresnik: There is one big issue and that is so-called globalisation. It is bad for the poor countries, I am thinking especially of Latin and South America and parts of Asia. All these vegetables and whatever else they produce go into a big container and they get paid a certain amount. They cannot sell their produce if they don't agree to the conditions.

Kolb: And what about 9/11?

Kresnik: Yes, perhaps, but up till now I have had so much to do.

Kolb: It is very often the case that the arts are the first to experience budget cuts...

Kresnik: There is also no resistance to this.

Kolb: Is the fact that choreographers and soloists are not organised, in unions for example, one of the reasons for this?

Kresnik: My company are not members of a union. They are represented by me and they have their days off and their spare time like any other company, maybe even more so. If I want to be a soloist then this is my business and not that of a union. With Pina Bausch and John Neumeier, no one dares to say to them that they cannot work on Sundays. They would reply 'Get lost!' Pina Bausch sacks at least a third of the company each year and engages new people.

Kolb: But if all choreographers worked together, if they were organised, would you not have more power?

Kresnik: It is not possible. I have tried it for years, to no avail. They all plough their own furrow. No one gets upset when someone is sacked in St. Pölten or somewhere else. No one. Not a line in a newspaper. They [the dance critics] are the death of German dance theatre. Earlier on I invited critics in open letters to come to me and to help out as dramaturgs to search for content, but no one accepted. But when I removed them from the auditorium they were very fed up. I told them that they don't need to write about me any more. Kill Kresnik by silence, it is all the same to me. But they couldn't do that. The *Süddeutsche* phoned me: 'You won't admit critics to your performances?' I said 'No, I don't need these wankers'. 'But who shall we send then?' they asked. 'As far as I am concerned, someone who hasn't studied drama', I said, 'someone who is interested in theatre'. And everyone trembles at what these stupid critics are going to say.

Klimke: The only consolation is that by behaving like that they abolish themselves. The less dance there is, the fewer dance critics will be needed.

Kolb: You spent some time in Latin and South America. Where exactly did you go?

Kresnik: Sao Paolo, Colombia and other places. I treated very hot political topics there – no one else dared to touch them – for instance in *Plan Via* in Colombia. It referred to Plan Colombia,[16] a ten-point-programme which the Americans and the Colombian politicians negotiated to ensure that the whole field of agriculture is improved: the fight against drugs, fight against terrorism and things like that. The Germans have given 8.6 billion to the

---

16   On the website of the U.S. Department of State, this 1999 mission is described as
      follows: 'Plan Colombia was a comprehensive program to combat narco-terrorism;
      spur economic recovery; strengthen democratic institutions and respect for human
      rights; and provide humanitarian assistance to internally displaced persons' (<http://
      www.state.gov/r/pa/ei/bgn/35754.htm> accessed 28 June 2010). Kresnik alleged
      in his choreography that the financial aid did not go towards democratisation and
      reagrarisation of the country but instead was used to subsidise armament and war.

Colombians to fight all these things and the Americans have given them 2.6 billion worth of weapons. What did the terrorists, who constitute the Left here, do? By kidnappings, by drug trading and so on they increased their arsenals. Two weeks later the first Hawkins fighter plane crashed, because what the Americans delivered to the Colombians was all rubbish. And I did *Plan Via*. In Colombia no one knew about it. It was such an enormous success that after every performance there were about five hundred people outside wanting to discuss these things. Based on my choreography they have created a saying: 'I want to die my own way'. That was written on all the walls, everywhere – that, for me, is political success. And in a press conference in Berlin I was asked 'Well, why don't you emigrate to Colombia?' I really wanted to belt him one, such an arsehole!

Kolb: Would it be possible for you also to criticise a left-wing government?

Kresnik: Of course. I know Gregor Gysi and Oskar Lafontaine[17] very well. Unfortunately the Left don't have a plan for the economy or for the money. That is the damn problem.

Kolb: You must be quite satisfied with the new developments in South America, with the new communist parties.

Klimke: They are being built up and knocked down. They are being allowed to become dictators and then get swept from office so that their resources can be accessed.

17   Gregor Gysi, a lawyer, was a major figure in the post-reunification Partei des Demokratischen Sozialismus (Party of Democratic Socialism), PDS, and is now a leading politician of the socialist political party Die Linke (The Left). Oscar Lafontaine is former chairman of the Sozialdemokratische Partei Deutschlands (Social Democratic Party), SPD, former Prime Minister of the State of Saarland, and former co-chairman of Die Linke.

Kresnik: Same as they built up the Taliban in Afghanistan. It is all controlled by the Americans, even the politicians are installed by them. [...] The choreographers forget all these things – the fact that there is a world outside the theatre. There is more than just the ballet studio and the stupid steps which give you cramps. One of these days I might invent a new step. The politicians use the directors, the directors use the choreographers – just keep everything running smoothly, just don't *do* anything. [...] There will be very difficult times for dance in Germany. I can only say the politicians share a large part of the blame. Perhaps I am quite wrong in my opinion of what dance should mean, that it must have to do with content. A fresh start is needed – the theatre has to become political again. But how can one motivate young choreographers to do that? Yes, there are fantastic choreographers like Mats Ek who interpreted *Swan Lake* quite differently. But where is the theme about fascism in Sweden, where are the pieces about women, for instance the clitoral mutilation of women in Africa? About Che Guevara? People don't dare to do that. One could also do a choreography about how all our culture in Germany is going to be ruined. They have studied ballet like mad, modern dance, and now they are without a job. Why doesn't anyone do a piece about this?

Figure 1 Johann Kresnik. Photograph: Alexandra Kolb

Figure 2 Linda Ryser (as Ulrike Meinhof), Daniela Greverath, Bibiana Jimenez, Pedro Malinowski, Sarka Vrastakova-Hildebrandt and Przemyslaw Kubicki (as terrorists) in *Ulrike Meinhof* (1990/2006) by Johann Kresnik. Theater Bonn. Photograph: Thilo Beu.

Figure 3 David Dorfman in the lunge position, in *Underground* (2006) by David Dorfman. Courtesy of DeBartolo Performing Arts Center.

4 Terror without End? Choreographing the Red Army Faction and Weather Underground

Introduction

One night in 1990, I was startled from my sleep by the screeching tyres and wailing of fire engines rushing out of the station across the road.[1] The shrieking noise was incessant. Shortly afterwards, the car of a friend who lived just a few blocks away towards the river Rhine was being searched. What had happened? A high-ranking manager and politician, Karsten Rohwedder, who lived in a villa on the river, had been cold-bloodedly murdered, hit by bullets fired through his windows from the allotments below. A letter that was later found claimed that a deceased member of the left-wing terrorist organisation, the Red Army Faction (RAF) was responsible. If the murder was indeed executed by this group, as the evidence suggests, it was done by its third generation: the RAF, operating between 1968 and 1998, was an offshoot of the 1960s student protest movement that shook a number of leading industrial countries including the US, Germany and France.

While examinations of 1960s and 1970s left-wing extremism have invariably focused on the national specifics of the phenomenon, it was a truly global affair and often rooted in student movements. In his comparative case study of American and German youth rebellions, Jeremy Varon (2004) points out the many commonalities between the events in these

---

1   I am grateful to Suzanne Little and Luke Purshouse for instructive comments on earlier drafts of this essay.

countries. With radical force and the optimism of youth, American and German students in the 1960s lined the streets and barricaded universities to challenge political and cultural authority, oppose oppression and protest against the war in Vietnam. They were influenced by the same ideological undercurrents – notably such thinkers as Karl Marx, Herbert Marcuse and Mao Tse-Tung – and upheld an anti-imperialist and anti-capitalist stance, levelling protest at the alleged exploitation and injustices attendant on the market system.

The student movement in both countries incorporated a militant faction which did not shrink from violence and even engaged in terrorist acts, waging guerrilla campaigns in the attempt to give their citizens a taste of the wars fought abroad in their names. In Germany, the RAF, some of whose members had been involved in activist circles of the student organisation SDS (*Sozialistischer Deutscher Studentenbund*), became a symbol of extreme New Leftist activism. The Weathermen – later renamed Weather Underground – which led the armed struggle in the US, was an offshoot of another SDS (*Students for a Democratic Society*). Several decades on, the issue of 1960s and 1970s left-wing terrorism is again experiencing a peak of public attention, undoubtedly spurred by the recent wave of terrorist attacks, and has reached both the popular cinematic and theatrical stages. Widely disseminated films include Green's and Siegel's *The Weather Underground* (2002), and *Baader-Meinhof Komplex* (2008) by Uli Edel.

Less well known is the fact that the topic has also served as the inspirational source for a small number of dance choreographies. This paper analyses contemporary choreographic responses to 1960s and 1970s left-wing terrorism in Germany and the US. I shall use Johann Kresnik's *Ulrike Meinhof* (1990), which centred on the famous founder-figure of the RAF, and *Underground* (2006) by David Dorfman about the Weather Underground group to examine how choreographers have tackled the highly contentious subject of violent anti-state activism. Like myself, both choreographers share individual memories of 1960s and 1970s terror organisations: Dorfman remembers the Weathermen from his childhood (David Dorfman blog 2009) while Kresnik – almost twenty years Dorfman's senior – was actually a political activist during this time: he joined the Communist Party first in Austria and later in Cologne. My discussion will be underpinned by the writings of Frankfurt-school theorists who question the boundaries between the aesthetic and political, in particular the 1970s contemporary Herbert Marcuse. I will finally offer a comparative analysis of the differences and similarities in the approach taken to New Leftist terrorism in the two works.

Art, Revolution and Terror

While documentaries about terrorist organisations are common and maintain a reassuring, news-like distance from the events, choreographic contributions on this topic are highly intriguing. Beauty, taste and the sublime are common concepts in aesthetic thought. While many dance works have transgressed conventional aesthetic ideals to embrace political issues, the idea of beauty and the social disengagement of dance – whether in Théophile Gautier's nineteenth-century reviews of the romantic ballerina or the twenty-first-century notion of the ideal dancing body – are persistent themes of dance criticism and, indeed, shape the expectations of significant sections of audiences. Arlene Croce's damning 1994 non-review of Bill T. Jones's *Still/Here* in *The New Yorker* demonstrates that for some more traditionalist commentators, (re)presentations of suffering, death and the 'ugly' sides of human existence remain unacceptable sights on Western theatre dance stages.

On such accounts, terrorism and dance may be irreconcilable: the former, a nasty, bloody and messy affair and extreme form of political rebellion, invokes intense psychological angst and has little in common with the aesthetic pleasure that 'should' result from an engagement with the arts. However, as I argued in a recent article, a range of significant analogies can be drawn between performance and terrorism (Kolb 2009).[2]

---

2   See also Sabbatini's differentiation between 'theatre' and 'performance' in this context (1986).

While terrorism is clearly not straightforward theatre, there are overlaps in terms of reception theory, 'author' intention or purpose, and dramaturgic structure. The performative and aesthetic aspects of terrorism, for instance, have lent themselves to close scrutiny in the past. Walter Benjamin and Theodor Adorno both diagnosed that in certain forms of totalitarian state terrorism, such as in Hitler's Germany, the terror of the regime was concealed by colourful aesthetic spectacles – not least, displays of body culture: 'The more torture went on in the basement, the more insistently they [Hitler's empire] made sure the roof rested on columns' (Adorno 1997: 49). Following Benjamin (1968: 243), this phenomenon has been labelled the aestheticisation of politics.

In a similar vein, terrorist minorities also aestheticise politics, but in their case primarily to maximise audience perception. The actions of small anti-establishment organisations are often dramaturgically planned to achieve maximum effect (the composer Karl-Heinz Stockhausen called the 9/11 attack 'the greatest work of art there has ever been', cited in Bell 2003: 7) and target a specific audience; for instance a government, nation, or the entire Western world. Also like many types of performance, terrorist acts often contain didactic impulses in the attempt to convert the public to their cause; and, as in the case of the period between the mid-1960s and '70s, terrorists may artistically or rhetorically construct an alternative reality, often in the attempt to debase the existing one.[3] In the famous trial of 1967 which saw several future RAF members taken to court for an arson attack colloquially termed the 'department store fire', defence witnesses testified that the event displayed artistic patterns, thus qualifying it as (performance) art rather than crime.[4] It is arguable, furthermore, that

3   See for instance Rolf Bachem's analysis of an open letter by the RAF which suggests
     that the group used theatre-based metaphors to undermine the state's 'official' version
     of reality as a farce (1978: 68).
4   There are also more recent illustrations of this phenomenon. When on 24 November
     2006 the Irish paramilitary loyalist Michael Stone, a previously convicted murderer,
     broke into the parliament building in Stormont (Northern Ireland) equipped with a
     knife and several pipe bombs, he claimed his action was an example of performance
     art rather than the attempted murder he was later charged with. In his defence, his

such extremist groups are prone to constructing dramatic narratives; for instance they may believe that they are enmeshed in a mythical struggle between good and evil. In these narratives they cast themselves as performers to give context to their collective experiences, i.e. a sense of belonging and significance.[5] Vice versa, the 1960s theatrical scene reacted to the upheaval and riots on the streets by seeking to collapse the clear separation between the realms of art and political life through such forms as anti-art, street and other alternative or experimental theatre. All this goes to show that both spheres 'borrow' from each other, in some cases making boundaries so fluid that they become virtually indistinguishable.

The collapse of boundaries between performance and the 'real' entailed a reorganisation of the ways in which an art work's form and content are related, in particular where the transference of political messages is concerned, and triggered wide-reaching discussions on the dependence of art works' political potency on their structure and content. Herbert Marcuse, a German-Jewish refugee who emigrated to the US in 1934 and taught at Columbia, Harvard and Brandeis, was among the intellectual fathers of the student movement in both countries. Marcuse famously addressed the connection between art and revolution in his writings accompanying, and commenting on, the contemporaneous student revolts. In *Counterrevolution and Revolt* (1972: 85), he argues that there is a contradiction between the political goals of the rebellion and its cultural theory and praxis. He critically discusses the tendency of contemporary (i.e. 1960s and 1970s) works of art to negate and shatter aesthetic forms, for instance in anti-art and street performance, which challenges traditional art's creation of beautiful illusion and artistic harmony. While this tendency was seen by many artists of the time as complementing the revolutionary upheaval on the streets, Marcuse by contrast contends that art must ultimately and by

---

lawyer Arthur Harvey announced that: 'It was, in fact, a piece of performance art replicating a terrorist attack' (Stone's Attack, 2006). The fact that Stone's lawyer deemed this argument a viable line of defence illustrates that terrorism deployed in artistic or theatrical spectacle is often not easily distinguishable from terrorism, as Anthony Kubiak puts it, 'in culture *as* theatricality' (Kubiak 1991: 24).

5   I am grateful to Carl Leichter for this observation.

virtue of its nature remain antagonistic to radical practice (ibid.: 122). In the 'transformation of reality into illusion, and only in it appears the subversive truth of art' (ibid.: 98). Only in a sphere removed from life can we find a source of resistance to that reality.

In *The Aesthetic Dimension*, Marcuse expanded and clarified some of his previous remarks formed in response to the 1960s events. His much-cited indictment of political art in the Preface to this work is noteworthy:

> The political potential of art lies only in its own aesthetic dimension. [...] The more immediately political the work of art, the more it reduces the power of estrangement and the radical, transcendent goals of change. In this sense, there may be more subversive potential in the poetry of Baudelaire and Rimbaud than in the didactic plays of Brecht (1979: xii–xiii).

Later on he grants that art works which renounce autonomy and attempt to reflect reality might, perhaps, most adequately mirror our fragmented and shattered society. However, 'the rejection of the aesthetic sublimation only turns such works into bits and pieces of the very society whose "anti-art" they want to be. Anti-art is self-defeating from the outset' (ibid.: 49). Thus, artistic practices such as collage, montage, or the juxtaposition of media are inadequate critical responses to reality as they ultimately integrate and reproduce the given order. They make 'the artist superfluous without *democratizing* and *generalizing creativity*' (ibid.: 51–52). The purpose of art, according to Marcuse, should be to open up another dimension of existence which is not like life itself: a liberated universe which transforms and stylises the order in society.

Marcuse was criticised by proponents of activist and politically engaged art for diminishing art's political potency. In a typically postmodernist vein, Grant Kester argues against all attempts to ground art in a sphere distinct from the public one, labeling this project a 'disabling domesticity' (1998: 9). Certain genres of modern art, such as Yves Klein's leap or de Kooning's slashes, Kester claims, register protest against political or cultural conditions (such as fascism) through withdrawal from the public political sphere and resort to a holistic expression of man's creativity. Post-modern theatre, on the other hand, is regarded as pursuing the importance of actuality on stage and mirroring the political landscape of the time (see Lehmann 2006). (However, the oft-expressed view that postmodernist choreographies were

of a political nature, as exemplified by Sally Banes's claim with reference to
Judson Dance Theatre that 1960s US-American art embodied democracy
(Banes 1993: 10), is questionable. There are reasons to believe that such
labels were at times unjustifiably imposed on them.[6])

Choreographers examining political matters, such as Kresnik and
Dorfman, are faced with a dilemma. If they seek openly to disseminate
political content and spread a revolutionary message by abandoning traditional aesthetic forms and concepts such as 'rhythm, contrast' (Marcuse
1972: 81) or 'order, proportion, harmony' (ibid.: 94), they are vulnerable to
Marcuse's criticism of failing to transform the order prevailing in society
through the intrinsic power of the conventional aesthetic. Marcuse's claim
that the shock tactics of contemporary art works and the shattering of
(un)consciousness do 'not break the oppressive familiarity with destruction; they reproduce it' (1972: 112), appears to deprive art of any political
power. Intriguingly, this resonates with reservations that André Lepecki
has more recently expressed regarding Kresnik's choreographic style: he
maintains that Kresnik merely reiterates external happenings in the misguided belief that 'the reproduction of trauma is enough to overcome the
cruelty of the traumatizer' (1995: 18).

If, on the other hand, choreographers rely on the transformative
power of the aesthetic alone, they may fail to deliver an unambiguous
socio-political content, and be accused either of escapism or of a return
to an undesirable cultural conservatism. For instance, neither Kresnik nor
Dorfman opt for the street or other alternative venues; rather, they stage
their productions in conventional theatre spaces. Are they thereby refusing any direct confrontation with the 'real' socio-political world outside
the theatre's enclave? Are they construing their audiences as passive and
elite groups of spectators, and thus undermining the 'democratic' process
of activist performance? Perhaps we are left in doubt about their political
intent (after all, as Marshall McLuhan famously stated in *Understanding
Media* (1964: 7), 'the medium is the message'). However, in addressing
the legacy of two of the foremost terrorist organisations of this era, both

6   See Steve Paxton's 2006 email communication to this effect, published in the intro-
     duction to this book.

Kresnik and Dorfman clearly emphasise, albeit to differing degrees, the direct political messages of their pieces and make no bones about their left-wing sympathies with the root causes of the 1960s rebellion. Moreover, the use of collage techniques and non-linear narratives, or indeed the abandonment of narratives altogether correspond, as Germanist Birgit Haas has argued with reference to Kresnik's *Ulrike Meinhof*, to a post-modern theatrical stance whereby 'politics need to be presented in a fragmented manner in order to produce a critical political message' (2008: 191). Following this line of argument, only the explosion of conventional structures enables the political message to be successfully conveyed – a position diametrically opposed to Marcuse's. This position is influenced by Hans-Thies Lehmann's influential *Postdramatic Theatre* in which he argues that 'it is not through the direct thematization of the political that theatre becomes political but through the implicit substance and critical value of its mode of representation' (2006: 178). Here, Lehmann is agreeing with Marcuse about the essential political value of art as inherent in the art work's form rather than content, but locates it in what the latter termed 'desublimated art', which implies a rejection of conventional aesthetics in order to convey a political message (see for instance 1972: 81).

Notwithstanding these philosophical issues, dance might be seen as a prime medium through which to achieve social liberation. While Marcuse may have been dismissive of openly politicising art, he did advocate the role that art might play in overcoming an underdeveloped sensuality and suppressed drives. While sensory qualities have been dismissed in a tradition reaching back to Plato who saw the disembodied activity of philosophy as the ultimate human ideal (and indeed by Karl Marx, who distanced himself from sensory qualities so as to appear suitably scientific and objective), Marcuse valued the hitherto constrained and mutilated senses as belonging to the counterculture's reassessment of social values. As Jürgen Habermas put it in his reflections on Marcuse, the 'emancipation of consciousness has to go along with the liberation of the senses' (1983: 166). The New Leftists in both the US and Germany embraced this trend toward sensory liberation by emphasising physicality with their outdoor demonstrations, sit-ins, meetings, support for sexual promiscuity, physical attacks on others, and a dissociation from abstract, purely academic theorising.

Advocacy of the emancipation of the senses and the 'search [...] for art forms which express the experience of the body' (Marcuse 1972: 82) make choreography an excellent avenue through which to express 1960s perspectives. As artists using the sensual body to convey a revolutionary (social) message, Kresnik and Dorfman's pieces are at least potentially exemplary manifestations of the 1960s passion for art that depicts the fight for liberation through corporeal means. Suzanne Carbonneau has noted that the Greek word *kinema* (motion) relates to both the body and body politic (2007), and thus to bodily and political movements alike.[7] Thus, while the two choreographers adopt a largely post-modernist aesthetic opposed to Marcuse's stance, the very fact that they rely on the sensory and physical qualities of dance makes their works ideal avenues to express a 1960s perspective with hindsight. However, even within an essentially corporeal medium, the choreographers draw on its physicality to different extents, as will be specified below.

Johann Kresnik: *Ulrike Meinhof*

Ulrike Meinhof was premiered in 1990 in Bremen when the RAF was still in existence, but later restagings of the ninety-minute piece, such as its 2006 production at Bonn Theatre, were designed to remind audiences – in particular younger theatregoers – of the historic significance of the RAF in Germany's post-war era. The work is named after, and focuses on, the famous founder-member of the group: the socially aware, intellectual journalist and mother-of-two turned terrorist Ulrike Meinhof. The piece

---

7   This does not mean, however, that dance is intrinsically revolutionary, as suggested by Ann Cooper Albright's speculation in her study guide to *Underground* (2006). Even though it is fair to claim that the desire for change is inherent in the activity of motion, this might similarly apply to other actions, even including such mundane ones as housework. More importantly, besides serving revolutionary causes, dance can also be aligned with and representative of conservative regimes.

draws a panorama of her life, dividing the role into three personae performed by different dancers. The first Meinhof character to appear represents the woman returning to post-reunification Germany posthumously
in 1990, only to find German society fundamentally unchanged; characterised by gluttony, consumer culture and superficial entertainment. The
second Meinhof dancer is the left-wing journalist, wife and mother, and the
third represents the terrorist who during her subsequent prison sentence
committed suicide by hanging herself by a rope in her cell. The work also
adopts, alongside the main protagonist, other central characters from the
real-life RAF: notably Meinhof's husband, the editor Klaus Roehl; and
fellow terrorists Gudrun Ensslin and Andreas Baader.

The RAF, whose members had predominantly Marxist or other leftist
leanings, was highly critical of German society and levelled harsh criticism at its cultural and political structures. It persistently attacked the
alleged continuity between the Nazi regime and post-war Germany, cultural indoctrination, the US-American involvement in Vietnam and the
Federal Republic's complicity in this campaign, state and police brutality, and authoritarian societal structures. The RAF was influenced by the
urban guerrilla tactics of the Bolivian revolutionary Carlos Marighella and
adopted some of his methods, such as physical removal of police leaders
and other alleged 'fascists' in hit-and-run actions and 'expropriation' of
big business-owned resources by means of thefts and robberies. Its high-
profile targets were mostly drawn from the spheres of banking, police and
military, politics and business. RAF members did not shy away from the
most extreme violence, claiming responsibility for a number of killings
and kidnappings.

The state reacted to the threats posed by the RAF with particularly
harsh measures and at times exaggerated (or simply overestimated) the size
of the group. The number of active members who operated underground
over all three generations between the 1970s and 1990s in fact did not
exceed one hundred.[8] The intense hype surrounding the RAF was perhaps
caused by strong concerns that the newly-established democracy could be

---

8   The complete list of RAF members is publicly available on the Internet; even on the
     internet dictionary Wikipedia. See entry under Red Army Faction.

blighted (with the sad demise of the Weimar Republic and the subsequent takeover by the Nazis still in everyone's vivid memory), or possibly because leftism was associated with the tabooed East German state and therefore seen as ideologically unacceptable. In the public mind, equally, the spectre of the RAF was widespread, and those who expressed sympathy for its causes quickly ran the danger of being suspected of being *Sympathisanten*: a negative and somewhat contemptuous term denoting an unsavoury alliance with, and support for, criminal elements.

With this in mind, it is unsurprising that Kresnik's production was seen to be highly unconventional, not to say controversial; indeed, the piece itself sparked a bomb threat before its premiere.[9] While most media coverage and the 'official' view of RAF deeds normally focused on the victims of terrorism, the communist Kresnik offers a remarkably sympathetic vision of the terrorist Meinhof herself, even going as far as to depict her as the victim of an inhumane society. Taking a fairly straightforwardly Marxist view, he takes sides with her aim to overthrow the regime of capitalist economic exploitation, which in the piece is portrayed by a range of drastic imagery. The opening scene, for instance, depicts Meinhof having to step over rubbish from fast-food meals and being force-fed, while German citizens wind their ways through the wrappers like reptiles, picking up the remains of junk food and vomiting it out in the process. In later sections, German citizens are shown attending church services in fur coats, displaying inappropriate luxury, and in other scenes Kresnik takes aim at mass culture by presenting impersonations of highly popular German *Schlager* singers (a popular song genre) of the 1970s and '80s. Easily-digestible mass culture, as a product of a highly developed consumerist society, is of course seen, in good Frankfurt-school tradition, as distracting the masses from their own suffering under the dominant capitalist system. As Adorno argued: 'The easy pleasures available through consumption of popular culture made people docile and content, no matter how terrible their economic circumstances' (Adorno 1978: 280).

<hr>

9   See the 2006 interview with Kresnik conducted by Marion Kretz-Meingold and that conducted by myself, published in this book (80).

Kresnik's images – many of which are more theatrical than dance-based in any traditional sense – are choreographic representations of the classical critique of consumerism, which is expounded in texts by left-wing thinkers such as Pier Paolo Pasolini, Erich Fromm and Herbert Marcuse. 'Consumption terror' refers to the repression and enslavement which results from the market system, which is characterised by the 'overwhelming need to produce and consume useless things [...] there is a fundamental obligation to consume' (Marcuse 1968: 27; my translation). Consumers lack autonomy because their desires are manipulated by the retail and advertising industries, rather than being freely formed on the basis of their own rational judgements of what is valuable. Still more negative light is shed on bourgeois capitalist culture in a notable scene where a naked fat couple in padded costumes, bowler hats and with fake, oversized protruding sexual organs physically and sexually assault an Ulrike Meinhof who seems very petite by comparison. This scene is reminiscent of the characterisations of the moneyed German bourgeoisie which the visual artist George Grosz captured in a series of poignant sketches. These depict fat capitalists in black suits which Grosz contrasts with tired, skinny proletarians.

While in the first part of the piece Meinhof is depicted as a victim of society and patriarchal culture, her victimisation is extended to her later imprisonment when she becomes a direct victim at the hands of state authorities, and even her fellow inmates from whom she was rumoured to be separated (see among others Varon 2004: 197). The prison scenes reflect widely-discussed allegations by RAF sympathisers that the state used torture methods against RAF prisoners, such as solitary confinement and force-feeding during hunger-strikes. Kresnik uses poignant imagery, for instance humiliation rituals (stripping prisoners naked before 'cleansing' them with huge hosepipes, and providing food out of a dog's bowl) and outright torture (by use of gigantic pliers) to convey his contempt for the measures aimed at bullying RAF detainees.

Purposefully raising concerns in the viewer about the 'justice' offered in the supposedly democratic West German state, one scene depicts Meinhof being hung up horizontally on oversized meat hooks (see Figure 2). This image is reminiscent of the iconography of the pietà, transferred into a profane context: Meinhof's body position strongly resembles that of conventional visual-arts depictions of Jesus in Maria's arms after the crucifixion.[10] Thus, Kresnik establishes parallels between Jesus and Meinhof, yet he redeploys (if not perverts) the original religious message: both figures, this scene could imply, were tortured and ultimately killed as a result of uttering societal criticism and attempting to change the world for the better. Even more poignantly, in the final tableaux Meinhof cuts off her tongue in a gesture reminiscent of the death of Cicero[11], and is finally placed between two large glass panels for apparent 'preservation'.

The merit of Kresnik's piece lies in its overt political struggle against oppressive social structures. *Ulrike Meinhof* clearly does not aim at displaying beauty and resists any attempt to construe dance in conventional aesthetic paradigms, in particular where the depiction of (alleged) state machinations is concerned. The representation of political power structures (the 'System') oscillates between two extremes: while promoting capitalist excess and superficial entertainment as leisure-time activity, the state presents a model for authoritarianism and the disciplining of bodies in the prison scenes. In both cases, bodies are portrayed as abject, associated as they are with physical and psychical violence such as vomiting, rape, vulgar allusions to sexuality, humiliation and torture, and often aligned with (petit) bourgeois, conservative values.

Kresnik's piece, then, embraces an aesthetic of the 'ugly'. Most dance studies scholars view dance as providing 'corporeal pleasure in shared kinaesthetic events' (Fensham 1997: 14) – scientifically underscored by the fact that the activity of dancing releases endorphins – and/or audience pleasure through aesthetic appreciation or kinaesthetic empathy. However, Kresnik undermines any such associations, instead depicting bodies gone rampant, much in line with his theme of terrorism. Furthermore, he uses dance styles eclectically to represent certain political functions while their aesthetic (beautifying) function is assigned no or insignificant importance.

10 Michelangelo's 1499 marble sculpture in St. Peter's Basilica is one such example.
11 Republican Roman senator who opposed many of his city's ruling elite; following his assassination on Mark Antony's orders, his tongue was allegedly pulled out by Antony's wife Fulvia and stabbed with a hairpin to symbolise their triumph over his renowned powers of speech and rhetoric.

A *Schuhplattler* (German 'slap' dance), for instance, is taken to signify Nazism, a Jewish dance symbolises (anti-) Semitism, while the Polonaise is employed to connote West German commodity culture. Corporeal pleasure is obstructed through alienation: the dramaturgical and choreographic means (such as exaggeration) being designed to make the audience distance themselves from, and reject, what is depicted on stage. The RAF members provide a certain counterpoint to this as they often use contemporary dance vocabulary whose greater flexibility and openness sets them apart from the 'capitalist' figures, aligning them with revolutionary causes.

Kresnik's extreme choreographic perspective can be explained with recourse to the historical determinants of German post-war dance, in which merry or beautiful dance (in particular that which moves outside the internationalist parameters of classical ballet) may have been regarded as ideologically suspicious for several reasons. First, beauty, especially where politically-engaged art is concerned, seems incompatible with post-war resistance to the fascist aestheticisation of politics and to Hitler's cult of the honed, beautiful body. Clearly the unhappy alliance between several German modern dancers, such as Mary Wigman and Rudolf von Laban, and the Nazi regime contributed to this. Secondly, the German avant-garde has been greatly influenced by leftist thinkers such as the Frankfurt School. Specifically, Adorno's dictum about the 'barbarity' of producing poetry after Auschwitz (first noted in *Prismen*, 1955) had an enormous impact on cultural production in Germany. He returned to this topic in *Noten zur Literatur*, in which he wrote:

> The sentence, to write a poem after Auschwitz is barbaric, does not have universal validity, but [it is certainly true] that afterwards, because it was possible and may indefinitely remain a possibility, no cheerful art can be imagined (1984: 603; my translation).

In the dance world, the indictment against 'cheerful' art and similar arguments advanced by the Frankfurt School could readily be understood as an attack on dances of an entertaining or amusing character, along with those that are affirmative of the existing social order. (Moreover, because Third Reich propagandists such as Joseph Goebbels believed the essence of dance was to entertain and embrace grace, lightness and harmony, 'beautiful' dance had become doubly suspicious on ideological grounds).

There may also be a third reason for Kresnik's choreographic strategy. *Ulrike Meinhof* explicitly draws parallels between the history of the RAF and the tensions between East and West in post-reunification Germany. From the perspective of the German political left, the fall of the Wall robbed them of the hope of an (at least potentially) superior society to that of the capitalist Federal Republic. Rather than witnessing the demise of capitalism after a proletarian revolution, as predicted in Marxist circles, the left-wing intelligentsia experienced reunification as resulting in a takeover and incorporation of the socialist GDR by the free-market West German state, which might partly explain the bitterness of Kresnik's vision.

Unsurprisingly, Kresnik makes no attempt to bring his audience members into line with the dominant state ideology. As Anthony Shay (2002) has shown, dance companies and folk dance forms can showcase nations; furthermore, dance is often used as a medium of unity, to boost ethnic pride or heighten citizens' patriotic spirit. Kresnik, however, choreographs *against* the nationalist community-building function of dance. While he uses a plethora of national symbols and images (such as the German flag and colours, and popular songs with which the general public identify), he evokes a sense of nationalism only in order to denigrate it. Nationalism here is portrayed as a divisive and exclusive mechanism: the state, rather than being glorified, is depicted as the 'real' terrorist culprit. The actions of the anti-state terrorist Meinhof, on the other hand, seem to be largely defended and justified.

At the time of the piece's premiere, Kresnik's unorthodox view was potentially dangerous, as evidenced by the bomb threat. However, with the growing distance from the traumas of the original events and a changed perception of the RAF by younger generations, treatments of the organisation have either become more factual, or indeed positively nostalgic and 'chic'. Intriguingly, reviews of the later stagings of the piece show that in 2006, even right-wing tabloids often conceptualised Meinhof as a martyr or icon; thus echoing Kresnik's perspective in an interesting historical twist (see also Kolb 2009: 143).

Kresnik's artistic achievements lie in the undermining, challenging, resignification and subversion of established models of political thought and constructions of reality (in his case according to reasonably orthodox neo-Marxist models). His strength, perhaps, is in pointing out the deficiencies of the status quo, rather than developing a viable alternative societal model. His artistic techniques evoke terrorist strategies, notably with respect to audience reception inasmuch as his piece invokes fear, shock and disbelief; hence, the choreography's form and content appear to coincide. In this regard, he militates against Marcuse's insistence that the true political potential of art must lie in its transcendence of reality – a position which indeed deviates from orthodox Marxism. Perhaps Paul Virilio is right when critically observing that 'avant-garde artists, like many political agitators, propagandists and demagogues, have long understood what TERRORISM [sic] would soon popularize: if you want a place in "revolutionary history" there is nothing easier than provoking a riot, an assault on propriety, in the guise of art' (Virilio 2003: 31). However, Kres-nik's radical choreographic perspective is undoubtedly symptomatic of the intense frustration experienced as a result of the critical impasse of leftist intellectual thought after German reunification, which left capital-ism as the only apparently feasible model for the country's political and economic future.

David Dorfman: *Underground*

Underground, first performed at the Brooklyn Academy of Music in New York City in 2006, begins as the audience enter; hence no formal bounda-ries (apart from the distance between stage and auditorium) separate the dance from the viewers. For roughly the first fifteen minutes, Dorfman continuously performs repetitive sequences of dance and casual move-ments on stage: these include a lunge resembling a revolutionary pose – right arm lifted with fingers balled into a fist, left knee on the floor (see Figure 3); casual walking across the stage diagonally; crawling across the floor; kneeling in a position with hands 'tied' behind the back; and throw-ing of imaginary objects, perhaps stones or grenades. These movements, some of which later appear intermittently as leitmotifs throughout the piece, are performed with increasing intensity. Only the darkening of the auditorium, a semiotic sign signalling the entry of the audience into the imaginative sphere of the art work, finally breaks this blurring of 'reality' and performance.

In the 2006 BAM recording which I have viewed, Dorfman used a group of approximately twenty community dancers in addition to the nine performers from Dorfman Dance Company, all clad in casual streetwear. His montage is diverse; without adhering to any narrative or chronology, he uses a kaleidoscope of mixed media and a collaged soundtrack incorporating a number of musical genres and texts. Film projections and stills of scenes from Siegel's and Green's *Weather Underground* documentary, by which the work was inspired, underpin and illuminate sections of the choreography. Hand symbolism plays a central role in Dorfman's piece; a massive handprint projected onto the back wall suggests sensual experience and touch as opposed to purely cognitive reasoning, but in certain contexts the 'bloodied palm' image has also been used to accuse governments of state-sanctioned murder (see Felshin 1995: 8). The clenched fist recurs throughout. A common salute among political activists of left-wing or anti-capitalist orientation (Moss 2006), it is seen as an expression of unity, defiance and strength. It was employed symbolically both by the German Sozialistischer Deutscher Studentenbund (for instance on the book cover of *Die Strategiediskussion des SDS von 1963–66*), and by the recent Students for a Democratic Society in the US, a re-establishment in 2006 of the 1960s left-wing student movement.

Like the German RAF, the Weathermen were a far-left organisation originating as a faction of the student activist movement in America. Their political fervour and revolutionary ideals were fuelled by anti-capitalist, anti-imperialist, feminist and anti-racist convictions. They saw the US as a highly repressive state dominated by conservative middle-class white supremacists, though it was the reaction against the Vietnam War and associated abuses of American power which prompted many of a series of rallies and bombings targeting banks and government buildings, including the Pentagon in 1972. The symbolic value of attacking America's centre of military power was of course reiterated in the 2001 Pentagon attack by Al-Qaeda.

The Weathermen felt that years of non-violent activism had failed to bring an end to the killing and maiming of innocent civilians in Vietnam. They therefore undertook a series of violent actions, entitling their first waging of war on the US establishment 'The Days of Rage', when in October 1969 they held demonstrations in Chicago which saw six Weathermen shot and a number of policemen and protestors injured. The accidental death in 1970 of three of their members whilst preparing a nail bomb in a Greenwich Village house led, according to some historians (such as Varon 2004: 13), to a rethink and subsequent rejection of lethal acts against the person, though not of violence *per se*. The Weather Underground's later underground activities were marked by guerrilla warfare, although by 1977 the organisation had disintegrated.

Dorfman's *Underground* begins, after the choreographer's solo 'prelude', with a dialogue between the two leading dancers. Karl Rogers raises an abstract question: 'Does what you do make a difference?' and Jennifer Nugent responds: 'What would you do?' This sets the tone for the work, which is a melange of verbal scenes engaging the audience in moral discourse, interspersed with group assemblages in which dancers launch into series of glissades, leaps and runs. The movement often conjures up images of frantic climbing, jumping, clambering in tense situations; or in others the hurling of imaginary projectiles. In two of these scenes, dancers run around in circles, paired with one partner grasping the other in a chokehold. While this image can be read multitudinously, the backdrop – a digital outline of protest footage and police arrests in the midst of riots – suggests an allusion to the Days of Rage, with the choke-hold presumably representing police brutality against activists.

The most memorable scenes are those which employ verbal communication. In Rogers's second appearance, he confronts both the audience and dancers with further questions of an ethical nature: 'Are you a pacifist?', 'Is violence ever justified?', and 'Is your country worth killing for?' One dancer begins chanting 'I'm apathetic', and the double entendre is noteworthy as it can also be understood as 'I am pathetic'. In his third appearance as an 'interviewer', Rogers wonders: 'Have you ever marched in a demonstration?', 'Can we live without war?' and ultimately 'Would you stand up?' The dancers respond by taking one step forward or backward, representing yes or no answers. In an email correspondence with myself Dorfman noted that these were mostly the dancers' reflections of their actual views, adding: 'The dance has been a wonderful and vulnerable peeling layers of [sic] collective and individual views within the company. In the end, the piece is not intended to be prescriptive to anyone – more of an exploration of views' (Dorfman 2009a). The theme of unwillingness to challenge the societal status quo is further addressed in a section where one dancer admits he used to vent his anger through protest demonstrations and organising his community. But now, he concludes, he would rather live a peaceful existence as he was told it was 'cool' to be apathetic.

Dorfman here highlights important issues of both historical and contemporary US-American interest, namely political disengagement and civic responsibilities. The Weathermen, like the German RAF, had announced their intention to 'bring the war home' in an attempt to cause sufficient trouble to stir the general public out of their perceived indifferent stance towards the conflict in Vietnam. In apparent admiration for the organisation, whose actions he first witnessed as a teenager, the choreographer announces to the audience: 'This is the first communiqué of a huge fan of the Weather Underground [...] You made a difference [...] You changed something.' While he seems unable to pinpoint the nature of this change, he still 'feels a sense of the irrational hope' (from *Underground* recording).

Dorfman's main conceptual themes – as he puts it 'apathy, concern, action and empathy' (Dorfman 2009a) – were timely issues to raise in 2006, when the military involvement in Iraq, including accounts of various types of violence against prisoners in Abu Ghraib, the legality of detentions, and torture techniques employed in Guantanamo Bay prison camp came under increasing scrutiny in the media. Various American choreographers have tackled similar issues in the last decade, for instance Victoria Marks in *Not about Iraq* (2007). Scholarly accounts of this phenomenon have also become quite commonplace: for instance, Nina Eliasoph's 1998 book sought explanations of contemporary political apathy in the US, notably the historically very low voter turnout[12] and people's ignorance about basic political matters. Though reasons for this are various, the author points

---

12   Voter turnout can be seen as an indicator of both the extent of the population's political participation and their faith in political institutions.

out that foreign policy issues are often 'not close enough to home' (1998: 2) and that citizens have 'learned' to avoid confrontational public political debates. Dawn Moon (2004) corroborates this view, maintaining that most US-Americans define politics as threatening and view it overwhelmingly negatively. She argues that voicing of political demands tends increasingly to be justified on grounds of their impact on the individual citizen rather than more socially-based commitments of an ideological or public-policy nature (ibid.: 231).

These recent findings, and Dorfman's concerns, would have been grist to the mill of the Frankfurt School theorists, who argued as early as in the 1940s that consumerist society (of which the US is clearly a prime exponent) tends to encourage political apathy. Adorno and Horkheimer cite two interrelated reasons for such apathy in highly developed capitalist systems. First, the manipulation of the consumer through mass culture and superficial entertainment distracts from the tedium of bourgeois existence and is simultaneously a phenomenon of, and cover for, the power-politics of the capitalist state. It thus 'confirms the validity of the system' (Adorno & Horkheimer 1979: 129). Secondly, people feel that political participation 'can alter their actual existence only minimally. Failing to discern the relevance of politics to their own interests, they retreat from all political activity' (Adorno 2001: 192). The bourgeoisie's proper form of existence is the private world (Adorno & Horkheimer 1979: 96). This is in tune with Moon's observation that people only muster the energy for political action when private or local concerns are at stake.

Dorfman's part-choreographed, part-verbal commentary on our individual responsibility for scrutinising and actively challenging corrupt political systems contains a double address. While the work ostensibly deals with a 1960s subject matter, the choreographic strategy also enables audiences to read an in-between-the-lines comment on contemporary US-American foreign policy under the Bush administration.[13] Parallels are drawn

---

13   Although no mention is made of Bush in *Underground*, reviewers have continually noted by association its relevance to the contemporary US political context. In one scene, upon hearing the question 'what would you do?' a dancer breaks into a frantic fit of anger before suddenly beginning to weep. The critic Mary Ellen Hunt notes: 'It's an instantly recognizable embodiment of the same response that perhaps you

between the 1960s and '70s, and more recent conflicts: notably the 2003 US-invasion of Iraq and the country's ongoing military involvement in the Middle East. In our correspondence Dorfman emphasised that he intended to comment on more recent politics: 'The wars in Iraq and Afghanistan were weighing on my mind. I wanted to look at the similarities in that and our time as far as decisions and actions by our government and citizens [are concerned]' (2009). Dorfman has previously admonished the Bush regime: 'I feel burned by the elections of 2000 and 2004 and the shameful behaviour of our government' (Felciano 2006).

The work's final scene foregrounds his view more explicitly. Three female dancers are puzzled by a solidified activist who stands frozen in a revolutionary 'lunge' posture. Upon realising what the man is, they excitedly exclaim he needs to be moved and attempt to rejuvenate him. The whole dance cast then congregate on stage and support the revived activist who begins throwing imaginary grenades. Dorfman finally joins on stage copying, and hence moving in unison with, the activist's movements. In this iconographically somewhat simplistic scene, Dorfman makes a propagandist move to encourage his audience, and by implication the public, to 'revive' the revolutionary and non-conformist spirit of the 1960s. The choreographer here seems to echo the views of Herbert Marcuse, who suggested in the early 1970s that activism was an appropriate means to challenge the current US government:

> The slogan 'let's sit down and reason together' has rightly become a joke. Can you reason with the Pentagon on any other thing than the relative effectiveness of killing machines – and their price? [...] Reasoning 'from without' the power structure is a naïve idea. They will listen only to the extent to which the voices can be translated into votes. [...] There is a level on which even the unintelligent action against them seems justified. For action smashes, though only for a moment, the closed universe of suppression. (Marcuse 1972: 132–133)

---

or I might feel, say, while watching a presidential press conference' (2006). Other critics have highlighted the points of connection between the 1969 Days of Rage in Chicago and 2006 Iraq (Swift 2006), while George Anderson (2006) points out that the logic of (lethal) violence against people to save others – verbalised in one scene – also justifies the use of torture in Guantanamo Bay.

Intriguingly, Dorfman's final tableau of grenade throwing and its plea for activism, which seems to suggest violent action as a possible means of resistance, is at odds with his declared pacifist stance. While he believes 'in a more radical approach to change than is usually afforded by corporate backed legislators' (Dorfman 2009a), he aims predominantly at provoking thought, and rejects violence. He supports a form of activism which promotes 'active consideration of citizenship' and is based on 'radical diplomacy, maximal transparency, and a softer humanity emerging' (ibid.).

Comparative Analysis and Conclusion

By transcending their individual memories of the 1960s and '70s movements and taking the historical theme of terrorism into the public artistic domain, Dorfman and Kresnik help remind their societies of their collective memories; in particular aiding younger generations to (re)construct an aspect of their countries' 'alternative' and marginalised cultural and political identities. The choreographies moreover frame these recollections within contemporary politics, using similar strategies to shed light on contemporaneous political developments through the lens of past events. Both artists acknowledge the point that history repeats itself. The image Kresnik presents of Helmut Kohl's reunified Germany resembles that conjured up by the RAF and student activists in the 1960s, which was predominantly marked by evocations of aggressive imperialism and greedy capitalism. Kresnik is, moreover, candid about his dislike of chancellor Kohl, even calling him a 'pig' in the 2008 interview published in this book. Similarly, Dorfman likens America's post-millenial military conflicts to those opposed by the Weathermen in the late 1960s and 1970s. Like Kresnik, he is openly sceptical of his country's government and points an accusing finger at contemporary apathy.

        Neither of the two pieces discussed has a straightforward narrative or gives a chronological, factual account of historical events. Kresnik's position is markedly anti-capitalist, reflecting a relatively orthodox left-wing perspective. Researchers have noted his work's essentially emotional appeal (see Haas 2008: 192–193); it is more dramatic and comprises a bolder message than *Underground*. Like conventional political protest, it is loud, intrusive, spectacular and corporeal. The aesthetic of the ugly distances people from the characters to diminish any possible empathy, and makes a visceral impact on spectators. Dorfman's piece, on the other hand, is more constrained and subtly, rather than openly, critical of the current regime. It is in many scenes, as critics have also noted, 'essentially verbal' (Anderson 2006) and therefore less directly sensual, presenting a broadly intellectual and somewhat less emotionally-charged take on its subject matter (Hunt 2006, MacMillan 2009). The use of speech also carries with it a degree of objectification of the issues addressed. Dorfman used local community dancers because he 'wanted to actually involve folks in the communities to which we travelled, instead of just making a piece about involvement and participation' (Dorfman 2009a), thus translating his democratic ideals directly into choreographic practice.

With regard to both form and content, the two choreographies provide examples of the 'desublimation' of art (Marcuse 1972: 81). And to be sure, postmodern choreographic strategies and the urge to revive the spirit of the 1960s justify these choices. However, the audacity of Dorfman's work, noted by its reviewers, seems muted in comparison with Kresnik's more radical piece in terms of both iconography and the latter's absolute prioritising of content over form. Indeed, the political message in *Underground* is often not directly expressed but evoked through its ethical questions, symbolic scenes and the backdrop film footage. One must, though, bear in mind the different historical contexts: perhaps in Germany it is more acceptable to criticise and debase the state and its ideology as a consequence of the country's fascist past, and in particular from the 'safe haven' of art which tends to harbour left-wing ideas. (Indeed, intellectual life in post-war Germany has arguably been dominated by a leftist consensus, for instance in the Frankfurt School philosophy). The left has held a stronghold in the German post-war and post-reunification political landscape too, as is evidenced by the strength of the leftist party *Die Linke* which achieved remarkable success in the 2009 parliamentary elections, obtaining almost twelve per cent of the national vote. By contrast left-wing thought, and associated values such as collectivism, have traditionally been marginalised outside artistic and intellectual circles in the US. This is illustrated, for example, by Post-World War II McCarthyism with its anti-communist purges, the lack of any major party professing socialist views, and even the recent discussions about health reform.

In his book on the RAF and Weather Underground, Varon (2004: 12–13) writes: 'Their comparison elicits a basic question of political morality: when and under what conditions may one assume dominion over life and death and kill another human being on behalf of a political goal or idea?'. Dorfman's piece raises this question explicitly. While the RAF approved of and embraced political murder, the Weathermen prohibited lethal violence when on the brink of it after the Greenwich explosion. Notably, *Ulrike Meinhof* and *Underground* engage with questions about politically-motivated killing by asking if and when violence and suppression are permissible in various contexts: state actions against terrorists, terrorist actions against states, and wars between states.

While both choreographies seek to destabilise the complacency of the status quo, they negotiate the tension between excess and limitation in different ways. Indeed, Kresnik's and Dorfman's choreographic choices reflect the activist practices of their countries' respective 1960s terrorist organisations in terms of the vigour by which they approach their subject matter. Dorfman's more bridled piece echoes what Varon has termed the Weathermen's 'internally constrained practice' (2004: 13); perhaps reflecting the more ambivalent approach to violence shown by the political group itself. Dorfman refuses to sensationalise the political, preferring to use authentic historical film footage of the events alongside verbal commentary. Kresnik's work, by contrast, deliberately transgresses many boundaries of theatrical 'decency' in its endeavour to express the artist's dissatisfaction with the political status quo and his defence of Meinhof. The recklessness and shock-tactics of his work mirror the RAF's uncompromising political terrorism through what one might term his 'terroristic' choreographic practice. Thus, his strategy is an extension of the logic of excess wherein political murder features as the ultimate transgressive act.

Works Cited

Adorno, T. 1978. On the Fetish Character in Music and the Regression of Listening, in *The Essential Frankfurt School Reader*. Edited by Andrew Arato and Eike Gebhardt. Oxford: Blackwell: 270–299.

Adorno, T. 1984. Noten zur Literatur IV, in *Gesammelte Schriften* 11. Edited by Rolf Tiedemann et al. Suhrkamp: Frankfurt am Main.

Adorno, T. 1997. *Aesthetic Theory*. Edited by Gretel Adorno & Rolf Tiedemann. Newly translated by Robert Hullot-Kentor. Minneapolis: University of Minnesota Press.

Adorno, T. 2001. Free time, in *The Culture Industry: Selected Essays on Mass Culture*. Edited by Theodor Adorno and J. M. Bernstein. London/New York: Routledge: 187–197.

Adorno, T. & Horkheimer, M. 1979. *Dialectic of Enlightenment*. London and New York: Verso.

Anderson, J. 2006. *Dorfman among the Weathermen*, Review from 17 November. Available: <http://www.nytheatre-wire.com/jao6117t.htm> [14 September 2009].

Banes, S. 1993. *Greenwich Village 1963: Avant-Garde Performance and the Effervescent Body*. Durham, NC and London: Duke University Press.

Bell, J. 2003. Performance studies in an age of terror. *TDR* 47(2): 6–8.

Benjamin, W. 1968. The Work of Art in the Age of Mechanical Reproduction, in *Illuminations*. New York: Harcourt, Brace & World: 219–253.

Carbonneau, S. 2007. *David Dorfman Dance. Days of Rage, Days of Hope. David Dorfman's 'Underground'*. Available: <http://www.batesdancefestival.org/Artist-Notes/dorfman07.php> [15 April 2009].

Cooper Albright, A. 2006. *Study Guide for Underground*. Available: <http://www.daviddorfmandance.org/uploads/Study%20Guide%20underground.pdf> [3 September 2009].

Croce, A. 2000. Discussing the Undiscussable, in *Writing in the Dark, Dancing in the 'New Yorker'*. Gainesville: University Press of Florida.

David Dorfman Dance, Underground. 2009. Denver News. Blog posted 11 February. Available: <http://www.americantowns.com/co/denver/news/david-dorfman-dance-underground-141671> [1 January 2010].

Dorfman, D. 2009. Email communication with Alexandra Kolb. 12 November.

Eliasoph, N. 1998. *Avoiding Politics: How Americans Produce Apathy in Everyday Life*. New York: Cambridge University Press.

Felciano, R. 2006 Weather channeling. David Dorfman's latest finds inspiration in activism. *San Francisco Bay Guardian online*. On website of David Dorfman Dance company <http://www.daviddorfmandance.org/articles.php> [13 August 2009].

Felshin, N. 1995. *But Is It Art? The Spirit of Art as Activism*. Seattle: Bay Press.

Fensham, R. 1997. Dance and the Problems of Community, in *Dancers and Communities*. Edited by Helen Poynor and Jacqueline Simmonds. NSW: Australian Dance Council: 14–19.

Haas, B. 2008. Terrorism and Theatre in Germany, in *Baader-Meinhof Returns. History and Cultural Memory of German Left-Wing Terrorism*. Edited by Gerrit-Jan Berendse/Ingo Cornils. Amsterdam/New York: Rodopi: 191–210.

Habermas, J. 1983. Herbert Marcuse: On Art and Revolution (1973), in *Philosophical-Political Profiles*. Translated by F. G. Lawrence. Cambridge, MA/London: The MIT Press: 165–170.

Hunt, M. E. 2006. *David Dorfman: underground*. Review 5 October. Available: <http://www.kqed.org/arts/performance/article.jsp?essid=11020> [4 October 2009].

Kester, G. 1998. Ongoing Negotiations: *Afterimage* and the Analysis of Activist Art, in *Art, Activism, and Oppositionality. Essays from Afterimage*. Edited by Grant H. Kester. Durham, NC and London: Duke University Press.

Kolb, A. 2009. Theatricalising Terrorism. Johann Kresnik's *Ulrike Meinhof* and the Red Army Faction. *About Performance* 9: 127–148.

Kretz-Meingold, M. 2006. *Grelle Szenen eines Lebens*. Interview with Johann Kresnik, 12 February. Available: <http://www.wdr.de/themen/kultur/theater/ulrike_meinhof/interview_kresnik.jhtml> [31 October 2007].

Kubiak, A. 1991. *Stages of Terror. Terrorism, Ideology, and Coercion as Theatre History*. Bloomington and Indianapolis: Indiana University Press.

Lehmann H.-T. 2006. *Postdramatic Theatre*. Translated and with an Introduction by Karen Jürs-Munby. London/New York: Routledge.

Lepecki, A. 1995. How (Not) to Perform the Political. *Ballett international/tanz aktuell 1*: 15–19.

MacMillan, K. 2009. '*Underground*' digs into protest. Posted 3 February. Available: <http://www.denverpost.com/entertainment/ci_11815291> [5 December 2009].

Marcuse, Herbert. 1968. *Der eindimensionale Mensch. Studien zur Ideologie der fortgeschrittenen Industriegesellschaft*. Neuwied/Berlin: Luchterhand.

Marcuse, H. 1972. *Counterrevolution and Revolt*. Boston: Beacon Press.

Marcuse, H. 1979. *The Aesthetic Dimension. Toward a Critique of Marxist Aesthetics*. London: Macmillan.

McLuhan, M. 1964. *Understanding Media: The Extensions of Man*. New York: McGraw Hill.

Moon, D. 2004. *God, Sex and Politics: Homosexuality and Everyday Theologies*. Chicago: University of Chicago Press.

Moss, St. 2006. What's in a clenched fist? *The Guardian online*, 30 May. Available: <http://www.guardian.co.uk/film/2006/may/30/cannes2006.cannesfilmfestival> [10 October 2009].

Sabbatini, A. 1986. Terrorism, Perform. *High Performance* 9(2): 29–33.

Shay, A. 2002. *Choreographic Politics: State Folk Dance Companies, Representation and Power*. Middletown, CT: Wesleyan University Press.

Stone's Attack 'Performance Art'. 2006. 19 December. Online. Available: <http://news.bbc.co.uk/2/hi/uk_news/northern_ireland/6193169.stm> [3 August 2009].

Die Strategiediskussion des SDS von 1963–66. 1972. Amsterdam: PacoPress.

Swift, O. 2006. *David Dorfman 'underground' review*. The News and Observer, 13 June. [Online]. Available: <http://www.h-artmanagement.com/Press_PDF_files/DDD/DDDCompletePress.pdf> [2 January 2010].

Varon, J. 2004. *Bringing the War Home: The Weather Underground, the Red Army Faction and Revolutionary Violence in the Sixties and Seventies*. Berkeley: University of California Press.

Virilio, P. 2003. *Art and Fear*. London/New York: Continuum.

PART II

Dance of Enemies

5 Death and the Maiden: Mary Wigman in the Weimar Republic

Introduction

Mary Wigman (Hanover 1886 – 1973 Berlin), one of the greatest artists of the twentieth century, set an agenda in modern dance – performance, choreography as well as education. 'What is dance?' asked Wigman in 1921 and answered: 'Space, symbol; the finite with the eternal, formed, penetrated, built' (Wigman 1921). Her dance, which 'realised the human body as tension in space', was 'absolute' (Wigman 1921, Michel 1924), 'pure' and 'essence in space' and therefore removed from any exterior influence; it was 'Selbstzweck' – an end in itself (Wigman 1925:19);[1] it was beyond reality and politics. The dancer had to serve the movement idea and had to reject exterior milieu and former histories, such as ballet and its technique, as outdated. So she insisted from her first days in Germany in the early 1920s.

Her dance was 'a living language that was spoken by and announced the human being – an artistic message that lifts itself to the skies, above base reality in order to speak in images and metaphors of that which moves man in his innermost being [...]' (Wigman 1963/1986: 10).[2] Not concrete reality, which would have been constricting, but liberating imagination inspired dance and choreography (Wigman 1925: 12). Contemporariness revolved around the laws and forces of eternity. To dance meant to be

---

1 Wigman also used the term 'angewandter Tanz' – applied dance (connected to other arts or dependent on music and stage practices) – as a counter-concept to pure/ absolute dance.

2 All translations are mine unless stated otherwise.

called, to witness, to be asked by some higher authorities and to answer them (ibid.: 18). The autonomy of the art form would have been impaired had too much reality invaded dance. That was true in 1921, when Wigman defined dance and it was true in 1963 when she contemplated dance and her entire career in one of her most comprehensive, written essay collections: *Die Sprache des Tanzes* (*The Language of Dance*). The evolution of her ideas and performance practices seems to have followed a strict logic; she never abandoned it but merely refined and narrowed down what she considered the 'essence' of the art of movement.

Wigman lived under four political regimes: she was born in 1886 into the middle class of the German Empire that socialised and educated her. Its values and mores dictated her upbringing. But the years of the Weimar Republic saw her rise to success and fame. Between 1918 and 1933 she established herself as the dominant figure of German Modern Dance, in Germany and abroad. When the Nazis came to power she recognised the opportunities open to her own career and that of the new dance. She easily integrated and collaborated with the Nazi bureaucracy. Finally, after the German defeat in 1945 she had to find a place in a country that would be defined by the politics of the Allied forces and had to adjust to an unfamiliar democracy. German Empire, Weimar Republic, Third Reich and post-war West-Germany thus were the four political regimes she experienced. Like every citizen, she reacted to her political milieu – she had to – but did she act consciously within it?

At the outbreak of World War I in 1914 Wigman was 28 years old. She had followed Rudolf von Laban to Switzerland in 1913 and spent most of her time in Zurich and Ascona, on the Monte Verità. She performed her first solo recital on 18 June 1917 in Zurich's municipal theatre. But she was still dependent on Laban. Only in 1918 did she manage to make the break after a long liberation process. Throughout 1919 she toured Germany and performed her dances, but she still resided in Switzerland. In 1920, after the Swiss authorities rejected her application for a long-term working permit (Müller 1986: 72), Wigman, now completely independent, with a growing artistic reputation, returned to Germany on her own mission; to dance, to choreograph, to teach, to introduce the new dance and make it a dominant culture. Laban too had moved from the Swiss paradise to German post-war chaos but their ways had parted.

Mary Wigman in the Weimar Republic

Wigman's professional coming of age coincided more or less with the proclamation of the Weimar Republic. But it would be a mistake to deem this concurrence more than a chronological overlap. Wigman left the safety and stability of Switzerland forcibly as her application for a visa and permanent right to reside was refused. Switzerland had been the place where the concept of a new dance had first materialised and where she had established herself as a teacher and performer. Her dance could have easily been perfected there. We can thus safely assume that it was not political sympathy with the Weimar constitution that instigated the relocation to Dresden. Berthe Trümpy, close friend and manager of the first school set up in Dresden in 1920, recorded the situation at that time: 'Under the window 18 trams rattled away and now and again there was bit of revolution with bullets going astray and flying around in the studio [...]' (Wigman 1925: 74). A bit of revolution: that was Trümpy's reference to the Kapp Putsch and the General Strike.[3] A striking and revealing summary of Wigman and her students' situation: something was going on beyond the studio but what really mattered was its inside space, teaching and dancing. Neither Wigman nor her students seemed to show the slightest interest in the young republic and the serious threat posed to it by the armed Freikorps and the Marinebrigade Ehrhardt who led the insurgency. On the surface this might characterise Wigman's attitude to politics: dance first, the rest later – and the rest encompassed an awful lot, including the turmoil outside, the rise and fall of Weimar democracy and eventually the ascent of Nazism.

The immensely popular playwright Carl Zuckmayer summarised Wigman's relationship to the Weimar Republic as follows:

---

3   The Kapp-Putsch was a military coup led by Reichswehr, i.e. army officers, to overthrow the Weimar Republic. The putsch was a right-wing monarchist and reactionary attempt to defeat leftist politics. In answer to the Kapp-Putsch, the social-democratic government called the German workers to defeat the insurgent army and paramilitary groups by a general strike, which received mass support and swept away the rebels.

Though the Weimar Republic provided Mary Wigman with the applause of its intellectuals, it did not give her a megaphone, nor a loud speaker, nor educational facilities and films, nor youth groups and oversize halls in which she could work on a gigantic scale with thousands of dancers moving to her enthusiastic rhythms and not merely twenty or fifty. (Zuckmayer 2002: 112)[4]

Thus a contemporary witness described that the Republic offered Wigman a space to work but not the place in which she developed identification with democratic ideals, in which she openly argued politics. The Republic provided her with a minimum of opportunities but not the maximum with which she expected to be rewarded; it did not give her 'enough' – not enough space, not enough people, not enough financial means, not enough recognition, not enough applause.

Was Wigman a political person? Aware of politics? Invested in any? In order to understand Wigman's relationship to politics we have to define the term and delineate those that Wigman represented and practised. There is a striking absence of the word 'politics' or 'political' in Wigman's writings at all times. In all of the roughly 120 pages of *The Language of Dance*, for instance, there is no mention of politics (Wigman 1963/1986). At no time did she discuss politics; she did not consider her actions and her behaviour political (Schumann 1986: 36–50).

If Wigman did not speak or write about POLITICS (writ large) should we then assume that politics did not matter to her? Her approach will not help us understand her position and she would not have appreciated the constant, indeed over-use of the terms politics and political in today's language. It is richly ironical that so many scholars attempt to analyse her social as well as aesthetic position under the rubric of politics of gender or modernism or this, that or the other when Wigman considered herself beyond politics. Hence we need to negotiate between Wigman's and our very different understandings of politics.

---

4   Carl Zuckmayer (1896–1977) went into exile after the Austrian Anschluss in 1938. His commentaries and portraits of famous and influential German artists were written for the Office of Strategic Services (OSS) in American exile in 1940.

During the Weimar Republic political involvement and affiliation were openly discussed and the atmosphere was fully charged with politics of left, right and centre. Wigman's stance thus cannot be deemed typical of this particular period. Politics were very much *en vogue* – for some. If one compares Wigman's writings and performance practices with those of her contemporaries who also concerned themselves with a new theatre, it very quickly becomes clear that the mere usage of the terms politics and political outlined a *Weltanschauung*. The experiments of Erwin Piscator or Bertolt Brecht (neither of whom she took too much notice of or supported) also targeted and invented revolutionary performance strategies. Piscator's and Brecht's *Epic theatre*, the *Lehrstücke* or the proletarian revues at the *Volksbühne* rested on a Marxist analysis of society.[5] Piscator's or Brecht's theatre[6] was fundamentally different from Wigman's dance performances for one reason above all others: their experiments were consciously political just as Wigman's were consciously a- or anti-political; Brecht and Piscator defined themselves through politics. Wigman refused to incorporate politics into her own work and recognise them as an aesthetically relevant force. Brecht's and Piscator's aesthetics tested the possibilities of an intervention in the social structure and integration of leftist, i.e. Marxist or communist theories into performance practices. At stake were class matters and that was the only way to interpret and counter politics: radicalise the arts and turn aesthetics into politics.

Or there were positions of a different political nature, taken for instance by the aristocrat Hubertus Prinz zu Löwenstein who involved himself in the defence of the Weimar political system. He commented on the reaction to his article on the rise of Nazism that he had written in the *Vossische Zeitung*, Berlin, 12 July 1930:

> For a young man of 24 years of age an editorial in the 'Voss' was something quite unheard of. I knew immediately that on 12 July 1930 a new stage of life began. The citizen of today cannot imagine what scandal I, with my family background, roused

5   The right-leaning press juxtaposed Wigman, an upright German artist, and Piscator, a capitalist theatre-dictator, supported by Jews (cf. Müller 1986: 147).
6   Cf. the evolution of Epic Theatre as political theatre of Piscator and Brecht.

by endorsing the Republic in the Vossische Zeitung. [...] Overnight my name was
known all over Germany [...] Goebbels wrote in the 'Angriff': So that's where the
worm in the apple, or rather in the garlic, was. The writer had stood up for the 'Jew
Republic'! (Loewenstein 1993: 8)

No comparable act is known of Wigman. As Wigman's own omission of
politics – a statement in itself – does not help us, we have to find a different
method to analyse her relationship to a phenomenon she denied. The
question for us, though, has to be how to appraise it, how to deal with
something that is missing.

We speak of politics fundamentally in three ways – first, 'as the theory
or practice of government or administration' or second, 'as the political
ideas, beliefs, or commitments of a particular individual, organisation,
etc.' and third, 'as actions concerned with the acquisition or exercise of
power, status, or authority' (OED-online 2008). These definitions will
guide us in our examination of Wigman's relationship to politics as an
interaction between her beliefs and the way in which she exercised them
to form an organisation, i.e. a dance group, and to choreograph and stage
her work. We have to stress again that Wigman would not have accepted
this perspective. She would have been loath to argue on political grounds
when artistic matters were in jeopardy. Art and politics were like fire and
water – incompatible. Her 'absolute dance' was a condensed version of
this attitude. Art was not about class or class wars, economics or democratic principles, it had to sustain its autonomy and address fundamental
existential problems, such as the identity of the dancing human being and
the link to its communal roots. Whereas class matters for instance were
political, community and culture were not. Dance was by its nature above
and beyond reality; it had to do with fate and meta-personal meaning
(Wigman 1963/1986: 910).

My first thesis in regard to Wigman's politics is: her refusal to acknowledge any influence as vital for the arts was symptomatic of a particular
class of people – the educated bourgeois intellectual leaning to the right.
Politics were the domain of the left who noisily let everyone know day-in
and day-out just how relevant political participation and attachment were.
My second thesis is: by comparing Wigman's attitudes to political events at

several stages of her life it is possible to assert that the first thesis is correct. Her aversion turned more against the left yet at the same time developed sympathies for the politics of the right. In the transition from Weimar Republic to Third Reich, which was prepared long before the actual take-over in January 1933, both aversion and sympathy manifested themselves in Wigman's words and deeds.

Wigman's artistic beliefs had evolved throughout her apprentice-ship with Laban in Switzerland and, fundamentally, within his notions of dance. They had diverged in several aspects to eventually form a modified but independent set of ideas. She deviated from Laban in her interpreta-tion of the ideological basis of dance: her definition of religion and the spiritual powers that inspired and directed dance were different as well as the place she ascribed to them; she addressed a different type of commu-nity, hence group or communal expression through movement together with a relevant leadership were of a different nature from that of Laban's groups and communities. Laban's groups, above all his movement choirs, gathered amateurs in order to instruct them in the canon of harmonic relationships that governed the world. Dancing communities, according to Laban's philosophy, would acquire harmonic knowledge and through movement theory practise its application. In the end, Laban's communal dancing bodies would transform an ailing civilisation and redeem man-kind (cf. Kant 2003).

Wigman had little interest in amateur dance politics; she was a profes-sional artist and educated future professional dancers and choreographers. But her high art, her 'absolute dance' too would redeem a sick Western soci-ety. Both deeply believed in a spiritual essence of the work of art; both also considered leadership of communities indispensable. Contrary to Laban, Wigman emphasised the necessity of an artistic elite, which had implica-tions for her aesthetic and pedagogical focus and the organisational and management styles to be practised. Unlike Laban, she had a stable national identity from which she could operate: German culture. She was German by birth and did not have to prove any allegiance to her heritage. She had it; she never wavered from, was questioned on or challenged by anyone on her Germanness. She defined it openly and provided the parameters of what it meant to be 'German' – it meant taking up the legacy of poet

Johann Wolfgang von Goethe as well as philosopher Friedrich Nietzsche and philosophical historian Oswald Spengler (Kant 1994). She was a Germanic 'Faustian' seeker (Müller 1986:58), she needed to battle with the elements that constituted life and she needed to get to the core of those things. Dance was the means to understand them; it was that elemental force that confronted space, time and energy (Wigman 1925), it expressed the 'human being as tension in space', torn between opposite existential tensions. Dance was 'the pure art of movement' (DAZ 1921). In and through it Wigman made visible the core of human nature (Michel 1935, Wigman 1935). If ethical or social tendencies stood in the foreground, then a work could be considered neither art nor dance, but should be labelled gymnastics (Wigman 1921). In gymnastics the body, though an expressive instrument as in art-dance, lacked the will to dance. It was moved, so to say, by an external political will. (But even in this passage Wigman used the word social and not political.)

Wigman and her young female friends and students danced because they entered into a new life through self-exploration and self-liberation (Wigman 1923 and 1929b) that, as far as they were concerned, had little or nothing to do with politics. Dance provided the means of expression for like-minded people, it offered itself as the language for that evolving, moving modern body (Die Musik 1933: 241, 272–274). Over the next decades her approach changed only insofar as she refined her aesthetics and adjusted them through artistic exploration to practical demands. She followed a strict programme, which is reflected in her writings, whether those of 1923 or 1933 or 1943 or later. In fact, Wigman's gift of retrospective and contemplative observations strengthened her theoretical stance and her practical sensibilities; it enabled her to pursue her grand vision and examine the way in which she realised it: to construct a concept of a new and contemporary life in a world of collapsed values – that was her mission and Wigman would achieve it through dance. Mission here is synonymous with quasi-theological belief, a programme dictated by religious fervour to transform reality.

Throughout the years of the Weimar Republic, we can see how Wigman encouraged an ensemble of young people to trust her, how that group turned into a discipleship and a community.[7] Throughout these years she also had to resolve the relationship between herself as a solo dancer and choreographer of the group that she collected around her. A distinct community, the 'Wigman-Gemeinde' (soon opposite to and opposed by the 'Laban-Gemeinde'), emerged from 1921 onwards – as a dance as well as a support group. Enthusiasts founded a *Society of Friends of the Mary Wigman Dance Group* in 1924, which supplied spiritual as well as material aid. After 1927 new Wigman-schools were set up and she as well as her devotees began to weave a fabric of Wigman teaching and performance networks. By 1928 *Die Deutsche Tanzgemeinschaft* had formed as an organised association, which also published a journal, *Die Tanzgemeinschaft*, with Felix Emmel as editor.

Her 'absolute dance' denied political involvement – a deeply political mindset itself – yet operated within political categories and lived through enacting visions that rested on the experience of contemporary political conflicts. The image of the dancer as an independent individual, guided by democratic desires for equality has been superimposed on Wigman and is used to justify *her* modernism of the 1920s as *our* modernism of the twenty-first century (cf. Santos-Newhall 2002). Yet Wigman's own explanations reveal her appropriation of totalitarian ideals: the process of intellectual clarification undertaken throughout the 1920s and 1930s focused on the aim of her art, the importance of Wigman herself as artistic creator and the place of the individual or the group in the course of the making of dances. This forceful relationship between individual and group is essential in assessing Wigman's politics for it is an enactment of and eventually a rejection of the Weimar democratic model. Let us follow this process of clarification. Several times in the early stages of her performance career Wigman articulated the logic that drove dance compositions. In 1925 composition was recognition of inherent law, detected and laid bare through the individual. She classified two types of works: applied compositions (the étude) and pure compositions (the dance, the suite). Pure or absolute dance

7   The critic Artur Michel wrote of Wigman's 'apostles' and her 'following' (Michel, 1923a and 1923b).

again fell into two different categories: functional and emotional dances (Wigman 1925). Her understanding still owed much to Laban's cosmos even though Wigman shifted focus and operated solely within the absolute dance idea. (Laban was described as the 'road sign', whereas Wigman was considered the 'path' or solution; Vogeler 1922.) In 1925, solo and group were essentially the same in regard to their choreographic content, only the format differed. She refined her attitude when she advanced towards more complex and demanding group compositions. By 1928 choric dance was the most complete interpretation of absolute dance, which she once more defined as the dance without any other meaning than that of expressing its own idea and content (Wigman 1928), the ultimate representation and expression of human movement, the transformation of the individual through movement into the member of a group or community and the acceptance of the leader.

Group dance had now taken on exactly the same properties which her solo performances initially had displayed. The tasks to solve the compositional and formal challenges of a choric dance work became clear to Wigman in all their power when she increasingly had to work for her dance group; she now had to satisfy her own aesthetic criteria as well as solve group dynamics and envisage more than one body in intricate spatial patterns that could no longer simply replicate the movements of the individual leading dancer. These problems became all too evident and no longer avoidable when she began sketching *Totenmal*. In 1972, when Wigman had successfully revised and omitted many events and incidents of her life and career, she remembered the difficult task of choreographing *Totenmal* in the late 1920s:

> Here it was – the choric challenge that I had tried so hard to tackle from my innermost being, without ever successfully taking that vital step from group to chorus [...]. *Totenmal* [...] the most mature and most ingenious of all my group compositions [...] was through and through symphonic, nothing but pure dance without any kind of underlying narrative... (Wigman 1963/1986: 90f)

Finally she could confront the crucial goal:

> That singular step from dance group to dancing chorus! It was crucial and had to
> be dared. This is no matter of pro and contra of forces struggling against each other
> [...]. Here the conflict is not battled out within the group. This is about the fusion
> of a group of human beings becoming one unified moving body that represents the
> present and the inscrutable at the same time, with one focus and one goal, accepted
> by all. No individual and fragmented actions any more. (Wigman 1963/1986: 92f)

Subjectivity in Wigman's sense, then, was not egocentric and hedonistic
individualism, ruthless and extreme independence of the individual will.
Neither was it mere 'self-fulfilment' and 'self-exploration'. Wigman had left
earlier assumptions of dance as 'self-exploration' behind. The self could only
be one element of dance as art. Towards the late 1920s dance embodied
the acceptance of being part of a community, the recognition of leadership together with the acceptance that the group required a leader. An
individual had to find her place within the group; the group had to admit
and admire the leader, the Führer-model of totalitarian Nazi ideology and
politics. Leaders turned the dark and faceless mass into a community for
only a leader could articulate and convince the group of its inner mission
and thus guide action. Without leadership, groups descended into chaos,
moral corruption, material depravity and consumerism. Wigman's sur-
roundings demonstrated the need for community every day. Taking on
leadership therefore became a fate, a tremendous burden that could lead
to complete dissolution of the individual – and her sacrifice.

Here is an example of the acceptance, appreciation and admiration
Wigman instilled in her group. We gain an insight into the translation of
theoretical/ideological definitions of leadership into practical, i.e. political,
application: Vera Skoronel, Wigman's student, assistant, and like Berthe
Trümpy, a close ally, praised her leadership as an artistic necessity. Wigman
organised and ran her dance group as a *Gemeinschaft* and she was its leader.
The dance group represented the *Gemeinschaft* on two levels: it was the
communal body that lived and worked together; it was also the performed
community, the community on stage as an aesthetic creation that projected,
embodied and enacted the cultural ideal:

> Mary Wigman is leader by her innate ability. She requires the dancing chorus for her
> ideas that explode the individual body; the world necessitates the dancing chorus
> [...]. To be a dancer means to carry out the holy battle... (Skoronel 1930: 4–6)

Skoronel's description affirms the total control of the leader over her community.

This interconnection cum interdependence of leader and community can be traced in the choreographies themselves and the tensions between solo and group works. An analysis of the titles that Wigman gave her choreographies confirms the thematic thread as well as the transformation of solo into group works in her creations: *Death, Death Call, Death Time, Death Dance, Lament, Sacrifice, Heroic Theme, Heroic Beginning, Funeral Lament, Song of Fate, Choric Movement.* 'Heroic' had figured prominently in her earlier writings as well as her choreographies (Wigman 1925: 15). *Fate* together with the *choric* form a constant in Wigman's creations; many other titles also include allusions to darkness, the night, despair, looming shadows, demons etc.

The terminology of heroism, the cultic and choric, death and lamentation brings us back to Wigman's cultural framework within which her politics unfold. We have to link these terms to the categories of culture and community; they enlighten us on Wigman's political intentions and goals. The analysis of ideological tenets identifies her politics. This is, once more, an indirect approach to Wigman's relationship to politics, but one necessary as a straight route cannot be taken. After all, her entire concept of 'absolute dance' consistently denied politics' direct influence on or relevance to her work.

The dance titles mentioned above reveal a strong preoccupation, if not obsession, with a certain type of death – the public death of a chosen person as the result of extreme tension. These 'deaths' evolved from the solo performances and embodied the sacrificial death as part of a necessary cultural renewal process. In *Totenmal* (1930) Wigman created such dynamic relationships between leader and group, individual and community.

The choreography of *Totenmal* confirmed the absolute necessity of choric dance, i.e. dance of the community. The move from solo and group to choric dance as dance of the communal body has to be understood as the decisive and qualitative step towards the establishment of the larger

German community (*Gemeinschaft*), envisaged by Wigman in the early 1920s but actually realised only from the late 1920s onwards. Its emergence confirms the continuity of Wigman's ideas and practices and it confirms that she was part of a greater stream of thought as well as practices that eventually merged into the Nazi 'People's community' in 1933. While the conservative right was clearing the way for the Nazis in the late 1920s and early 1930s, Wigman emphasised that a new dawn called for the dominance of the group. The future was for and in the communal group, whereas individual accomplishments, however ingenious they may be, were limited in their consequences and could never achieve more than personal satisfaction (Bach 1933: 59).

German culture was under constant attack and Wigman was on the side of those who would protect it and introduce its rejuvenation and rebirth. Germany suffered under the present regime of the Weimar Republic; it needed to be reconnected to an idealised past. The nostalgic harking back and re-imagining of better times provides a further indication of Wigman's deep conservatism. She hated the un-German attempts to dilute the superior cultural fabric of Germany. Her defence of German dance in 1929, answering the attack that the critic Andre Levinson launched after the 1928 Dancers' Congress and Wigman's appearances there, made her position transparent: a man 'impregnated with Latin culture and aesthetics' could only destructively and nastily condemn the efforts of the young German dance movement; he, who 'lacked German orientation', could never comprehend the essence of German dance (Wigman 1929a: 12f). Levinson had pointed out that: 'At its core the modern German dance is fiercely aware of its racial originality' (1929: 147). She did not renounce but confirmed the racial importance in her art by attacking Levinson's 'race' – he was of 'Latin culture', lacking 'German orientation'; indeed, the key to comprehending the disdain of German dancers for classical ballet also lay in their racial make-up. Ballet was 'rassenmässig wesensfremd' (racially essentially alien) (Wigman 1929a: 12).

Her response illustrates Wigman's relationship to democratic tolerance. She used vocabulary that would become part of Nazi language: 'vernichtende Gehässigkeit' (crushing nastiness) to locate the critic who was against her and her dance: 'wesensfremd, rassenmässig wesensbestimmt' (alien to one's essence, race-determined essence) etc. Criticism was 'Vernichtungswille' (the will to destroy) (Wigman 1929a: 13). Democracy was fine as long as it provided a working space, but far too narrow, vague and unreliable with respect to the categories on which her choreographic mission was based: the German community that carried and embodied German culture. Culture was not a matter of voting patterns, parliamentary decisions and should never depend on majority rule or criticism; it should certainly never be exposed to someone who 'lacks German orientation'. This particular answer demonstrates quite clearly that Levinson was not an individual or person but a type – the hostile Jew, member of the anti-German race; it reveals the roots of her anti-semitism that would make integration into the Nazi system so easy.

'Absolute dance' has to be placed within German intellectual traditions that pitched society against community, pinned its hopes on culture of the national community, and declared them the pillars of national values. For Wigman, as well as other representatives of this ideological tradition a battle was being fought between a national culture as the basis upon which a community rests versus a society with an eroded and commercialised art. This battle juxtaposing national 'culture' against international 'civilisation' extended far beyond the dance or even cultural field; it was part of a long running German debate that began with the publication in 1887 of Ferdinand Tönnies' work *Gemeinschaft und Gesellschaft*, in which he attacked modern life – society – as mechanical and artificial compared to 'organic community' or *Gemeinschaft*. Wigman's teacher Laban too favoured a dancing community and sought to establish it through dance and rhythmic movement. His assaults on Weimar democracy and its institutions were direct and crude. He hated parliamentary debates, found them useless and compared them to Punch-and-Judy shows. Weimar Germany suffered and produced a sick environment with 'false civilisation claims', 'sick degeneration' (Laban 1920: 134) and a modernity he despised. He only saw 'rottenness and decadence of our so highly praised culture' (Laban 1975: 42). Laban also knew how to heal it – with a turn toward a new religion and mystical incarnations (Laban 1920). Wigman did not directly attack the political system though her concerns and actions undermined it in a different manner.

Wigman had embarked on an extremely ambitious undertaking: restore German culture, create a German choric community. (The name of the new dance – *German Dance* – accepted and advanced by Laban as well as Wigman had stressed the German cultural component from their emigration to Germany in the early 1920s onwards.) Nietzsche's writings, in particular his *Birth of Tragedy* and Spengler's *Decline of the West* had made a vital impact on Wigman and had given her that larger cultural framework within which she could function and orientate herself. Christian Schad recalled Wigman and Laban 'drumming and dancing to Nietzsche' in 1915 in Zurich; he disliked the 'primitive writhing of their beautiful souls' (Schad 1985: 163). According to her diaries and other written testaments she returned to these authors for guidance and comfort throughout her life.

Nietzsche's *Birth of Tragedy* of 1872 suggested a 'rebirth' of culture through reinvention of ancient Greek tragedy. This tragedy, if inspired by the spirit of music, would establish what had been lost to humanity. Nietzsche followed the historical demise of the genre 'tragedy'. The balance between the Apollonian and Dionysian forces determined tragedy; once their balance was disturbed and the Apollonian won over the Dionysian, the downfall of the tragedy had begun, and with it the slow deterioration of Western culture. In order to restore the balance of the creative forces, tragedy had to be reborn. Nietzsche, initially under the intoxicating influence of Wagner's operas, imagined that the spirit of music was best suited to instil such profound cultural renewal.

Nietzsche saw in his own modern culture a worrying representation of the supremacy of 'Alexandrian culture', i.e. theoretical and overly rational Apollonian culture (Nietzsche 2000: 110f). The supremacy of Apollonian intellect had undermined the possibility to create art. Only the rediscovery of the Dionysian would rectify this dreadful and evil state of affairs:

> My friends, you who believe in Dionysian music, you also know what tragedy means to us. There we have tragic myth reborn from music – and in this myth we can hope for everything and forget what is most painful! What is most painful for all of us [...], is – the prolonged degradation in which the German genius has lived, estranged from house and home, in the service of vicious dwarfs. (ibid.: 142)

I argue that Wigman accepted all of Nietzsche's propositions and insights – except one: it would not be the spirit of music but that of dance (i.e. movement) that would redeem modern existence and culture. Through Nietzsche Wigman discovered the chorus and its tragic hero as the origin and essence of Greek tragedy. Chorus and heroic leader were expressions of the two interwoven artistic impulses, the Apollonian and Dionysian. The duality drove the conflict (ibid.: 81); it also drove Wigman's choreographies, her performances in which she acted out the drama between Dionysus and Apollo, and it drove her writings in which she reflected the Nietzschean dichotomy (ibid.: 48) over and over again as that between bodily materiality and movement form.

Wigman intended to re-balance the upset dichotomy of Apollonian and Dionysian; she, 'the Dionysian-Apollonian genius' (ibid.), would create the tragic chorus and be its heroic leader, she would put herself through 'the mystery of union', she would compose the mythical work, that '[...] epic event and the glorification of the fighting hero' (ibid.: 140). Absolute dance as 'tension in space' embodied the struggle of the two Nietzschean creative forces, these tensions guided her through the compositional process and led her towards conquering the tragic form. They made it possible to give form to 'the chaotic mental exertions' and turn them into creations of 'shaped dance gesture' (Wigman 1925: 9). Following Nietzsche's advice, she shielded from the critical rational eye her instinctive desire to make something (ibid.: 10). Her dance converted innermost invisible agitation into bodily visible movement. Expression was the breaking out of unconscious mental processes and their alteration into conscious physical conditions (ibid.: 12). Her entire descriptions of expression, function, theme, structure, dynamics, nuance, ornament (all Wigman's terms) were appropriations of the Apollonian and Dionysian and the attempt to clarify the way in which the struggle between the powerful, demonic and overwhelming subconscious and the equally powerful desire to form and tame the instinctive and threatening as well as fascinating forces formed an equilibrium.

The critic Artur Michel beautifully captured this tenuous balance in Wigman's dances: 'stretched between heaven and hell, superbly and demonically possessed she conceived the idea of creative dancing as oscillation of a human being between external poles of tension, thus transplanting the dancing body from the sensually existing sphere of materialism and real space into the symbolic supersphere of tension space' (Michel 1935: 5). Every composition, creative act, demanded a new detection of timeless internal laws; every time the creative urge came upon her Wigman had to battle it out and throw herself into the eternal confrontation of Apollo fighting Dionysus and vice versa (Wigman 1925: 11). What Nietzsche wrote about the dithyramb is applicable to Wigman's definition of absolute dance: 'it is a chorus of transformed characters whose civic past and social status have been totally forgotten: they have become timeless servants of their own god who live outside the spheres of society...' (Nietzsche 2000: 64).

As soon as Wigman had integrated the decisive communal factor into her choreographies and performances, Nietzsche's ideas, his concept of cultural rebirth through tragedy, could be carried out. It gained not only philosophical but also technical-formal momentum. Wigman had started her career by exploring, through her own, personal, individual body, new and unknown modern forms of dance expression. Once she had trained herself, she could also train a group. Once she had a group she could transform that group into a community. Dance, filtered through such a community, became the carrier of national identity and had to be realised accordingly. Form informed content and content determined form. Dance could only flourish within a system that re-established cultural primacy in the face of modern civilisation that tended to destroy national identity and artistic integrity (cf. Wigman 1929a, 1936).

Through *Totenmal* Wigman attempted to realise the grand vision of Nietzschean tragedy. In the libretto of Albert Talhoff, Wigman found all the ideas that Nietzsche had articulated and systematised: a modern culture, a community with its leadership and existential reinvention through death. The narrative brought back the horrors of war, but also its patriotism and heroism. Talhoff's ideas, transmitted in written and spoken language, music, lighting etc. supplied Wigman with the basis from which she could find the equivalent bodily language to turn Nietzsche's tragic idea into dance. She had to shape her movement so that it would become the spiritual foundation for the tragedy of modernity. She needed to convince her contemporaries that her dance-movement initiated the renewal according to Nietzsche and that art-dance was also the means through which radical ideas could be expressed and a decaying world would be fed new, unspoilt cultural values.

Wigman and Laban were 'creat[ing] dance anew' (Laban 1920: 24) for
current Weimar society was in need of rebirth and renewal. Nietzsche's philosophy strengthened Wigman's anti-democratic impulses. Her Nietzsche
interpretation placed her within the larger debate around the concepts
of *Gesellschaft-Gemeinschaft* (society versus community), which begun
around the turn of the century and quickly turned into a political confrontation between defenders of rational and liberal values and anti-rational
reinforcers of cultural and völkisch values. Wigman represents a variation
in this battle of ideas and politics as she combined reactionary concepts
with feminist notions. If Nietzsche placed his hopes on a super-man, then
Wigman celebrated and suffered as a super-woman.

Mary Wigman in the Third Reich

By the late 1920s her own ideals cultivated the celebration of the cultic
essence of the community, of the leader fronting the group and guiding it
towards its calling and fate. To be a leader also included preparing oneself
for self-sacrifice in the name of a greater cause – that could be war or the
cause of dance, art or the community.

Throughout the Weimar years she had systematically nurtured a modernist yet conservative, increasingly nationalist ideology and had followed
politics that eventually brought her closer to the Nazis than the social
democrats who could not protect the republic. Zuckmayer concluded his
assessment of Wigman:

> She who in her artistic perceptions, in her stylistic feelings, in her spiritual and
> personal structure, tends towards the choric, the group-like, the collective, to the
> embodiment of the communal experience or the effect of rhythmically ascertainable
> communal forces rather than to individual expression, to communal ethos rather
> than individual responsibility, to mass seizure rather than effect within a personal
> living centre – for such a person the national-socialist cultural propaganda offered
> enormous possibilities... (Zuckmayer 2002: 113)

We know how much Wigman became an ally of the Nazi cause, how much she supported the nazification of the arts carried out by the new bureaucracy with the help of artists themselves. Her collaboration rested on the artistic experience that she gained and political alignment that she underwent during the Weimar Republic. Weimar and its politics radicalised her, as it did many of her contemporary fellow artists and it made her partake in the aims of those who would bring down the Republic: the conservative and right-wing nationalists. Her political actions during the first phase of the Third Reich from 1933 to 1936 were in tune with Nazi ideological demands. She met and fulfilled national-socialist principles in several vital points: in their and her emphasis on a unified, homogenous national, i.e. 'People's' community; in their and her belief of the necessity of a 'Führer', leader of that community; in their and her anti-semitism. These were ideological tenets that translated into political actions.

The focus on *Gemeinschaft*, community, and the acceptance of its Nazi interpretation in the form of *Volksgemeinschaft*, the 'People's community' grew out of her desire to rescue German cultural values in the disintegrating world of Weimar Germany. The 'People's community' seemed to represent exactly what Wigman had been searching for. It seemed to offer her secure state support. She imagined that the Nazi administration would accept and incorporate her version and her experience in the new community-building endeavours. In 1935 Wigman stressed the individual – her own – contribution in the emergence of a modern German dance in an essay for the American readership: 'It is only the carriers of the great works of art who determine the artistic worth and the cultural meaning of a creative current [...] the new German dance should be judged [...] by the work of its truly great representatives...' (Wigman 1935: 20); whereas one year later she reminded her German audience of 'the calling of the blood' and, above all, of the *Volksgemeinschaft* as the core principle that would renew art, theatre and life (Wigman 1936: 11, 64, 67). At that moment she and the Nazi ideal had fused. The differences in articulation between German and American publications meant she was fully aware of what was 'politically correct', desirable to project publically and advantageous in two different political settings. She sensitively responded to different political expectations.

Several passages in *Deutsche Tanzkunst* paraphrased personal notes and
published accounts of her work around *Totenmal*, performed in 1930.

> The oft-abused term community (Gemeinschaft) does not denote a delusion. We
> do not err when we ascribe to our times the power of community. At the core of
> community in its most productive meaning lies an idea that is accepted by all partici-
> pants. Community demands leadership and recognition of the necessity of leader-
> ship. The masses that refer only to themselves can never constitute a community...
> (Wigman 1936: 64)

In both essay as well as book Wigman referred to characteristics and aspects
of group and community make-up, and to the force of the 'cultic' and
'heroic' shaping choric dance – but with a slightly different slant (Wigman
1935: 20; 1936: 76). She had fostered and accepted the 'Führer principle',
leader and leadership, embodied ultimately by Adolf Hitler whom she
greeted with great enthusiasm (cf. Wigman 1933), within her own dance
group and she had nurtured and exhaustively examined the possibilities
in which it could be carried out in a community of dancers. Many of her
musings as well as the reports from her students confirm her strict belief
in the exceptional leader – that could be the genius-artist or the charis-
matic politician.

Wigman's anti-semitism belongs to the most distasteful political displays of Nazi-sympathy. Her racial objectives had emerged in the mid- and
late 1920s. In the answer to André Levinson in 1929 they were fully articulated and her concept of a German culture stood in juxtaposition to less
worthy, Latin, international, cosmopolitan, i.e. Jewish or other cultures. Her
ideological anti-semitism had nothing to do with instructing Jewish students. The choice to include Jewish students in her schools dignified them
('aryanised' them) and made membership in her community viable.

Her appalling treatment of one of her most devoted supporters, Artur
Michel[8], is another example of her anti-semitism in action. Michel promoted her dance as well as her personality relentlessly and uncompro-

---

8   Artur Michel, 1884–1946, responsible for the feuilleton ('arts and culture section')
     of, and dance critic for, the *Vossische Zeitung*, one of the powerful daily newspapers
     in Germany.

misingly. He, more than any other critic, appointed her to the status of German dance-goddess; she epitomised the future of dance. Without his reviews and analyses she would not have had such systematic public exposure. Her last letter to him dated from 9 November 1933. He was trapped in Berlin until early 1941, desperately trying to get out and rescue his life. How could Wigman be silent and ignore his fate? Only in 1946, when Michel contacted her from his New York exile, did she begin a new correspondence, pondering her terrible life under Nazism and exploiting his 'anti-fascist' credentials.

The denunciation of *Der Tanz*, originally edited by Joseph Levitan but in the process of being 'aryanised', is another example of her anti-semitism. *Der Tanz* had included an article in which Wigman was criticised by former student and advocate of 'Zionist ideas' Friedl Braur, who had attacked Wigman's German dance. It is also an example of her political savviness:

> Would you regard it as appropriate in the present situation if I were to write to the journal in question to forbid them absolutely in future to publish my photograph or that of my dance group? I am of the opinion that the German dance community as a whole should break off all relations with the magazine, but how and through whom should it be carried out? (Karina/Kant 2003: 228)[9]

She alerted the councillor in the *Propagandaministry* to 'Zionist', 'Jewish' assaults on her and asked for advice – 'I am particularly concerned to have your view of the matter as soon as possible and thus in the appropriate circumstance to send my letter at once to the editors' (Karina/Kant 2003: 228). She demonstrated her acceptance of party racism yet she would not act without ministerial guidance and then let the politician decide and take appropriate actions for her.

One of the most public political acts lay in her endorsement of the extreme organisation *Kampfbund für Deutsche Kultur*, founded by the chief-ideologist of Nazism, Alfred Rosenberg. In April 1933 she, the foremost figure of German Dance, urged all her pupils to join the most radically

9   Letters written by the director of the Wigman School and by Wigman herself to the ministerial bureaucrat in charge of dance politics, Keudell on 24 October 1935.

nationalist and racist cultural organisation in Germany. This membership resulted in the elimination of all students who could not prove their 'Aryan' ancestry. She expelled all Jews without having been asked to – nobody forced Wigman to enact Nazi ideology and Nazi rules to this extent at that time. The fact that she did demonstrates her political orientation and her adaptation to the demands of changed political principles.

Conclusion

I have argued that Wigman's refusal to acknowledge any political influence on the arts was symptomatic of a certain type of conservative German intellectual. This refusal as a profound attitude towards the arts, I concluded, can be studied by comparing Wigman's writing and speeches as well as her aesthetic responses to political events at several stages of her life. Wigman's definition of absolute dance was based on the separation of dance from any exterior influence as formative force, in other words: dance was placed above politics. In the transition from Weimar Republic to Third Reich, which was prepared long before the actual takeover in January 1933, both aversion to and sympathy for political powers manifested themselves in Wigman's words and deeds. The Weimar Republic allowed Wigman to experiment with a set of political agendas and define her own programme. Though she never claimed to belong to any particular political camp and waivered in her support of specific parties, and though she considered herself above and beyond politics, she nevertheless behaved and acted in a political way. The denial of politics is political in itself. Wigman's politics – her preferences for a set of beliefs – can be isolated through her choreographies and the writings reflecting on them. She revolutionised movement patterns and compositional dynamics; she focused on the aesthetics of her art form and exclaimed that therefore she evaded political entanglement. The desire to keep her art pure was impossible to accomplish.

Her explicit choice of an ideology based on Nietzschean categories and ideas that favoured a homogenous community and despised ethnic inclusion and national tolerance put her firmly in the political mainstream of conservatism and nationalism. By adopting her chosen ideology she also spoke in a recognisable and politically inspired language. We can therefore affirm that politics influenced Wigman's oeuvre, her activities, her decisions – in short, that politics permeated her entire life.

Works Cited

Bach, R. 1933. *Das Mary-Wigman-Werk*. Dresden: Carl Reissner Verlag.

Deutsche Allgemeine Zeitung (DAZ). 1921. Mary Wigman, die den Tanz als reines Bewegungs-Kunstwerk auffasst, errang im Blüthnersaal grosse Erfolge. Bilderchronik No. 10. 6 March.

Die Musik. 1933. Special issue *Dance*, January 25(4).

Kant, M. 1994. Mary Wigman – Auf der Suche nach der verlorenen Welt. *Beiträge zur Musikwissenschaft (Beihefte der Berlinischen Musikhefte)*, 9/2: 25–36; and *Tanzdrama*, Seelze-Velber: Kallmeyersche Verlagsbuchhandlung, 1994(2): 14–19, 1994(3): 16–21.

Kant, M. 2003. Laban's Secret Religion. *Discourses in Dance*, 1/2: 43–63.

Karina, L., & Kant, M. 2003/2006. *Hitler's Dancers: German Modern Dance and the Third Reich*. Oxford & New York: Berghahn Books.

Koegler, H. 1973. Mary Wigman, Tänzerin der Weimarer Republik. *Theater heute*, 11: 1–4.

Laban, R. von. 1920. *Die Welt des Tänzers*. Stuttgart: Walter Seifert.

Laban, Rudolf von. 1975. *A Life for Dance. Reminiscences*. Translated and annotated by Lisa Ullmann. London: Macdonald and Evans. (Original German edition 1935, *Ein Leben für den Tanz*).

Levinson, A. 1929. The Modern Dance in Germany. *Theatre Arts Monthly*, 13/12: 143–153.

Loewenstein, Hubertus Prinz zu. 1993. Das Dritte Reich, in *Deutsche Intellektuelle im Exil: ihre Akademie und die 'American Guild for German Cultural Freedom'*. Edited by Werner Berthold, Brita Eckert & Frank Wende. Exhibition & catalogue of the Deutsches Exilarchiv 1933–1945 der Deutschen Bibliothek, Frankfurt/Main. Munich: Saur: 8.

Manning, S. 1993/2006. *Ecstasy and the Demon*. Berkeley: University of California Press.

Michel, A. 1923a. Der Aufschrei. *Vossische Zeitung*. Berlin. 22 November.

Michel, A. 1923b. Tänzer der Zeit. *Vossische Zeitung*. Berlin. 10 October.

Michel, A. 1924. Der Absolute Tanz. *Vossische Zeitung*. Berlin. 5 February.

Michel, A. 1935. The Development of the New German Dance, in *Modern Dance*. Edited by Virginia Stewart. New York: Weyhe: 3–17.

Müller, H. 1986. *Mary Wigman. Leben und Werk der großen Tänzerin*. Weinheim, Berlin: Quadriga Verlag.

Nietzsche, F. 2000. *Die Geburt der Tragödie aus dem Geiste der Musik*. Leipzig: E. W. Fritzsch. English translation: The Birth of Tragedy Out of the Spirit of Music, in *Basic Writings of Nietzsche*. Translated and edited by Walter Kaufmann. New York: The Modern Library.

Oxford English Dictionary (OED). [Online]. Available: <http://dictionary.oed.com/entrance.dtl> [13 September 2008].

Reynolds, D. 1999. Dancing as a Woman: Mary Wigman and 'Absolute Dance'. *Forum for Modern Language Studies*, 35/3: 297–310.

Santos Newhall, M. 2002. Mass Movement and Modern Totalitarianism. *Dance Research Journal*, 34/1: 27–50.

Schad, C. 1985. Zurich/Geneva Dada, in *The Era of German Expressionism*. Edited by Paul Raabe. New York: The Overlook Press.

Schumann, G. 1986. Interview Mary Wigman, in *Positionen zur Geschichte und Gegenwart des modernen Tanzes*. Edited by Marion Reinisch & Hannelore Renk, Arbeitshefte der Akademie der Künste der DDR Vol. 36. Berlin: Akademie der Künste.

Skoronel, V. 1930. Mary Wigmans Führertum. *Die Tanzgemeinschaft. Vierteljahresschrift für tänzerische Kultur*, 2/2: 4–6.

Spengler, O. 1963. *Der Untergang des Abendlandes. Eine Morphologie der Weltgeschichte*. Munich: C. H. Beck.

Tönnies, F. 1887. *Gemeinschaft und Gesellschaft*. Leipzig: Fues's Verlag.

Vogeler, E. 1922. Mary Wigman. Ein Kapitel über Tanzkunst. *Berliner Tageblatt*, 29 April.

Wigman, M. 1921. Der Tanz als Kunstwerk. *Deutsche Allgemeine Zeitung DAZ* 1–2, 9 March.

Wigman, M. 1923. [No title]. *Vossische Zeitung*. Berlin: No.154, April 1.

Wigman, M. 1925. *Kompositionen*. Ueberlingen: Seebote.

Wigman, M. 1928. *Der neue künstlerische Tanz und das Theater*. Speech held at the Dancers' Congress in Essen.

Wigman, M. 1929a. Das Land ohne Tanz. *Die Tanzgemeinschaft. Vierteljahresschrift für tänzerische Kultur*, 1/2: 12–13.

Wigman, M. 1929b. Weibliche Tanzkunst. *Blätter der Staatsoper und der Städtischen Oper.* Berlin: 10/6: 14–16.

Wigman, M. 1933. Tagebücher. Mary Wigman Collection Akademie der Künste Berlin.

Wigman, M. 1935. The New German Dance, in *Modern Dance.* Edited by Virginia Stewart. New York: Weyhe: 19–23.

Wigman, M. 1936. *Deutsche Tanzkunst.* Dresden: Carl Reissner.

Wigman, M. 1963/1986. *Die Sprache des Tanzes.* Stuttgart/Munich: Battenberg.

Zuckmayer, C. 2002. *Geheimreport.* Edited by Gunther Nickel & Johanna Schrön. Göttingen: Wallstein Verlag.

GUNHILD OBERZAUCHER-SCHÜLLER

6 Dramaturgy and Form of the 'German Ballet': Examination of a National Socialist Genre

As a beginning!
During the years when National Socialism was fighting for the soul of
the German people – which today it possesses completely – the opponents of the national renascence repeatedly sought to discredit National
Socialism by alleging that it was lacking in culture. But nothing could
be more wrong than what these unobjective enemies claimed. Because
nowadays everyone in Germany agrees: the nation has never before had
a government which was so driven by a fanatical commitment to culture
as that of the people's chancellor, Adolf Hitler.
— *Ministerialrat* OTTO LAUBINGER (1934: 57),
President of the *Reichstheaterkammer* (Reich Theatre Chamber)

For the present challenges of the German theatre, the period from 1934
to 1944 does not have any artistic significance in the history of drama.
— HUGO GAU-HAMM (1945/48: 8), *Genossenschaft Deutscher
Bühnenangehöriger* (Association of German Stage Employees)

This chapter concerns the situation of German dance during the years
lying between the two statements quoted above.[1] Using the broad, diverse
German dance scene before 1933 as a point of departure, I shall pursue the
question to what extent National Socialism developed an independent genre
of dance. While up to now, examinations of dance under National Socialism

---

1   Translated by August Obermayer, this chapter is a modified version of 'Dramaturgie
    und Gestalt. Versuch über eine nationalsozialistische Gattung', 2010, in *Blickpunkt
    Bühne. Musiktheater in Deutschland von 1900–1945*. Edited by Th. Steiert & P. Op
    de Coul. Cologne: Dohr.

have predominantly focused on the fate of *Ausdruckstanz* (German expressive dance) and its leading exponents,[2] the intention of this chapter is primarily to examine the development of dance at the *Dreispartentheater*.[3]
When following the ideological debates which accompanied the process of the monopolisation of dance by the newly created cultural policy organisations, one might form the impression that the development of traditional ballet in the Third Reich came to a virtual standstill. In particular the discussion about *Ausdruckstanz*, which was especially dominant after the National Socialists came to power, but also the official party representatives' negative attitude towards classical ballet might lead to the assumption that ballet was only of minor importance in the overall National Socialist dance scene. However, a glance at the programmes of German theatres reveals a completely different picture. It becomes obvious that there was a veritable repertoire of newly created ballet works, which can be viewed as distinctively National Socialist.[4]
The obvious discrepancy between theoretical demands and theatre practice points to the difficulties and problems the National Socialists faced in the realm of dance. Disorientation and disputes over respective areas of authority impeded a target-oriented implementation of the theory into practice, so that the gulf between aims and actual production remained significant. Irrespective of the ideological controversies, the ballet masters of the leading *Dreispartentheater* created a 'German Ballet'. Although it was continually subject to criticism, it not only won recognition as a representative genre but, with its most important works, remained the foundation of German theatre programmes up until the late 1950s.
In order to examine this situation – characterised by contradictions and conflicts – in more depth, it is crucial to recapitulate the main features of the dance scene during the first third of the twentieth century. The German dance scene of that time was characterised by two parallel developments, which were stylistically entirely different and essentially 'hostile' to one

2   See in particular Koegler 1972, Koegler 1973, Müller/Stöckemann 1993, Karina/Kant 1996 and Guilbert 2000.
3   Theatres which comprise the three genres of opera, drama and dance in their repertoire.
4   Compare the list compiled in 1942 for the Reich Ministry of Propaganda, reprinted in Karina/Kant 1996: 314–316.

another. While after 1900 the musical genres of opera, operetta and ballet remained tied to the court and municipal theatres, a 'free' scene developed over the years outside the theatres and independently of such institutions. This scene became the arena for new dance trends which were referred to by a number of different terms: 'new dance', 'free dance', 'modern dance', or 'expressive dance'.[5] The ballet, which continued to operate within the institutions, was thus confronted with two enemies: the first was the sister-genre, opera, which tried – partly for economic reasons – to push traditional ballet more and more into the background, and the second was the increasingly successful movement of *Ausdruckstanz*. The situation finally came to a head when the opera – the institution as well as the genre – began to integrate *Ausdruckstanz*, which operated outside the institutionalised theatre, into their new art of production. The subsequent phase of the takeover of the position of 'ballet master'[6] at opera houses by free dancers has already been commented on extensively (Oberzaucher-Schüller 2000).

Up to the early 1930s, the following genres of stage dance were in existence:

1) The ballet as a form of stage dance, which developed in the seventeenth century at first as an integral part of opera using a codified language. From the second half of the eighteenth century it developed as an independent genre but was still tied to the institution of opera. Certain forms of ballet outside of opera can be found on the popular stage (in light entertainment theatre).

---

5 For a detailed discussion of the development of dance during this period see Oberzaucher-Schüller 2000.

6 It has to be noted that the term 'ballet master' – the person in charge of the ensemble with responsibilities not only for the repertoire but also for its production – was retained after 1918 and that exponents of free dance sometimes held such a position. Rudolf von Laban, for example, was 'ballet master' of the State Opera Unter den Linden in Berlin from 1930 to 1934. In many cases, however, new terms were introduced: 'head of modern dance', 'head of the dance choir', 'dancing master and teacher of expression', 'head of choreography', 'movement director' and 'dancing director'. During the period of National Socialism the terms 'dancing master' or 'dancing mistress' were preferred.

2) *Ausdruckstanz* as a form of stage dance, which – mostly performed as solo acts – developed from 1900 as a countermovement to the 'high art' of ballet outside the institution of opera.

3) Chamber dance, an ensemble dance performed by dancers of *Ausdruckstanz*, which can be found inside as well as outside the traditional institutions of theatre.

4) Theatre dance which developed in the 1920s and comprised classical as well as free dance. Theatre dance was broadened by integrating forms of light entertainment theatre.

'... to be German means to be simple and clear!'[7]

The artistic variety of the 1920s dance scene posed numerous problems for the new rulers. The free scene of *Ausdruckstanz* in its various groupings and manifestations as well as the institutionalised theatre dance and ballet were incompatible with the beliefs of those responsible for cultural policies. From the perspective of National Socialist cultural guidelines, criticism was levelled, on one hand, at the distinct individualism of expressive dancers, who as 'creator-interpreters' pursued their own artistic concepts and could not be subjected to all-encompassing, obligatory aesthetic ideals. Ballet, on the other hand, was criticised because of its foreign origins and internationalism.

Right from the beginning, a swift monopolisation and ideological co-ordination of the dance scene was impeded by conflicts of competence between the various organisations. The leading institutions, aiming for re-orientation of the dance scene, were the *Reichskulturkammer* (Reich Culture Chamber) which was founded in November 1933 with Joseph

7   Cunz 1938: 20.

Goebbels as president, and the *Kampfbund für Deutsche Kultur* (Fighting
League for German Culture) under Alfred Rosenberg, founded as early
as 1929. As the structure of the Reich Culture Chamber shows[8], dance
had not been assigned its own Chamber but had been integrated into the
Deutscher Chorsängerverband und Tänzerbund (German League of Choir
Singers and Association of Dancers), a subsection of the Reich Theatre
Chamber. At the same time, the Fighting League for German Culture controlled parts of the dance scene, which were combined in the *Fachgruppe
Körperbildung und Tanz* (Physical Education and Dance Section) headed
by Rudolf Bode.[9] In 1934, Goebbels was able to prevail in the conflict
with the Fighting League and consolidated the subsection known as the
German League of Choir Singers and Association of Dancers, which was
part of his fiefdom, to become the central organisation for dancers. In the
following year, this section was incorporated into the newly created *Fach-
schaft Bühne* (Stage Division), which now united all the artists' associations
within the Reich Theatre Chamber.

This administrative restructuring, which was designed to define the
scope and the fields of activity of dance artists, was accompanied by an
aesthetic and ideological debate aimed at bringing the various manifestations of the dance scene into line and placing them within a superordinated
umbrella framework. The guidelines of the Fighting League for German
Culture, published in the journal *Der Tanz*[10] under the title *Die geistigen
Grundlagen für Körperbildung und Tanz im Nationalsozialistischen Staat*
(The Mental Principles for Physical Education and Dance in the National
Socialist State) contributed vitally to this discussion. Their aim was to
define the relationship between dance and National Socialist ideology and
to postulate a reformation of dance in Germany on the basis of a number
of principles:

8   For an overview of the structure of the Reich Culture Chamber and the role of dance
     as part thereof see Deutsches Bühnenjahrbuch 1934: 117–120, 869–873.

9   After separating from his teacher Émile Jaques-Dalcroze, Rudolf Bode developed
     his own type of 'Rhythmic Gymnastics', which proved to be very popular and is still
     in existence today.

10   For information on the journal and its editor Joseph Lewitan, see Dahms 1997:
     74–82.

1) Dance is to be viewed as an expression of the health and strength of the people.

2) Two expressions of the health and strength of the people – the 'eruptive' and the 'gently binding' – lend dance its characteristics.

3) The cohesion of separate beings can express itself only though collective motion. The people come together in dance, in the circulating, pleasure-oriented movement of the whole, but without abandoning the existence of the individual – as all dance is grounded in Eros, meaning the power of the capacity to experience the innermost expression of one's fellow human beings.

4) All dance is very closely connected with music. It is impossible to want to create a dance culture where music is debased as mere 'accompaniment', rather than forming, in polar tension, a unity with movement which originates from the human soul.

5) All art dance [*Kunsttanz*] must have its origin and echo in the joy of movement and the language of movement of the people.

6) All teachers of the art of dance must fulfil the same requirements as any other person who works as an educator towards the reconstruction of the folk.

7) The training for stage dance is to be structured in such a manner that the severe demands of the stage accord with the requirement of the most direct impact possible on the spectators. Any relapse into old ballet techniques is to be combated in the same way as any falling victim to the feeble, insipid surrender of the self which has – in ignorance of the elemental principles of dance – unfortunately been passed off as art dance in the last decade. (Geistigen Grundlagen 1933: 2–3)

I would like to stress that these principles demonstrate the comprehensive understanding of dance by the National Socialists. They not only address the three types of dance – folk dance, social dance and stage dance – but also the relationship between dance and music, and the training of dancers and choreographers. These guidelines were officially decreed and signed by *Staatskommissar* (State Commissioner) Hans Hinkel[11] and Rudolf Bode. As early as 25 April 1933, Fritz Böhme had initiated an ongoing debate with his article *Ist das Ballet deutsch?* ('Is Ballet German?') in the newspaper *Deutsche Allgemeine Zeitung*. A much more significant event, however, which did not produce the kind of reaction we would expect from a modern-day perspective, was the publication of the *Richtlinien für die Aufnahme von Nichtariern in die Fachverbände der Reichsmusikkammer* (Guidelines for the Admission of Non-Arians into the Professional Associations of the Reich Music Chamber) almost exactly a year after the notorious *Gesetz zur Wiederherstellung des Berufsbeamtentums* (Bill for the Re-establishment of a Professional Public Service). A special edition of the *Amtliche Mitteilungen der Reichsmusikkammer* (Official Memorandums of the Reich Music Chamber; 1934: 48) announced the mandatory general guidelines for the admission of non-Arians into the professional associations of the Chamber.[12] The aforementioned publications, *The Mental Principles for Physical Education and Dance in the National Socialist State* as well as Böhme's critical analysis of the traditional ballet, might be seen as polemical documents which had a determining influence on the future development of the National Socialist dance scene.

11   Hans Hinkel was Reich-administrator for culture in the *Reichsministerium für Volksaufklärung und Propaganda* (Reich Ministry of People's Enlightenment and Propaganda).

12   Directive 1 states: 'Non-Arians are not to be regarded as suitable stewards and custodians of German cultural assets and therefore have to provide evidence of their reliability and suitability under §10 of the I. Executive Order of the Reich Culture Chamber Act.' Directive 2 said: 'The respective professional associations are therefore – in the spirit of the Decree for the Re-establishment of a Professional Civil Service dated 7 April 1933 – obliged to check up on a Non-Arian person who applies for membership. The professional association must ensure that all Non-Arians (i.e. those who are already members and those who apply for membership) fill in the enclosed questionnaires which are the same for all professional organisations' (Amtliche Mitteilungen 1934). The accompanying sample of a questionnaire for the admission of Non-Arians requests information about the person and their ancestors back to their maternal and paternal grandparents.

In 1934, the first practical steps were undertaken to reorganise the dance scene. The *Deutsche Tanzbühne* (German Dance Stage) was founded with the intention of uniting the various groupings of expressive dancers under an umbrella organisation. Rudolf von Laban was named as its head and its most urgent task was the realisation of the dance festivals of 1934 and 1935 at the Berlin Theatre on Horst-Wessel-Platz. During these events, the renowned soloists and ensembles of the German dance scene were able to present themselves in their aesthetic variety, but they were also subjected to the increasing criticism of cultural functionaries. For the dance festival of 1935, the selection of works was already severely regimented. Through inclusion of an array of training and further education programmes, the German Dance Stage was integrated into the *Deutsche Meisterwerkstätten für Tanz* (German Master Workshops for Dance), which were founded in 1936 under Laban's management and became the central training institution for aspiring young dancers.

Standing somewhat aside from this scene, Lizzie Maudrik at the Berlin State Opera Unter den Linden and Rudolf Kölling at the Deutsche Oper had assumed positions of ballet masters. The future protagonists of the 'German Ballet' had thus entered the stage. Maudrik and Kölling, along with Pia and Pino Mlakar, who at that time were still working in Zurich, had already produced the ballets which can be regarded as prototypes of National Socialist ballet:

- *Die Barberina* (Barberina), choreography: Lizzie Maudrik, music: Herbert Trantow after masters from the eighteenth century, Berlin 1935;
- *Der Teufel im Dorf* (The Devil in the Village), choreography: Pia and Pino Mlakar, music: Fran Lhotka, Zurich 1935;
- *Die Gaunerstreiche der Courasche* (The Roguish Tricks of Courage), choreography: Rudolf Kölling, music: Richard Mohaupt, Berlin 1936;
- *Der Stralauer Fischzug* (The Stralau Fish Haul), choreography: Rudolf Kölling, music: Leo Spies, 1936.

In the introduction to the 1937 *Jahrbuch Deutscher Tanz* (Yearbook of German Dance), which marked a turning point towards the genesis of an independent National Socialist genre of stage dance, the publisher Max Liedtke wrote:

> Music, theatre and dance are three great possibilities to depict the German soul, and dance plays by no means the most humble role among them. In fact it will play a key role, because dance, correctly understood, is nothing less than the cry of the soul for space. Therefore dance must be racially tied and can only reach us and free emotional energies in the spectator when it presents the people's soul, the racially characteristic [*arteigene*] soul of the dancer. This is why again and again we learn by experience that dance which receives its energy and expression from racially uncharacteristic [*artfremd*] music does not speak to us, but that we are only moved by dance which is the presentation of our racially characteristic soul. It is not true that one dances just to any music but the emotional energy revealed in dance is of utmost importance. Therefore it will only be possible to reach the highest emotional representation in dance if the dancer creates the melody of his dance from within himself and the composer uses this melody as the basis for his composition. Herein lies a wide field for German composers and also a great task for the future, whereas nowadays the gifted dancer has to search for a composition which is appropriate for his dance. (1937: 7)

Liedtke's text is noteworthy both as a summary of what had thus far been achieved and as an appeal for further initiatives; the new ballets performed before 1937 conformed to his ideas, and leading contemporary composers had finally begun to perceive ballet music as a potential field of activity.

With Rolf Cunz succeeding Otto von Keudell as the civil servant in charge of the *Reichspropagandaministerium* (Reich Ministry for Propaganda), the policy changed again: Keudell had favoured Laban, who was now being pushed out of the dance scene. The demands articulated by Cunz, which had already been met to some extent, were yet to form the basis for changes and criticism in the following years: Cunz, who acted as an appointee of *Reichsdramaturg* (Reich Dramaturg) Rainer Schlösser penned an important résumé which emphasised the process of restructuring and what had so far been achieved in the process of 'standardisation'. As there was no longer supposed to be any differentiation between two realms of dance, ballet in its new form was emerging as a form of music theatre with a popular emphasis, primarily as an entertainment genre.

Cunz thought that the dance festivals of 1934 and 1935, which had placed 'the free art dance into the centre of the theatre programme of the Reich's capital' (ibid.: 9), had helped to clarify the situation. Of the remaining 'free dancers', the works of Lotte Wernicke, Lola Rogge (with some reservations) and Mary Wigman (also with reservations) were regarded as suitable, while the school of Dorothee Günther was praised unreservedly. The 'accompaniment of a flexible body of instruments' (ibid.: 13), which referred to Orff's instrumental range, was given special mention. Palucca's work was *per se* 'problematic' (she was half-Jewish). Harald Kreutzberg on the other hand was celebrated as a 'trendsetter'. According to Cunz, among the works of the 'stage dancers', those by Inge Herting, Lizzie Maudrik and Helga Swendlund were particularly outstanding.

In principle Cunz does not argue in favour of a specific type of dance or genre (though he defines both in detail), but he points out what has so far been missing: namely, that all 'German concert dance [...] completely ignores' the vital *'Volkskulturbestrebungen* (overall aims of a people's culture)' (ibid.). Together with the demand for the inclusion of folk art, he again emphasises a rejection of ballet. At the dance festival in November 1935, there may have been 'ballet images in the classical operatic style' which were 'appropriate for our time' but they were nevertheless 'stuck in the cul-de-sac of a dance technique determined by foreign countries' (ibid.: 12).

We cannot determine the extent to which the rapid 'Germanisation' of French terminology[13] was also applied in everyday stage life, but photographic documents prove that classical dance developed a different image through intensive use of folk and social dance. (In this, another of Cunz's demands had been anticipated). The choice of the new genres – divertissement, genre piece, dance suite – corresponded to these demands; but the shift to *ballets d'action* in several acts did not. The basis for a work was again a libretto, a kind of 'visual scenario' which was also called a *Tanzspiel* (dance play).

---

13   Compare the examination regulations for German dancers and teachers of artistic
       dance in 1934, reprinted in Karina/Kant 1996: 217–225.

As becomes evident from Liedtke's introduction to the 1937 *Jahrbuch Deutscher Tanz*, the new 'German Ballet' was classified as belonging to the new music theatre; composers were thus instructed to compose music for this new ballet. These included not only musicians such as Trantow, Mohaupt and Spies, but also Julius Weisman, Hermann Reutter, Rudolf Wagner-Régeny, Boris Blacher, Heinrich Sutermeister, Carl Orff[14] and Werner Egk, who viewed the genre of ballet as an opportunity to realise their conceptions of a contemporary music theatre on stage.

Populism, Verve and Easy Comprehensibility

Let us consider the careers of these choreographers Maudrik and Kölling, who set out to develop a new genre virtually unnoticed by the party officials. Both of them were ballet masters in the traditional sense of the term. Maudrik had trained in ballet and, after a stint as dancer and ballet master in several German cities, was engaged as ballet master at the *Städtische Oper* in Berlin in 1926. In 1934 she was employed by the *Berliner Staatsoper* and remained there until the *Theatersperre* (closing of theatres in 1944).

Rudolf Kölling had been trained as a dancer at the ballet school of the Hanover Opera but, following the general trend of the time, had also studied with Laban and Wigman. In 1924 he became a principal dancer at the *Berliner Staatsoper*. He belonged to the group of dancers who were sacked by Laban, who was the ballet master there. Kölling had toured Germany as a member of 'The Six of the State Opera'.[15] In 1934 he became ballet master at the *Deutsche Opernhaus* in Berlin where he remained until

---

14   Orff's *Schulwerk* (School Work), which is still regularly performed today, can be regarded as one of the few remnants of *Ausdruckstanz*.

15   'The Six of the State Opera' were Elisabeth Grube, Genia Nikolajewa, Daisy Spies, Rolf Arco, Jens Keith and Rudolf Kölling. The six dancers had their debut in the Berlin Varieté Wintergarten in Autumn 1931.

the *Theatersperre*. Over the years Kölling acquired the same influence and power as Laban had held previously. In 1941 he was appointed head of the German *Meisterstätten des Tanzes* and of the *Deutsche Tanzbühne*.

As proven experts in the dance repertoire, Maudrik and Kölling remained familiar with those ballets which had been performed before *Ausdruckstanz* invaded the opera houses. A number of ballets from the nineteenth century, in particular *Coppélia* and *Die Puppenfee*, had been preserved and were being shown more often again. Additionally, the works of the 'great' masters were consistently put on the programme despite the (theoretical) debates about the value of the *ballet d'action*. These included ballets by Gluck, Mozart, Beethoven and Richard Strauss. Surprisingly, the programmes also included some works from the repertoire of the Ballets Russes and the Ballets Suédois.

The integration of folk dances became more and more important for Maudrik's and Kölling's creations. They were proven experts in this genre. Having worked at opera houses for many years they were thus very familiar with the arrangement of dance interludes in operas and operettas. The verve with which these scenes were performed is evident from still photographs and filmic documents. Dancers such as Daisy Spies, Ilse Meudtner, Liselotte Köster, Manon Ehrfur, Rolf Arco, Werner Stammer, Jockel Stahl, Rolf Jahnke and Harald Kreutzberg (as a guest) were among the stars of ballet performances at both opera houses in Berlin. Cunz's repeated call in 1938 for an increased use of 'national and character dance' thus seems somewhat redundant: 'The classical dance in our time is being returned to its essential basic form through the use of national and character dances. It thus aligns itself with the modern art dance, which obtains its most valuable energy from its reflection of folk dance' (Cunz 1938: 14).

As far as ballet music was concerned, Maudrik and Kölling, like all the other choreographers working at that time, strictly observed the prescribed parameters. They either rearranged popular music from the nineteenth century, for example music by Schubert and the Strauss dynasty; or else composers, such as those mentioned above, provided new ballet scores. It appears that the genre of ballet in particular was 'deregulated' and used as an experimental ground for the type of contemporary music the party was just about willing to tolerate. Consequently, composers such as Orff, Egk, Blacher and his pupil Gottfried von Einem were jointly responsible for the success of those ballets which, up until 1944, might be regarded as 'National Socialist' or 'German' ballets. The best-known examples of this genre are – along with the aforementioned *Barberina, Der Teufel im Dorf, Die Gaunerstreiche der Courage*[16] and *Der Stralauer Fischzug*:

- *Landsknechte* (Lansquenets), choreography: Tatjana Gsovsky, music: Julius Weismann, Essen 1936;
- *Die Kirmes von Delft* (The Parish Fair of Delft), choreography: Sonja Korty, music: Hermann Reutter, Baden-Baden 1937;
- *Der zerbrochene Krug* (The Broken Jug), choreography: Lizzie Maudrik, music: Rudolf Wagner-Régeny, Berlin 1937;
- *Fest im Süden* (Festival in the South), choreography: Ellen von Cleve-Petz, music: Boris Blacher, Kassel 1937;
- *Das Dorf unter dem Gletscher* (The Village under the Glacier), choreography: Valeria Kratina, music: Heinrich Sutermeister, Karlsruhe 1937;
- *Carmina Burana*, production: Oskar Wälterlin, choreography: Inge Herting, music: Carl Orff, Frankfurt 1937;
- *Catulli Carmina*, production: Hans Niedecken-Gebhard, choreography: Tatjana Gsovsky, music: Carl Orff, Leipzig 1943;
- *Joan von Zarissa* (Joan of Zarissa), production: Heinz Tietjen, choreography: Lizzie Maudrik, music: Werner Egk, Berlin 1940;
- *Prinzessin Turandot* (Princess Turandot), choreography: Tatjana Gsovsky, music: Gottfried von Einem, Dresden 1944.

From this itemisation as well as the repertoire lists (Kant/Karina 1996: Documents), we can identify the following genres of dance during the period of National Socialism (1933–1944):

1) Divertissement or dance-suite
   A loose medley of dances of diverse origin. This type of dance was also of special importance for the entertainment of troops.

---

16   After Richard Mohaupt had left Germany, this highly successful ballet was banned.

2) German Ballet
Although regularly subject to criticism in theoretical discussions by
the party hierarchy and at best just tolerated, the genre of 'German
Ballet' nevertheless continued to develop in the theatres. It is defined
by the topics treated, the dramaturgy and the applied means.
3) Expressive dance (*Ausdruckstanz*) of the National Socialist variety
   a) Solo dance
   A dance-solo, choreographed and danced by an outstanding dance
   artist. Creative artists who stayed on good terms with the National
   Socialists were allowed to continue with their solo careers. In return,
   they incorporated new topics and themes into their dances and watered
   down their own dance vocabulary.
   b) Chamber dance (also called 'concert dance')[17]
   An ensemble-dance, led by an expressive dancer, and mainly presented
   in theatres. As far as the topics and the structure of these dances are concerned, it corresponded to the aesthetics of the National Socialists.

Dramaturgy of the 'German Ballet'

In the early 1940s the key elements of a dramaturgy of 'German Ballet' were
finally assembled. The impulse for a new work might have come from a
choreographer or theatre director, but the selection and concept, including
the structure of the ballet, the dramaturgy and the means used – such as
the blending of the classical vocabulary with folk dance elements – had to
conform to party ideology. This conformity was checked by a commission
which could accept or refuse a new work.

The preferred genre was the divertissement (as 'Dance does not show
a plot but gracefulness, harmony, exhilaration', Goebbels, November 1936,
in Reuth, vol. 2, 2000: 736), and also genre pictures with outlines of a plot.

17   See Karina/Kant 1996: Document 27: 257.

The *ballet d'action* in several acts was controversial; a framework story for a dance suite was, however, permitted, because it gave 'an even greater popularity and plausibility to the whole'. Intellectually demanding pieces had to be avoided: 'One should refrain from a transposition of dramatic and intellectual content into dance. [...] Dance does not need any intellectual cooperation. Its theme should be dance itself, rhythm and movement, colour and beauty.'[18] 'Eccentricity' and symbolic 'secretiveness' were deemed undesirable. 'Absolute' dance was equated with 'expressionism' and therefore rejected. Important stimulation was to be derived from other forms of art (such as painting and literature) – that is to say, from models already accepted by the party. Themes comprised local tradition, fairy tales and legends, as well as German history (though, in this case, any anti-militaristic stance had to be avoided). Preference was given to popular heroes from the 'good old days' who were juxtaposed with the folk in their naïve earthiness. The story had to be told in a linear way; hence playing with different temporal layers was no longer possible. Experiments with space were jettisoned too; but the technical innovations of 1920s theatre were retained, albeit with a reintroduction of scenery and realism.

As far as ballet music is concerned, popular accessibility was considered desirable, which meant that the compositional means had to be 'simple'. For pieces with several acts, a coherent all-embracing 'action music' was called for which would use simple melodies, tonal colours and employ different groups of instruments for the different sexes. Dance interludes were permitted, or even encouraged, but they had to be quoted without distortion. The use of folk music, arranged for the theatre, was also promoted. There were calls for the 'strong melodician'. 'Harsh sounds', 'callous rhythms and drum kit parts' were to be avoided, while a 'motor crescendo' was said to achieve 'great enhancements to dance' (Karine & Kant doc. 71: 295).

---

18   Quotations taken from Karina/Kant 1996, Rainer Schlösser document 89: 308f; and document 90: 310f.

In addition to the music which was to be composed specifically to purpose, there were the ballets of the great masters Gluck, Mozart, Beethoven
and Richard Johann Strauss, and also adaptations and arrangements of
works by great or old masters such as Lanner and Strauss. Mediaeval or
baroque music was often the basis for compositions. The music of foreign
composers was banished, along with the performance of the folk dances of
'hostile' peoples, 'improper' dancing to the music of great masters, and to
music which was not specifically composed for dance. Because easy-listening
music was valued highly in the National Socialist state, a specialist group
of composers of ballet and light or popular music emerged.

In terms of the appreciation of dancers, there was a new positioning
of the 'artist' in general. The star dancer was placed on equal footing with
other National Socialist artists of the stage or film. They formed the top
of the pyramid of the new society. The reorganisation of dance and dancers followed the structures of the nineteenth century, which meant that
the hierarchy of the ensemble was restored, which in turn impacted on
plot and dramaturgy. Other elements, such as the different categories of
dance [*Tanzfächer*] and the corresponding assignment of roles to male and
female dancers, were also re-established. The standardisation of roles was
emphasised through costumes, which oscillated between offering historical
accuracy of details and slight abstraction, but in all cases made the work
more comfortable to dance.

For ballets on a larger scale, the action on stage was given such prominence that directors and choreographers often worked as a team, with the
director being responsible for the overall dramaturgy. The action was still
very often 'eventful' as was the case in 1920s theatre dance. With respect to
the direction of ensembles, the soloists and the *corps de ballet*, individualistic dance fashion and specialised aestheticism were to be avoided. There
was to be a focus on the people from whom the individual, the chosen,
the leader or the historic hero would emerge. In accordance with the new
relationship between individual and chorus, the construction of the latter
had changed: the *corps de ballet* was no longer organised according to the
principle of 'leading and following' (able to change repeatedly its form
and internal structure), but was now a self-contained, unchangeable and
symmetrically structured chorus, which was pitted against the individual,
the *Führer*. Body image, body language and movement vocabulary were

not connected with those of the 1920s; nuances in the characterisation and portrayal of the sexes and exaggeration into the grotesque, as was frequently seen then and even characteristic of that theatrical epoch, disappeared completely.

Choreographies now emphasised character dance of extraordinary quality. Pointe work was used, on one hand, as a means to showcase femininity (for 'dance has [...] to show beautiful female bodies', Goebbels, June 1937, in Reuth 2000 vol. 3: 1095), and on the other to demonstrate mastery of the craft. Audiences too underwent a restructuring. As they were now organised by the National Socialist association *Kraft durch Freude* (Strength through Joy), full houses were not only guaranteed but a unanimous positive response was virtually predetermined.

Continuity and the Return of Variety

Insofar as circumstances allowed, the theatres resumed their activities immediately after the war.[19] What is immediately noticeable within the blossoming dance scene is its continuity. With the exception of Lizzie Maudrik, who withdrew completely from the stage, and Pia and Pino Mlakar, who returned to the *Bayrische Staatsoper* only in 1952, many of the foremost choreographers of National Socialism were still in leading positions. These included, amongst others, Tatjana Gsovsky, who dominated the dance scene in East Berlin, and Rudolf Kölling and Jens Keith, who worked in the western part of the city. In Hamburg, Helga Swedlund continued working and in Vienna there was Erika Hanka. Only in Munich was a new appointment made: Marcel Luipart.[20] With the choreographers who remained *in situ*, their works were retained too.

---

19   For an extensive discussion of the post-war scene see Oberzaucher-Schüller 2002: 15–30; Müller, Stabel and Stöckemann 2003.

20   Luipart, until then known as a classical dancer, only began choreographing after the war. See also Poeschl 2002.

The dance scene that developed when the quadripartite agreement was introduced in Germany was tailored towards the special requirements of each occupied zone. Their common denominator, however, was the demand for classical dance. In spite of this, there was also a revival of *Ausdruckstanz*. By the mid-fifties, the stylistic and aesthetic spheres had been consolidated. The co-existence of two trends could be most clearly observed in Berlin. In the West of the city, a modern 'German' ballet was established by Tatiana Gsovsky. Gsovsky's work relied on the composers with whom she had already worked in the forties. In the East, the ballet of the Soviet repertoire was becoming more and more prevalent. The creations of National Socialism continued to be performed both in East and West. In the East, a number of these ballets even became the basis for the new stylistic tendency called Socialist Realism, a phenomenon which warrants further study.[21]

Particularly illuminating in this context are the accounts provided by Eberhard Rebling – one of the official ballet writers of the GDR – in his ballet guide *Ballett von A bis Z* (Ballet from A to Z), which was published in 1966. He writes that Pia and Pino Mlakar, with *The Devil in the Village*, had created 'for the first time a full-length artwork of dance, whereas since the end of the previous century – with the exception of the Soviet Union – the practice of short ballets had been dominant'. The 'naïve-folksy story depicting the triumph of human love over the power of the devil [...] is a rewarding task for the choreographer' (Rebling 1966: 436). Moreover, Rebling describes *The Roguish Tricks of Courage* as 'a successful translation of the ingenious German popular humour into a ballet'. It depicts 'the insanity and inhumanity of war in a burlesque guise and with satirical exaggeration'. The music by Mohaupt is said to be characterised by 'bawdy

---

21   See Stabel 2001. Stabel's remarks and the documents printed as an appendix to the book (321f.) – the 'Theses of the Theoretical Conference on the Art of Dance on 23/24 March 1935 in Berlin' – attest to the approach taken by those in charge of cultural affairs. The loosely formulated demands are empty clichés which could be given whatever content the situation required. This 'open-ended' approach may have been all the more appropriate given the need to be prepared for interventions from the Soviet Union.

humour, popular melodies and energetic rhythms' (ibid.: 132). *The Stralau Fish Haul* also remained on the programmes. Rebling maintains that 'the down-to-earth characters who dominate the streets at such a feast' (he refers here to a folk festival in Old Berlin) 'are brought onto the stage through dance and costume, displaying their humour and easily excitable earthiness' (ibid.: 426). *The Parish Fair of Delft* is, as Rebling writes, a work with 'a humanistic keynote' of 'hefty reality'; Reutter's music being distinguished by an 'unobtrusive tonal portrayal' (ibid.: 203). The ballet *The Broken Jug*, which was based on Heinrich von Kleist's work, is called 'delightful'. Above all, Rebling praises the 'joyfully satirical' music by Wagner-Régeny with which the composer quite consciously 'opposed' the kind of barbarism fostered by National Socialism (ibid.: 475). Furthermore, Rebling writes about *Joan of Zarissa* that the composer Werner Egk 'puts a humanistic idea into the foreground, which was especially important at the time of the ballet's premiere' (ibid.: 185). Finally, Rebling assesses Gottfried von Einem's music for *Princess Turandot* as a 'courageous avowal against brutality and tyranny in the midst of war' (ibid.: 314).

It is particularly illuminating to consider a voice from the West on these same ballets. In 1956, Otto Friedsrich Regner wrote about *The Devil in the Village* in the first edition of *Reclams Ballettführer* (Reclam's Ballet Guide): 'Credit has to go to Mlakart for having utilised the sheer inexhaustible abundance of southern Slavic folklore for the stage dance' (1956: 367). He notes about *The Roguish Tricks of Courage*: 'The rustic plot, the somewhat rough characterisation of the figures on stage and the music correspond to each other; the music is of a dramatic melodiousness, more stereotypical than differentiating, but altogether very effective, though almost lurid' (ibid.: 135). With respect to *The Parish Fair of Delft*, Regner merely notes that the work has been performed on more than eighty stages (ibid.: 219). He is full of praise for Egk's music to *Joan of Zarissa*. It is 'full of dancerly impulses and rhythmic energy', and Egk proves to be a 'predestined composer for the ballet' (ibid.: 202). Finally, Regner quotes a review of the ballet *Princess Turandot*, according to which Tatjana Gsovsky combined 'ecstatically inflated gestures with an impassioned unleashing of dance movements' (ibid.: 277).

The continuity observed as well as the startling similarity between the ballet of National Socialism and that of the newly emerging East zone of Germany will have to be investigated in more depth elsewhere. In the 1960s, the 'German Ballet' disappeared from both the West and East German programmes.[22]

Works Cited

Amtliche Mitteilungen der Reichsmusikkammer. 1934. Berlin, April 25. Vol. 1.

Cunz, R. 1938. *Deutsches Volkstanzbuch. Vom Tanzkreis zur Tanzgemeinschaft.* Dresden: Rudolph.

Dahms, S. 1997. Der Tanz – ein Leben. Friderica Derra de Moroda 1897–1978, in *Der Tanz – ein Leben. In memoriam Friderica Derra de Moroda. Festschrift.* Edited by Sibylle Dahms and Stephanie Schroedter. Salzburg: Selke Verlag: 9–116.

Deutsches Bühnenjahrbuch 1934. Vol. 45. Edited by the Genossenschaft der deutschen Bühnen-Angehörigen. Berlin: Bruno Henschel und Sohn.

Die geistigen Grundlagen für Tanz im Nationalsozialistischen Staat. 1933. Der Tanz, 2–3 November.

Guilbert, L. 2000. *Danser avec le IIIe Reich. Les Danseurs modernes sous le nazisme.* Brussels: Ed. Complexe.

Hamm, H.-G. 1945/48. Das deutsche Bühnenjahrbuch. *Deutsches Bühnenjahrbuch* 56. Berlin: Bruno Henschel und Sohn: 7–8.

Karina, I., & Kant, M. 1996. *Tanz unterm Hakenkreuz. Eine Dokumentation.* Berlin: Henschel.

Koegler, H. 1972. Tanz in die Dreißiger Jahre in *Ballett 1972. Chronik und Bilanz des Ballettjahres.* Edited by H. Koegler: 38–51.

Koegler, H. 1973. Tanz in den Abgrund in *Ballett 1973. Chronik und Bilanz des Ballettjahres.* Edited by Horst Koegler: 57–61.

Laubinger, O. 1934. Zum Beginn! *Deutsches Bühnenjahrbuch* 45. Berlin: Bruno Henschel und Sohn: 57.

Liedtke, M. 1937. Introduction. *Jahrbuch Deutscher Tanz.* Berlin: 7.

22 *Joan of Zarissa* remained on the programme for somewhat longer; Orffs's works are still frequently performed today.

Müller, H., & Stöckemann, P. (eds.) 1993. '*... jeder Mensch ist ein Tänzer*'. *Ausdruck-stanz in Deutschland zwischen 1900 und 1945*. Gießen: Anabas Verlag.

Müller, H., Stabel, R., & Stöckemann, P. 2003. *Krokodil im Schwanensee. Tanz in Deutschland seit 1945*. Frankfurt: Anabas Verlag.

Oberzaucher-Schüller, G. 2000. Theatralische Freie und Freie Theatraliker. Aspekte der Tanzszene im deutschsprachigen Raum 1918–1939. *tanzdrama* 56: 19–26.

Oberzaucher-Schüller, G. 2002. Am Beispiel Berlin, oder: Auch in der Tanzwissenschaft erweist es sich als sinnvoll, von einer Historiographie als Basis für weitere Forschung auszugehen, in *tanz. theorie. text*. Edited by G. Klein and Ch. Zipprich. Tanzforschung vol. 12. Münster: Literatur Verlag: 15–30.

Poeschl, Th. 2001. *Abraxas, Höllen-Spectaculum*. Teetz: Hentrich und Hentrich.

Rebling, E. 1966. *Ballett von A-Z*. Berlin: Henschel.

Regner, O. F. 1956. *Reclams Ballettführer*. Stuttgart: Reklam.

Reuth, R. G. (ed.). 2000. *Joseph Goebbels Tagebücher 1924–1945*. 5 volumes. Second edition. Munich: Piper.

Rosenberg, A. 1932. Der Kampf um die deutsche Kulturerneuerung. *In Deutsche Bühnenkorrespondenz. Nachrichtenblatt des Dramatischen Büros im Kampfbund für Deutsche Kultur* 1(16/17).

Stabel, R. 2001. *Vorwärts. Rückwärts, Seitwärts mit und ohne Frontveränderung. Zur Geschichte der Palucca Schule in Dresden*. Wilhelmshaven: Noetzel.

STACEY PRICKETT

7 Dancing the American Dream during World War II

With few exceptions, Western theatre dances inspired by war tend to convey an oppositional stance, either commenting on war's hardships and devastation or expressing overt ideological resistance.[1] Reactions to international conflicts since the end of World War II may make it difficult for current generations to appreciate the extent to which the public and artists rallied in support of the fight against fascism. Today's socially conscious dances can be seen to emulate the dominant relationship between dance and politics in American modern dance during the 1930s when protest often took dance form. Ranging from the agit-prop dances of Edith Segal and her Red Dancers to dancer-choreographers such as Anna Sokolow, Helen Tamiris and the members of the New Dance Group, socially conscious themes were dominant. The plights of unemployed, homeless or exploited labourers were joined by anti-fascist themes on the burgeoning concert dance stage in New York City. Once America entered World War II in 1941, however, second generation modern dancers adopted a different tone in dances that celebrated positive national archetypes, reinforcing the good in humanity rather than highlighting negative aspects of contemporary life. By the middle of the war, visions of American identity and heroic ideals became increasingly embodied in light-hearted and accessible themes, marking a change from the previous decade in terms of content and expanding the aesthetics associated with modern dance.

---

1   I would like to thank Ann Vachon of the José Limón Dance Foundation for her questions arising from a conference paper which fed into this chapter. Thanks also go to Andrew Hillier and Larraine Nicholas for their feedback on early drafts.

The visions of American spirit in the early 1940s continued to be aligned with international struggles demonstrating some similarities to the previous decade, but drawing on narratives and characterisations linked to popular entertainment and iconic national symbols rather than presenting a particularly 'proletarian' vision. Modern dancers also continued to view their choreography as socially significant, inspired by contemporary events, but their dances of celebration and entertainment appear at odds with the didactic and idealistic goals of the earlier years of the revolutionary dance movement. Jane Dudley, Sophie Maslow and José Limón all created dances evoking a gathering of forces against a common enemy, explored here in their under-researched choreography created during World War II. In wider society dancers, teachers and writers also argued that dance had a crucial role in the fight for democracy, calling for recognition of its value.

Multiple Identities and Ideologies

With the entry into war in 1941, US government policy became aligned with many left-wing activists and artists who began to express support for American ideals, its fighting forces, and the need to pull together as a community and nation at home. Central to the struggle was the articulation of diverse and often competing notions of identity, in response to cultural shifts which began in the 1930s and continued throughout the 1940s. The leftist dances of the 1930s have been examined by numerous scholars who consider how the potential for revolution in the early years of the Depression and appeal of communist and socialist ideologies was worn down gradually by multiple factors.[2] Dances about the socially and economically

2   For early published accounts of the left-wing dance movement see for example, Stacey Prickett (1989 and 1990); Ellen Graff (1997) and the collection edited by Lynn Garafola (1994). Other aspects of the period have been reassessed extensively in recent years, including publications by Mark Franko (2002), Susan Manning (2004) and Julia L. Foulkes (2002). Victoria Phillips Geduld's *Performing Communism in the*

marginalised shared the stage with works about the oppression of workers on the factory floor (seen for example in Dudley's *Time is Money* in 1934 and Anna Sokolow's *Strange American Funeral* in 1935). An international proletariat was represented predominantly by references to Eastern European and newly Soviet states, some of which were the homelands of first generation Jewish-American dancers. References to an American national identity were few and far between in the early 1930s, and couched in highly critical terms when present. With the People's War, as it became known, the end of isolationist policies signalled a convergence of ideologies, as choreographers had been challenging the fascist threat to world democracy as early as 1934 with the New Dance Group's *Van der Lubbe's Head*.

Analysing what is termed 'American exceptionalism' or difference, Stephen Fender (1993) notes that the emergence of an American character is found in its development as a country predicated on what was fundamentally a bourgeois dream. Early eighteenth-century travellers described the population as having 'a dominant middle class of craftsmen, traders and farmers' (ibid.: 1) that was independent and not bound by European extremes of peasantry and aristocracy. The differences helped set apart the young nation through the radical concept of the bourgeois dream, revealing qualities of 'enterprise, the accumulation and investment of capital, the taking of risk, the deferring of gratification, the faith in future possibilities' (ibid.: 12). The possibility of such aspirations in and of themselves had set Americans apart. A shared experience of emigration helped link together a disparate population and although the frontier provided the ability to move on, a strong need to conform became fundamental to the national character. The imagined community of an American nation, using Benedict Anderson's (1983) concept, came under particular threat during the Depression.

American Dance: Culture, Politics and the New Dance Group (2008) focuses on the relationship between modern dance and the Communist Party, drawing on CPUSA archives. She also highlights the ramifications of such associations for dancers in the post-war years as the anti-communist backlash reached its peak under the leadership of Senator Joseph McCarthy.

A myriad of symbols linked to national identity and representations of mythical personas became common, evident particularly in the dances created during World War II. Warren Susman's analysis of American culture in the 1930s highlights how myths contributed to the shaping of a national identity when phrases such as the 'American Way of Life' and the 'American Dream' came into vernacular usage. They emphasised the country's 'cultural visions: questions of life style, patterns of belief and conduct, special values and attitudes that constitute the characteristics of a special people' (Susman 2003: 155). Marxism was ultimately undermined, Susman argues, by Americans' search for a common identity found in symbolic expression of its 'folk', combined with the emergence of a consumerist culture stimulated by New Deal policies resulting in a 'culture of abundance'. The American folk embodied a heroic strength that stood in contrast to the failures of industrial capitalism and shifting social orders brought on by the Depression.

A shift away from 'the proletariat' to 'the people' occurred with the emergence of Popular Front policies in 1935 as the Communist Party sought to reinforce an ideological alignment with the American way of life, leading to what Susman perceives as anti-intellectualism among leftist and liberal ideologies. Fundamentally, the middle class rather than the working class, and its values became the cornerstone of an alternative to Marxism (Levine and Papasotiriou 2005: 3), as 'the people' replaced the 'proletariat' as dance subjects during the 1930s in part through the use of folk themes. Significantly, the conceptualisations of 'the people' offered opportunities to cross class boundaries, to celebrate broader values and national ideals while, to those on the political right, representations of the 'proletariat' stood in tension with the capitalist foundations of American society. Various identities were represented choreographically as explored below, ranging from the soldier, to the urbanite middle class to the rural small town inhabitant.

Offering another perspective on the cultural trends of the 1930s, Michael Denning asserts that the dominant emphasis on class conflict had 'obscured the divisions of ethnicity, race and gender in an imagined unity of the "people" and "people's culture"' (Denning 1997: 124). Unlike Susman, Denning perceives continuities between pre- and post-Popular Front cultural representations, investigating how the art of second and third generation Americans who were part of the revolutionary movement were infused with 'competing nationalisms' of 'new Americans', demonstrating 'pride in ethnic heritage and identity combined with an assertive Americanism and a popular internationalism' (ibid.: 130). Tendencies manifest in the evolution of a 'pan-ethnic Americanism' included the use of grand narratives and myths of the nation's past while embracing cultural forms from abroad, thus rejecting earlier isolationist policies. Such reaching out is exemplified politically by the campaigns for Spain. Rather than homogenising ethnic difference, dancers celebrated distinctive identities, among them Jewish and Spanish, in addition to representations of a mythologized American folk. In particular, Spain's civil war initiated multiple forms of collective action by American liberals, through fund-raising efforts and even volunteering for the Abraham Lincoln Brigade to fight the fascists, with solidarity evident in dances, paintings and plays. Activists and artists celebrated the ideals of democracy even as they were being challenged on multiple levels within contemporary society.

The desire to belong, to be a part of an organisation or institution that created change, reached what Susman defines as a culture of commitment evident in the 1930s, although he argues that the most powerful leftist political stances were predicated on negative issues such as 'Franco, fascism, [and the] dehumanisation of Depression America' (Susman 2003: 173). In contrast, positive images are linked to President Roosevelt's New Deal policies which utilised new technologies of radio and film to reinforce unified responses and commandeered 'a set of images, symbols, and myths with most meaning for the bulk of the American people' (ibid.: 179). These are also evident in artistic responses to war, marking a break from the left's close alignment with labour. Despite the popular support for the fight for democracy, historian Howard Zinn (2003) argues that it was a contentious time for America's workers who did not share in the economic benefits generated by the industrial war machine. Ironically, the highest incidents of labour unrest occurred during a time when the nation has been perceived as strongly united. He also reminds his readers of the USA's failure to sustain its own democratic ideals during World War II, notably in the three-year internment of 110,000 Japanese-Americans, continued government sanction of racial segregation and discrimination, and in the exclusion of women from policy-making roles despite their entry into men's employment.

In dance, a more populist legibility was evident in an attention to entertainment values and expansion of movement vocabularies away from modern dance techniques, only decades after the efforts undertaken by the form's pioneers and early practitioners to have the dance recognised as high art. As Sophie Maslow summarises in 1946,

> We're popular, if by 'popular' you mean 'of the people'. But this is the Age of the Common Man, and it is the common people who are the backbone and the strength and hope of our civilization and our culture. (cited in Hering 1946: 17)

The integration of national symbols in modern dance marks an interesting but temporary turn towards the popular and patriotic by those previously considered left-wing as they debated the most appropriate choreographic response to the intense crisis marked by the nation's declaration of war in December 1941. John Martin argued in the *New York Times* that:

> When there is peace there is no need to make art about it; it is when there is war that the enduring qualities that make for peace demand to be voiced. Let us by all means dance now about the nobility of the human spirit, the grace that is in us, the harmony that inheres in unity; that is the only way, indeed, that we can dance about war. (Martin 1943: X8)

Martin had criticised the musical and thematic choices of an all-Bach programme by Doris Humphrey and José Limón which led to a published exchange between critic and choreographer. Humphrey explained that '... the convulsive drama going on simply cannot be expressed in dance, at least not by me. Any attempt would be pallid and unconvincing'. Instead, her creations *Chorale Preludes* and *Partita in G Minor* evoked nobility and grace, giving dancers 'a chance to move harmoniously with each other, [to] say in my small way that there is hope [...] where unity prevails' (cited in Martin 1943, X8). Although expressing an indictment of the pain and suffering brought on by the global conflict, the celebration of diverse identities and positive ideals came to be labelled as American in character, aligning the modern dance field with dominant ideologies. Offstage, other avenues emerged for the promotion of dance as an integral part of the war effort.

Social Dance and Off Stage Activities

After Pearl Harbor, articles in New York periodicals and specialist journals reported on dancers' responses to the outbreak of hostilities. Readers were urged to rally behind the war effort to raise morale and to undertake practical tasks that would demonstrate dance's wider social relevance. Other articles chastised those who labelled dancers and other artists as 'non-essential [...] in a time of national crisis' (Dancer's War Fund 1942: 59), arguing that dance can generate a stronger sense of community and even reinforce the tenets of democracy through collaborative processes in the creative act (Radir 1942). Slogans such as 'Keep 'em flying – buy war bonds!' filled spaces of the *Dance Observer*. Activist-musician Woody Guthrie (1943: 114) joined in calling dancers to arms, claiming that

> ... the job of the dancer (or steel driver, or jackhammer man, or bomber pilot) is all the same. We're working to win the war [...]. Soldiers, sailors, marines, powder monkeys, dancers all wear different looking uniforms but its [sic] all the same fight.

Guthrie advocated accessible themes about 'the people', one comprised of diverse identities:

> If a dance don't tell you what kind of a fight is going on, and what caused it to break out and what kind of work you got to do to win out, the goods in your costume are wasted. (ibid.)

Dance has the potential to reveal truths, he argued, to increase understanding of each other and facilitate a more unified response to Hitler.

Letters published in *Dance Magazine* expressed gratitude from dancer-soldiers when back issues caught up with them at various fighting fronts. Whilst *Dance Observer* editorials made constant reference to the war effort and the need to mobilise as an artistic community, *Dance Magazine*'s articles made fewer mentions of the ongoing battles, although its July issues in 1943 and 1944 were devoted to dancers in the military. After victory in Europe was declared on May 8, 1945, entertainment troupes travelled to the former battle zones, their activities widely covered in the press. Articles about dancers such as Igor Schwezoff, a former Soviet ballet dancer, reflected on how their dance training related to their service training. Schwezoff declared basic training:

> ... a snap for the ballet dancer [...] and why not? He has been for years trained to make the best possible use of his body, and his sense of coordination and balance puts him far ahead of the average soldier. Army callisthenics [...] are as easy as A.B.C. to him. Why shouldn't he make a desirable solider equipped as he is? (Schwezoff 1943: 16)

The image of dancer as fighter was seen in features on dancers in uniform, such as tap dancer Johnny Seager who set a record time in learning the radio code needed for his new job as Naval Air Transport Pilot, because of his ear for rhythm (Marsh 1944: 5). Dancers, as artists and activists, put their efforts into the fight against fascism in multiple arenas, both on stage and off. Money was raised for relief agencies while social dances provided escape for military and civilian personnel. Beyond the morale boosting effects, the physical benefits of dance amongst factory workers and volunteers were publicised. Anne Green, President of the Dancing Masters of America, advocated how correct posture, breathing, walking, stretching and relaxing could be transferred from dancing to daily activities 'to prepare them for what lies ahead' (Green 1943: 6). Dance breaks for Red Cross volunteers included exercises to strengthen wrists and hands for rolling bandages, foot and ankle exercises for standing and improved posture to reduce backaches.

May Gadd reported on square dances and social dancing in the USO (United Services Organisation) in the *Dance Observer*, discussing new logistical problems posed by the dance gatherings. An increase in gender disparity at a military camp in Texas noted a ratio of 40,000 men to 300 female dance partners. But the form was deemed to be adequate to accommodate the imbalance:

> The simple technique of the [square] dance offers no barrier even to the most inexperienced dancer, while the spirit of friendly cooperation that it engenders is very helpful to the morale of the soldier or worker who has been uprooted from his familiar surroundings. (Gadd 1942: 118)

Country dances served as an icebreaker among strangers, alleviating the need for men to ask women to dance and risk rejection. As military programme consultant, Gadd ran training sessions for country dance leaders and classes for women to prepare them for local dance events. Such activities were deemed beneficial for the art form while improving the morale 'of fighting men and civilians through participation in this most democratic, sociable, recreative activity' (Gadd 1943: 90). Those in the dance community worked to publicise how vital the form is to society on a variety of levels, even as those working on the concert dance stage ventured into new territory artistically and geographically in support of the war effort.

The Dudley-Maslow-Bales Trio

In the professional field, dancers began to broaden their movement palette, drawing on diverse dance styles and populist choreographic themes. At the forefront of the left-wing dance movement of the 1930s, Jane Dudley and Sophie Maslow began choreographing and dancing as soloists and as members of the New Dance Group. At the same time they emerged as prominent performers in Martha Graham's company, creating seminal roles in early masterpieces. Their creative development occurred under the tutelage of Louis Horst's composition classes, their solos acclaimed for their expressive artistry and performed at benefits for a range of causes. The dancers' individual styles were distinctive yet complimentary, with Maslow noted for her lyricism and Dudley for a powerful presence and dramatic intensity. Eventually joining forces, they worked on collaborative duets such as *Caprichos* (1938), inspired directly by the Spanish Civil War.

While earlier works were an indictment on emerging fascist powers in Europe, the Spanish struggle became a rallying point for many fellow travellers who perceived links between their class struggle and the threat of fascism. Rather than rising to the defence of the Republicans as the democratically elected government, the anti-interventionists won the political battle when the USA's neutrality policy prohibited the sale of armaments to either side in the Spanish conflict. The Republicans were outgunned literally, as Italy and Germany rose to the support of the fascist forces led by General Francisco Franco (Carroll et al. 2006). Class conflict underpinned the struggle as explained in the 1942 *Caprichos* programme notes: 'The figure in red personifies the capricious and arrogant woman of the aristocracy – the figure in brown is the peasant, her serf.' A *Dance Observer* review noted the contrasts: 'Its figures might have stepped out of a Picasso canvas: a peasant woman, crushed by hunger and despair, and a harlot, equally tragic in spite of her mood of wild gayety' (Sabin 1942: 47). Danced solidarity with Spain re-emerges later in the war, but with a different emphasis as seen in *Llanto* (1944). The sections 'We shall avenge our tears' and 'This is our grief' focused on the anguish and grief of the conquered (Beiswanger 1944: 9) rather than the hope of victory.

Throughout the decade modern dance was moving towards the ideo-logical and aesthetic mainstream as the boundary between high art and popular stage was increasingly blurred by Broadway musicals.[3] Shifts to the centre are exemplified in the closure of the *New Theatre* journal which was a vital forum for the discussion of left-wing dance philosophies.[4] As Ellen Graff (1997) notes, *Dance Observer* broadened its readership base with the inclusion of articles on folk dance and college dance department activities. The editorial board became more directly involved in advancing the careers of young artists the journal deemed worthy, with Dudley and Maslow among those regularly praised.

The Dudley-Maslow-Bales Trio was created when the two Graham dancers were joined by William Bales in a 1942 concert inaugurating the *Dance Observer*'s production activities while reviews continued to chart

---

3   Beth Genné examines the strong links between theatre dance, Broadway and film during the war in *'Freedom Incarnate': Jerome Robbins, Gene Kelly, and the Dancing Sailor As An Icon Of American Values In World War II* (2001).

4   One reason the journal closed was the departure of its editor to serve as a correspond-ent in the Spanish Civil War. See Herbert Kline 1985: 363.

the group's progress and tours.⁵ Bales' Broadway success and balletic background proved a rich foil for the two women while increasing the range of themes available to them with the addition of gender diversity. Accompanist-composer Zoe Williams also became an integral part of the creative team. During Bales' academic breaks from a teaching post at Bennington College the Trio toured across the country, appearing under the auspices of *Dance Observer*, the USO and at colleges, universities and military service clubs, thus exposed to different audiences than the regular New York City concert dance attendees. In 1944, George W. Beiswanger (1944: 3) proclaimed of the Trio:

> They make one like dancing very much. They fill the stage with happy imaginings, delightful conceits, hearty sentiments and dance that sings. Warmth spreads over the footlights and takes the audience into its comfortable arms. People have a good time.

Dances inspired by the Spanish conflict remained a focus of new creations. However, inventive choreography on light-hearted themes gradually dominated, reflecting changes in performing environments undertaken during the early years of the group's existence.

The Trio's trajectory exemplifies trends amongst socially conscious artists of the period as support for the war rose among the left-wing. Close bonds between anti-government and pro-labour sentiments came under tension with many fellow travellers disillusioned by the Nazi-Soviet non-aggression pact of 1939. In an extreme example of shifting allegiances, a major ideological rift occurred when the Soviet Union was invaded by Germany in May 1941. According to Robbie Lieberman (1995), the Almanac Singers' first album released in March 1941, a staunchly leftist folksong group whose members included Pete Seeger and later Woody Guthrie, criticised President Roosevelt's war preparation and the institution of the peacetime draft. Musician Lee Hays recalled how they had to change the words to songs on the eve of a tour because of the need for unity:

---

5   Postponed from an earlier date, the inaugural *Dance Observer* concert occurred on 10 and 11 March, 1942 at the Humphrey-Weidman Theater.

> Our whole politics took a terrible shift from 'the Yanks ain't coming' to 'the Yanks *are* coming'. All of a sudden it became one war, instead of two, and there was a chance of beating fascism on its own ground, which everybody was for. But it sure knocked hell out of our repertoire. (Hays cited in Lieberman: 54)

Seeger later joined the military but a decline in popularity because of their initial anti-war stance led to the Almanac Singers' dissolution. During the 1940s rare expressions of patriotism by left-leaning artists replaced earlier creative challenges to hegemonic and governmental policies.

Dance critics commented on a trend towards literalism in modern dance singling out the Dudley-Maslow-Bales Trio as examples of aesthetic changes. The Trio's inaugural launch evoked high praise in the *Dance Observer* with Robert Sabin (1942: 47) writing of an authenticity in the dances:

> In emotional maturity, command of form and stage knowledge it was infinitely superior to the average product which the big managements still feed to the big public. And furthermore, it had a direct relationship with our times, our problems and our lives [...] their work was notably free from literalism and pantomime...

Edwin Denby (1943: IV) analysed how the group excelled at challenging 'fundamental questions of dance forms from all sorts of novel angles [...]. [They] developed highly interesting movements by emphasizing action in the arms, by extreme torso displacements that violently shift the body's weight'. Soon though, the Trio was criticised for being too accessible and entertaining, especially in what critic Margaret Lloyd (1946b) labelled as the 'pantomime pieces', *Furlough: A Board Walk Episode* and *As Poor Richard Says – A Colonial Charade* (1943). The latter used Benjamin Franklin's words spoken and written on a large written book prop (see Figure 4). Lloyd contended that the inclusion of literal pantomime undermined the artistic level of the creations. In their defence, the dancers argued that 'modern dance could with impunity incorporate all styles and forms, adjusting them to the needs of each dance, if they strengthened its purpose of emotional expression' (ibid.).

Increasingly the Trio's repertory was dominated by dances that integrated national symbols. Rather than flag-waving patriotism, however, they choreographed archetypes of American society, drawing from popular cultural forms, infusing modern dance technique with other dance influences and pantomime to develop strong characterisations rather than aiming for authenticity of style. Although Maslow drew inspiration from an American rural folk style, and flamenco influences were seen in heel taps, bodily stance and arm gestures in the Trio's Spanish themed dances, they were stylistic interpretations rather than attempts accurately to emulate other dance traditions. Thus their versions of Americana were not solely insular ones as international influences continued to inform their creations.

In what ways do the dances of the Trio in celebrations of American folk and international people stand as political commentary? How do they differ from the agit-prop impetus of the workers dance groups? Written in 1949, Margaret Lloyd's (1987: 178) seminal account of the period illustrates the shifting conceptualisations of 'the people' away from the proletariat and towards the folk, marked by the May 1941 concert 'America Dances', drawing together Margaret Mayo's American Square Dance Group, ballroom dance, the Lindy Hoppers and diverse modern dances on folk and jazz themes. Dudley's *Harmonica Breakdown* (1940) to Sonny Terry's harmonica with washboard backing and Maslow's *Folksay* (1942) to Earl Robinson and Woody Guthrie's accompaniment were indicative of a turn to folk culture for inspiration, also utilising Carl Sandburg's poem *The People, Yes. Dust Bowl Ballads* (1941) marked the representation of what Ellen Graff (1997: 146) labelled as a 'new mythic American' although there were never claims of authenticity of dance style despite drawing on different forms of social dance. Denby's 1943 review praised the extent to which they moved away from earlier representations of despair:

> In composing, they tend to avoid the modern effects of several years back – the harsh armthrust followed by a wait, the gloomy straddle, the solemn cramp, the long writhing on the floor. They would like dancing to look friendly for a change. (Denby 1943: IV)

New dances integrated various visions of Americana while after the war one of Maslow's older solos reappeared with a modified title. In 1935, Maslow choreographed *Two Songs about Lenin (In January he was born; In April he died)* to music that composer Alex North brought back from Tajikistan. In 1947 the dance appeared in the program notes as *Songs about a Soviet Hero* (Lloyd 1987: 184), thus shifting associations from a co-founder of the Bolshevik Party and the Soviet state to a celebration of Allied fighters.

While questioning the use of literal gestures, Lloyd (1987: 191) concluded that the Trio

> ... made modern dance unformidable, friendly, a language that could speak of contemporary and colloquial subjects without determined Americana or social-consciousness fisticuffs. The program glorified the folk, not as a picturesque people in native costume, but as We, the People, in whatever we had on. It was far from isolationist. It reminded the audience of people in other countries.

The true story of a dying Yugoslav guerrilla's unfinished letter to an unborn child provided the inspiration for Maslow's *Inheritance* solo in *Fragments of a Shattered Land* (1945). Tales of oppression continued to feature in the group's repertory, but were balanced by light-hearted, humorous works. Dudley's *Ballad of Molly Pitcher* (1939) had comical elements in its evocation of the spirit underlying the revolutionary war, while Bates' *Es Mujer* (1942) drew from Mexican rites of passage into womanhood. Bales' contributions to the repertory included *To a Green Mountain Boy* (1942). Dudley's *American Morning* (1943) with music by Marc Blitzstein and text by David Wolf was described by Lloyd (1987: 183) as 'a forward-looking group dance'. Critics pondered whether the Trio's artistic choices meant the modern dance form was compromised, although enthusiastic responses by audiences around the country attest to the group's success in blurring boundaries between entertainment and high art, an issue that continues to vex scholars, critics and creators. Crucially, Doris Hering's profile of the Trio in *Dance Magazine* quoted a soldier at an Army camp show as saying 'There weren't any words to follow, like in a play, but I understood them' (cited in Hering 1946:17). Such appreciation by an audience not educated about dance is also evident in Limón's work during the war years as he branched out into a new demographic of both audience and performers – the military.

José Limón

Limón's early choreography on themes of war and conflict and the dances
he created while a US Army conscript during World War II range from
anti-war statements to those perpetuating myths of the 'American dream'.
Aesthetic and ideological shifts appeared in Limón's choreography on the
theme of war and works choreographed during his years of military service
in 1943 and 1944. He created group dances with the Camp Lee Concert
Dance Group comprised of fellow soldiers, and 'Blueprint Specials' that
enabled 'soldier shows' to be produced independently under the guidance
of Special Services Divisions at various military bases. Like other young
modern dancer-choreographers of the 1930s, Limón's early works embodied
a social consciousness in dances responding to events such as the Spanish
Civil War (*Danza de la Muerte*, 1937) and Mexico's history of colonisation
and revolution (*Danzas Mexicanas*, 1939). In *War Lyrics* (1940), Limón
placed women's roles at the centre of an indictment of war's devastation.

During a 1940 dance summer session at Mills College in Oakland, California, Limón created the anti-war dance *War Lyrics* which explored three
female roles, the wife, nurse, and the 'harlot', all danced by May O'Donnell.
A comprehensive production team – designers, composers and musicians
– supported the choreography danced to a poem by William Archibald.
Student dancers functioned along the lines of a Greek chorus in interludes between duets by O'Donnell and Limón. Lloyd's account draws
from the production notes, highlighting the bitter ending of the verse to
which 'The Wife' sends her husband off to fight: 'You, the wife with need
of glory, give your husband to the dead' (Archibald, cited in Lloyd 1987:
204). Esther Williamson's piano and trumpet score contained variations
on the 'Taps' theme, and Lloyd described 'tempo changes from the main
funeral dirge theme, [with] each spoken line underscored by the pound
of heavy footsteps, and pantomimic dancing downstage' (ibid.: 205). The
Taps theme is the solo trumpet tune which accompanies the daily ritual of
lowering of the flag at US military bases around the world and is played at
funerals of military personnel. Its use in the dance created clear associations

with the armed forces. *War Lyrics* was later performed as a duet under the title of *Three Women* with different music and the omission of the poem, possibly due to the absence of the student chorus and changes in political sentiments in the midst of the war.

Of, by and for the Soldiers

As male dancers volunteered or were drafted into the military, they found innovative ways to continue dancing. Dancer-soldier Private First Class (Pfc) Barry Lynn reported in *Dance Observer* that he managed to integrate dance technique exercises into physical training regimes at the Pueblo Air Base in Colorado, which helped alter perceptions about dance (Lynn 1944: 6). Small dance groups performed at benefits and in various service clubs, and eventually on the front lines as highlighted in Lucile Marsh's report in *Dance Magazine* (Marsh 1944: 4–5, 29). Initially, rehearsals were conducted after completion of regular duties but more institutional support emerged with the formation of the Special Services Division of the Army (The Theatre and the Armed Forces 1943; Bernstein 1944: 654).

In addition to morale building and entertainment, the military's insti-tutionalisation of the performing arts was seen to contribute to the trans-formation of a collection of individuals from diverse locations, ethnicities and careers into a cohesive unit. In the early years of the war there was a perception that the public needed to be motivated into action due to the 'betrayal of the peace' after the end of World War I. As Olin Downes (1942) argued in *The New York Times*, there was

> the necessity of convincing the younger men of the nation, all over again, that there are things worth fighting for, and dying for too [...]. We have not only to win a war, but, as a people, to win back a faith.

The arts provided a tool to help stir America's fighting spirit.

Limón's performing career was interrupted when he was drafted in 1943. The dances created during his military service stand in sharp contrast to the dark sentiments evoked in *War Lyrics*. Stationed at Camp Lee, near Richmond, Virginia, Limón's duties began as a truck driver for the Quartermaster Corps until he was transferred into the Special Services Division. His new job involved work as actor, designer, performer and dance 'director' in productions ranging from a Christmas Nativity pageant to the revue *Mexilinda* which included *Spanish Dance* and *Western Dances*, comprised of theatricalised square dances. His debut was announced in the local newspaper (Dancer Makes Debut Saturday 1943), dancing with Diane Roberts who trained with Ted Shawn and Hanya Holm prior to becoming a WAC (Women's Army Corps) private.

The formation of the Camp Lee Concert Dance Group offered opportunities to develop group choreography, first seen in *Fun for the Birds*, a soldier show benefit for the War Bond Campaign in Richmond on September 5, 1943. Entrance was by purchase of $25 or $50 war bonds or one dollar 'war stamps' which bought balcony 'rush' seats. Local press notices reinforce the extent of racial segregation at the time. Tickets for the 'Negro' section could be bought at the Booker T. Theatre instead of the bond counters of two prominent department stores (Lindeman 1943b).

Fun for the Birds drew on the talents of two hundred military personnel to present humorous evocations of idealised camp life based on 'the dream of two homesick soldiers sleeping in their pup tent on a lonesome bivouac' (Camp Lee Stages Bond Revue 1943). Twenty variety acts poked fun at the day to day existence of life in uniform, with Limón's input just part of a large creative team. Dream sequences enabled the soldiers to subvert strict military hierarchy, with sergeants serving cocktails to privates, and fantasy scenes where movie stars and beautiful girls travelled to the front lines 'to sing and dance for the war weary soldiers' (Lindeman, 1943a). In *What does a Soldier Dream of* Limón danced to his own musical composition to convey the challenges of a new recruit (Jowitt, 2001: xiii).

The exception to the satirical tone is found in Limón's 28 minute dance, *We Speak for Ourselves* (see Figure 5). Set to a poem by playwright Lynn Riggs, whose book *Green Grow the Lilacs* was the basis for the Broadway musical *Oklahoma!*, Riggs drew on his own struggles in being transformed from independent individual to part of a military unit (Lindeman, 1943b). Riggs (1943a: 103) explained that the dance poem was

> conceived by soldiers [...] danced by soldiers, and *for* them [...] and intended to express the permanent complexity and drive of their actual feelings, their dismay, their disturbances, their searing memories, their faith arrived at through dark boredom and fire, through questioning and anguish.

Published in its entirety in *Theatre Arts* in December, 1943, Riggs' (1943b) words reflect on the difficulties in conforming to the discipline, lack of solitude and loss of individuality of the new recruits and draftees. The first section questions 'What am I doing here? Why? Why? I wonder if you ask that too'. A dance section followed, comprised of Limón as a soloist and a twelve-man corps, the movement 'based on close order drill, fatigue detail, police-up and so forth'. The poem focused on what was left behind: 'Remembering the street in my home town – my house there was two stories high, there was a maple tree and grass and kids playing hop-scotch, and an old dog named Flip that didn't belong to anyone [...]'. Memories of parents, a girlfriend, and church on Sundays fill out the imaginary scene with the narrator questioning the intrusion of the memories. A duet interlude followed, danced by Limón and Diane Roberts. In the third section, the reason for fighting was found in 'little unimportant things. [...] Those are the things I have lived for – that all of us have lived for – Not just the large great words: Peace and liberty and freedom...'. The archetypal American community is evoked in the words, with the narrator urging the audience to do their best, 'less than that is less than a man – *And we are men*'.

The final dance sequence by Limón and the corps was 'Challenge and affirmation', performed in 'fatigue and battle dress, with movements of attack and the forward surge of battle' (ibid.: 757). A US Army Signal Corps rehearsal photograph shows Limón in a fatigues uniform at the height of a powerful jump, one leg pulled up underneath him, his helmet partly obscuring his face. Eight bare-chested soldiers sit in a semi-circle on the ground behind him, their rifles hoisted above their heads. Another outdoor rehearsal photograph was featured on the cover of the July 1945 issue of *Dance Magazine*, with Limón in the foreground, one hand supporting him in a full body lift from the ground, holding aloft a rifle in his free hand. He is flanked by three soldiers, bare-chested but wearing helmets like Limón, who also raise their rifles and gazes skyward, echoing the powerful lines created by Limón.

On the surface, Riggs' poem shares some thematic elements with Archibald's vocal accompaniment for *War Lyrics* in reflecting on a life left behind and references to military rituals. Yet significant differences emerge in the underlying spirit of the two dances. *War Lyrics* ended with the soldier's death in the arms of the nurse, highlighting the futility of war and hinting at a loss of faith conveyed by the poem:

> But thank no god –
> No living god –
> No supernatural
> mystic god –
> no high
> all mighty
> gracious god –
> that you
> are here
> to
> dig.
> (Archibald cited in Lloyd 1987: 206)

In contrast, *We Speak for Ourselves* reinforced a sense of community, offering reasons for leaving their lives behind. Despite differences in their personal circumstances, the soldiers were drawn together by the American dream – the house in a tree-lined neighbourhood, religious faith, family relationships and romantic love in addition to grander ideals of 'peace, liberty and freedom'. Instead of ending with death and questioning faith, Riggs and Limón end with a rallying cry for unity.

An emphasis on camaraderie is also seen in Limón's choreography for *Deliver the Goods* which ran for three nights in April 1944, celebrating the work of the Quartermaster Corps, described in the show's program notes as the 'world's greatest supply agency' (*Deliver the Goods*, 1944). Extensive publicity photos appeared in the local press and the May 7, 1944 *New York Times Magazine* showed Limón and a group of soldiers in the dance *Machete Eddy*, described as 'a dance built around the flicking wrist motion of the machete' (New Wrinkle in Dance Routines, 1944). In one picture taken from above, in a strong wide-legged stance Limón holds a machete over his head, encircled by a group of kneeling soldiers with machetes in their outstretched arms touching him, like the spokes of a wheel. In another image, grasping a machete in his right hand, Limón is counterbalanced in a lean by two machete-wielding soldiers, their free arms raised and poised to strike, with a third soldier kneeling, all with bare torsos. The need to choreograph and rehearse the soldier shows in off hours, drawing on various levels of technical skill, meant that the group provided a foil for Limón's recognizable style. Writing about *We Speak for Ourselves*, Riggs (1943a: 103) noted Limón's 'familiar power and thrust, his slumberous subterranean flow, his spiritual elevation and warmth' along with his characteristic 'distinction and clarity of movement'.

'Blueprint' Specials: 'By the men ... for the men in the service'

In another type of soldier show, 'Blueprints' of camp shows were distributed to military units, providing stage directions, choreographic outlines, musical scores and costume patterns. A *Theatre Arts* article emphasised the multiple benefits gleaned from the production and performance activities: 'The very speed and violence of training, the very intensity of fighting in modern war demands its compensatory moments of release and relaxation', noting that 'It is no easy matter to make a fighting army out of some five to six million rampant individualists...' (The Theatre and the Armed Forces 1943: 149).

Limón helped create the musical comedy *Hi Yank!* utilising gender stereotypes, drag roles and popular cultural and ethnic tropes such as basketball players, ballerinas and Latin Copacabana dancers in the dance sections. Detailed dance plans, production directions and Alex North's musical score were circulated to Special Services units to facilitate the show's independent staging. The central character is Sad Sack, the gangly and inept cartoon soldier with a big nose, who constantly comes up against his superiors and is teased by his colleagues. In the 'Sports Section' Sad Sack is able to transcend his uncoordinated body – after futile attempts to throw a basketball through the hoop, a danced dream sequence transforms him. With the aid of five men dressed as ballerinas, his mood is transformed from 'sad and dejected' to 'light and gay' (*Hi Yank!* 1944: 12). Sad Sack provides a popular caricature engaged in mundane activities, attempting to come to terms with life in the military as were the musical's performers and viewers.

The second dance sequence in the 'Report from the Caribbean' section draws on Latin stereotypes, starring Ricardo and Conchita (based on Carmen Miranda) in a Rumba-Conga-Samba routine. A detailed floor plan guides the twenty-four dancers who surround the pair as they perform lifts and turns. Although it is left to individual dance directors to set the final movement details, the number of musical bars are provided, indicating how long to allow in moving from one pattern to another. The dance sequence lasts for 128 bars, building in intensity throughout to a final climax. While Susan Manning and Alan Bérubé examine the subversive potential of the drag element of army shows as an outlet for celebration of gay identities,[6] aspects of *Hi Yank!* also perpetuate a range of stereotypes and myths of the 'American Way of Life' and celebration of Latino vernacular dances.

Multiple symbolic layers loom large in Limón's works – the assertion of communities, the camaraderie of the creative act and the celebration of Hispanic identity. As numerous scholars such as Deborah Jowitt (2001: xvii) have noted, 'Mexico shaped Limón as a man and an artist, yet most of his choreography on Mexican themes turned on conflict and revealed a powerful ambivalence'. *Danza de la Muerte* (Dance of the Dead) was created in response to the Spanish Civil War. Revolution and death was a part of Limón's background, when his family home was caught in the crossfire during violent conflict between the Mexican government and rebel forces, killing an uncle. *Danzas Mexicanas* evoked historical tensions between

6   See Susan Manning 2004: 123, also see Chapter 3, 'GI Drag, A Gay Refuge', Allan Bérubé 1990: 67–97.

indigenous Indians and their Spanish conquerors: *Indio, Conquistador, Peon, Caballero* and *Revolucionario*. In his unfinished memoirs, Limón (2001: 8) wrote of being 'an exile in a strange country' when he moved to Los Angeles at the age of seven. He explained:

> ... for the rest of my life I was to be a translator and a conciliator. It would be my task to translate, perpetually, within myself, the tongue of Castile into that of the Anglo-Saxons, to reconcile many disparate and contradictory cultural habits and ways of living, and to resolve hostilities within and around me.

The act of translation can be seen in *Spanish Dance*, another Camp Lee Concert Dance Group production, in which the passionate yet formal style of Spanish dances is depicted in 'the struggle of two cavaliers for the favors of a lady' (ibid.: 137). The ambivalence seen in Limón's earlier works on Mexican themes is gone, replaced by a celebration of his heritage. Hispanic elements in his wartime choreography offer up a pan-ethnic Americanism, alongside choreography which communicated the grand narratives and myths of American identity. These are clearly grounded in the references to the American dream in *We Speak for Ourselves*, and the patriotic response to threats against the nation's ideological foundations of liberty and freedom. The expression of a patriotic spirit was temporary, however, as evidenced by the rest of his choreographic legacy. A convergence occurred during World War II, where the celebration of diversity coincided with expressions of support for the battle, distinct from a 'populist rhetoric of the right' dominated by a white America which felt itself under threat from foreigners and blacks (Denning 1997: 127). Denning sets out the parameters of a US nationalism that encompasses diversity and the working class, in which those who shaped the cultural front that arose out of the 1930s ideological debates did not shy away from interrogating questions of national identity and their relationship to it, embracing specifically the 'promise of the Lincoln republic' and its classless ideals (Denning 1997: 130–131).

Conclusion

The work of the Dudley-Maslow-Bales Trio and José Limón during World War II resonates with the argument for dance to be taken seriously not just as an art form but as an integral part of contemporary culture, including the war effort. The young modern dancer-choreographers matured artistically during the war years, moving away from representations of the proletariat as downtrodden, celebrating instead a spirit of survival and the power of people linked by a sense of community that transcended ethnic boundaries. There were some continuities in dance themes, but the treatment changed as more popular and accessible perspectives were adopted, causing concern that modern dance had reached a crisis point in 1944. As Gay Morris examines in *A Game for Dancers* (2006), some *Dance Observer* critics warned that the aesthetic goals of early modern dance had been replaced by commercial ones. The dances discussed here appear to have achieved a balance between reaching out to a wider audience and being inspired by socially aware issues. Choreographers turned away from the overt aims of the previous decade, no longer seeing their art form as a means to stimulate a specific social consciousness but rather to share visions of struggle and belief in the moral imperative to stop the spread of fascism. In limiting such expressions of patriotism to calls for unity in the battle against fascism, ideological continuity was retained with works created at the height of the left-wing movement during the 1930s. Dudley, Maslow, Bales and Limón continued to choreograph works that maintained fundamental links between a committed social consciousness and artistry.

Works Cited

Anderson, B. 1983. *Imagined Communities: Reflections on the Origin and Spread of Nationalism*. London: Verso.

Beiswanger, G. M. 1944. Reviews of the Month: Dudley-Maslow-Bales Trio. *Dance Observer* 11/1: 3, 9.

Bernstein, W. 1944. Report on *Hi Yank!* and other Soldier Shows. *Theatre Arts* 28/11: 654–660.

Bérubé, A. 1990. *Coming Out Under Fire: The History of Gay Men and Women in World War II.* New York: The Free Press.

Camp Lee Stages Bond Revue Tonight. 1943. *Richmond Times Dispatch*, 5 September. Limón Scrapbook, 1937–1945, New York Public Library for the Performing Arts Dance Division (NYPL-DD).

Caroll, P. N., Nash, M.& Small, M, eds. 2006. *The Good Fight Continues: World War II Letters from the Abraham Lincoln Brigade.* New York: New York University Press.

A Dancer-Soldier Speaks. 1943. *Dance Magazine*, February: 16.

Dancers' War Fund. 1942. *Dance Observer* 9/4: 59.

Dancer Makes Debut Saturday. 1943. 25 August. Limón Scrapbook, 1937–1945, NYPL-DD.

Deliver the Goods program, Limón Scrapbook, 1937–1945, NYPL-DD.

Denby, E. 1943. The Modern Dance: Dudley-Maslow-Bales. *Herald Tribune*, 5 December: IV. Clippings file, Dudley-Maslow-Bales Trio, NYPL-DD.

Denning, M. 1997. *The Cultural Front: The Laboring of American Culture in the Twentieth Century.* London and New York: Verso.

Downes, O. 1942. The Need of Great War Songs. *New York Times*, 23 August: X5.

Fender, S. 1993. The American Difference, in *Modern American Culture: An Introduction.* Edited by Mick Gidley. London: Longman Group, 1–22.

Foulkes, J. L. 2002. *Modern Bodies: Dance and American Modernism from Martha Graham to Alvin Ailey.* Chapel Hill, NC: University of North Carolina Press.

Franko, M. 2002. *The Work of Dance: Labor, Movement, and Identity in the 1930s.* Middletown, CT: Wesleyan University Press.

Geduld, V. L. 2008. Performing Communism in the American Dance: Culture, Politics and the New Dance Group. *American Communist History* 7/1: 39–65.

Gadd, M. 1942. Recreational Dancing and the U.S.O. *Dance Observer* 9/9: 118–119.

Gadd, M. 1943. Country Dancing with the Services. *Dance Observer* 10/8: 89–90.

Garafola, L., ed. 1994. Of, By and For the People: Dancing on the Left in the 1930s. *Studies in Dance History*, Vol. 1.

Genné, B. 2001. 'Freedom Incarnate': Jerome Robbins, Gene Kelly, and the Dancing Sailor As An Icon Of American Values In World War II. *Dance Chronicle* 24/1: 83–103.

Graff, E. 1997. *Stepping Left: Dance and Politics in New York City, 1928–1942.* Durham, NC: Duke University Press.

Green, A. 1943. The Dance in the Defense Program. *Dance Magazine*, January: 6–7.

Guthrie, W. 1943. People Dancing. *Dance Observer* 10/10: 114–115.

Hering, D. 1946. Dudley-Maslow-Bales. *Dance Magazine*, May: 17.

Hi Yank! Blueprint Special No. 2. c. 1944. US Army Service Forces, Special Services Division, Headquarters, Army Service Forces, Washington: 12.

Jowitt, D. 2001. Introduction, in *José Limón: An Unfinished Memoir*. Edited by Lynn Garafola. Hanover and London: Wesleyan University Press.

Kline, H. 1985. Afterword, in *New Theatre and Film 1934–1937*. Edited by Herbert Kline. New York: Harcourt Brace Janovovich: 363–367.

Lieberman, R. 1995. '*My Song Is My Weapon': People's Songs, American Communism and the Politics of Culture, 1930–1950*. Urbana and Chicago: University of Illinois Press.

Limón, J. 2001. *José Limón: Unfinished Memoirs*. Edited by Lynn Garafola. Hanover and London: Wesleyan University Press.

Lindeman, E. 1943a. Camp Lee's *Fun for the Birds* Usher in War Bond Campaign. *Richmond Times Dispatch*, 31 August. Limón Scrapbook, 1937–1945, NYPL DD.

Lindeman, E. 1943b. Author of Soldier-Produced Dance Poem Visits Richmond. *Richmond Times Dispatch*, 4 September. Limón Scrapbook, 1937–1945, NYPL DD.

Lloyd, M. 1946a. This Changing Modern Dance, Part I. *The Christian Science Monitor*, 19 January, Jane Dudley Clippings File, NYPL DD.

Lloyd, M. 1946b. This Changing Modern Dance, Part II. *The Christian Science Monitor*. 2 February, Jane Dudley Clippings File, NYPL DD.

Lloyd, M. 1987. *Borzoi Book of Modern Dance*. New York: Dance Horizons, orig. pub. 1949.

Lynn, B. 1944. To the Editor, March 30, 1944. *Dance Observer* 11/6: 75.

Manning, S. 2004. *Modern Dance, Negro Dance: Race in Motion*. Minneapolis: University of Minnesota Press.

Marsh, L. 1944. Men in Uniform Dominate the Dance. *Dance Magazine*, July: 5.

Martin, J. 1942. The Dance: Americana. *New York Times*, 9 December: X5.

Martin, J. 1943. Choreographing Bach. *New York Times*, 14 February: X8.

Morris, G. 2006. *A Game for Dancers: Performing Modernism in the Postwar Years, 1945–1960*. Middletown, CT: Wesleyan University Press.

New Wrinkle in Dance Routines to be Feature of 'Deliver Goods', *Lee Traveller*, 19 April 1944, Limón Scrapbook, 1937–1945, NYPL DD.

Prickett, S. 1989. From Workers' Dance to New Dance. *Dance Research* 7/1: 47–64.

Prickett, S. 1990. Dance and the Workers' Struggle. *Dance Research* 8/1: 47–61.

Radir, R. 1942. Moving Backwards. *Dance Observer*, February: 20–21.

Riggs, L. 1943a. A Note on 'We Speak for Ourselves'. *Dance Observer*, November: 103.

Riggs, L. 1943b. 'We Speak for Ourselves', A Dance Poem. *Theatre Arts* 27/12: 755–757.

Sabin, R. 1942. Reviews of the Month: Jane Dudley, Sophie Maslow, William Bales. *Dance Observer* 9/4: 47, 50.

Schwezoff, I. 1943. A Dancer-Soldier Speaks. *Dance Magazine*, February: 16.

Susman, W. I. 2003. *Culture as History: The Transformation of American Society in the Twentieth Century*. New York: Smithsonian Books, orig. pub. 1973.

The Theatre and the Armed Forces. 1943. *Theatre Arts* 27/3: 149.

Zinn, H. 2003. *A People's History of the United States 1492-Present*. Third edition. London: Pearson.

Figure 4 Jane Dudley (standing), Sophie Maslow and William Bales in
As poor Richard says – a Colonial charade (1945). Photograph: Valente,
Courtesy of the New Dance Group Collection, Music Division, Library of Congress.

Figure 5 José Limón rehearsing *We Speak for Ourselves* (1943), Camp Lee, Virginia. Photograph: US Army Signal Corps. Courtesy of Jerome Robbins Dance Division, The New York Public Library for the Performing Arts, Astor, Lenox and Tilden Foundation.

Figure 6   Pape Ibrahima N'Diaye (Kaolack) in *Fagaala* (2004)
by Germaine Acogny and Kota Yamazaki, JANT-BI Company.
Photograph: Thomas Dorn. Courtesy of JANT-BI.

PART III

Dancers, Rights and Wrongs

NAOMI M. JACKSON

8 Dance and Human Rights

> No dance can have exclusive rights. Human rights begin with tolerance.
> Tolerance in the dance world begins in dance schools, performance groups,
> and on the tiniest stage. Dance can flourish in any society, whether demo-
> cratic or dictatorial; human rights cannot. Dancers, choreographers,
> performers – they too are responsible for making a society that accepts
> the ideals of 'freedom, justice, and peace' and takes responsibility, moral
> and political responsibility, for the ideas that their dances promote.
>
> — MARION KANT 2008: 18

Introduction

Throughout history, and across the globe, dance has been engaged to promote strict adherence to repressive ideologies, incite violence and celebrate
the spoils of war.[1] Dance has also been a powerful vehicle for revealing,
resisting and rectifying differing forms of abuse and injustice, whether
through intentionally choreographed work, therapeutic forms, or as part
of broader social movements that engage in wider struggles for justice and
peace. As a profession and as an amateur activity, dancing has frequently
been regulated through laws, bans and other means, and individual dancers have been humiliated, detained, imprisoned, tortured and sometimes
killed because what they symbolized and did mattered. Within the dance

---

1   I would like to acknowledge the extensive efforts of Toni Shapiro-Phim in formulating
     some of the ideas expressed in this text, as drawn from the introduction of our co-
     edited volume *Dance, Human Rights, and Social Justice* (Scarecrow Press, 2008).

field, dancers have often been bullied, embarrassed and treated as unfeeling tools by choreographers. Dancers have also united to demand greater respect, establish standards of treatment and promote harmony and fairness in the workplace.

The extent of the convergence of dance and human rights is breathtaking, even if at first glance obscure. As this article aims to demonstrate, there are multiple ways that the two subjects relate, often in examples that are heart wrenching in their pathos, or rousing in their ecstasy of achievement: a gun is trained at a colored man as he is ordered to dance before a lynching; a torture victim is finally able to regain fully a sense of well-being after months of careful work with a movement therapist. Dance appears at the center of experiences of humiliation and oppression, as well as during times of extreme compassion and emancipation.

This article provides an introduction to the notion of human rights and its connections to dance. It achieves this by first examining the nature of human rights, and considering how concerns about dance and dancers relate to the Universal Declaration of Human Rights and related documents, followed by an overview of three broadly conceived ways that dance intersects with human rights:

1) Regulation and/or exploitation of dance activity and dancers by governments and other groups with authority,
2) Participation in dance as a means of empowering and healing victims of trauma, societal exclusion, and human rights abuses, and
3) Broad-scale social/political movements in which dance plays a powerful role in providing people with agency in fighting oppression.[2]

What most clearly stands out in the following discussion is that, as Eleanor Roosevelt so aptly reflects, human rights begin 'in small places, close to home – so close and so small that they cannot be seen on any maps of the world' (1958). The abuse or promotion of human rights occurs everyday

2   These categories are drawn from the introduction to *Dance, Human Rights, and Social Justice: Dignity in Motion* (Jackson and Shapiro-Phim 2008: xxii).

in our 'dance schools, performance groups, and on the tiniest stage' (Kant, 2008: 18). It is not easily achieved, and requires vigilance, negotiation, and patience. It is this realization that is our starting point, and provides the frame for the following analysis. No matter how far afield we travel in this essay, and how extreme the cases of human rights abuses we examine, there are always examples 'close to home' that should demand our immediate attention and motivate our action.[3] The reader is encouraged to locate those examples and reflect on them in light of the material presented.

The Nature of Human Rights

Recognition of the inherent dignity and of the equal and inalienable rights of all members of the human family is the foundation of freedom, justice and peace in the world... (Universal Declaration of Human Rights 1948)

The idea that people have inherent, inalienable rights solely because they are human is part of a deontological tradition of ethics which holds that moral worth is an intrinsic feature of human actions, shaped by necessity, duty or obligation. Rather than assessing worthiness or goodness in relation to other factors (such as the consequences of actions, or the virtuousness of someone's character, for instance), those who are strong believers in human rights tend to assert that human beings are due certain fundamental rights regardless of their specific situations, outcomes of their behavior, or personalities. They are human beings, so they are due certain rights – most usually recognized as rights that both protect people from interference so that they may flourish (known as 'negative rights'), as well as 'positive rights' that actively provide individuals with those goods and services that

---

3   This is especially true, as Robin Lakes has observed, for a Western dance tradition in which many artists 'conduct their classes and rehearsals as demagogues' (2008: 109).

promote the highest quality of life.[4] It is the passionate belief of human rights advocates that protecting and implementing human rights is the 'foundation of freedom, justice and peace in the world'.

While there is debate as to the origins of the notion of human rights, the Western tradition traces them to ethical and philosophical ideas evolved by the Greeks, and in the Torah and New Testament (Ishay 2004). In terms of modern thought, which most influences current practice, the concept has existed under several names since the thirteenth century and the time of the Magna Carta, which enumerated a number of what later came to be thought of as human rights. These included the right of the church to be free from governmental interference, the rights of all free citizens to own and inherit property, and principles of due process and equality before the law.

In the eighteenth and nineteenth centuries, in particular, several European philosophers, the most influential of whom was John Locke, proposed the concept of 'natural rights'. Such rights belonged to a person by nature and because he was a human being endowed with reason (and by implication knew right from wrong), not by virtue of his citizenship of a particular country or membership in a particular religious or ethnic group. Locke formulated the classic trinity of these natural rights as life, liberty, and property.[5]

While the idea of 'natural rights' became increasingly challenged along philosophical lines that threw into doubt the underlying assumptions regarding natural law, the first humanitarian organizations took hold in the 1800s and they kept the basic notion alive. These organizations grew up in relation to a number of important social movements that strove to address certain fundamental inequalities between people. These included

4   Examples of negative rights include: freedom from violent crime, slavery, and torture. Examples of positive rights include the right to food, healthcare, education and access to the arts.

5   In the late 1700s two revolutions occurred which drew heavily on this concept: in 1776 the American Revolution, which led to the formation of the United States' Declaration of Independence, and in 1789 the French Revolution, which culminated in the Declaration of the Rights of Man and of the Citizen.

the abolitionist movement, the women's suffrage movement, and the labor movement, which addressed issues such as brutal working conditions, starvation wages, and child labor.

Nevertheless, it was not until the horrors of World War II and the Holocaust that the notion of 'universal human rights' was asserted within an international political arena with the approval of the Universal Declaration of Human Rights in 1948. This document asserted for the first time that human rights crossed borders and transcended individual state sovereignty. In thirty succinct articles it laid out a complete set of civil, political, economic, social, and cultural rights. Since that time there have been six international human rights treaties that have elaborated the various aspects of the initial declaration in more detail.[6]

Today there are many nations, institutions, and individuals committed to human rights, yet there are also significant problems in their implementation let alone consensus over the best approach to achieve them. Challenges are rooted in fundamental disagreements over the universal existence of human rights, over their precise definition, and/or the means to their successful achievement. Such disagreements may be between countries with differing traditions and views, or between organizations and people of conflicting outlooks. Such debates are important to recognize and value, for they indicate that there are no easy answers in the realm of human rights. While this article takes as its premise the importance of human rights in creating a world that offers individuals and communities circumstances within which to thrive, it also presents the view that detailed, context-sensitive interpretations and analyses of specific peoples and their situations and practices will yield the clearest insights into people's struggles to realize their individual and collective dignity, justice, and peace, whether it be through more time-honored or innovative means.

6   These are: the Covenant on Civil and Political Rights; the Covenant on Economic, Social and Cultural Rights; the Convention on the Rights of the Child; the Convention on the Elimination of All Forms of Discrimination against Women; the Convention on the Elimination of All Forms of Racial Discrimination; and the Convention against Torture and Other Cruel, Inhuman or Degrading Treatment or Punishment.

Dance and Human Rights: Tracing Connections to the Universal Declaration

Everyone has the right freely to participate in the cultural life of the community, to enjoy the arts and to share in scientific advancement and its benefits. (Article 27 (1), Universal Declaration of Human Rights 1948)

One of the first questions one might ponder when thinking about dance and human rights is the basic question: is dance a human right? When looking for an answer in the Universal Declaration of Human Rights, it becomes clear that while there is no specific mention of dance, there are several assertions that resonate strongly with the dance field and provide a framework for starting to think about this and related questions concerning the relationship between dance and human rights.

The first, found in Article 27 (1), stresses that everyone has the right freely to participate in the cultural life of the community and specifically to enjoy the arts. Here, and in later covenants and recommendations crafted under the auspices of the United Nations, is a key recognition of 'cultural rights' as being equally indispensable to human beings as civil and political rights. These cultural rights first and foremost seem to pay recognition to the contributions of different art forms and artists, and the right of all citizens to have access to artists and their creations. The 1980 (UN) Recommendation concerning the Status of the Artist fully develops this notion of the central position played by artists; it is an extremely detailed text that recognizes the 'essential role of art in the life and development of the individual and of society'. It provides recommendations concerning the participation of artists in decisions concerning quality of life, the vocation and training of artists, and the employment, working, and living conditions of artists, including professional and trade union opportunities.

Indeed, the right of artists to practise their art form freely and produce their work without interference is highlighted in Article 27 (2) of the Universal Declaration of Human Rights, which states: 'Everyone has the right to the protection of the moral and material interests resulting from any scientific, literary or artistic production of which he is the author' (1947). Article 15 of the International Covenant on Economic, Social and Cultural Rights furthers this idea and stresses the need to 'respect the freedom indispensable for [...] creative activity' (1966). The 1980 Recommendation concerning the Status of the Artist also echoes this assertion and states that member states have a duty to 'protect, defend and assist artists and their freedom of creation'.

Considering this initial set of claims, it is possible to begin to articulate an answer to the question of whether dance is a human right. What emerges is the following: it is a human right for dance artists to practice their dance forms, and it is a human right for other members of society to participate in these dance forms. A question arises, however, when dance is engaged in outside of a clearly demarcated 'artistic' framework, or by the general populace in other contexts, such as social, entertainment, or therapeutic settings. Are these other kinds of dance also a human right?[7]

In terms of looking beyond the realm of dance as art to dance more broadly conceived, there is also important direction provided in the human rights literature. Indeed, there are many times that the Universal Declaration and its antecedents strongly recognize the significance of cultural rights in a more expanded sense concerning culture with a small 'c' – as the sum total of the customs, social relations, values and practices of individual members that give a society a unique sense of identity (Jackson 2004: 6). Article 19, for instance, states, 'Everyone has the right to freedom of opinion and expression; this right includes freedom to hold opinions without interference and to seek, receive and impart information and ideas through any media and regardless of frontiers.' Article 22, meanwhile, insists that everyone, as a member of society, is entitled to the 'realization, through national effort and international co-operation and in accordance with the organization and resources of each State, of the [...] cultural rights indispensable for his dignity and the free development of his personality'.

7   Under the United States Constitution, it is worth observing, first amendment protection is afforded to art dance, but not social dancing; exotic dance, meanwhile, is regarded as a special case, also not fully covered by the first amendment, even though it often involves trained professionals performing set choreography (Hanna, 2008).

The right of all human beings to be free to express themselves through different cultural forms is found more fully developed by UNESCO in their 1976 Recommendation on Participation by the People at Large in Cultural Life and Their Contribution to it. Here it is acknowledged 'that culture is not merely an accumulation of works and knowledge which an elite produce,' and that 'culture is, in its very essence, a social phenomenon resulting from individuals joining and co-operating in creative activities'. This document makes it clear that 'participation by the greatest possible number of people and associations in a wide variety of cultural activities of their own free choice is essential to the development of the basic human values and dignity of the individual'.

In this way, then, the Universal Declaration also supports the notion of dance as a human right in the broadest possible sense – as the right of every person in fulfilling their human potential and participating in, and contributing to, their culture. What is critical, however, is the linking of these rights to fundamental notions of dignity and freedom. Article 1 of the Declaration begins, 'All human beings are born free and equal in dignity and rights. They are endowed with reason and conscience and should act towards one another in a spirit of brotherhood', and Article 5 asserts, 'No one shall be subjected to torture or to cruel, inhuman or degrading treatment or punishment.' It is with such claims that the discussion moves us from dance as an art form in the narrowest definition of the term, to dance as a basic form of human bodily expression. For, in its assertions regarding the inherent dignity of the human being, and in forbidding torture and other assaults on the body, the Universal Declaration also provides an important argument regarding individuals' right to control their own bodies, and by extension their right to freedom of movement and dance.

Ultimately, therefore, the right to dance is supported by the Universal Declaration, and is rooted in a fundamental belief that to ensure that human beings are treated with dignity they must be free to move expressively and creatively, and do so without censure in a context that also promotes individual and collective expression, and values including non-discrimination, fairness, compassion, and peace. As we proceed to examine the various ways that dance and human rights have converged over time and place in different parts of the world, this insight will be of particular importance, for it illuminates a claim that has often been ignored, suppressed, and manipulated, as much as it has been promoted, fostered, and celebrated.

Regulatory and Exploitive Moves

Reforming the cabaret laws can seem like this abstract thing, but we're really after
something simple: the right to dance. (Eric Demby of Legalize Dancing NYC,
quoted in Brown 2002)

If the human rights literature points to an understanding of dance as a fundamental human right, historical and global analysis suggests otherwise.
Throughout time, and from so-called first world to third world contexts,
dance has been heavily regulated through laws, bans, public censure, and
other means. It has been viewed as everything from a frivolous waste of time
leading to dissolute behavior, to the blatant work of the devil and something
to be prohibited by any means. At the same time, many of those in power
have also seen dance as something to be manipulated to attain particular
political and ideological ends. The flip side of restraining dance behavior
has been harnessing it to further the agendas of especially repressive regimes.
In this section I consider these dual approaches to dance through several
different examples, and what they further suggest regarding the nature of
dance and its relation to human rights.

The first example of dance being repressed is from the heart of the
Western world. Since 1926 it has been illegal for three or more people to
dance socially – or move in 'synchronized fashion' – in New York city, if the
bar, nightclub, or music hall does not have the appropriate 'cabaret license'
(Springer 2006: 117). These difficult-to-obtain, costly licenses require the
establishment to follow strict codes and be located in an area that is zoned
for dancing, mostly on the outskirts of the city. In many places 'No Dancing Allowed' signs have reigned, and if the NYPD catches people dancing
in an unlicensed club, the business may be fined and padlocked for days or
weeks at a time. This was particularly evident during the mid-1990s through
2001 when then Mayor Rudolph Giuliani created a multi-agency Nightclub
Enforcement Task Force to enforce his 'Quality of Life' campaign.[8] As a

---

8   The 1994 Criminal Justice and Public Order Act that passed in the United Kingdom
    has been used in a similar manner by police to disperse or prohibit unlicensed rave
    parties which involve music and dancing.

result of his efforts various groups have fought to overturn the law, including Legalize Dancing and Metropolis in Motion. However, in 2007, New York's Supreme Court's Appellate Division maintained that social dancing is not a form of expressive communication worthy of first amendment protection, and upheld the city's right to assign cabaret licenses, which the city argued was necessary to protect neighbors from noise, overcrowding, littering, and rowdiness.[9] As of 2009, the law remains on the books, although steps to repeal or 'reduce' it continue to be intimated by the government.

Another example comes from a sector of the Islamic world, where government officials and organs such as the Taliban in Afghanistan, until their defeat in October 2001, and the Islamic Republic of Iran, mount attacks against dance as a public performance activity, as well as a private social pursuit that happens behind closed doors (Shay 2008: 68). Official and quasi-official goon squads, known as the *pasdaran* and *basij*, patrol the streets listening for the sounds of dance music, native or Western, not hesitating to break into people's homes to physically assault and arrest people whom they find dancing. Stage or professional dancers who try to work are often arrested, detained, and tried, with fines and prison sentences as a result. In the celebrated case of Iranian-American dancer Mohammad Khordadian, he was formally charged with corrupting the morals of youth. Most often, the concern is that dance is 'frivolous' and sinful because it will unleash dangerous sexual emotions and longings. Although there are signs of small rebellious acts occurring throughout Iran, an underlying fear of dance – or 'choreophobia' as it is aptly referred to by scholar Anthony Shay (1999) – remains strongly in place.

Finally, a historical example references how dance has often been severely limited and frequently obliterated in contexts of colonialism. In the late nineteenth century, dancing among Aboriginal peoples in the North West Territories of colonial British Canada was banned as part of a colonial project to assimilate indigenous culture, replacing it with European customs and values (Glass 2004; Doolittle and Flynn, n.d.). These

---

9   See the actual ruling at the Supreme Court of the State of New York – New York County website: <http://decisions.courts.state.ny.us/fcas/FCAS_docs/2006APR/ 30010872420051SCIV.PDF>.

bans were enacted through amendments to the Indian Act of 1876. In 1884, an amendment expressly forbade the cultural practice known as potlatching, a gift-giving ceremony that included dancing. In 1894 the prohibition was extended to dances of the Plains Indians. Again in 1913, the act was amended to prohibit any dancing outside native reserves. These laws proved extremely difficult to enforce, but still many dancers were imprisoned or forced to perform hard labor. Drawing from simultaneous 'antidance' sentiments characteristic of Christian Europe, government officials and clergy attacked native dances because they symbolized laziness, savagery, paganism, and debauchery (Aldrich 2008: 29). As scholars Lisa Doolittle and Anne Flynn observe, 'aboriginal dance obscured the desired image of Canada as an empty but bountiful capitalistic haven and projected the undesirable image of a raw primitive land full of gesticulating savages. In the colonial project of turning aboriginals into "Canadians" dancing had to stop' (Flynn and Doolittle, n.d.).[10]

The above examples illuminate related ways in which dance has been viewed as an evil necessary to contain, and in some cases eliminate from human society. The examples cross over social dancing, dance created for the stage, and dance performed as part of a people's cultural identity closely connected to daily life. While existing on a continuum of intensity, the reasons given for dance's need for restriction lie in its perceived triviality, lasciviousness, and contribution to wanton human behavior. Indeed, the argument seems to be that it makes people less enlightened and civilized; in some ways, less 'human' than the societal ideal – which is indeed a serious charge, especially for those who wish to champion dance as a fundamental and significant right. However, what can also be argued is that the reason that dance has come under such serious and sustained attack is that it is recognized as such a potent medium by those in power. Rather than being in itself evil, it is characterized as such to further specific ideological agendas.

10   Each of these examples clearly exists against the backdrop of different cultural contexts and varied human rights records. While many argue that Taliban rule, for instance, is highly repressive, American culture is seen as highly protective of individuals' rights. This likely explains why the example of the 'cabaret laws' seems so surprising; what is most significant, however, is the widescale regulation and repression of dancing across a broad spectrum of societies, both present and past.

Consider why it is that in Iran, for instance, even though most forms
of dance are banned, regional folk dances are promoted. Since the death of
Ayatollah Khomeini in 1989, men have been permitted to dance regional
folk dances in front of all male audiences. The government has even encouraged the video recording of these dances referred to as *raqs-ha-ye mahalli-ye
Iran*. Anthony Shay observes that this is because of the performers' ability
to legitimize the new Islamic regime through the patriotic messages of the
music, and their emphasis on athletic prowess and displays of masculine
strength – both symbolic of desirable qualities associated with the state
(Shay 2008: 77). Similarly, in many other parts of the world, and throughout history, dance has been engaged as a propaganda tool to solidify state
legitimacy. When viewed in this way, it is possible to recognize just how
extensively dance has been embraced by leaders in their quest for power
as much as it has been denounced. Looking at a couple of such examples
provides an alternative perspective on how dance has been perceived in
relation to human rights.

The first example comes from Nazi Germany and relates to the use
of dance to inculcate children and teens in Nazi ideology. By 1940 membership of the Hitler Youth became mandatory for boys, with girls joining such organizations as the *Bund Deutscher Mädel* (League of German
Girls). As part of these groups the youth would sing songs devoted to the
Führer, go on hikes in the country, and perform folk dances. They would
also sometimes participate in the mass rallies that celebrated the new Reich
as well as other spectacles related to the regime. Mary Wigman, an early
Nazi collaborator, contributed to one such mass dance for the opening of
the Olympic Games in Berlin in 1936. Collaborating with other famous
stage dancers Gret Palucca, Harald Kreutzberg and Dorothee Günther,
Wigman choreographed a scene of *Olympische Jugend* (*Olympic Youth*),
which as a whole involved more than ten thousand performers. Susan
Manning observes that this work 'epitomized the fusion – and confusion
– of nationalism and internationalism', and 'fulfilled Goebbels's ideal of
"invisible propaganda," staging the body politic of the Third Reich' (Manning 1993: 195).

Another chilling instance of the use of dance as state propaganda comes
from Africa. *Animation politique* was a nationally observed, compulsory
activity in Zaire during President Mobutu Sese Seko's rule (1965–1997),

one of the core objectives of which was to inculcate citizens with notions of Zairian national identity through daily activities involving dancing, singing and chanting of praises to Mobutu, his family, his ancestral village, or some aspect of his political agenda. The dances drew heavily on gesture and pantomime, and appropriated aspects of traditional dances. They were also accompanied by lyrics that blatantly praised the new regime.[11] These dances were enacted in schools, offices, stadiums, street corners, and by everyday citizens as well as officially trained performers known as *animateurs* and *animatrices*. A presidential company, Ballet Kaké, traveled with Mobutu and presented professional versions of the dances. In this way, *animation* was a tool used to 'develop and to educate people in the ideology of the new state, a means of mass and rapid political enculturation' (Huckstep 2008: 52).

These examples illustrate how dance can be highly effective in campaigns of ideological indoctrination and the galvanizing of group feeling in favor of a particular individual or community. This has been true both of dance performed as part of everyday life by regular citizens, and of highly choreographed works developed by renowned artists and performed by professionals. The key in these cases, and the countless others they stand for, seems to be that dance is viewed as a wholesome, exuberant activity that people fundamentally enjoy and that humans dance to express themselves, especially in relation to a broader community. Dictators and other aggressors consequently turn to dance as a persuasive means of recalling and forging group loyalty.[12] Indeed, there seems to be nothing so binding

---

11   One person recalls that every morning when he was in elementary school, the first fifteen minutes were dedicated to dancing and shouting the name of the president. 'We had to recite one party, one country, one father, Mobutu, Mobutu... It was ridiculous. You knew it but you could not do anything about it. Not to sing and dance was to commit suicide. You just went along with it' (French 1997).

12   The recognition that dance is a primary medium through which to express joy of life is likely why so many use it as a form of humiliation. There are countless instances involving people being forced to dance while they are simultaneously shamed, harassed, beaten, tortured, or murdered. Human Rights Watch is an excellent source for such examples. For a few examples see: 'Rebel Abuses Near Sierra Leone Capital' <http://www.hrw.org/press/2000/02/sl0303.htm>; 'Russian Federation; Serious Violations of Women's Human Rights in Chechnya', Human Rights Watch report,

as a simple communal dance, infused with folk, nationalistic, or ritualistic rhetoric, which can unite a person with those around him/her. This is the power of dance in action.

What we have seen in this section, then, is that dance is sometimes perceived as something to be banned and at other times an activity to be exploited. Rather than being viewed as a universal human right to be protected and fostered, dance is frequently carefully manipulated – either limited, or promoted – by those wielding authority. But what does this imply in terms of the nature of dance? What is this power wielded by dance, and what does it really mean regarding how dance relates to human rights concerns?

A Moment of Suspension: The Right to Dance?

In the opening quote by Marion Kant, it is asserted that 'dance can flourish in any society, whether democratic or dictatorial; human rights cannot.' Why is this statement significant? The answer lies partly in the above discussion. Dance, it seems, is a potent medium that can easily and effectively be utilized by nefarious regimes to further their abuse of human rights. While dance and dancers can certainly be themselves the targets of these regimes' restrictions, dance can equally play a role in oppressive regimes' strangling of individuals' rights. During the Nazi period, and Mobutu's reign, there were, for instance, rampant mistreatments of human beings, including arbitrary arrest, torture, mass murder, and genocide. Dance and some individual dancers greatly helped to solidify the ideology that supported this behavior, and created the enthusiasm that surrounded its implementation.

(January 2002), <http://www.hrw.org/backgrounder/eca/chechnya_women.htm>; Guantánamo – Torture and Other Ill-Treatment <http://web.amnesty.org/library/Index/ENGAMR511892006?open&of=ENG-2M4>.

In the human rights literature it is emphasized that for cultural rights to be regarded as valid rights, they must be engaged in through 'free choice'. People, in other words, must freely choose to dance in order for dance to be seen as a right that is appropriately being nurtured by society. So, one might argue, in those cases where people are forced to dance, it is not so much a case of dance being at fault as an example of dance not being truly recognized and protected as a fundamental human right. The Nazis, in coercing youth to participate in folk dancing, were trampling on their cultural rights – but the right to dance remains, and should remain, in place as a human right.

But is this argument really sustainable? While it is certainly true that in certain instances people are made to dance against their will in oppressive contexts, it is also frequently the case that individuals willingly take part in these same occasions. For many, dancing as part of nationalistic causes provides a sense of great pride and opportunity for celebration of group identity. The extent to which this is the case can be seen in the long history of dance being the medium of choice for expressing joy after a successful battle – when people celebrate conquering a foe by dancing.[13] Consider, for instance, the pyrrhic dance of the ancient Greeks (Kyle 2007), the victory or scalp dance of the Plains Indians (Goodrich 2002), or the Ohafia war dance of Nigeria (McCall 2000). The ubiquity of dancing as a symbol of superiority is also suggested by the massive popularity of folk and national dance and music in oppressive contexts lacking a systematic and central-ized use of these elements as government propaganda. For instance, during Serbia's aggression in Bosnia and Croatia in the 1990s, 'turbo folk' – with its sadistic, aggressive, and pornographic iconography – became extremely popular (Kronja 2001). People were not necessarily coerced into embrac-ing this music/dance/lifestyle – they willingly chose it.

What this suggests, then, is that there is nothing inherently virtuous about dance that makes it a human right. Rather, dance has certain quali-ties that need to be recognized before fully understanding what it means

---

13 A recent study suggests performative displays of victory are innate to all primates. (See: Tracy & Matsumoto 2008: 11655–11660).

for it to be considered a basic human entitlement. These qualities consist of the following: dance holds the power to create a sense of community and shared perspective, displays sensuality and sexuality, embodies memories in a tangible medium, sustains and communicates cultural values that are held dear to a group, and expresses deeply felt emotions including the agony of loss and the exuberance of life and/or transcendence of spirit. Given these characteristics, it is critical to realize the multi-layered power of dance, and how that force can be used to uphold the dignity of all individuals and their complete set of civil, political, economic, and cultural rights, or to assist in destroying those rights. Dance, in other words, is not necessarily and inherently related to ideals such as dignity, equality, justice, and peace. The connection must be made by those who engage with it (dancers, teachers, choreographers, producers, critics, etc.) in order for dance to earn its place as a human right.

Returning to Marion Kant's statement that dance can flourish in any society while human rights cannot, it is possible to see the profundity of this assertion. Human rights, at their core, are about recognizing, valuing, fostering and protecting the inherent dignity of *all* human beings equally – not just a select few. It is only when the thread is interwoven between dance, dignity, equality, justice, and peace, as articulated in the Universal Declaration, that dance might truly be said to function as a human right. And it is only when individuals, groups, and governments recognize, value, foster, and protect dance in the context of this broader awareness, that dance can and should be celebrated as an important contributor to the discourse of human rights. Otherwise, one is justified in questioning the right to dance as an unqualified, universal dictum.

The rest of the article considers approaches that foster this perspective, first looking at those instances where access to, and use of, dance by particular individuals empower and heal the participants, and then considering broader-scale social/political movements in which dance plays a privileged role in providing people with agency in fighting oppression. In these cases, the various claims of the Universal Declaration finally come to life, as moves are made to promote participation in the arts and culture as an expression of human dignity, as opposed to its opposite.

Access, Healing and Empowerment

> Community dance artists share a set of ideals that emphasize collaboration, diversity, and participation – all essential to a society that truly values democracy, and fundamental human rights. (Fitzgerald 2008: 258)

It is inspiring and heartwarming to learn of the vast number of people worldwide engaged in the emancipatory and healing nature of dance especially as related to advocating cultural rights – providing access to the arts within a community, and promoting participatory and restorative justice, opportunities for social participation, recognition of dignity, well-being and citizenship. For these individuals, who see these efforts as indispensable for human dignity and the development of a complete personality, the articles of the Universal Declaration and its antecedent covenants and recommendations resonate strongly.[14] Overviews of activity offer convincing evidence that whether the forms are traditional in nature or more avant-garde, indigenous or Western, within the context of a therapy session or part of a theatrical performance, participation in dancing within a nurturing context can and does provide people with the means to live more fully and self-reliantly, as productive members of a society.

Many efforts in this arena are heavily influenced by sacred or ritually based performance traditions, dance or movement therapy, and the community arts movement. Within the United States, the pioneering efforts of individuals such as Katherine Dunham, Marian Chace and Anna Halprin, to name just a few, have played a vital role in drawing on dance to heal and empower individuals and communities. However, it is clear that

---

14   It is important to recognize that while accounts of fundamental human rights generally include democracy, democracy does not necessarily entail fundamental human rights. The connection is often problematic when the electing majority enforce their views on a minority or individual as is, and has often been, the case. This is why it is so important to recognize the limitations of democratic processes and the consequent need for human rights instruments that protect everyone, especially those in the minority.

there exists a global effort in this realm (see Jackson and Shapiro-Phim 2008). Indeed, extensive international work related to children and teens uses the arts as a way of promoting ideals of freedom, justice, and peace for future generations. Two examples follow that provide insight into these approaches. The first relates to the work of Amber Gray, an internationally renowned specialist in the area of movement and dance with survivors of torture and trauma. The other focuses on the work of Dance Arizona Repertory Theatre (DART), a community dance company, which for almost a decade forged community partnerships with at-risk youth in the surrounding city.

In her work, Gray draws on her extensive training in Western dance/ movement therapy along with her familiarity with traditions of healing from Haiti and West Africa.[15] She argues that because 'dance/movement therapy focuses therapeutic work directly on the body and its movement, it provides a uniquely targeted therapy modality for survivors of extreme and ongoing stress and violence, albeit one that must be modified to be culturally congruent and non-invasive' (Gray 2008: 225). Dance/movement therapy theory posits that the health-dysfunction continuum is reflected somatically, in the body, and that when the organized, sequential manner in which humans develop is disrupted through torture and trauma, therapists can work to safely reestablish well-being. This can occur for a variety of reasons related to the fundamental role of movement in human development, and the relational aspect of dance/movement therapy – how it addresses interpersonal relations and reestablishes trust between victims and those

15   Amber Gray is an internationally known somatic psychotherapist and dance/move-ment therapist specializing in treatment of survivors of torture, combat and war trauma, street children, and former and current child combatants. From 1998 to 2003 Gray was a senior therapist and clinical director at the Rocky Mountain Survivors Center in Denver, Colorado. In 2004–2005 she established and directed Haiti's first program for victims of organized violence and torture, and since 2001 has worked there as a dance/movement therapist with street children and child combatants. She was co-director of New Mexico's Alliance for Child Traumatic Stress, and as Director of Restorative Resources Training & Consulting, she addresses law enforcement, combat veterans and victims of trafficking. She is also an *initiate* and *sevito* in the Fran Guinea tradition of Vodou.

around them. It also relates to the creative, symbolic, and sacred aspects of dance that allow individuals to express deeply held feelings in a safe and nourishing manner. Many indigenous dance forms work to reinforce these insights through their emphasis on the healthy integration of the individual into community and the cosmos. Gray observes, 'in my work in Haiti as both a dance movement therapist and an initiate, I have learned that the dance *is* the healing and expresses the continuum that exists between the spiritual world and the world of humans' (ibid.: 228).

In her article, Gray also considers the rich partnership between Vodou and classic dance/movement therapy as healing modalities for children who suffer from multiple forms of violence. For instance, she considers how in both traditions the circle formation creates a safe container for group expression, process, and healing, and how the mirror is an important concept – as an act of witnessing by another person or by ancestral spirits – that allows a person to reclaim their dignity and standing in a community. The article touches on her work with a seventeen year old victim of torture, whose developmental movement appeared to be truncated at a fixated, frozen shoulder. Through their sessions his upper body began to relax and he was able to develop more relational behavior and increase emotional expression. Gray also outlines her successful interaction with a group of street children, with whom she assumed the role of a facilitator rather than a traditional leader. She emphasizes the importance of sharing and co-creation in the ultimate success of her work since these processes allowed her to recognize the empowering role of the dances of Vodou, and that 'they relate to the continuum of existence we are all part of' (Gray 2008: 232).

Gray's and other movement therapists' emphases on respect, collaboration and empowerment are strongly reflected in community dance practices in Europe and America that are focused on socially and economically disenfranchised members of society. While not usually addressing blatant human rights abuses, community artists often concern themselves with what Jean Harvey refers to as 'civilized oppression' (Harvey 1999) – 'the vast and deep injustices some groups suffer as a consequence of often unconscious assumptions and reactions of well-meaning people in ordinary interactions which are supported by the media and cultural stereotypes as well as by

the structural features of bureaucratic hierarchies and market mechanisms'
(Deutsch 2005). With influences from the Settlement House Movement
and Works Progress Administration (WPA), community dance efforts
have blossomed since the mid-1970s, with a notable proliferation in the
United States, Britain, Canada, and Australia. In the US, some of the most
renowned organizations include the Liz Lerman Dance Exchange, David
Dorfman Dance, Urban Bush Women, Pat Graney and Dancers and AXIS
(a company for dancers with and without disabilities).

One particular company directed by Mary Fitzgerald and Jennifer Tsu-
kayama, between 1998 and 2007, illustrates some of the ideals and features
of this work (Fitzgerald 2008). DART was a community dance company
housed in the Department of Dance at Arizona State University, which during
the course of this period partnered with several youth organizations in the
Phoenix metropolitan area, including one for homeless youth. During each
academic year, DART met with its partners for multiple sessions, exploring
improvisational concepts, collaborating on choreography and/or working
with guest choreographers, such as Deborah Hay, Marlies Yearby, Arthur
Aviles and Pablo Cornejo. In these interactions everyone was expected to
memorize and fully embody complex phrases, polish the work with a professional attitude, and contribute their ideas to the creative process. The content
of the guest artists' pieces tended to explore themes of identity, togetherness,
and spirituality, and highlighted the individuality of the cast members. Yearby,
for instance, explored each person's internal pulse and how it connects us all,
providing opportunities in her final piece for smaller groups to be highlighted
as well as building a strong sense of ensemble and 'community'.

As in the community arts movements discussed above, DART
embraced a set of values that allowed diverse populations to assert a presence in the arts, and ultimately the culture at large. These values included a
belief that artistic expression can serve as a means to emancipation from the
socio-economic constraints of such aspects as gender, race, poverty, physical ability, sexual orientation, and age, and that culture itself is a dynamic
and ever-changing whole. The company operated under the premise that
the boundaries typically constructed in culture – such as the dichotomies
of white/black, high vs. low art, rich/poor, etc. – are artificial and of little
value. Fitzgerald argues that:

Exchanging knowledge through dance allows new relationships to form within society, and some of the borders that normally exist between different communities begin to blur, allowing for an expansion and redefinition of personal worlds, as well as of the overall cultural fabric. By joining the creative forces of youth (ages six through fourteen) with college-aged students (ages eighteen through thirty) for intensive workshops each year, DART served as a vehicle for artistic expression and participation in the society as a whole. (Fitzgerald 2008: 259)

Dance as Insurgency

Actions conducted in public spaces by people who have been rendered marginal or abject are necessarily rebellious [...] At a time of crisis, the performance of corporeality and the enactment of choreography are the most effective means available for a community to assert itself and to state its demands for action and change. (Gere 2008: 336)

Choreographers have long created works for the stage that represent and recreate a sense of the horror, suffering, and courage of the victims of human rights abuses, as well as the brutality of the victimizers. Several of the most celebrated of these pieces within Europe and North America include: *The Green Table* by Kurt Jooss (1932) about the horrors of war, *Dreams* (1961) by Anna Sokolow about the Nazi concentration camps, *Soweto* (1977) by Mats Ek about apartheid in South Africa, *Ghost Dances* (1983) by Christopher Bruce, about the Chilean military coup, *Fagaala* by Germaine Acogny about the Rwandan genocide (see Figure 6) and Liz Lerman's *Small Dances About Big Ideas* (2006), reflecting on genocide and the Nuremberg Trials following World War II. There are many other works, familiar to audiences in specific communities and deserving of broad recognition and analysis, that have not enjoyed international exposure.

What this last section of the article shifts to consider, however, is how broad scale social and political movements engage dance within the public sphere to fight discrimination and injustice.[16] The emphasis here is not so much on individual dance professionals, choreographic works, or special projects, as on how dance brings visibility and bears witness in crisis situations where people are often made invisible; how through highly visible acts of dancing – acts of making and doing – people strive to reclaim their humanity. In the cases discussed below, the right to dance is held precious, not just because it provides access and empowerment for limited groups of people, but because it works symbolically at a monumental level to decry mistreatment and call for social justice. Here, dance is in effect promoted as a fundamental human right because of its ability to lobby for human rights.

A spokesperson for this perspective might be seen in David Gere, author of *How to Make Dances in an Epidemic: Tracking Choreography in the Age of Aids* (2004). In this book and elsewhere Gere examines the relationship between civic, choreographed acts of intervention, and the sense of frustration born from being marginalized by mainstream, official discourses. He explains, 'The importance of choreographic insurgencies in the AIDS era becomes clear when considering the dearth of response from the United States government to the AIDS epidemic and the violation of basic human rights in relation to prevention and treatment of the disease' (Gere, 2008). Referencing the work of art critic and theorist Douglas Crimp, Gere argues for the necessity of turning normally privately expressed grief into public activism – and the value of such activism in times of urgent distress. For instance, Gere includes a close reading of the symbolism of the unfurling of the AIDS quilt at the Washington Mall in the heart of the US capital. During this event hundreds of white clad performers ceremoniously carry, unfold, billow, and lay sections of the enormous quilt in a pedestrian but nevertheless highly choreographed spectacle. Gere sees such 'danced acts of intervention not in a soft, disempowered, or enervated condition, but rather in a dynamic insurgent relationship to oppressive monumentalities. These performances stand against the established order, against stone edifices as well as the invisible conditions of oppression' (2008: 336).

16   Theatrical work is not addressed in this article since it is the aspect of dance and human rights most frequently analyzed in other sources. For those interested in stage choreography and human rights, see Jackson and Shapiro-Phim (2008).

Another superlative example of mourning linked with activism and dance is the *cueca sola* performed by female members of the Association of the Detained and Disappeared as a form of protest against human rights atrocities in South America. The *cueca sola*, traditionally a dance for couples, is performed as a solo, with photographs, or men's shirts, symbolizing the women's missing partners – husbands and sons – who 'disappeared' during the years of military dictatorship (1973–1990) in Chile. The women perform the dance in streets, plazas and theaters as part of larger demonstrations. Scholar Marjorie Agosín discusses the radical nature of these women's reinterpretation of the country's national dance in a culture where women are traditionally sequestered in the private, domestic sphere. Dancing the *cueca sola* in the streets is simultaneously a reminder of torture and of hope; the performance suggests 'a strategy of revealing oneself before the oppressive power as well as appropriating the language of the body in a public space' (Agosín 2008: 297–298). She writes that it is 'the story of the mutilated body of the loved one. Through their movements and the guitar music, the women also recreate the pleasure of dancing with the missing person. When the women step onto the dance floor, they invoke the dead and perform a dance of life for them' (ibid.: 299). Indeed, she argues that 'this dance-remembrance, permits the body to free itself from all bonds. Through the *cueca sola* and its movements full of soft and delicate cadences, the women are representing the free body, the body that hasn't been tortured [...] the concept of homeland assumes a female identity; one of the slogans of the women who fight for human rights is "freedom is the name of a woman"' (ibid.: 300).

Final Reflections

I learned two nights later [that] in the 1860s, three whaling vessels pulled up next to this little island in the Northern Marianas, and the crews disembarked and slaughtered every male on the island and took the women as their wives and taught them this jig. And for those people, the presentation of this jig at a Festival of Pacific Dance was a statement that their race will never be exterminated, that they will continue to live, and they hate those people, but those people are also their fathers now, and so they are not allowed to hate them. So the tone with which this jig is executed – not spirited, not sad, just perfectly poised – is the key to their own sense of continuity in their own lives. (Sellars 1989: 12)

The pleasure and sense of freedom often experienced when dancing are profound. As we have seen, it is a strong argument for dance's standing as a human right and as an adversary of human rights abuses. So too are the ways in which dance engages a language of the body and movement that seems fundamental to human development and resonates across cultural divides. Individual dances also appear as symbolic, performative acts that build healthy relationships, provide visibility for the otherwise marginalized, and counter hegemonic discourses of oppression. The efforts of those committed to dance as closely connected to the ideals of dignity, freedom, peace and justice cannot and should not be underestimated. They bring the words of the Universal Declaration to life, and provide inspiring examples for us all.

At the same time, the complexity with which dance interfaces with human rights concerns must not be ignored. In the case of the *cueca sola*, Agosín at one point admits the irony that the dance represents the same nation that has deprived the dancers of their husbands and children. In the example referred to directly above by the director Peter Sellars, people performed a jig at a Festival of Pacific Dance that at one and the same time represented their history of genocide and their courage of continuity. Sometimes, these examples suggest, dance is ambivalent and experienced on a variety of levels by those who create, participate, and view it. Sometimes, dance is neither a straightforward friend nor enemy of human rights abuses, as many would see it, but a medium that can be engaged to either end simultaneously or be interpreted in a variety of ways.[17]

17   An excellent example is found in the enforced cabarets and revues staged in the concentration camps like Westerbork or Theresienstadt by Jews for Jews and Nazis. Some saw these performances as an insurgent form of political commentary and satire; others as a shameful charade masking murder. Were these performances an opportunity for the artists to practice their art and find respite from the horror around them, or a means for the Nazis to find pleasure in their forced puppetry/ entertainment? All are likely interpretations. (See Ingber 2005.)

Once again, then, we return to the realization that no matter how much we would love for dance to be considered an *a priori* unconditional human right, it seems that such a claim is ill conceived. Perhaps instead it is more important to consider the question basic to normative ethics, which asks 'how *should* we live?' by inquiring 'when *should* dance be regarded as a human right?' For it is when considering the answer to this question that one engages more fully with the issues at the heart of matter: issues of dignity, equality, freedom, and justice, and the way dance relates to a broad range of civil, political, social, economic, and cultural rights. When asked by each of us in relation to our practice and theorizing in the field of dance this question highlights the moral implications of our efforts, so critical to achieving a more humane and just society.

Works Cited

Agosín, M. 2008. The Dance of Life: Women and Human Rights in Chile, in *Dance, Human Rights, and Social Justice: Dignity in Motion*. Edited by Naomi Jackson and Toni Shapiro-Phim. Lanham, MD: Scarecrow Press: 296–303.

Aldrich, E. 2008. Plunge not into the Mire of Worldly Folly: Nineteenth-century and early Twentieth-century Religious Objections to Social Dance in the United States, in *Dance, Human Rights, and Social Justice: Dignity in Motion*. Edited by Naomi Jackson and Toni Shapiro-Phim. Lanham, MD: Scarecrow Press: 20–33.

Brown, E. 2002. Let's Dance!, in *New York*, July 29. Available: <http://nymag.com/nymetro/nightlife/barsclubs/features/6265/?loomia_ow=t0:a41:g29:r10:c0.5:b18277140> [3 May 2010].

Deutsch, M. 2005. The Nature and Origins of Oppression, in *Beyond Intractability*. Edited by Guy Burgess and Heidi Burgess. Conflict Research Consortium, University of Colorado, Boulder. March. Available: <http://www.beyondintractability.org/essay/nature_origins_oppression/> [3 May 2010].

Doolittle, L., & Flynn, A. (n.d.) *Assimilating Bodies: Regulatory Moves in Canada's Choreography of Nationhood*, unpublished paper.

Fitzgerald, M. 2008. Community Dance, Dance Arizona Repertory Theatre as a Vehicle for Cultural Emancipation, in *Dance, Human Rights, and Social Justice:*

Dignity in Motion. Edited by Naomi Jackson and Toni Shapiro-Phim. Lanham, MD: Scarecrow Press: 256–269.

French, H. W. 1997. Anatomy of an Autocracy: Mobutu's 32-Year Reign, *New York Times*, 17 May. Available: <http://www.diversityjobmarket.com/library/world/africa/051797zaire-mobutu.html> [10 March 2008].

Gere, D. 2004. *How to Make Dances in an Epidemic: Tracking Choreography in the Age of AIDS*. Madison, WI: University of Wisconsin Press.

Gere, D. 2008. Monuments and Insurgencies in the Age of AIDS, in *Dance, Human Rights, and Social Justice: Dignity in Motion*. Edited by Naomi Jackson and Toni Shapiro-Phim. Lanham, MD: Scarecrow Press: 333–341.

Glass, A. 2004. The Thin Edge of the Wedge: Dancing Around the Potlatch Ban, 1921–1951, in *Right to Dance: Dancing for Rights*. Edited by Naomi M. Jackson. Banff, Alberta: Banff Centre Press: 51–82.

Goodrich, T. 2002. *Scalp Dance: Indian Warfare on the High Plains, 1865–1879*. Mechanicsburg, PA: Stackpole Books.

Gray, A. 2008. Dancing in our Blood: Dance/Movement Therapy with Street Children and Victims of Organized Violence in Haiti, in *Dance, Human Rights, and Social Justice: Dignity in Motion*. Edited by Naomi Jackson and Toni Shapiro-Phim. Lanham, MD: Scarecrow Press: 222–236.

Hanna, J. L. 2008. Right to Dance: Exotic Dancing in the United States, in *Dance, Human Rights, and Social Justice: Dignity in Motion*. Edited by Naomi Jackson and Toni Shapiro-Phim. Lanham, MD: Scarecrow Press: 86–108.

Harvey, J. 1999. *Civilized Oppression*. Lanham, MD: Roman and Littlefield.

Huckstep. J. 2008. *Animation Politique*: The Embodiment of Nationalism in Zaire, in *Dance, Human Rights, and Social Justice: Dignity in Motion*. Edited by Naomi Jackson and Toni Shapiro-Phim. Lanham, MD: Scarecrow Press: 51–66.

Ingber, J. B. n.d. Dancing Despite the Scourge: Jewish Dancers During the Nazi Period, unpublished paper. A version is available in the *Proceedings of the International CORD Conference on Dance and Human Rights*, Montreal, Canada, 12–13 November 2005: 62–67.

International Covenant on Economic, Social and Cultural Rights. 1966. Available: <http://www.unhchr.ch/html/menu3/b/a_cescr.htm> [3 May 2010].

Ishay, M. R. 2004. *The History of Human Rights: From Ancient Times to the Globalization Era*. Berkeley: University of California Press.

Jackson, N. (ed.) 2004. *Right to Dance: Dancing for Rights*. Banff, Alberta: The Banff Centre Press.

Jackson, N., & Shapiro-Phim, T. (eds.) 2008. *Dance, Human Rights, and Social Justice: Dignity in Motion*. Lanham, MD: Scarecrow Press.

Kant, M. 2008. Practical Imperative: German Dance, Dancers, and Nazi Politics, in *Dance, Human Rights, and Social Justice: Dignity in Motion*. Edited by Naomi Jackson and Toni Shapiro-Phim. Lanham, MD: Scarecrow Press: 5–19.

Kronja, I. 2001. *Smrtonosni sjaj: masovna psihologija i estetika turbo-folka* (The Fatal Glow: Mass Psychology and Aesthetics of Turbofolk Subculture). Beograd: Tehnokratia.

Kyle, D. 2007. *Sport and Spectacle in the Ancient World.* Malden, MA and Oxford: Blackwell.

Lakes, R. 2008. The Hidden Authoritarian Roots in Western Concert Dance, in *Dance, Human Rights, and Social Justice: Dignity in Motion.* Edited by Naomi Jackson and Toni Shapiro-Phim. Lanham, MD: Scarecrow Press: 109–130.

Manning, S. 1993. *Ecstasy and the Demon: Feminism and Nationalism in the Dances of Mary Wigman.* Berkeley: University of California Press.

McCall, J. C. 2000. *Dancing Histories: Heuristic Ethnography with the Ohafia Igbo.* Ann Arbor, MI: University of Michigan Press.

Recommendation concerning the Status of the Artist. 1980. Available: <http://portal. unesco.org/en/ev.php-URL_ID=13138&URL_DO=DO_TOPIC&URL_ SECTION=201.html> [3 May 2010].

Recommendation on Participation by the People at Large in Cultural Life and Their Contribution to It. 1976. Available: <http://portal.unesco.org/en/ev.php-URL_ID=13097&URL_DO=DO_TOPIC&URL_SECTION=201.html> [3 May 2010].

Roosevelt, E. 1958. *In your Hands.* Address delivered to the United Nations on the tenth anniversary of the Universal Declaration of Human Rights, 27 March 1958.

Shay, A. 1999. *Choreophobia: Solo Improvised Dance in the Iranian World.* Bibliotheca Iranica. Performing arts series, no. 4. Costa Mesa, CA: Mazda Publishers.

Shay, A. 2008. Dance and Human Rights in the Middle East, North Africa, and Central Asia, in *Dance, Human Rights, and Social Justice: Dignity in Motion.* Edited by Naomi Jackson and Toni Shapiro-Phim. Lanham, MD: Scarecrow Press: 67–85.

Sellars, P. 1989. *The New Territory.* Keynote address at the Dance Critics Association conference, San Francisco, 10 June. Most of the text was published as 'Sellars in Criticland', in the *DCA News* (Fall 1989): 12.

Springer, D. 2006. The Right to Move: An Examination of Dance, Cabaret Laws, and Social Movements, in *Proceedings of the Society of Dance History Scholars,* Twenty-Ninth Annual Conference, Alberta, Canada, 15–18 June: 117–123.

Tracy, J. L., & Matsumoto, D. 2008. The Spontaneous Display of Pride and Shame: Evidence for Biologically Innate Nonverbal Displays. *Proceedings of the National Academy of Sciences 105*: 11655–11660.

Universal Declaration of Human Rights. 2008. Available: <http://www.unhchr.ch/ udhr/lang/eng.htm> [3 May 2010].

9 About *Not About Iraq*

In Fall 2007, I premiered a dance piece entitled *Not About Iraq*. An ensemble work for six dancers plus myself, the piece used spoken word and dance to deliver conflicting layers of information. *Not About Iraq* is about the manipulation of meaning and I, the choreographer, sometimes stood in for larger (political) forces of meaning making. Since the premiere, performances have taken place in Sweet Briar (Virginia), Los Angeles (my home town), Chicago, New York, Washington, DC, Helena, Minneapolis, and Long Beach.

I welcome the opportunity to write about this dance, to understand what it is, and to know better where I am having made it. But to write about the discoveries and questions *Not About Iraq* gave rise to, is also to consider the phenomenon of a dance: Its lack of fixity and its multiple ways of being apprehended.

Spreading her arms wide, Taisha Paggett says: *This is a dance.*

Whether purposeful or not, a dance is a staging of both the imaginative world of its creators and of the public imaginary.

Looking at the audience, Taisha says: *This is looking at you.* A dance is a mirror.

A dance takes its place in history and serves as its own bookmark for a moment in shared time. It whispers or shouts what a group of people care or cared about.

It is an archeological finding.

In 1994 New York choreographer Neil Greenberg premiered *Not-About AIDS-Dance*. In Neil's piece, dancing was accompanied by projected subtitles: fragmentary personal narratives that revealed the unfolding of lives and relationships in the midst of an epidemic. Neil's piece made me aware of the way the making of a dance is always informed by what is going on outside the room and in dancers' lives. While I did not wish to imitate the choreographic processes he used in *Not-About AIDS-Dance*, I did want to refer to the way a dance acknowledges its relationship with the larger world. The title *Not About Iraq* is homage to Neil Greenberg's piece, and particularly to the idea that it would be impossible to make a dance in 2007 that was not about Iraq.

To be in history is to identify context and connection. Modern and post-modern dance choreographers and their contemporaries value(d) innovation. That tradition of individuality and invention is complicated by a real world in which dance knowledge is passed from person to person, taught by the doing of things together. We take class together, and we set out of an evening to see one another's work. Choreographers and dancers learn from each other. Our work is part of an ongoing public conversation about embodiment and authorship. This conversation sometimes occurs across a table, in a studio, or while traveling home together after a performance. But mostly it permeates the air and is unspoken. It is in the way we work together, warm up, and think of what a dance can be or do. Yet given how much we learn from each other, I don't think it's customary for one artist to publicly say to another: I learned this from you.

Neil, I learned this from you: One can never separate a dance from the world in which it lives.

***

In the studio the question was: How to begin moving? What actions to inscribe in space? While critical of my unrelenting interest in 'making movement that is beautiful', I tried to make that 'beautiful' movement. I had a hunch that if I began with something that I loved and kind of knew how to do, but about which I was also very critical, I would eventually find a connection to my questions about a dance's ability to address the world beyond it.

I liked the way Taisha moved: slow, considered and elegant. I decided to work on creating combinations of spiraling movement. I watched Taisha thoughtfully attending to different orchestrations of action in her core and in her hips and shoulders as she corkscrewed in and out of herself in unexpected ways.

From the audience, I proclaim: *This is beautiful. This is so beautiful. Isn't this beautiful?*

Initially I sit in the audience while Taisha moves on stage. Later I move onto the stage. I interrupt her actions from time to time to coo about the beauty, sexiness and truth of the dance/her actions, or perhaps of Taisha herself. As she executes a turning jump, early in the piece, I pop out of my seat and shout: *That! It's the truth.*

In this statement I am addressing the way we often speak of dancing, or the physics of an action, as 'the truth'. As I query the philosophical notions of truth that are associated with dancing (somewhere between physics and human mortality), I am also thinking about the transmutability of 'truth' that surrounds me. It is impossible to separate a dance from the contexts in which it operates. The context is that as an American citizen, I have ceased to be able to recognize the truth.

While I was making *Not About Iraq* I felt horrified and also helpless. I was simultaneously affronted by the double-speak and the knowledge of lives being destroyed at home and also far away. Could I make a dance that directly confronted the current political moment without being didactic? Could a dance be a forum in which to better understand my own problematic sense of citizenship?

I knew that I wanted to find a way to make a dance in response to the war, or my feeling of helplessness about the US deployment to Iraq, or my lack of trust in and total suspicion of the moral integrity of our political leaders. I wondered: Could a dance do that?

As time went on, of course, I became clearer about my path. In *Not About Iraq* I deliberately set myself the task of making a dance that was a restaging of the way US government and news agencies were communicating in the period preceding and immediately following the invasion of Iraq. In response to this replication of Bush administration violence, I also hoped to provide an antidote: to offer a possible solution. My theory is that in spite of the contradictions and the absence of information, we understand the moral imperatives before us. So, as the lights begin their final fade out and Taisha backs away from the audience brushing the 'dust' of the dance off, she repeats: *You know what this is. You KNOW what this is. You KNOW what this is.*

***

Our clean wood-floored studio looked out on the Federal Building where groups were congregating to demonstrate against the war. (Another choreographic action.)

Dance has always acted for me as a place to make corrections, to rehearse a set of possibilities, to become other than as I am, and to say what cannot be said otherwise. You could say a dance is a place to step out of the circumscribed automatic and daily choreographies, to make a new and alternative dance.

Bodies, whether at the Federal Building or on the stage are never without their subjectivity. They are never generic or universal. On stage, however, trained and virtuosic bodies are often positioned so. There seems to be a correlation between training and an abstraction of the body such that these bodies are removed from markers of their unique histories and subjectivities.

I ask myself why it was that in the making of *Not About Iraq* I wanted to work with dancers capable of exceptional technical mastery. In hindsight, I will explain my choice by saying: I wondered if virtuosity could be highlighted – made to stand out, even though it is a professional standard and a conventional means to visual pleasure?

In the second act of *Not About Iraq* dancing becomes associated with the presentation of smooth, untroubled and exceptional surfaces that undermine our ability to think and feel. For me, this unquestioning self-absorption of dancing worked as part of the larger matrix in which meaning is corrupted. Happy go-go-ing and pony-ing dancers gingerly step over bodies rolling on the floor. The sheen of happiness and heroics stands in for a kind of anesthesia. This is the same anesthesia that led George W. Bush to respond to Sept 11 by counseling Americans: 'Get on board. Do your business around the country. Fly and enjoy America's great destination spots. Get down to Disney World in Florida. Take your families and enjoy life, the way we want it to be enjoyed'.

***

Like an orange, a dance can be understood as a record of its own process of creation. It's the fruit inside that you are concerned with; and its juiciness and sweetness are all about the rain and the sun of the previous hundred days.

There were many chapters in the creation of *Not About Iraq*, as it was developed in sections over a period of three years. The dancers who worked with me: their movement proclivities, their imaginations and their intellect were inscribed in the dance, as were their relationships with one another and with me. Funding and lack of funding is written in the dance, as was what was going on around me, in the news and in the studio.

Once it was premiered, *Not About Iraq* changed substantially. These changes were initially catalyzed by the deportation of a French dancer/cast-member who had temporarily left LA and was trying to re-enter the country on a tourist visa (because we could not afford an artist visa). As a result, I learned that only US citizens are permitted to dance in *Not About Iraq*. Soon after, we lost another dancer to injury. Losing artists at the last minute made it necessary for performers to learn new roles, and for me, to make significant choreographic changes. Economics and citizenship imprint choreographic production.

But beyond the vulnerability of dancers who are the center of choreographic labor, dances change because they are changeable. Why shouldn't we take what we learned yesterday and apply it to the ending this evening? There is so much to study, as we experience the piece in performance. (See Figure 7.)

***

I have begun to see a dance like a comet. It whips by a geographical loca-
tion at high speeds, leaving a flaming trail of memory and experience. Its
own shape and density changes as it travels. It is not the same thing in
Minneapolis as it was in Chicago. A dance, though tensile is also hyper-
mobile, depending on a set of agreements between dancers whose main
characteristic is a readiness for motion and change.

So, as I consider *Not About Iraq*, I wonder which iteration of the piece
I should write about.

But even on a single night, what *Not About Iraq* purported to do was
different for different audience members. As with all dance (or phenomena,
for that matter), it was different based upon who saw it, the constellation
of their experience, and what they understood to be its intentions. In a
post-performance discussion in Minneapolis, the audience argues about the
central narrative of meaning in the work. One African-American university
scholar describes the piece as a dance about race and the inability to make
reparations in America. Another audience member sees the piece telling
the story of Iraq. And finally, for another audience member, a curator and
presenter, the piece is indeed, NOT about Iraq. It is about war.

Because all dances employ non-linguistic processes of meaning making,
they are consummate laboratories for studying the very production of
meaning. What happens and when it happens shapes the way we experience what we see. *Not About Iraq* (2007) and the leaner and more potent
redux presented in Fall 2008 makes the alchemy and disabling of meaning
its central quandary. Rather than attempting to create coherence, I worked
to study the fracturing of meaning that we encounter in our lives. I thought
about the White House spin-doctors who skilfully craft reality, and the
cracks in that reality which unavoidably appear.

The dance is NOT intended to be about Iraq. Not directly. I am more
interested in focusing on the process of making meaning in these times
when we are required to be adept at reading through and around information, and to knowingly ask what the motives for the 'information' are.
There are no dead bodies. And also, there are. There are weapons of mass
destruction and also it doesn't matter if there are not.

I say: *Words are so, so... (make a bad face). But the body...! (exultant gesture)*

In fact, I don't believe that words are so, so (icky) and the body is so, so (yum).

If I initially set myself up in the piece as an authoritative figure who comments knowingly about the dance (first from the audience and then from the stage), the dance quickly undermines this dynamic, drawing attention to my own unreliability. But neither does the dance rest on the reversal of this dyad. The body, the dancers' bodies, though compelling, are not set up as the site of monolithic truth and reliability. How could they be? Light-years away from the world Martha Graham spoke to when she said 'A body never lies', meaning and truth are moveable feasts.

Describing a melting back-bend action, Taisha says: *This is a confession. This is a cupcake. This is a joke.*

To be honest... in a back bend, the extreme opening of the belly side of the body, gradually collapsing upside down toward the ground, conjures the vulnerability of a body in a confession. And the convex rounded surface of the top shape does make me think of a cupcake. And the act of renaming an action in this way may indeed seem like a joke. But it is also not a joke.

In a dance we don't assign an individual meaning to an individual action. Standing on two feet with arms stretched to each side, elbows bent and palms up, Taisha says: *This is justice. This is balance. This is 'I don't know'.*

In a constellation of stars, each star is understood as not only uniquely itself, but also through its relationship to the heavenly bodies around it. And if gravitational forces shift such that the stars are re-constelled, the individual stars themselves will take on new identities. (Writing in Los Angeles, I can't help wondering if you are thinking, 'Why does everything have to be about Hollywood?' So be it.) Any one thing or any one body is understood as a result of the orchestration of everything around it. The moment of 'understanding' then is not fixed, but is hugely fluid and dynamic, contingent upon numerous factors.

Where meaning is always unstable, we live in an age where it has also become a commodity. The engineers of public information control what we know and when we know it, attempting to orchestrate (choreograph) our behavior for the endgame of their public policies. Evidence that might work against these plans, bodies coming home from Iraq, veterans on city streets, or citizens in New Orleans, is rendered invisible. Public inquiry and reasoning are usurped by urgent agendas of patriotism. I am made docile by my confusion. Could this be choreography?

But this is a new (Obama) era. Isn't it?

***

And then, here I am attempting to distill from my recent work a few fragments of intention, a sense of the way dancing and politics merge. I know that we as dancers, dance makers, writers and viewers continually apply ourselves to the reading of bodies that move at high speeds past our fields of vision. *(You know what this is.)* Like the spin-masters, we study the apprehension of bodies, real or virtual, in action.

At the end of the duet in *Not About Iraq*, Taisha says, with arms and legs spread wide like Da Vinci's Vitruvian Man: *This is evidence.* She then flutters her hands back and forth in front of her body so rapidly that they become a blur. It is as if her body is drawn on a piece of paper and she is trying to erase herself. Erasure is, of course, impossible. (See Figure 8.)

I figure that we (you and I) are left with the complex task of interpreting the evidence, finding truths (however impermanent) and then taking action accordingly. We will do this, whether we choose to or not, knowingly or not, through our daily choreographies at work and at home, as well as in the dances we make. If citizenship is about understanding and interpreting the complex events (actions) that surround us, and finding *our* 'right' actions on behalf of our communities, local and global, then dance is an excellent primer for the work ahead.

I recognize that my efforts to write about *Not About Iraq* have left an incomplete map at best. If, in the beginning of this essay, I initially set myself up as an authoritative figure who could comment knowingly about my own dance, it was a case of optimism. I am still learning about the dance. So now the choreographer who attempts to be reliable and who does and does not know what she has done, has come to the end of this essay, at least for the time being.

As the lights begin to fade, Taisha says: *Wait. Stop!*
This is not the end of this dance!

Figure 7 Phithsamay Linthahane in *Not About Iraq* (2007) by Victoria Marks. Photograph: Jeff Zucker.

Figure 8   Taisha Paggett in *Not About Iraq*. (2007) by Victoria Marks.
Photograph: Steve Gunther.

Figure 9 *Black Milk* (2006) by Douglas Wright. Wright recreates Abu Ghraib's iconic pyramid of flesh and adds another form of imprisonment. Photograph: John Savage.

Figure 10 *Black Milk* (2006) by Douglas Wright. Wright inserts a quasi-religious figure into his Abu Ghraib inspired sequence. Photograph: John Savage.

SUZANNE LITTLE

10 Re-presenting the Traumatic Real: Douglas Wright's *Black Milk*

> How can political awareness and social engagement be conveyed without falling back into the rhetoric of ecumenical allegories already programmed by the same political realm one is trying to critique/destroy?
>
> — LEPECKI 1995: 5

Over a decade later, Andre Lepecki's question continues to reverberate, highlighting the struggles and dangers for those choreographers and dance artists who wish to enter into wider political and social discourses through their work. In 2006, Douglas Wright, one of New Zealand's most respected and awarded choreographers, made reference to the infamous photos of prisoner abuse and torture at Abu Ghraib in his dance theatre piece *Black Milk*. The performance toured New Zealand (25 March – 8 April 2006) and went to the Sydney Opera House (12–13 April 2006) in Australia, receiving critical acclaim. While *Black Milk* contained much of Wright's hallmark stunning choreography, provocative imagery and disturbing themes, the Abu Ghraib sequence appeared a precarious practice, considering the difficulties, ethics and potential for 'blow back'[1] involved in representing the traumatic 'real'. Wright's utilisation of the images as the basis for a live action sequence aimed at critique seemed perversely to reinscribe the original humiliation tactics and power hierarchies of the political realm that created them. This was clearly not Wright's intention and for that matter it did not seem that other members of the audience, while shocked and disturbed by the scene, were aware of this possibility or read it as such, and nor did the many critics who wrote about the show.

---

1   A military term referring to the negative effects incurred by one's own weapons.

Most reviewers either failed to mention the sequence or described it as an exploration of power (Smythe 2006, Horsley 2006: 47). The preference was to speak of the performance in wider and loftier terms: 'Malevolence in its various guises asserted power [...]. It preyed on the body; the young violated by desire, adults degraded for sadism, others exposed or headless, dizzied by circling mirrors' (Horsley 2006: 47). Perhaps this is because the framing of pieces as 'art works' often seems to discount or deter criticism relating to ethical and political matters. In a letter to the editor of the *The Listener*, one viewer did see the sequence as a 'reenactment of the Abu Ghraib prison events' that 'diminished the horror of the original' (Temple 2006: 8). However, this viewer was in the minority. This disparity has prompted further investigation of the representation of the traumatic 'real' in performance, utilising Wright's *Black Milk* as a starting point.

In a production that aims to explore physically the 'intangible boundaries of love, death, fear and memory' (*Black Milk* Programme 2006: 4), reference to the atrocities of Abu Ghraib would seem relevant and worthy of critique. However, the exploration of the images and their content and meaning appeared highly problematic, begging the question of how does one, or indeed, should one represent the 'real' suffering of others in artistic works and to what ends? This chapter will attempt to unpack some issues surrounding this contentious area, with particular reference to the specific complexities and dangers of dealing with the Abu Ghraib images in performance. While the overarching focus is the difficulties involved in representing the traumatic 'real' in performance, the working contention underlying this discussion is specific to the Abu Ghraib images. That is, that while the images (and the actions surrounding their creation) require criticism, there is something about the nature of these particular photographic records that makes artistic representation of them an inherently precarious practice.

The photographs have inspired a great deal of theoretical writing and debate across multiple paradigms since their release. The writing has reflected the concerns and perspectives of the respective individuals and their paradigms. Most admonish, but in seeking to understand or unpack the images a wide variety of causes, inspirations and links have been identified. Sontag (2004) and others link the images to a history of racial abuse in the US; art historian Eisenmann (2007) states that the guards did not need to seek out inspiration because the prototypes have long existed in Western art and its depictions of 'beautiful suffering'; theatre historian Thompson links the images to the practices of racialised othering on the early modern stage (2008) and Baudrillard and others see pornography and the treachery of the spectacle and image (2006: 86–87). Alternatively, human rights and medical theorists link the images to a history of sexualised abuse in war (Oosterhoff et al. 2004). In a sense, each is a reductive response to the images, but arguably all are variously valid in their own right. What this variety does highlight is the complexity and generative nature of these images.

While the exposure of the images to the public via the mainstream media burned them into our memories, the photographs continue to be generative in their ongoing reproduction and availability through print and Internet sources. The images continue to resonate, despite the fact that we have been increasingly bombarded with images of war to the point where, adapting Hannah Arendt's phrase (1970), Mirzoeff argues that the Second Gulf War marked the emergence of 'the banality of images' (2005: 67). To create a context for discussions here it is necessary to revisit briefly the history and content of the images.

In April/May 2004, photographs of prisoner abuse and torture at Iraq's Abu Ghraib prison by American guards came into public view on CBS's *60 Minutes II* and in a series of *New Yorker* articles written by Seymour Hersh and subsequently disseminated around the world. The photographs feature American soldiers humiliating and torturing prisoners and forcing them to perform sexualised acts. The fact that the photos were staged by, and often included images of the smiling American guards giving a 'thumbs up' while standing next to their victims, adds another level of reprehensible horror to the scenario.

During the era of Saddam Hussein, Abu Ghraib was considered one of the world's most notorious prisons, known for its appalling living conditions, torture and weekly executions (Hersh 2004: 1). Following the overthrow of Saddam's regime in 2003 by the US-led coalition's 'preventive'[2]

---

2   Tétreault maintains that the Iraq war was part of an ongoing US plan post 9/11 to demonstrate power in a spectacular way (2006: 33). The Secretary of Defense,

(Tétreault 2006: 33) war on Iraq, the prison was looted, deserted and then converted into a US military prison to hold a mixture of several thousand 'common criminals; security detainees suspected of "crimes against the coalition"; and a small number of suspected "high-value" leaders of the insurgency against coalition forces' (Hersh 2004: 1). The revived use of Abu Ghraib was in a sense an ironic move and considered by some a display of 'the most cynical form of neo-colonial reason, when the only remaining justification for the invasion was to close the torture rooms'[3] (Mirzoeff 2005: 180).

Subsequent reports into conditions at Abu Ghraib, which were leaked to *The Wall Street Journal*, concluded that there was widespread abuse of Iraqi detainees by the US military at Abu Ghraib, which in some cases was 'tantamount to torture' (Murphy 2004: 594). Some of the intentional acts of abuse listed include:

> ... Videotaping and photographing naked male and female detainees [...] Forcibly arranging detainees in various sexually explicit positions for photographing [...] Forcing detainees to remove their clothing and keeping them naked for several days at a time [...] forcing naked male detainees to wear women's underwear [...] Forcing groups of male detainees to masturbate themselves while being photographed and videotaped [...] Arranging naked male detainees in a pile and then jumping on them [...] positioning a detainee on a [...] Box, with a sandbag on his head, and attaching wires to his fingers, toes, and penis to simulate electric torture [...] Placing a dog chain or strap around a naked detainee's neck and having a female soldier pose for a picture... (Murphy 2004: 594–595)

Donald Rumsfeld, described it as a campaign of 'Shock and Awe' based on a concept developed by military strategist Harlan Ullman (Schifferes 2003: 1). Tétreault further observes that the passage into the war had been pre-prepared by a formal policy statement issued from the White House in 2002. The statement included the option to undertake preventive war without the imprimatur of the United Nations. The war was launched in March 2003 (2006: 33).

3   A number of reasons had been given for invading Iraq including the threat of Saddam Hussein's 'weapons of mass destruction' and the desire to close down the torture rooms of various Iraq prisons. During the extended campaign no weapons of mass destruction were found and many of the other touted reasons for going to war were also considered suspect.

The American government tried to minimise the damage of the photographs by claiming that it was only a small group of soldiers that had participated in the incident. Regardless, the effect of the images did greatly unsettle the 'attempt to claim the Iraq invasion as an unfolding narrative of progress and freedom' (Zuber 2006: 283). The use of the refined torture technique known as the 'Vietnam' (the hooded prisoner being forced to stand on a box while connected to wires believed to hold electrical current) has become an iconic symbol of the Abu Ghraib atrocities and arguably also functions as an exposé of historic techniques:

> This mode of torture used to be preferred precisely because it left no visible marks but the digital cameras and computers that were so central to the success of the US-led invasion have now 'blown back' the sight of Americans as torturers. (Mirzoeff 2005: 180)

Controversially the US powers claimed that the treatment was 'abuse' and not 'torture' (Sontag 2004: 24). The techniques are arguably in contravention of the 1949 Geneva Convention Relative to the Treatment of Prisoners of War which dictates that prisoners 'must at all times be humanely treated...' (in Murphy 2004: 591). The treatment was also in conflict with The Convention against Torture to which the US is also a party. Among other strategies the White House introduced new legislation, modifying portions of the War Crimes Act and releasing a final version of the Military Commissions Act (MCA) of 2006, citing the need to foil terrorist attacks. The legislation defines an 'unlawful enemy combatant' (as opposed to a 'prisoner of war') as someone who 'purposefully and materially supported hostilities against the United States' (in Otterman 2007: 186). This potentially places the individual outside of the protection of the Geneva Convention.

The MCA also stipulates a ban on torture but defines it as 'acts that must be *specifically intended* to cause severe mental and physical pain' and that must inflict serious 'bodily injury' (original emphasis, ibid.: 187). Hence, torture becomes difficult to identify and prove and the lesser term of abuse is invoked. With respect to the sexualised torture that is a major focus of this discussion, up until World War II, rape and violence had been seen as 'inevitable by-products of war' or acts ascribed to renegade soldiers

(Ooosterhoff, Zwanikken & Ketting 2004: 71). Sexualised violence was first acknowledged in the Geneva Convention, but its first legal recognition as torture occurred later (ibid.: 71). In 1998, The International Criminal Tribunal for Rwanda (ICTR) enlarged the legal definition of sexual violence stating that it 'is not limited to physical invasion of the human body and may include acts which do not involve penetration or even physical contact' (cited in ibid.: 72). Aside from arguments about the veracity of the photographs, there is a *prima facie* case that sexual violence was being practised at Abu Ghraib, yet recognition of this depends on the perspective of the viewer.

Right-wing American commentator Rush Limbaugh considered the photographs to be little more than a college fraternity prank and condoned the behaviour: 'You know, these people are being fired at every day. I'm talking about people having a good time, these people, you ever heard of emotional release? You ever heard of need (sic) to blow some steam off?' (A. S. & G. W.: 2004). However, the sexualised nature of the torture and other aspects of the practice pointed to a project of interrogation, humiliation and 'othering',[4] specifically designed to have maximum and ongoing impact on the Muslim prisoners. While the photographs betray a 'vicious sexism and homophobia' amongst the guards (Eisenmann 2007: 18), the treatment also plays directly on some Islamic sensibilities and beliefs. Although law in Iraq protects homosexuals, attacks and intolerance are common with violence escalating to assassinations (UNAMI 2006). The deliberate humiliation, dehumanisation and enactments of taboos were designed to dishonour the victims to such a degree that return to their communities would be impossible (Eisenmann 2007: 29).

The photographic recording of the prisoners in sexualised positions provided another level of torment and humiliation with the threat that the images would be sent to prisoners' families and friends. Additionally, the photographs became trophy-like records that were circulated amongst military and civilian personnel. The staging and photographing of the victims is also tantamount to a performative 'othering', placing the victims in

---

4   Process that involves securing one's own, or a group's positive identity and potentially power and superiority through the stigmatisation and marginalisation of an 'other'.

the role of the 'savage' other. Whereas J. L. Austin identified performative situations, such as the wedding ceremony, where 'to *say* something is to *do* something' (original emphasis, in Schechner 2006: 110–111), in the case of these photographs to *show* something is to *do* something. While homosexual acts and public nudity were abhorrent to most Arab prisoners, the acts were also being inscribed as deviant by a number of their captors. In the military trials of the US guards that ensued, witness Specialist Matthew Wilson testified:

> SFC Snider grabbed my prisoner and threw him into a pile. [...] I do not think it was right to put them in a pile. I saw SSG Frederick, SGT Davis and CPL Graner walking around the pile hitting the prisoners. I remember SSG Frederick hitting one prisoner in the side of its [sic] ribcage. The prisoner was no danger to SSG Frederick. [...] I left after that.

When he returned later, Wilson testified:

> I saw two naked detainees, one masturbating to another kneeling with its mouth open. I thought I should just get out of there. I didn't think it was right. [...] I saw SSG Frederick walking towards me, and he said, 'Look what these animals do when you leave them alone for two seconds.' I heard PFC England shout out, 'He's getting hard.' (cited in Hersh 2004: 2)

As such, the motivation and methodology behind the photographs was the construction of a 'social reality' of sexuality and race deemed inferior to the captors. This construction served multiple objectives beyond the stated intentions of 'information gathering' and 'softening up'. The photographs appear to have both intended and unintended performative functions, in that the images work to construct images of, and record acts of, a perceived inferior racialised and sexualized identity. In their exposure, the photographs also 'blow back' the actions of the guards, revealing the US military to be practitioners of torture. In this respect, the images have a certain treacherous and active quality, a performativity that speaks despite the absence of words and live action. This active and potentially generative quality appears intrinsic to the images and is arguably still present in representations or stagings of the photographs in performance. Wright's *Black Milk* provides a viable case study for examining this phenomenon.

The Performance: Description

The choreographer's decision to include reference to the photographs in his performance resulted in part from his position as a HIV positive homosexual. Hence, the performance response is a blending of personal and political worlds. Wright is uneasy about the role of the political in art. In an email to me from December 2008 he writes:

> Everything is political, but I do think that it usually kills a work as 'art' for it to have a strident political message and try to avoid it usually! Dance can do nothing to change the world except perhaps help one person at a time to open their minds and hearts and BREATHE. (original emphasis, Wright 2008)

Regardless of these concerns, Wright does venture into the political realm. He discusses his reaction to the images and his approach to representing them in an interview with Kim Hill on National Radio (New Zealand).

> WRIGHT: When I think about Abu Ghraib I weep. The fact that it's as if someone took the pulse of mainstream, the world and the pulse said that homosexuality is still the most disgusting thing that one human being, you know to make someone simulate homosexual acts is still the most disgusting and humiliating act you can perform on another human being. Yeah, I find that heart-wrenching.

And in response to his appearance on stage during the scene:

> WRIGHT: I'm only dancing because there is a particular scene – the torture scene which is particularly difficult and I thought that it needed a metaphorical sort of level to it.
> HILL: This is the torture scene with resonance (sic) to Abu Ghraib?
> WRIGHT: Yeah and I thought that it needed a metaphorical image in it to leaven the brutality at the beginning so [...] I do a short dance myself just standing on the spot [...] and I'm happy to go on stage for those three to four minutes or whatever it is. Oh god, I was going to say something ridiculous.
> HILL: Go on what was it?
> WRIGHT: I was going to say for God. (Wright 2006b)

In an interview with myself, Wright maintained that he did not just seek to comment on the demonisation of homosexuality but wished to also acknowledge the 'hell' that the prisoners went through and wanted the piece to act as a 'prayer' (2008). While undoubtedly well intentioned, his response does not appear to consider and accommodate the Muslim religious and cultural sensibilities regarding homosexuality that were deliberately targeted and exploited in the torture. This is undoubtedly a difficult issue to traverse, involving a critique of belief systems held by some in that culture which are inextricably linked to negative perceptions of homosexuality. Additionally, Wright spoke of the desire to stage it in 'real time' to combat the media tendency to present everything in still images between shampoo advertisements (ibid.). This is a bold move as he is choosing to animate highly contentious and provocative still images, the ramifications of which will be returned to later.

Within the realm of the wider performance of *Black Milk*, the Abu Ghraib sequence thematically, at least, is not a wild departure as it is interspersed between multiple 'taboo' sequences. The programme dutifully warns of nudity and 'scenes that may disturb' (*Black Milk* programme 2006: 4). *Black Milk* is intentionally provocative, highly creative and often hauntingly beautiful. It moves from images and sequences of delicate beauty relating to the nature and flow of intimate relationships to violent dysfunctional and often sexual attacks, to themes of child molestation and castration and from there into sequences that humorously deconstruct and parody the nature of dance construction, interpretation and intentionality.

This is a sophisticated work, which often briefly embraces literal representation, only to undo and undercut it with poetic abstraction in the next moment. Wright forms stage pictures that are visually arresting. Operating on a largely metaphorical level, the work often has a dream-like or nightmarish quality. To provide the audience with cognitive hooks and/or to provide Epic Theatre style critical distancing, Wright provides placards or signs, hung from above, carried on by the dancers or written on set pieces. The written text serves to frame the designated sequence, characters and in some cases objects. For example, the house that the pedophilic ventriloquist shares with his dummy/child is painted with words such as 'house', 'lair' and 'flesh' that describe and label the structure.

There is a certain rhythm to the piece frequently involving a silent dance segment followed by a scene with spoken text. The show's preset includes a large sign hanging above the stage stating 'Pain examined without prejudice is metamorphosis'. Below the sign a male blow-up doll lies on a bed of nails atop a downturned coffin. In a semblance of breath, an unseen pump propels air in and out of the doll. The confrontational tableau frames what is to come.

During the show up to ten highly skilled male and female dancers are on stage at any given time. There are also the relatively well-defined characters of the pedophilic ventriloquist and his child/dummy, as well as Wright himself, who appears during the Abu Ghraib-inspired sequence. Running at nearly two hours, the show is epic in scale. Its pared back staging artfully uses sheer and opaque red curtains, lengths of black plastic for moving objects and people on and off stage, a moveable closet/home for the ventriloquist and his dummy and a huge silk cocoon/womb/breast, which hangs down over the stage, serving as something of a metaphoric birth canal in a number of scenes. *Black Milk* is performed on a proscenium arch stage. The audience sits some distance from the action in the darkened auditorium. However, the stage apron is used regularly throughout in what seems to be a deliberate ploy to implicate the audience in the stage action.

The characters of the ventriloquist and his child/dummy both engage the audience via direct address and repel the audience through their pedophilic relationship. Often their conversations provide clues as to the thematic reasoning in the piece through poetic language, for example when the ventriloquist says 'Death is a monstrous spider. It has black milk'. The 'storyline' of their relationship, including the dummy giving 'birth' to a tiny 'mummy' (of the ancient Egyptian sort) and its 'death' and the 'death' or transcendence of the dummy itself shifts between the abstract and naturalistic and serves as a narrative structuring device for the whole performance. A sequence where their voices are heard from within their closet is particularly disturbing, as it appears to be playing out a scene of child sexual abuse. Outside two male dancers masturbate in response to what they hear. Two females roll on the floor in a sexual embrace and another takes photographs of the voyeurs, including the audience. This may be an early metaphor for the sexual abuse at Abu Ghraib. However, it seems more likely that it is thematically linked to wider notions of power, control, 'othering' and sexualised abuse and works to prefigure and, to an extent, prepare the audience for the explicit and literal content of the Abu Ghraib-inspired sequence that appears in the latter half of the show.

Ultimately, the juxtaposition of the two sequences (the child abuse and the Abu Ghraib-inspired scenes) is jarring. Instead of blending together to create a coherent summative semiosis commenting on the wider themes, the two sequences remain decidedly separate. The first involving the ventriloquist and his child/dummy, while mimetic, does not call upon 'real' and almost universally viewed photographs, whereas the latter sequence works to animate such images. As a result, the Abu Ghraib sequence has the capacity to jolt the viewer out of the world of the performance and into current political, social and ethical issues. The jolt may well be Wright's intention but whether it results in critique, reinscription, disgust or titillation is the subject of this analysis. To examine this it is useful to look at the sequence in some detail.

It begins with quiet piano music. A red and black sign is lowered with the words 'somewhere – now' emblazoned in white handwritten letters. A group of ten male and female dancers shuffle into the dimly lit space. They wear plastic bags over their heads – mimicking the sacks used at Abu Ghraib. They are naked, save for the females who wear prosthetic penises, presumably to indicate that they should be read as male as well. The dancer-prisoners take tentative and unwilling blind steps, hiding their genital regions with their hands. They form a line along the back of the stage, and invert themselves by flipping their legs over their heads. We see their exposed backs and their arms dangling at their sides. In this position they look uncannily like plucked chicken carcasses. The effect is heightened as they inch forward in this position, like a line of animated headless chickens. The moment seems comic and does not appear to relate, at this stage, to existing images of Abu Ghraib.

The choreographer, Wright, walks into the space. He is dressed entirely in white and carries a spray can that he uses to assign numbers from one to ten to the backs of the individual dancers. While he does this, his altered electronic voice booms out from the sound system, listing the numbers in reverse order, counting down from ten to one. The voice has been distorted to sound powerful and harsh and its amplification through the speakers in the auditorium lends it a god-like omnipotence. Wright appears to be wearing a transparent half mask over the lower half of his face. After spraying the dancers he sprays a 'o' on his own shirt and then moves to the side where he assumes a position of command. We hear the sounds of dogs barking and the closing of heavy metal doors. This relates to Abu Ghraib and the use of dogs to terrorise prisoners (Taguba in Murphy 2004: 594–595). He lurches in front of the dancer-prisoners, gesturing and miming to the pre-recorded voice: 'Stand up you bastards, stand up, get up Number Four, Number Four come forward, lie down'. He repeats the directive as the dancer-prisoner moves into place. Then 'Number Eight come forward, lie on top...' He also beckons Numbers Three and Two. 'Get on top you fucking idiot [...] now wriggle around like a pack of worms [...] you gay white bastards [...] Wriggle!' Wright's body contorts in agony or pleasure (it is difficult to determine which). His eyes are closed, arms rigid and his wrists are locked backwards as he swings and turns his arms in a movement pattern reminiscent of a musical conductor.

While the voice seems connected to the character Wright is playing, its detachment from the physical body gives it an otherworldly quality that suggests a form of external possession. Nonetheless, the strident voice dominates the space and renders all those on stage small and vulnerable. In an email to me, Wright clarified that he plays two characters within the scene and considers this first character to be the owner of the voice who is 'torn apart by the proceedings' (2008). In this he seems to be referencing the testimony of those guards at Abu Ghraib such as Specialist Matthew Wilson who wanted no part in the torture (Hersh 2004: 2).

The commands continue, variously ordering the dancer-prisoners to take on a number of sexualised positions. While the actions seem in tone with those undertaken at Abu Ghraib, it is difficult to judge where poetic license has taken over from 'real' references. The whole sequence is an extension on the photographs. The stage action has moved beyond animating the two-dimensional image presented in the photographs and is proposing likely scenarios, some seemingly recycled from earlier historical methods of dehumanisation, such as the reduction of prisoners to numbers and the inscribing of marks on the body, as employed in the death camps of Auschwitz. It is interesting to consider the implications of this collage of references. On one hand, it may help the audience to create cognitive and emotional links between traumatic events, but it also risks suggesting spurious equivalencies between different historical events and reductive viewpoints and rationalisations relating to universal notions of suffering.

As the performance continues Wright re-emerges dressed in a quasi-religious robe of white. A large white cross covers his head (see Figure 10). An apparently enormous erection presses against the robe from underneath. The costume and image is evocative of the Ku Klux Klan and also of Christian priests and penitents. While the voiceover does not alter in tone or volume, it would appear that Wright's role and character has changed. Where previously he could have been seen as a tortured torturer, this incarnation is more obviously enjoying the experience and the erection suggests the enjoyment is motivated by sexual power. Wright discussed the character in an email to me. The 'cross-head, Ku Kluxish figure I see as the sort of gloating overlord and repository of the matrix (patrix?) of meanings inherent in the scene, one being the hatred of the body and homosex as taught by the Church (sic)' (2008). In the scene, he moves amongst the dancer-prisoners miming the voice as it issues orders to create other oral and anal sexual scenarios. Wright places his hands on either side of the cross in a gesture of seeming ecstasy. This sense of enjoyment in directing and observing the scenario reflects, to an extent, the attitude of the smiling guards at Abu Ghraib. However, the overt sexual arousal of Wright's character inadvertently highlights and reinforces the pornographic aspect of the images and their construction.

The Abu Ghraib photographs have been described as pornographic (Baudrillard 2006: 86, Tétreault 2006: 38). Hence, it would not seem unreasonable for a live action performance based on the images to have pornographic appeal to some individuals. Indeed, despite the artist's best intentions, audience members may be titillated by the scene rather than experience and come to a deeper empathic understanding of the prisoners' plight. Wright's own performance within the scene embodies a sexually aroused response to the action. Hence, despite the fact that he is attempting a critical symbolic reference to individuals and institutions he perceives to have deleterious impact on perceptions of homosexuality, the character's actions also performatively inscribe the situation as pornographic.

The scene continues building to a recreation of one of Abu Ghraib's iconic images. The dancer-prisoners are told to get down on their knees, put their heads on the floor, their hands on their heels and crawl forward. This would seem a direct reference to the stress positions used at Abu Ghraib and Guantanamo Bay. Wright's character instructs them to squeal like pigs then to form a line. He singles out Number Seven to remain forward. Loud bangs are heard as chairs are hurled at the individual from the wings of the stage. The dancer-prisoner tries to move back but is told to lie face down. Again we hear dogs barking. The directive is given 'Get on top of him you fucking animals', at which point the others (now approximately six dancers) slowly pile on top of him to reenact Abu Ghraib's famous pyramid of flesh.

Three dancer-prisoners emerge from behind the curtains wearing large wooden boards around their necks, reminiscent of the stocks used for imprisonment and public humiliation (see Figure 9). The three are bent over with the weight of the boards as they move forward into a growing light downstage. This is another departure from Abu Ghraib where there was no apparent use of stocks. The three dancer-prisoners pass the pyramid, which disappears behind a curtain. The voice announces 'Ladies and gentlemen here we have murderers, child molesters, drug addicts, traitors, sodomites, Christians, lawyers, suicides, thieves, necrophiliacs, whites, vampires...' Some of the categories are difficult to distinguish due to the electronic distortion. By this point, the three have come to a stop on the apron of the stage facing the audience. The ever-inclusive listing of 'criminals' is comprehensive enough to be seen as an attempt to undermine processes of 'othering'. The taxonomy implies that the 'crimes' of these individuals are commonplace and perpetrated by many in society, including those present in the auditorium. As such it is another device employed by Wright to critique the underlying philosophies and actions exemplified in the Abu Ghraib images. Notably the voice, which had been directed previously at the dancer-prisoners, now seems to be addressing the audience. Thus, as the curtains reopen to re-reveal the sign 'somewhere – now' and the three dancer-prisoners edge their way slowly off stage, the sequence returns us to the present and its implications for us.

Black Milk: Critique or Reinscription?

Wright's piece makes for deliberately uncomfortable viewing. However, the success of his critique would seem partial at best. Outwardly, the piece does little to overturn the demonisation of homosexuality, largely because in trying to capture the 'hell' experienced by the prisoners Wright presents a grim and harrowing scenario. It is difficult to imagine how the Abu Ghraib example could be used to advocate against the demonisation of homosexuality because what is generally identified first in the situation is torture and abuse. As discussed earlier, this particular form of sexualised abuse was contrived specifically to have maximum impact on the cultural group targeted (Otterman 2007: 170–171 & Eisenmann 2007: 29). Thus, while the American guards are clearly demonising homosexuality and may be held accountable, the case of these particular Iraqi prisoners is complex. Accusations in the latter case would involve castigating the victims.

With respect to the 'hell' of the prisoners, there is certainly a sense of suffering and degradation but whether this approximates to that of the original prisoners is questionable. It is theoretically possible to read the sequence without identifying pain or trauma. Elaine Scarry in her book *The Body in Pain: the making and unmaking of the world* has argued that pain is not visible to the outsider:

> For the person whose pain it is, it is 'effortlessly grasped' (that is, even with the most heroic effort it cannot *not* be grasped); while for the person outside the sufferer's body, what is 'effortless' is *not* grasping it (it is easy to remain wholly unaware of its existence; even with effort, one may remain in doubt about its existence or may retain the astonishing freedom of denying its existence; and finally, if with the sustained effort of attention one successfully apprehends it, the aversiveness of the 'it' one apprehends will only be a shadowy fraction of the actual 'it'. (original emphasis, Scarry 1985: 4)

If this is the case, it may be considered that it is not possible adequately to represent or approximate suffering. Many Holocaust theorists maintain that extreme suffering is un-representable and that artistic renditions not only fail to capture the experience but do a disservice to the victims. Patraka contends:

(t)he dangers of staging the visual in the theatre of the Holocaust are double-edged: first that the anguish of suffering bodies will be conveyed on stage as 'real' and somehow comprehensible, manageable, able to convey what is actually an immeasurable absence, or second conversely, that the suffering mediated by 'the toy gun,' will have the seduction of the unreal. (1999: 101–102)

Similarly, Adorno criticises a number of artists for presuming to speak on behalf of the victim. In response to Schoenberg's *Survivor of Warsaw* (also known as *Survivor from Warsaw*), a combination of music, choral singing and spoken voice, he claims that there is

> something embarrassing in Schoenberg's composition [...] the way in which, by turning suffering into images, harsh and uncompromising though they are, it wounds the shame we feel in the presence of the victims. For these victims are used to create something, works of art, that are thrown to the consumption of a world which destroyed them. The so-called artistic representation of the sheer physical pain of people beaten to the ground by rifle-butts contains, however remotely, the power to elicit enjoyment out of it. The moral of this art, not to forget for a single instant, slithers into the abyss of its opposite. The aesthetic principle of stylization, and even the solemn prayer of the chorus, make an unthinkable fate appear to have had some meaning; it is transfigured, something of its horror is removed. This alone does an injustice to the victims [...]. Works of less than the highest rank are also willingly absorbed as contributions to clearing up the past. (1980: 189)

This raises the question of whether it is possible to represent the traumatic 'real' in performance, or does the aesthetic process inevitably change and mediate the suffering, transforming it into something else entirely (which may look the same) – something that works to hide and relegate to the past that which the artist is seeking to highlight? These issues have been debated across a number of cultural realms including Dance and Theatre studies. In the case of *Black Milk*, despite the gritty and confronting nature of the Abu Ghraib sequence, the process of staging involves a process of aestheticisation. While Wright's work maintains a similar confrontational quality to that possessed by its source material, it is difficult to argue categorically that it does not create some, if not all, of the outcomes outlined by Adorno. My own initial reactions did follow along similar lines. Perhaps it is because the transformative nature of performance can, as Patraka (1999) maintains, make the unmanageable manageable, that the ethical and political ramifications of representation are often overlooked.

In effect, the context of the performance event may also work against the aims of the artist. Wright's dancers, unlike the prisoners at Abu Ghraib, have beautiful healthy bodies, which are routinely willingly objectified in and for performance. The context of aesthetically pleasing bodies, framed within an arguably 'high art' night of culture, is difficult to transcend. In this setting and situation, it is difficult to apprehend the atrocities of Abu Ghraib. Phenomenologically experienced aurally and visually, the relentless violence of the piece may promote a visceral and reflexive re-response to the material (Abu Ghraib) that the viewer is familiar with outside of the theatre. However, within this lies the possibility of creating something of a hermeneutic surplus. Through the processes of decontextualisation and recontextualisation involved in 'reading' the segment, the reader may choose to close off reading or recontextualise what is experienced as a purely aesthetic or isolated episode. Wright is thus in a double-bind. For his segment to create his preferred reading it needs both to evoke the 'real' and function as performance.

In this particular instance, the 'real' is also bound up with performativity. The photographs are not simply a representation but a performative act of 'othering' undertaken in the original site of Abu Ghraib prison. The photographs were also taken to perpetuate that 'othering' through the continued existence and circulation of the images. As such they are not simply documentary evidence (often of staged tableaus) but also evidence of blackmail and an ongoing act of identity-construction of 'actual' human beings. And as Sontag observes, 'the pictures will not go away. That is the nature of the digital world in which we live' (2004: 42).

In evoking the images in performance there is the risk that the photographs will continue to operate in a performative manner and, as a result, reinscribe those hierarchies of power that facilitated their creation, as well as perpetuating the constructions of identity used to torture and blackmail the victims. The victims' presence, virtually captured in the photographs, is arguably re-summoned in a performance that references the images. Theoretically, to avoid this would involve avoiding any form of literalism, any form of representation that could evolve into re-presentation.

This resonates with cautions that Lepecki offers regarding the use of the political in dance. He identifies three operational fallacies:

1. The exposure of the body is enough to dignify it (and redeem the oppressor)
2. The reproduction of trauma is enough to overcome the cruelty of the traumatizer
3. The expression of one's rage is enough to destroy the agents and mechanisms of repression. (1995: 8)

Repetition does not equal allegory, or critique for that matter, but in the case of the *Black Milk* segment there is more than simple repetition at work. While Wright makes no claim to veracity or docudrama, the 'real' aspect of his source material and indeed his desire to acknowledge the 'hell' of the prisoners does result in a 'reality' tinged performance. However, as Baudrillard points out, the 'real' captured in the photographs is elusive:

> The bulk of media or photographic images today portray only human violence and misery. But the more meaning this misery and violence is granted, the less troubling it becomes. It's a total non-sense, the very opposite of meaning. For us to be directly affected by its content, the image has to move us, impose on us its peculiar language (once again, the image is more important than what it means). If transference to the real is to occur, there must be a definite counter transference of the image. (2008: 42)

To clarify, in the rush to ascribe meaning the image becomes lost under the 'weight of reality', obscuring its uniqueness in its complicity with the 'real' (Baudrillard 2008: 41). Baudrillard maintains that '"realist" photography doesn't capture *what is*, but *what shouldn't be* [...]. Behind their so-called "objectivity", photographic images are the witness of a profound denial of the real, but simultaneously a denial of the image' (ibid.: 42, original emphasis). In the case of the Abu Ghraib photographs, which are staged constructions that simultaneously document 'real' suffering, the path back to the original situation and trauma becomes ever more convoluted and susceptible to slippage and misreading.

When a temporal aspect is added to the spatial (the two-dimensional image), other layers of complexity and potentiality in meaning-making emerge. In an email to me, Wright reflects that 'showing something so disturbing in real time was a major test of our commitment' (2008). In animating the pictures, Wright does make the audience endure the violence in real time and it does have the advantage of 'liveness' to decrease distance from the event. At the same time, being allowed to sit in the dark and watch makes possible the consoling illusion that by attending such events, one is doing something about them. Alternatively, the individual may benefit from a cathartic release that diffuses a desire for change (Taylor 1990: 168). There is also the possibility of desensitising the individual to an image through repeated viewings. Hence, Wright may either nullify response with his re-presentation of the images or be confronted with audience members already desensitised to the source images. The nature of individual reception makes it impossible to determine whether nullification or catharsis will occur. Nonetheless, the possibility of such reactions does offer an ethical dilemma for artists intent on creating decidable meaning.

In choosing to stage the Abu Ghraib images, Wright also risks the backlash of a triple-revulsion. In response to the images, Sontag proclaimed 'the horror of what is shown in the photographs cannot be separated from the horror that the photographs were taken' (2004: 26). While avoiding further exploitation is clearly an aspect to be considered in future presentations, the risk of another revulsion at the Abu Ghraib atrocities does not appear sufficient reason to avoid their use, particularly if it culminates and aids in effective critique. Yet the use of these images remains highly problematic, working time and again to reinscribe that which is being criticised.

The US touring exhibition *Inconvenient Evidence* (2004) comprised sixteen of the infamous Abu Ghraib torture photographs with four images aimed at providing a 'counter-discourse to the dominance and voyeurism of both the American media and the soldiers taking the photographs' (Hesford 2006: 31). Hesford claims that the exhibition represents 'an overdose on the antidote', utilising trauma theorist La Capra's phrase, and argues that 'it reproduces the moral distance that spectacle enables and simulates the obsessive attraction to dominance and the temptation to excess in popular and military cultures' (ibid.: 34).

Baudrillard observes that the images of Abu Ghraib atrocities are depictions of something that is the opposite of an event, a non-event of obscene banality, the degradation, atrocious but banal, not only of the victims, but of the amateur scriptwriters of this parody of violence [...] pornography becoming the ultimate form of the abjection of war which is unable to be simply war, to be simply about killing, and instead turns itself into a grotesque infantile reality-show, in a desperate simulacrum of power. (2006: 86)

In his condemnation, Baudrillard acknowledges that although banal, the images are linked inextricably with power, war and myriad other cultural and political issues. This also contributes to the photographs' peculiarly active and provocative power beyond their representation of suffering.

Indeed, what causes the use of these particular images to be a precarious practice is not one factor, but many. Any performance involving representation of the images will invariably aestheticise the source images and the situation that created them. This opens up the possibility of lessening their horror, endowing them with a constructed meaning, making the suffering depicted enjoyable or titillating, rendering the atrocities manageable and promoting catharsis and/or desensitisation. Along with this is the notion that pain and trauma cannot be fully apprehended by the onlooker, thus challenging their very presence. The spatial and temporal characteristics of the artistic performance form are generative and mediate representations of the 'real'. The performative nature of the form, and of the images themselves, also make it possible for the original power hierarchies and practices involved in the creation of the Abu Ghraib photographs to be re-presented and reinscribed in performance.

Ultimately, Wright's critique through performance is not successful because, like the theorists writing about the images, ultimately (and perhaps inescapably) it underestimates the power of the images and presents them as 'less than what they are'. The piece while provocative and well-intentioned does not accommodate the images' complexity. Wright is unable to stop the generative, performative nature of the images, and the practices that created them, from perversely reinscribing their original aims in his performance. In this, he has ironically fallen prey to the images' treacherous power in a similar way to the US guards and government that spawned them. 'Do you want to acquire power through the image? Then you will perish by the return of the image' (Baudrillard 2006: 86–87). While many of these dangers are immanent in any attempt to represent the traumatic 'real', it should be recognised that these images possess a particularly generative performativity due to their form and the nature of their original production. Therefore, any attempt to utilise, represent or reference them in performance will remain a precarious practice.

Works Cited

Adorno, T. 1980. Commitment, in *Aesthetics and Politics*. Edited by Ernest Bloch and Ronald Taylor. Translated by Ronald Taylor. London and New York: Verso: 177–195.

Arendt, A. 1970. *On Violence*. New York: Harcourt, Brace and Ward.

A. S. & G. W. 2004. Limbaugh on Torture of Iraqis: US Guards Were 'Having a Good Time', 'Blow[ing] Some Steam Off'. [Online]. Media Matters for America. Available: <http://mediamatters.org/items/200405050003> [15 December 2008].

Black Milk Programme. 2006. Douglas Wright Dance.

Baudrillard, J. 2006. War Porn. *Journal of Visual Culture* 5: 86–88.

Baudrillard, J. 2008. The Violence of Images, Violence Against the Image. *art US* 23/3: 38–45.

Eisenmann, S. 2007. *The Abu Ghraib Effect*. London: Reaktion Books Ltd.

Hersh, S. 2004. Torture at Abu Ghraib: American Soldiers Brutalized Iraqis. How Far up Does the Responsibility go? *The New Yorker*. [Online]. Condénet. Available: <http://www.newyorker.com/archive/2004/05/10/040510fa_fact> [14 December 2008].

Hesford, W. 2006. Staging Terror. *TDR: The Drama Review*, 50/3 (T191): 29–41.

Horsley, F. 2006. Malevolence. *The Listener* 203/3441: 47.

Lepecki, A. 1995. How (not) to Perform the Political. *Ballett International*, January: 15–19.

Mirzoeff, N. 2005. *Watching Babylon: The War in Iraq and Global Visual Culture*. New York and London: Routledge.

Murphy, S. D. 2004. US Abuse of Iraqi Detainees at Abu Ghraib Prison. *The American Journal of International Law* 98/3: 591–596.

Oosterhoff, P., Zwanikken, P., & Ketting, E. 2004. Sexual Torture in Croatia and Other Conflict Situations: An Open Secret. *Reproductive Health Matters* 12/23: 68–77.

Otterman, M. 2007. *American Torture*. London: Pluto Press.

Patraka, V. 1999. *Spectacular Suffering: Theatre, Fascism, and the Holocaust*. Bloomington: University of Indian Press.

Scarry, E. 1985. *The Body in Pain; The Making and Unmaking of the World*. Oxford: Oxford University Press.

Schechner, R. 2006. *Performance Studies: An Introduction*. London: Routledge.

Schifferes, S. 2003. Analysis: US 'Shock and Awe' Tactic. *BBC News*. [Online]. BBC. Available: <http://news.bbc.co.uk/2/hi/middle_east/2874075.stm> [15 February 2009].

Smythe, J. 2006. 'Black Milk' in Wellington: Darkness and Life. *Theatreview*. [Online] Available: <http://www.theatreview.org.nz/reviews/review.php?id=154> [9 December 2008].

Sontag, S. 2004. Regarding the Torture of Others. *The New York Times Magazine*, May 23: 24–42.

Taylor, D. 1990. Theater and Terrorism: Griselda Gambaro's 'Information for Foreigners'. *Theater Journal* 42/2: 165–182.

Temple, P. 2006. Dance Carded. Letters to the Editor. *The Listener* 203/3442: 8.

Tétreault, M. A. 2006. The Sexual Politics of Abu Ghraib: Hegemony, Spectacle and the Global War on Terror. *National Women's Studies Association* 18/3: 33–50.

Thompson, A. 2008. *Performing Race and Torture on the Early Modern Stage*. New York: Routledge.

UNAMI (UN Assistance Mission for Iraq), Human Rights Report, 1 November – 31 December 2006, 16 January 2007. [Online]. UNHCR Refworld. Available: <http://www.unhcr.org/refworld/docid/4693430f27.html> [18 February 2009].

Wright, D. 2006a. *Black Milk* (dance/theatre performance). Regent Theatre Dunedin: Douglas Wright Dance.

Wright, D. 2006b. Interview on *Saturday Morning with Kym Hill* (radio), National Radio New Zealand 18 March, 09h05.

Wright, D. 2008. Interviewed by Suzanne Little. 16 December.

Zuber, D. 2006. Flânerie at Ground Zero; Aesthetic Countermemories in Lower Manhattan. *American Quarterly* 58/2: 269–299.

PART IV

Dancing to Market Forces

11 Performative Intervention and Political Affect: De Keersmaeker and Sehgal

This chapter investigates the potential for dancing bodies to intervene in the political.[1] It does this by analysing two recent but very different dance works: Tino Sehgal's performative installation *Instead of allowing something to rise up to your face dancing bruce and dan and other things* (2000), and Anne Teresa De Keersmaeker's solo *Once* (2002). As I will show, each work cites the memory of the 1960s in order to draw attention to current political concerns. *Once*, which was made during the build up to the 2003 invasion of Iraq, reflects on opposition to war, while the conceptual strategies articulated in *Instead of allowing something to rise...* address the effects of capitalist overproduction. These two dance works, however, not only cite particular political issues but intervene performatively within them by acknowledging affective aspects of the political. These works do not attempt to propose solutions to the problems to which they draw attention. Instead, as I shall show, each generates a sense of shame at the violating effects of political processes. By doing so they put their beholders in positions where they might begin to reflect on where they themselves stand in relation to the violence of war (*Once*) or the degradation of the physical and social environment (*Instead of allowing something to rise...*). These kinds of violence are the effects of power on individuals. As Michel Foucault observed, power is 'a relationship between two individuals, a relationship which is such that one can direct the behaviour of another or determine the behaviour of another' (2007: 134–5). This, he argues, is

---

1   Parts of this chapter have been presented in 2007 and 2008 during the Maska seminar in Ljubljana, and have developed out of discussions with Valerie Briginshaw and Bojana Kunst.

what governments do, and he defines governmentality as 'the group of relations of power and [the] techniques which allow these relations of power to be exercised' (ibid.: 135). This chapter investigates the biopolitical ways in which the dancing bodies in Sehgal and De Keersmaeker's works constitute sites of resistance against these violating relations and techniques of governmentality.

The question of the relationship between politics and violence is central to the recent emergence of a discourse about biopolitics. For Hannah Arendt 'violence is a marginal phenomenon in the political realm' (1973: 19) because it silences people. It is marginal because, in her view, politics is about free speech and democratic debate. But, as Chantal Mouffe notes: 'Arendt envisaged the political as a space of freedom and public deliberation, while others see it as a space of power, conflict, and antagonism' (2005: 9). Foucault developed the idea of biopolitics to account for the way the state seeks to normalise and regularise individuals as embodied subjects. These sometimes violating acts of governance largely operate through silence rather than speech. Arendt argued that 'violence itself is incapable of speech, and not merely that speech is helpless when confronted with violence' (1973: 19). Giorgio Agamben (1998, 2005) has brought together Arendt and Foucault's insights to suggest that modern states repeatedly exercise their sovereign power to declare permanent states of exception (states of emergency) that deprive their citizens of their rights. This leaves them unable to engage in the human interactions that constitute the political realm. Agamben likens this to the position of the 'homo sacer' in ancient Roman law who was an outsider, expelled from society and declared legally dead though physically alive so that it was not a crime to kill him. Agamben nevertheless believes that a recognition of the impossibility of having any rights under present political regimes is a first step towards realising a new libertarian politics. In some ways, in making and performing *Once*, De Keersmaeker seems to be refusing to accept the foreclosure of the space Arendt envisaged for democratic involvement. Sehgal's artistic choices, I will suggest, seem to have something in common with the kind of libertarian counter-politics that seeks to generate alternative, non-hierarchical social and political structures outside the state's regimes of regularisation and normalisation. Both pieces present choreographed performances of powerlessness and vulnerability that create a space in which to express what remains unspeakable and invisible under the states of exception through which we are currently living.

Sehgal's *Instead of allowing something to rise...* cites and reflects on the development of conceptual art in the late 1960s and De Keersmaeker's solo *Once* takes as its starting point Joan Baez's now classic 1963 album *Joan Baez in Concert, Part 2* for a reflection on the changing nature of politically committed art practices. The memory of 1960s radicalism has taken on particular meanings during the 1990s and 2000s which have seen a lack of political will concerning the destabilising effects of globalisation, environmental degradation, and the erosion of human rights. Philosopher Simon Critchley suggests there is currently a mood of political disappointment in response to 'the corrosion of established political structures and an unending war on terror where the moods of western populations are controlled through a politics of fear managed by the constant threat of external attack' (2007: 3). These sources of disappointment perhaps feed into growing voter apathy within long-established democracies, and contribute to the rise of right-wing populist nationalist groups in many countries. Looking back from the 2000s, the appeal of the 1960s lies in the memory of a time when large numbers of young people became actively involved in protests against repressive aspects of the state. One of the songs to which De Keersmaeker dances in *Once* is a recording of 'We Shall Overcome' from a concert Baez gave at Miles College in Birmingham, Alabama in May 1963. That week during Martin Luther King's Birmingham campaign there had been mass arrests of Civil Rights demonstrators. The political relevance of that song in that place at that time gives a particular affective charge to Baez's recording.

This positive idea of the radicalism of the 1960s is, of course, a contested one. As Judith Butler recently noted, in the aftermath of the September 2001 attacks in New York and Washington, editorials in the *New York Times* criticised anyone trying to understand the reasons for the attacks as 'excuseniks' exploiting the echoes of 'peaceniks' understood as naive and nostalgic political actors rooted in the frameworks of the sixties' (2004: xiii). *Once*, I shall argue, engages in a sophisticated reflection on the relation between political naivety and a belief in justice. While the conceptual

art works that Sehgal's piece cites were not in themselves politically motivated, they belong to a historical moment when conceptual artists were
challenging the institutions of the art world by producing works that had
no intrinsic value as objects; some people naively believed that these would
not therefore circulate within the art market. Sehgal's piece is a sophisticated
reflection on the efficacy of such institutional critique from the point of
view of recent libertarian politics.

What is at issue here is not just the explicit political content – *Once*'s
appeal against war or Sehgal's critique of capitalist overproduction. My
aim in this chapter is not only to interpret these works in relation to the
specific contexts to which they refer, but also to evaluate the affective
political landscape that each imaginatively proposes. Each work opens
up a potential for communication between performer and beholders, by
making the latter aware of their own material presence within the gallery space or theatre. By doing so, each challenges its beholders to find
new ways of experiencing and valuing the work. As Jonathan Crary has
recently observed: 'We are now in a material environment where earlier
20th-century models of spectatorship, contemplation and experience are
inadequate for understanding the conditions of cultural creation and reception' (2003: 6). A general recognition that 'art must reconfigure itself in
relation to transformed modes of cognition and experience' (ibid.) has, in
Crary's view, led artists to create 'unanticipated spaces and environments
in which our visual and intellectual habits are challenged and disrupted.
The processes through which sensory information is consumed become the
object of various strategies of de-familiarization' (ibid.: 7). I aim to show
that a key aspect which the works by Sehgal and De Keersmaeker have
in common is that, while making the kind of challenge Crary describes,
they each produce a paradoxically passive, vulnerable performative presence which draws attention to affective qualities within current political
experience that otherwise remain hidden.

Neo-liberalism and Political Affect

While I was working on this essay in October 2008, I was also following the news of a global financial crisis. In the light of these events, I reread a lecture that the sociologist Anthony Giddens gave in 1999 about globalisation. In this he recalls his experience as a chance witness of the opening of the Berlin Wall in November 1989. He happened to be in Berlin for a meeting on 9th November when they heard that the Wall was on the point of being opened. Quickly making his way to part of the Wall with a small group, he found:

> Ladders were being put up against it and we started to climb up. But we were pushed back by television crews who had just arrived on the scene. They had to go up first, they said, so that they could film us scaling the ladders and arriving at the top. They even persuaded some people to go back down and climb up twice, to make sure they had good television footage. (1999: 67)

Reflecting on this incident, Giddens notes that 'television not only gets there first, but also stages the spectacle' (ibid.: 68); but in this case he suggests it had a right to do so because of the role it had played in bringing about the end of communism. As part of the open network of global communications, he argued, Western television undermined the communist political system because of the latter's dependence on control of information. In Giddens's neo-liberal view, the opening of the Wall exemplifies the positive benefits of fast, free, globalised flows of information twenty-four hours a day, seven days a week. The 2008 financial crisis has called Giddens's optimistic view of globalisation into question. De Keersmaeker and Sehgal's works draw attention to more complex and conflictual sets of responses to the impact of these fast free flows on individual and collective experience. I shall argue that these works use the affective power of dancing bodies to interrogate the effects of globalisation in ways that problematise the kinds of neo-liberal views that Giddens, Ulrich Beck, Scott Lash and others advocate.[2]

2   See for example Lash and Urry 1994; Beck 1997; Giddens 1991; Thrift 1996.

The Belgian political theorist Chantal Mouffe has recently criticised this kind of neo-liberal thinking. She argues that 'the mistake of liberal rationalism is to ignore the affective dimension mobilised by collective identifications and to imagine that those supposedly archaic "passions" are bound to disappear with the advance of individualism and the progress of rationality' (2005: 6). Giddens, Beck, Lash and others have argued that the increasing load of information generated by globalised communications and economics has generated a need for face-to-face interactions in order to facilitate the development of interpretative communities. As Mouffe points out, these neo-liberals believe that this has resulted in greater social and institutional reflexivity (ibid.: 43). In her view however this leads to the denial and suppression of the political:

> An idealised view of human sociability, as being essentially moved by empathy and reciprocity, has generally provided the basis of modern democratic political thinking. Violence and hostility are seen as archaic phenomenon, to be eliminated, thanks to the progress of exchange and the establishment, through a social contract, of a transparent communication among rational participants. (ibid.: 2–3)

In the aftermath of the 2008 economic crash, newspaper commentators have been challenging the idea that those working in the world's financial markets are rational agents with independent and well defined but selfish goals which they pursue with intelligence and consistency. There has been much discussion about the unpredictability of the markets and the need to re-establish confidence within them. Confidence is affective rather than rational. It is my contention that, through the way in which Sehgal and De Keersmaeker articulate memories of the 1960s, *Instead of allowing something to rise...* and *Once* each creates spaces in which to articulate political affects that are inadmissible within neo-liberal thinking.

There are levels within contemporary communication that are 'aesthetic' in the original sense of being open to sensation. As Susan Buck-Morss has pointed out: 'The body can *sense* when reasons have become rationalization and culture is a euphemism for oppression' (Buck-Morss 2002: 257). She makes this point in a discussion of the work of some Russian philosophers including Elena Petrovskaia, Valerii Podoroga and Mikhail Rylkin, with whom she was collaborating on academic research during the period leading up to the opening of the Berlin Wall and the collapse of

Soviet communism. This was a time when it became possible to investigate aspects of the Stalinist period that had previously been unacknowledgeable. Valerii Podoroga argued that, during periods of political oppression, certain art works have the potential to 'rediscover, or to be more exact, *invent* the catastrophic spaces and times that official culture covers over' (in ibid.: 258). While one cannot make a direct comparison between the USSR under Stalin and Western countries in our current globalised times, there are nevertheless violent effects of contemporary political and economic policies that today remain unspeakable. The kinds of catastrophic spaces and times that Podoroga identifies, I suggest, come into being during performances of *Instead of allowing something to rise...* and *Once*. Both works present a performance of powerlessness and vulnerability. I do not mean that these works advocate passivity and inaction as responses to the problems and challenges of political events. What these works demonstrate, I suggest, is the strategic value of using a performance of passivity to suggest alternatives to current political practices. In *Once*, as I will show, De Keersmaeker's theatricalisation of vulnerability foregrounds people's interdependence and hence their responsibility for one another. In Sehgal's work, a conceptual performance of vulnerability challenges and disrupts notions of reflexivity through defamiliarising contexts in which one might otherwise expect communication to take place. *Instead of allowing something to rise...* strips the human down to a minimum of motor activity thus suggesting a situation where dancing bodies are sufficiently free from the violence of governmentality so that they can become potential sites of resistance against such violence.

Once

Once was first performed in September 2002 just twelve months after the terrorist attacks in New York and Washington, and during the build up to the invasion of Iraq in March 2003. Some commentators have argued this represented a (failed) attempt by conservative business interests at global political and economic domination of the Middle East and its oil reserves. In this context, *Once*, like *Instead of allowing something to rise...*, addresses the violent effects of globalisation. As I noted earlier, the hour-long solo is danced to the classic 1963 album *Joan Baez in Concert Part 2* which was released at the height of the US Civil Rights movement. As Deborah Jowitt, reviewing *Once* in the *Village Voice* in November 2005, noted: 'Baez's 22-year-old voice floats out ravishingly in folk songs like "Once I Had a Sweetheart," fresh as the new world we hoped for in 1963' (2005: n.p.). Two statements by De Keersmaeker herself make clear the social and political values she hoped her solo would express. As she told Claire Diez:

> Joan Baez spread a profound belief in social change. She fought for human dignity, for a sense of well-being devoid of materialism. The word 'together' was supposed to mean something and its force made everything seem possible. Today, society is so atomised, problems are so complex that we don't know where or with what to begin, and that sometimes gives us such a feeling of powerlessness! (Diez 2002: n.p.)

Once is not, however, about powerlessness but seems to raise the question whether people can still feel as strongly about justice today as they did at the time when Baez's album was recorded. De Keersmaeker touches on this in an interview printed in *The New York Times*:

> There are a number of things set in those songs, which I really do believe in, maybe values that were proper to a certain time, which maybe would be considered utopian or naive. I don't think it's ridiculous to express a certain feeling that love, compassion and justice are values which are worth more than ever to defend. (La Rocco 2005: n.p.)

What makes *Once* such a powerful piece is the complex, multilayered way in which these political affects are expressed.

Joan Baez in Concert Part 2 is an album which has very personal associations for De Keersmaeker who knew it well as a child in the 1960s. Using it for her solo therefore combined the personal and the political. *Once* was not only premiered during the build up to the invasion of Iraq but also at a time when De Keersmaeker's company *Rosas* was about to reach its twentieth anniversary. Rather than making a celebratory piece with her company, however, De Keersmaeker's response seems to have been to turn introspectively back on herself and her past. Claire Diez writes that De Keersmaeker heard the album for the first time in 1967: 'Brand new and incongruously offered as a gift celebrating the birth of her sister, the record was proudly displayed next to a bouquet of flowers in the maternity ward' (2002: n.p.). It became the soundtrack of her childhood and adolescence, and she learnt to sing along with its words before she could understand the languages in which Baez was singing.[3]

The idea of memories, De Keersmaeker's own and those of the audience, is central to the solo's conceptual structure. Talking to her audience between songs, Baez tells them she feels so at home she hopes they won't mind if she takes her shoes off. As De Keersmaeker's audience hear this in the middle of *Once*, many of them will no doubt have remembered the solo's startling opening when De Keersmaeker walked on stage, abruptly kicked off her shoes, tensely eyed the audience and said 'Once'. After eyeing them for an uncomfortably long time, she slowly began dancing in silence, gradually introducing the audience to the movement vocabulary she had developed for the piece. This slipped idiosyncratically between contemporary dance steps, ballet extensions, and naturalistic gestures. Deborah Jowitt appreciated

> the many nuanced ways in which she twists, curves her arms, turns one foot in, sinks down, circles her elbows, tosses a leg into the air, skips lightly, spins, stands poised at the edge of the stage [...] as if she might jump off. Once Baez begins to sing, De Keersmaeker inserts subtly pantomimic, often playful gestures, hints of character, and enigmatic private responses. (2005: n.p.)

When Baez's music was finally played, I thought that De Keersmaeker had perhaps been dancing in silence while running through Baez's songs, or parts of songs, in her memory. Moreover, during some of the songs, whose words were projected onto the canvas backdrop, De Keersmaeker seemed to be tentatively lip-syncing with them. Deborah Garwood suggests that De Keersmaeker created

---

3   The album contains Spanish and Brazilian folk songs as well as ones in English.

the impression that a young girl was dancing alone to a record she loved [...]. By playacting the private world of an adolescent listening to a quintessential peace movement album, de Keersmaeker disarmed (an appropriately Peace Now kind of verb) the audience and swept it into an updraft of adult emotion. (Garwood 2006: 78)[4]

In this complex, multi-layered way, *Once* folds the present dancer into her memories of her younger self. At the same time it raises questions about memories of the strong political affects aroused in the 1960s and their relationship to the political landscape of the 2000s.

While for most of *Once*, De Keersmaeker danced to Baez's songs in the way Jowitt described, there are two songs where she staged a much more complex layering of ideas and theatrical actions. These are 'We Shall Overcome' in the middle of the piece, and 'With God On Our Side' at the end. As I have already noted, Baez's performance of 'We Shall Overcome' was recorded during a historic Civil Rights campaign of non-violent action in Birmingham, Alabama. Campaigners opposed the city's policies of segregation and racial discrimination in public accommodation, employment and education. The week that Baez performed at Miles College, thousands of people had been marching. Press reports and photographs recorded appalling scenes where firemen turned hoses on demonstrators, and police dogs were set on them. Censure at a national and international level helped to create a receptive political climate that led to the enactment of the 1964 Civil Rights Bill.

De Keersmaeker's treatment of 'We Shall Overcome' was striking. After Baez announced the song, she hummed its melody through. De Keersmaeker danced along with this introduction using what was now a familiar repertoire of movements. Just as Baez began to sing the first verse, however, the volume suddenly dropped so that Baez's recorded voice was almost inaudible. De Keersmaeker stopped dancing and began tentatively to mouth the words, occasionally quietly singing along with them, checking over her shoulder where the words were projected on the back wall. I found the effect here quite painful to watch and others have told me

---

4   'Peace Now' was used as a slogan in protests against the Iraq war although it is also
      the name of an Israeli peace organisation.

that they felt the same. In contrast with Baez's beautifully clear voice, De Keersmaeker's face looked tense and strained, her forehead furrowed as if ashamed of what she was trying to do. For one verse she, at last, sang the words resonantly, stumbling over one phrase during the performance I attended, her strong Belgian accent contrasting with Baez's American one. On one level, as Garwood suggests, De Keersmaeker might be restaging the adolescent's private world. De Keersmaeker's anguish, however, might also point to the distance separating the naive optimism of the 1960s from the political disappointment of the early 2000s.

This distance between naivety and experience also emerges at the end of *Once*. From the moment when Bob Dylan, rather than Baez, began to sing 'With God On Our Side', the performance shifted mood and became much more fragmented. While De Keersmaeker's dancing and other actions had always seemed to engage with Baez's singing, she seemed completely disconnected from Dylan's nasal twang as he sang his ballad of an anonymous everyman from the mid-west telling the history of his land.[5] Dylan's narrator noted that for each war – against the American Indians, the Spanish Americans, in the civil war – God had been on 'our' side. As the narrative shifted closer to the present, the wars became increasingly horrific. The song mentioned weapons made of the chemical dust and, in 2002, UN weapons inspectors were searching for just such weapons in Iraq. At the end, after the narrator questioned whether God had been on Judas Iscariot's side and said he felt confused, he concluded that if God is on our side he'll stop the next war. In September 2002 when *Once* was first performed, for campaigners in many countries the 'next war' against which they were protesting was the invasion of Iraq.

For much of this song De Keersmaeker sat in the shadows, getting up to spread out a grey blanket neatly on the floor only to roughly bundle it back up and discard it. Similarly she unfastened her hair and painstakingly

---

5   Baez, I suggest, sings 'With God on Our Side' in a way that empathises with the narrator and makes the latter's gradual dawning of political awareness believable. Dylan's performance, however, has an edge to it that suggests a certain ironic detachment. It is as if he is aware of the narrator's naivety, particularly in his use of 'we' and 'our', and gives more emphasis than Baez to the narrator's confusion at the end.

shook it free only to tie it quickly up again at the back of her neck. When Dylan sang the last verse, she got up and went over to a gramophone at the side of the stage. Dropping the needle into her parent's original, fragile, vinyl copy of Baez's record, she searched for the spot where Baez herself sings this last verse. The audience heard the key line about God stopping the next war a second time and then the 1963 audience's rapturous applause. A scene of the US Civil War from D. W. Griffiths's 1915 film *The Birth of A Nation* was then projected on the back wall and De Keersmaeker stripped off her dress to dance in her black panties in front of it, the shadow of her naked female body interrupting the unstoppable flow of black and white images of soldiers and gunfire.

Like 'We Shall Overcome', De Keersmaeker's performance in this final section is disturbing to watch, coming perilously close to the edge of the black hole of marginality and incoherent madness. Off stage De Keersmaeker is one of the best known Belgian artists who directs not only the Rosas company but also P.A.R.T.S., the internationally renowned dance conservatoire. She is a strong enough person to risk being thought unfashionable: for making an explicitly committed, political dance; for using Baez's perhaps now dated music; and for referring to essentially feminine experiences such as childbirth, girlhood, adolescent shame, and maternal grief at the senseless termination of human lives. Part of what makes the audience's experience in *Once* an awkward one is this focus on potentially unpopular causes and negative affects.

At the end of Dylan's ballad, although De Keersmaeker performed as if she was as weary and confused as its narrator, her dancing suggested grief at war and killing. Judith Butler has argued that what grief displays 'is the thrall in which our relations with others hold us, in ways we cannot always recount or explain. [...] Let's face it. We're undone by each other. And if we're not, we're missing something' (2004: 23). De Keersmaeker's uncomfortable and disturbing performance of powerlessness, I suggest, generates affects that are both political and ethical. They remind audience members of their own potential to be in thrall and undone through their relations with each other. This is where the sense of shame that De Keersmaeker reveals during the piece becomes transferred to the beholder. This sense of shame for her turns into shame at the inadequacy of our own response to the ethical demands made by the other. By doing this, I suggest, *Once* has the potential to invent what Valerii Podoroga describes as the catastrophic spaces and times that official culture covers over (Podoroga in Buck-Morss 2002: 258). Its affective charge compels us who behold it to reflect on our own responsibility for the violence of history.

Instead of allowing something to rise up to your face dancing bruce and dan and other things

Sehgal's *Instead of allowing something to rise up to your face dancing bruce and dan and other things* is a work made for exhibition in a public art gallery or museum in which a single performer rolls slowly on the floor of a gallery that is empty except for a typical museum label giving the artist's name, the title of the work, its date, and the name of its owner. The rolling movement, which looks relatively loose and free, comprises a partly improvised sequence that takes about six minutes to complete and is repeated ad infinitum. Its movement quality cites the new American dance of the late 1960s and early 1970s, while the work and its title cite US conceptual art of the same period. A single man or woman executes this limited range of rolling movements on a small part of the floor whenever a visitor is present in the gallery. The piece has no beginning or end but is presented in a continuous loop during opening hours. For the duration of the exhibition, a team of dancers, or interpreters as Sehgal calls them, replace one another at two and a half hour intervals. *Instead of allowing something to rise…* is therefore a work that installs dancing bodies within a space associated with visual art practices in ways that make critical interventions within normative modes of aesthetic appreciation. In doing so it can make beholders aware of the way they themselves are situated as embodied subjects in relation to the installation. It thus seems to open up possibilities for the beholder to become involved and in some way interact with the performers on the level of embodied experience. But the actual movement material performed is so minimal that it challenges normative ideas about involvement and interaction.

Tino Sehgal studied dance in London and in Germany and has also
studied economics. He currently lives and works in Berlin. After choreographing and performing a few works for conventional theatres, he turned
to creating pieces for art galleries, museums, and private collectors. Like
Instead of allowing something to rise..., these have no material existence other
than the interpreter's actions. Although it is possible to find unauthorized
photographs and video clips of some of Sehgal's work on the world wide
web, none of his works are documented by the artist himself either through
video, photographs or writing. In Sehgal's piece for the 2003 Frieze Art
Fair in London, a boy and girl, both around 8 years old, pretended to be
art dealers and invited visitors into their stand, explaining: 'We are only
documenting works which are not installed in the fair'. As Adrian Searle
explains: 'After each bit of perfectly choreographed business, they sing the
titles and the prices... If anyone tries to photograph the kids, they fall to
the ground and yell "We don't think it appropriate to take pictures of our
work"' (Searle 2003). In Sehgal's piece for the German pavilion at the 2005
Venice Biennale, the unsuspecting visitor found three uniformed gallery
attendants sashaying towards her wagging their finger and chanting in a jolly
way: 'This is so contemporary, contemporary, contemporary'. My impression was that most visitors smiled broadly at the attendants' song and dance
act. Elsewhere in the German pavilion, Sehgal had arranged for another
attendant to invite visitors to discuss the effects of global economics. In an
earlier work *This objective of that object*, a group of philosophers perform
a highly choreographed invitation to the gallery visitor to ask a question.
If the visitor responds and poses one, they then analyse and debate it in a
ritualistic and ironically rigorous manner.

Making gallery attendants, who are usually invisible, the subject of
the exhibition is on one level ironic. A similar ironic strategy operates in
Sehgal's works with children. As well as his piece for the 2003 Frieze Art
Fair, he also used children who were between 6 and 8 years old in his 2007
show at the ICA in London which had two alternative titles: *This Success*
and *This Failure*. For this a group of children (with an adult supervisor)

involved gallery visitors in school playground games.[6] Beholders were thus offered the possibility of comparing the theoretically sophisticated refinement with which they generally approach 'advanced', conceptually based installation art with the children's more direct and un-intellectual approach to being in the gallery. Sehgal's use of children and gallery attendants may not widen the public for installation art, but goes some way towards making people aware of those who do not belong within this narrowly defined public and are normally thus rendered marginal and invisible within this privileged space.

Sehgal's creation of participatory work aligns him with a number of artists who, since the early 1990s, have engaged in a kind of critique of art galleries and museums as institutions. They do this by problematising the role these institutions play in bringing together artworks, art practitioners, art theory, and members of the public in relational situations. The works these artists create generate opportunities for interactivity and collaboration that can often dematerialise creative outputs, resulting in the development of what Nicolas Bourriaud has called a relational aesthetic. Bourriaud, who is himself an exhibition curator, suggests that: 'Meetings, encounters, events, various types of collaboration between people, games, festivals, and places of conviviality, in a word all manner of encounter and relational invention thus represent, today, aesthetic objects likely to be looked at as such' (2002: 28). As Claire Bishop (2004) points out, Bourriaud has in effect proposed one of the most useful frameworks for discussing the art practices of the 1990s and early 2000s. She is one of a number of scholars who have criticised Bourriaud's propositions from theoretical or socio-political points of view.[7]

The kinds of activities that Bourriaud lists can, in general terms, be identified in some recent European dance works: the collaborative proc-

---

6   Eliza Williams, reviewing this piece in *Flash Art* reported that: 'On entering, a child appears and immediately announces the show to be a success or a failure, depending on his or her mood, before encouraging you to join in a range of chaotic childhood games' (2007: 127–8). This did not happen during the twenty or so minutes while I was in the gallery.

7   See also Halsall, Jansen and O'Conner 2006, Ross 2006 and Kunst 2006.

esses which Thomas Lehman initiates and the places of conviviality and encounter that Felix Ruckert creates might be seen as instances of the kinds of encounter and relational invention Bourriaud discusses. In a very different way, the interactive question and answer section at the end of Xavier Le Roy's *Product of Circumstances*, and the kinds of activities generated as part of his *E.X.T.E.N.S.I.O.N.S.* projects (1999–2001) exemplify the use of critical tactics that bring about the new kinds of aesthetic relations that Bourriaud identifies. The game-like structures of Le Roy's *Project* (2003) – in which Sehgal performed – might be seen as a performative representation of such strategies.

While acknowledging the pertinence of Bourriaud's insights into the recent emergence of these kinds of artistic activities, Bojana Kunst suggests that the institutional positioning of this relational work requires further interrogation. Many of the projects Bourriaud writes about, she argues, 'belong to an institutional community of work that fetishises mobility, participation and communication' (Kunst 2006: 83). Kunst is pointing out that such relational art works resonate with the kind of social and institutional reflexivity that Giddens, Beck, Lash and others suggest is characteristic of globalisation. In Kunst's view, Bourriaud's analysis is in danger of affirming and celebrating a particular stage of globalised capitalism. Any critical potential that these recent artistic practices may have, Kunst warns, becomes lost in Bourriaud's account of 'the fluid multiplicity of ways of doing things together' (ibid.). Although subjectivities may dynamically interact in such work, they seem to do so as empty circulating signs. Kunst reminds us of another form of contemporary mobility experienced by the '"non-belonging" people or groups of people [who] move in the invisible and deadly channels of illegality, poverty, invisibility, and escape' (ibid.: 82). These include, for example, illegal immigrants whose non-productive, servile labour is not only not valued but largely invisible within wealthy Western countries. Rather than celebrating new artistic forms of mobility and participation in an uncritical way, Sehgal's work resists recuperation by the processes of institutionalisation and global capitalism because of the kinds of people he involves in their interpretation. This is particularly obvious in his use of children and gallery attendants. The interpreters of *Instead of allowing something to rise...* are anonymous and strangely isolated from the beholder, their execution of Sehgal's movement material allows them no possibility for either self expression or any demonstration of skill or virtuosity. There is I suggest a similarity between the interpreters and those who are alive but invisible and whose illicit status too often means they do not enjoy any rights. By staging this performance of powerlessness within the privileged institutional space of the art gallery, the work disrupts the kind of reflexivity that Bourriaud uncritically celebrates.

I saw two different interpreters of the piece during an exhibition of works by Sehgal at the Institute of Contemporary Arts, London, in January 2005: a man when the gallery first opened around midday, and a woman when I returned in the early evening. I could see that both were executing the same rolling movements in very similar ways, but each had a very different energy in the way they moved. The woman was not as tall as the man and had a bigger, rounder pelvis. She seemed to move more smoothly and continuously. His interpretation, in comparison, was more austere and used less momentum. He sometimes seemed almost to come to a standstill and then to make the minimum possible effort to just about keep going. But in both interpretations there were moments of hesitation when a rolling movement reached a stable midpoint. It was as if the interpreter was thinking about whether to carry on with the same movement or to make some small change of direction.[8] Dancers who improvise often use such mid points to check themselves and try to break out of patterns of repetition by attempting to find something new and unpredictable. The interpreters, in my opinion, were doing the opposite. It was as if they were ensuring that they were not introducing anything new into their execution but just staying within set parameters. I do not know what Sehgal's reasons for imposing these kinds of limitations to their expressivity may have been, but the effect for me was to render the interpreters anonymous, servile and almost disturbingly deindividuated.

---

8   I also saw a third interpreter when I visited the exhibition a few weeks later. This was a man who seemed to have less experience of the kind of relaxed, image-based, improvisational way of moving with which, in my opinion, the previous two interpreters had seemed familiar. Nevertheless I saw the same stages in his interpretation.

Their eyes closed, the interpreters each confined their movements on and around a restricted patch near the wall. Every five minutes or so (or maybe longer) their turns brought them close to the wall and they then rolled round to face up towards the ceiling. With their head pushing slightly back against the wall, they appeared almost to be looking down the length of their body and out into space. One could see most of their face for the first time. At this point their elbows were bent, and their two hands, having come up free from underneath their body, seemed to be moving together towards their face, just below the chin. This, I suggest, is a key moment in the movement sequence whose significance lies in the way it cites early conceptual art works.

Bruce and Dan in the piece's title are the visual artists Bruce Nauman and Dan Graham. In the late 1960s Nauman made a series of videos including *Floor-wall positions* (1968) and *Elke Allowing The Floor to Rise Up Over Her, Face Up* (1973), which document simple actions he or an assistant executed in front of a video camera in his empty studio. These drew on his knowledge of the new dance of Anna Halprin, Simone Forti, and members of Judson Dance Theater. Dan Graham admired Nauman's videos and, hearing by word of mouth about these dancers, tried to find out everything he could about them (Graham 1999: 99). His installation *Roll* (1970) consists of two films projected onto facing walls. One shows him rolling on the floor holding a camera, while the other shows the film shot with his camera facing towards the other static one. *Roll* thus restages Nauman's videos in a way that acknowledges the presence of the camera. When I saw Sehgal's piece, the figure rolling on the floor at the far end of the gallery bore a strong resemblance to photos of Graham in *Roll*. Later, looking at these photographs of Graham with a camera, I was particularly reminded of the recurring moment in Sehgal's piece when the interpreter's hands seemed about to rise to the face. I realised it was as if there was an invisible camera between their hands.

Sehgal has recently said that *Instead of allowing something to rise...* is a critique of these videos and films. He defines dance as a mode of production that is a transformation of action. These videos and films, in Sehgal's opinion, turned dance into a material object by transposing a transformation of action into a transformation of material: '[Nauman and Graham] took up dance and placed it in the museum but as video or film, whereas I'm interested in placing a transformation of action as a transformation of action into the museum' (Griffin 2005: 219). In the 1960s and 1970s, it was generally accepted that conceptual artists like Graham and Nauman were subverting art as an institution by not creating conventional art objects. Sehgal, however, says his work is not intended as an attack on art as an institution. He is quite happy to work within the museum: 'I'm just trying to define the way in which it does what it's there for... I am not against its address or celebration of the individual, but I am against its continuous, unreflected-on celebration of material production' (ibid.). Not only does Sehgal prefer not to create any material objects, but his work also troubles conventional ideas about production. He points out that: 'If one does a movement or sings or speaks, then one is obviously producing something. But immediately as a note ends or the movement stops, it is gone; it deproduces itself' (ibid.: 218). His work, he says, exists in the simultaneity of production and deproduction. The stable mid point in the roll, which I described earlier, and the absent camera each, in different ways, exemplify this. Sehgal's work will not, of course, put a stop to the economic system of unsustainable overproduction by simultaneously producing and deproducing itself. It does not provide an answer to present problems but prompts beholders to reflect on where they themselves stand in relation to them.

When I saw *Instead of allowing something to rise...*, the interpreters were each maintaining a blank, neutral performance. Their eyes were closed, and they were seemingly unaware of any beholders, as if they had been instructed to be careful not to look at them. When I attended a talk by Jens Hoffmann, the curator who had organised this exhibition, this was given in the gallery at the same time that an interpreter was performing the piece. I was struck by the way the audience, as they listened to the talk, sat with their backs to her, seemingly ignoring what she was doing. It was as if the installation were an object whose presence they had registered and which they knew would still be there to look at should they choose to turn and see it. The interpreter was objectified and rendered entirely anonymous; this is in marked contrast to a dance performance in which the programme generally gives dancers' names and brief biographies.

Sehgal himself has acknowledged how troubling this can be. When the work was first shown in a gallery at S.M.A.K. in Ghent, he recalled that

> the reactions of the people were really quite strong, I realized they were experiencing exactly what the work is about. They were shocked that this was not an object. Some people even thought it was a puppet or a robot. It was very strange. So I was motivated even more than before to keep on going, since I felt that I had found a form which can produce an experience which has something to do with the point of the work and not just talk *about* a certain point. (Sgualdini 2005: n.p.)

Sehgal's argument is that, because gallery visitors expected the exhibition to contain objects, they were troubled when they found themselves looking at an objectified human body. Although the interpreters of Sehgal's piece were alive, their isolation and inability to communicate with the gallery visitor placed them in a particular socio-political space. Involved in servile, non-productive labour, the interpreters were active and alive but not part of the community, their state of silent non-communication rendering them barely human, like those Agamben calls 'homo sacer'. Yet, as I noted earlier, the 'homo sacer' is also a starting point for a new libertarian politics. To quote from another Bob Dylan song 'when you ain't got nothin' you got nothin' to loose'.

Sehgal himself acknowledges that, in his work, the visitor is made aware of his or her own presence in the situation created by the installation. As he told Tim Griffin,

> you cannot be uninvolved, somehow, when there's this other person who can look back at you. The viewer in my work is always confronted with him- or herself, with his or her own presence in the situation, as something that matters, as something that influences and shapes this situation. This experience that his or her own presence has consequences can kind of empower the viewer. (Griffin 2005: 219)

If, as he suggests, this self-awareness can empower the viewer, this is usually done in an ironic, witty way. As far as I am aware, *Instead of allowing something to rise...* is the only piece by Sehgal that does this through isolation and non-communication. Sehgal's piece generates a sense of shame that involves interpreter and gallery visitor with one another in a physical, embodied way. Writing about theatrical performance, Nick Ridout argues that 'there is something in the appearing that takes place in the theatre that seems capable of activating in an audience a feeling of our compromised, alienated participation in the political and economic relations that make us appear to be what we are' (2006: 94). In a similar way, the gallery visitor beholding Sehgal's piece is also made aware of their participation within these relations. We are compromised by the unsustainable consumption that our society perpetrates. *Instead of allowing something to rise...* doesn't analyse or seek to understand the state we are in. What it does prompt us to ask is where we ourselves stand. Whereas *Once* shames us into taking a stand against the violence of history, Sehgal's piece prompts us to imagine an impossible future in which we might no longer participate within these political and economic relations.

Conclusion

Like Sehgal's *Instead of allowing something to rise...* the critical potential of *Once* lies in the way it draws attention to affective aspects of current political experience that otherwise remain hidden. As I have shown, the performative means that each uses to do this are very different. Sehgal developed a conceptually dense but technically simple, anti-theatrical performative installation. De Keersmaeker, by contrast, drew on her considerable experience as a highly trained theatrical performer and exploited sophisticated technical resources for sound, lighting, and decor. Each piece reflected on memories of the 1960s in order to develop a critical position in which to explore the problems of the 2000s. Faced with the bewildering complexity of experience within the current state of globalisation, these two pieces reminded us that, as Susan Buck-Morss puts it, the body can *sense* when reasons have become rationalization (Buck-Morss 2002: 257).

The figure that Giorgio Agamben calls 'homo sacer' has informed the readings I have offered of these two pieces. The 'homo sacer', as someone who has been condemned to be an absolute outsider, has the status of being legally dead and so his actual death cannot be mourned. In the final section of *Once*, where De Keersmaeker danced in front of the film, she was resisting the gradual acceptance of the inevitability of war, and with it the death of soldiers and what is euphemistically called 'collateral damage'. The affective power of her performance challenged the audience to feel the sense of justice that comes from the recognition that all lives, including those that like the 'homo sacer' are not supposed to count, are equally valuable. But the 'homo sacer' is also a site of resistance against the relations and techniques of governmentality. The affective power of *Instead of allowing something to rise...* recalls the ambivalent fear and fascination with the possibility of imagining libertarian alternatives outside the state's regimes of normalisation and regularisation. Both De Keersmaeker and Sehgal's pieces therefore remind us of the need to reconstitute the political, and demonstrate the potential of dancing bodies to open up new affective spaces in which to do so.

Works Cited

Agamben, G. 1998. *Homo Sacer: Sovereign Power and Bare Life.* Stanford, CA: Stanford University Press.

Agamben, G. 2005. *State of Exception.* Chicago: The University of Chicago Press.

Arendt, H. 1973. *On Revolution.* Harmondsworth: Penguin.

Beck, U. 1997. *The Reinvention of Politics: Rethinking Modernity in the Global Social Order.* Cambridge: Polity Press.

Bishop, C. 2004. Antagonism and relational aesthetics. *October* 110: 51–79.

Bourriaud, N. 2002. *Relational Aesthetics.* Paris: Les Presses du Réel.

Buck-Morss, S. 2002. *Dreamworld and Catastrophe: The Passing of Mass Utopia in East and West.* Boston, MA: MIT Press.

Butler, J. 2004. *Precarious Life: The Powers of Mourning and Violence.* London: Verso.

Crary, J. 2003. Foreword, in *Installation Art in the New Millenium: The Empire of the Senses.* Edited by Nicolas de Oliveira, Nicola Oxley and Michael Petry. London: Thames & Hudson: 6–9.

Critchley. S. 2007. *Infinitely Demanding: Ethics of Commitment, Politics of Resistance.* London: Verso.
Diez, C. 2002. *Once* [Online]. Rosas. Available: <http://www.rosas.be/once.html> [3 August 2004].
Foucault, M. 2007. *The Politics of Truth.* Los Angeles: Semiotext(e).
Garwood, D. 2006. Dancing against War. *PAJ* 83: 76–9.
Giddens, A. 1991. *Modernity and Self Identity.* Cambridge: Polity Press.
Giddens, A. 1999. *Runaway World: How Globalisation Is Reshaping Our Lives.* London: Profile books.
Graham, D. 1999. *Two-Way Mirror Power: Selected Writings.* Boston, MA: MIT Press.
Griffin, T. 2005. Tino Sehgal an interview. *Artforum International* 43/9: 218–20.
Halsall, F., Jansen, J.& O'Conner, T. 2006. Editorial Introduction: Aesthetics and Its Objects – Challenges from Art and Experience. *Journal of Visual Culture* 5/3: 123–126.
Jowitt, D. 2005. Channelling the Sixties. *Village Voice*, 8 November: n.p.
Kunst, B. 2006. Sodelovanje in proctor (The collaboration and space). *Maska* 21/101–102: 80–87.
La Rocco, C. 2005. How to Turn 45 Gracefully: With Civil War Battles on Naked Torso. *The New York Times*, 6 November . [Online]. Available: <http://www.nytimes.com/2005/11/06/arts/dance/06laro.html> [30 October 2008].
Lash, S. & Urry, J. 1994. Economies of Signs and Space, Reflexive Modernization: Politics, Tradition, and Aesthetics in the Modern Social Order, in *Reflexive Modernization: Politics, Tradition And Aesthetics In The Modern Social Order.* Edited by Ulrich Beck, Anthony Giddens and Scott Lash. Cambridge: Polity Press.
Mouffe, Ch. 2005. *On The Political.* London: Routledge.
Ridout, N. 2006. *Stage Fright, Animals, and Other Theatrical Problems.* Cambridge: Cambridge University Press.
Ross, T. 2006. Aesthetic Autonomy and Interdisciplinarity: A Response to Nicolas Bourriaud's 'Relational Aesthetics'. *Journal of Visual Art Practice* 5/3: 167–181.
Searle, A. 2003. One pair of children for sale, $6,000. *Guardian*, 20 October. [Online]. Available: <http://www.guardian.co.uk> [12 February 2005].
Sgualdini, S. 2005. The objectives of the object: an interview with Tino Sehgal by Silvia Sgualdini, in *E-Cart Contemporary Art Magazine*, 6 August. [Online]. Available: <http://www.e-cart.ro/ec-6/silvia/uk/g/silvia_uk.html> [29th October 2008].
Thrift, N. 1996. *Spatial Formations.* London: Sage Publications.
Williams, E. 2007. Tino Sehgal. *Flash Art* 253: 127.

12 Politicizing Dance: Cultural Policy Discourses in the UK and Germany

Introduction: Politics and Performing Arts Policies in the UK and Germany

In their introduction to *Dance Discourses*, Susanne Franco and Marina Nordera regard the keyword 'politics' as opening

> ... a wide field of investigation that ranges from the relationships of the dancers with political and cultural institutions, to the communication, performance, and reception of a dance work, to the ways in which dance connects with the individual, the collective, society, the state, and power. (Franco & Nordera 2007: 4)

In this context this chapter raises a number of questions of importance for dance as an art form, at an individual, organisational and institutional level. These stem primarily from cultural policy measures instigated by governments, in this case by the UK and German governments, which examine the effect of such measures on dance practice, its funding and positioning in the performing arts sector. Furthermore the influence of the current, pervasive *creative/cultural industries* debate is examined in the light of growing demands to make the arts in general more appealing to mass audiences, particularly where they are dependent on subsidies. This in turn raises increasingly familiar questions about the quality and the benefits provided by the art form in a social and artistic context.

In the UK, as we shall see, a policy vacuum has resulted in dance being 'attached' to other governmental policy objectives in order to gain and maintain financial support. This has generated much debate on the role of dance organisations and the organisational and indeed individual competences that they must display in order to receive funding. This situation is compared and contrasted with Germany where, despite immense upheavals in the cultural sector as a consequence of the reunification of East and West Germany in 1989, a clearer commitment to dance as an art form is visible.

In recent decades the emergence of cultural industries and dance's positioning within this sector has led to a reappraisal of its role as a form of expression and set of bodily practices. Whereas in the 1980s much of the work carried out in the field of dance anthropology focussed on the politics of dance and the relations among culture, body and movement, the more recent appropriation of dance for economic and social welfare purposes has turned attention from direct discussions of power and resistance in relation to ethnicity, class or gender and towards its contribution to achieving very specific policy objectives. The politics of dance now include a debate over its very nature and role in society. Reinterpreted as a social, that is, not only as a bodily, practice, dance finds itself treated often merely as a means to an end. As Mark Franko puts it, 'Politics are not located directly "in" dance, but in the way dance manages to occupy (cultural) space' (Franko, in Franco & Nordera 2007: 13).

Contemporary dance, including contemporary ballet, occupies particularly sensitive cultural space in that the decidedly experimental and unconventional character of the genre limits its commercial attractiveness. Often the size and programming of such organisations is a major factor in making it difficult to create a broad appeal amongst audiences. This makes companies active in this arena dependent on funding, both public and private, and tends to result in a variety of objectives to be met that can include increasing audience participation or promoting social benefits through the medium of dance.

While Germany and the UK have both articulated policies and implemented initiatives to support dance there are discernible differences in emphasis. Some are the result of historical and cultural as well as political influences that have shaped and still inform policy-making for the arts in both countries. What is clear is that the institutions that administrate arts policies and distribute public funding in both countries operate with varying degrees of autonomy and have somewhat diverse perspectives on the degree to which cultural policy can and should be instrumentalised to achieve economic or even ideological objectives. The adoption of non-cultural objectives for arts management is in many ways dependent on three key dimensions, namely funding policy, cultural policy objectives and the concomitant impact on artistic practice. These dimensions also form the comparative basis for the following evaluation of (contemporary) dance and politics in the UK and Germany. The key similarities and differences are shown in Table 1.

Comparative Criteria	UK	Germany
Cultural Policy	Highly centralised and closely related to the 'Creative Industries' debate promulgated in the late 1990s	Federated model with a significant degree of autonomy for the regions enshrined in the constitution. Federal government acts as a conduit for negotiations and debates at EU level
Funding	Two main sources: Government and the Lottery. Distributed through the ACE using a variety of selection criteria closely related to Government social policy objectives	Almost exclusive use of a public funding model, with some use of PPP-type models and foundations. Funding tends to be largely independent of artistic programming objectives
Artistic Practice	Increasingly project-based with growing competences in management and administration. Dichotomy between artistic and social practice increasingly evident	Artistic integrity still the main priority for the arts. Reinforced by regionalised model of organisation of the arts.

Table 1: Comparison of Contemporary Dance and Politics in the UK and Germany

Cultural Custodians and Changing Missions

Dance in the UK began to receive public funding only after the Arts Council of Great Britain (ACGB) was set up in 1946. The purpose behind the ACGB was to ensure support for arts activities that would otherwise not survive on their own in a purely commercial environment. Even then the Arts Council only supported three dance organisations, all of them ballet companies. This limited scope has its roots in the social distinctions made between the two main forms of theatre in the UK during the nineteenth century. As Jeanette Siddall observes in her assessment of the evolution of dance management in Britain, 'This period saw the establishment of a new distinction between "art" and "entertainment", in which the former was elevated and the latter denigrated. Dance was firmly identified with the latter' (Siddall in Jasper & Siddall 1999: 7).

Dance only began to become respectable when Diaghilev and his Ballet Russes arrived on the scene. Their performances attracted wealthy, influential patrons and helped to raise the status of ballet in the UK. This development did not, however, extend to modern dance. Despite guest appearances of modern dancers in the UK like Isadora Duncan, modern dance in the UK never experienced the same degree of interest or, indeed, development as it did in mainland Europe. Most attempts to popularise the modern dance form during the 1920s in the UK were short-lived and even as late as the 1950s attempts to introduce new techniques to the British public were very poorly received.

However, during the early 1960s there came a renewed interest in contemporary dance forms. American modern dance companies in the form of Merce Cunningham, Alvin Ailey and Paul Taylor descended on Britain and helped to spark serious interest. The momentum created by this revival continued throughout the 1960s and by 1970 the London School of Contemporary Dance had been founded. Public sector funding for UK dance began to increase significantly and enabled a variety of festivals such as Dance Umbrella and more culturally diverse dance forms to emerge. New professions were created, e.g. the animateur and dance began to be offered as a higher education qualification.

Whilst the funding of and participation in dance has steadily increased over the years, the question of the definition of dance has taken on political aspects that have implications for future public sector funding and the artistic integrity of the art form. In the case of the UK the reappraisal of dance by policy makers began during the Thatcher era, spanning most of the 1980s. In 1986 the Arts Council of England (ACE) published a document entitled *A Great British Success Story* that promulgated an economic case for public arts funding in terms of the 'indirect', or as economists would put it, 'multiplier' effects of spending on and in the arts industry. Although the ACE's 1996 *Policy for Dance* document still emphasised dance as a creative art form, more and more weight was being placed on the commercial returns to be 'earned' from the arts.

Whereas the ACE's 1996 document concerned itself with dance as a professional art form, by 2004 the emphasis had noticeably shifted to a discussion of dance's contribution to healthy living and its kinship with sporting physical activity (HC 587-I, 2004). This change of emphasis has brought subtle role changes for many of the parties involved in the funding, production and performance of dance. Funding and distribution agencies such as the ACE are no longer simply enablers, supporting the producers of dance works and events in the pursuit of excellence, but are required to use their resources to develop a wider, more diverse, i.e. populist audience for dance and the arts in general (Caust 2003: 58). Equally many dance (both modern and ballet) companies find themselves becoming progressively more involved in educational programmes as a means to secure funding. Interestingly, this is sometimes at odds with the needs of experienced dancers and established companies for actual performance funding. Touring is another activity encouraged by policy makers as a way of attracting a broader, regionally based audience. Again, this affects both contemporary and ballet dance in that it reflects an attempt to divest dance of its elitist image.

The debates on the arts increasingly imply two things, namely that creative art forms must be able to justify their public funding and that they must serve a useful social purpose. These criteria apply to the arts generally, but are particularly relevant for those cultural activities that have limited commercial appeal, such as ballet and even more so contemporary dance. Whilst ballet requires extensive, long-term training to achieve the standards necessary for public performance, contemporary or modern dance is often viewed as a more 'flexible' dance form that can be extended to complement popular music such as rap and that is also more easily practised and reflects a variety of ethnicities. Furthermore the use of a variety of dance-type 'exercise' regimes in fitness gyms has served to make the association between dance and healthy living more overt.

However, much of this development has occurred without a formal governmental policy on dance that has left this sector of subsidised culture in the UK particularly vulnerable to so-called 'policy attachment', a phrase coined by Clive Gray (2002) and also taken up by Eleonora Belfiore (2006) in her essay for the Policy Exchange think-tank. The term refers to policy sectors with limited or low-priority political influence that are obliged to meet their objectives by emphasising their contribution to the achievement of more 'worthy' aims. However, by attaching extra 'value definitions' to subsidised culture in order to obtain funding there is the danger that the sector's ability to be innovative and truly creative may be seriously constrained (Caust 2003).

The situation in Germany is somewhat different, due in part to the federal system of government, which recognises a significant degree of political autonomy on the part of its states. In the case of cultural policy-making it is not the federal government that devolves decision-making authority to the Länder; rather, such authority already exists as part of the constitution of the states themselves and extends to cultural policy development as well. In fact, such is the strength of the Länder in cultural matters that they reserve the right to be represented by their own special delegate at EU level (Burns & van der Will, 2003).

Moreover, dance in Germany has a much more politically overt image than in the UK. This is partly a legacy of a tendency to use the theatrical stage for national or political debate dating back to the eighteenth century (Weber 1991: 44). With the societal upheavals that occurred in the aftermath of World War I the emergence of *Ausdruckstanz* signified the deep social and cultural changes that were underway in the country. This was the first of two distinctly German dance forms that developed that could be seen as being a part of a national dance identity. The second national dance form emerged after World War II in the shape of the much more politically vocal *Tanztheater*.

Today, contemporary dance has eschewed the overtly political in favour of works that tend to be either fairly conceptual in nature and represented by choreographers like Xavier Le Roy or more light-hearted and juvenile in style, led by Constanza Macras and Sascha Waltz (Heun 2007: 6). Performing arts organisations at a regional or municipal level are usually run by directors who have been appointed by the state or city council. The ensemble is made up of staff and performers on a mix of permanent and short-term contracts, with choir and orchestra members tending to have permanent contracts, whilst soloist singers are likely to be on short-term contracts only. In the case of ballet dancers contracts are often just for one or two years. Budgets and individual remuneration tend not to be linked to the relative success of programming decisions and there is little need to worry about competition from other cultural offerings or venues.

However, such publicly funded organisations are not immune to budget cuts and although much of the attention of the policy makers is centred on the major performing arts such as opera and the theatre, Germany has recognised the need to protect dance in the face of budget cuts that have proved unavoidable over the last few years in many Western economies. The initiative *Tanzplan Deutschland* (Dance Plan Germany) is a five-year plan that was devised by the Federal Cultural Foundation in 2005 to create a sustainable improvement in the arena of international dance, specifically in the areas of training, performance, production and theory. 12.5 million Euros were allocated to fund a number of activities and investments, including the 2006 *Ständige Konferenz Tanz* (Permanent Conference for Dance) dance congress, new dance academies, innovative teaching tools and publications.

In its 'manifesto' in 2006 the *Ständige Konferenz Tanz* announced that

> The Ständige Konferenz Tanz sees itself as a lobby for dance in Germany. It oversees the coordinating of concerns related to artistic dance nationwide, and commits itself to dance-related matters on a political level and in the administrative sector. The goal is to improve dance appreciation nationally and internationally, to make this art form accessible to a broader public, and to anchor it as a lasting fixture in society.

For some observers this may be Germany's response to its lack of a true national identity in the field of dance. The regional power in cultural matters and the tainted legacy of the National Socialists, as well as the different directions followed by the Federal Republic and East Germany after the war hindered efforts to create a unified, national approach to dance. There is no national ballet and only now, with the creation of the *Tanzplan*, has a country-wide focus been established for the profession. The threat to funding is now also shaking dance-makers out of their complacency and forcing them to re-appraise their roles as both performing artists and social practitioners.

Where the cultural discourse in Germany differs markedly from that in the UK is in the absence of an overt 'economic advantage' argument for the promotion of the arts: the emphasis in Germany remains on the aesthetic, creative, social and cultural benefits of dance. Even where references are made in the '10 maxims for dance', issued by the *Ständige Konferenz Tanz* (2006), to social welfare benefits, they are subtler than in the ACE documentation and form part of a broader cultural training agenda that argues for a place for dance in the educational system alongside art, music and literature.

Although both the UK and German systems consider quality to be an important determinant factor, the manner of interpretation is somewhat different with the 'value in use' argument often being applied to the subsidised arts sector in Germany and the 'value in exchange' line of reasoning used to justify commercially oriented productions, as is the case in the UK. Proponents of both subsidised and commercial systems claim superior quality for their output, but measuring quality in a quantitative, objective manner and relating it to available capacity and programming constraints has so far proved elusive (Gerlach 2006; Neligan 2006; Traub & Missong 2005).

This difficulty in measuring the value (economic or otherwise) of cultural outputs has generated an extensive literature in an attempt to determine whether or not subsidised performing arts produce better products than commercial organisations. What many of these studies fail to take into account properly is the nature of the audience. While productions intended for mass audiences require little or no effort to understand or appreciate, work representing the sphere of 'limited cultural production' such as contemporary dance or ballet presupposes educational and social credentials that enhance the viewer's ability to comprehend and enjoy the work. Thus, quality judgements become very personal and strongly associated with a viewer's previous knowledge of the subject matter.

The Price of Legitimating Dance in the UK: The Creative Industries Discourse

The 'Creative Industries' discourse that has permeated so much of the policy and cultural debate over the last two decades was enthusiastically taken up in the UK and can be seen as a natural extension of the 'new public management' discourse; the response adopted by many Anglo-Saxon-based economies such as New Zealand, Australia, the United States and the UK to public funding cuts. In the case of the UK the continuation of the 1980s Conservative experiments in managerialism[1] in various public services such as health and its extensive use of quantifiable targets as measures of policy success have led to a diffusion of such rhetoric into other areas of public life.

However, as the general public in the UK becomes increasingly sceptical about direct political interventions in matters of social, economic or cultural interest the practice of 'policy attachment' has become increasingly prevalent. The disillusionment with the managerial discourse that characterised the previous Tory government led the 1997 Labour administration to look for other 'benefits' that could temper the underlying policy objectives of value-for-money and economic efficiency. Thus, public art is widely used as a means not only to reflect, but also promote the regeneration of deprived areas (Appleton 2006). Political policy has reinforced this

---

1   SOED (Sixth edition) definition: Managerialism is (belief in) the use of professional managers in conducting or planning business or other enterprises.

practice and caused the relativisation, if not subordination, of the arts to other objectives, something exemplified recently by the comments by the then Culture Secretary, Tessa Jowell that

> The Olympics will provide an opportunity like no other to showcase not just sports, but also arts and culture. The investment is not just in sport and the regeneration of east London but also in the cultural Olympiad. (BBC News, 2007)

Moreover, the juxtaposing of culture and sport in this way has enabled the government to justify a sum of £1bn of national lottery funding intended for arts and heritage causes to be reallocated to pay for the 2012 Olympics.

Where, then, has this call for economic justification of the arts come from? Observers like Hesmondhalgh and Pratt (2005) see its origins in the commercialisation of the so-called cultural industries during the twentieth century. In fact, the very use of the term 'cultural industry' was intended to draw attention to the perceived commoditisation that many observers saw emerging from the development of mass forms of cultural production. Adorno and Horkheimer coined the term 'culture industry' in their 1947 publication *Dialectic of Enlightenment*[2] to illustrate the growing demand for cultural outputs that would satisfy the tastes of the masses.

Such systemization of culture removes the historical separation of high from low art, a separation distinguished by the need to possess more extensive cultural knowledge and understanding in order to be able to 'consume' high or elite art forms. Furthermore, the intrinsic value of the content of culture is replaced by its economic value such that '... the entire practice of the culture industry transfers the profit motive naked onto cultural forms' (Adorno 1991: 99), consequently eroding the autonomy of various art forms by demanding an economic return on any investment made in them.

The Arts Council England is, as a strategic public body for the arts, a leading proponent of the current political agenda and makes this quite clear through its selective use of wording in its policy documents for the arts and dance. Vocabulary relating to culture is frequently juxtaposed with that of the market, with references to the 'creative economy' or defining

---

2   Published as *Dialektik der Aufklärung*.

an art form as a 'distinct industry with its own economy' (ACE 2006a). This language is also applied to the UK subsidised dance sector in the hope of creating an understanding that dance needs to become less reliant on public sector funding and seek new means of supporting itself. For example, in Jeanette Siddall's 2001 document *21st Century Dance*, published by the ACE, direct references were made to the possibilities offered by digital technology to commoditise dance and the prospect that the existing subsidy and funding model provided '... neither the potential for gain nor a baseline of security' (Siddall 2001: viii). With the commercialisation of culture has come the increased use of business planning and performance measures as a way of demonstrating increased value for money, managerial competence and improved accountability.

In Germany, the debate over the role of culture and its relative value to society in general began during the late 1960s. Prior to that, cultural policy, in an attempt to distance itself from the legacy of the Nazi regime and its wilful reinterpretation of culture for ideological purposes, attended firstly to 'the mediation of the German and European traditions of high culture in music, drama, literature and art and the rebuilding of the cultural infrastructure' (Burns & van der Will 2003: 141).

A major development came in the early 1970s when the German Foreign Office called for a radical realignment of cultural policy such that it could become more integrated with the concerns of civil society and reflect those concerns in new ways. This was taken up wholeheartedly at the municipal level, most enthusiastically by cultural policy makers in Frankfurt and Nuremberg, who began to view culture more dynamically, as a source of communicative practices and not just as a medium for content dissemination. One of the most high-profile exponents of this approach was Hilmar Hoffman, the head of Frankfurt's Cultural Department between 1970 and 1990. His book *Kultur für alle*, first published in 1979 is regarded by many as a seminal work on social inclusion and the arts. The success of such measures encouraged a reassessment of the role of culture in Germany in general and precipitated huge increases in public spending on the arts. Despite cuts to funding in the intervening years this has nevertheless resulted in the state becoming responsible for financing some 90% of cultural activity in Germany.

Changing the Meaning of Dance

Interestingly, the ambiguity of much of the language surrounding culture in the UK requires assumptions to be made about the true meaning of the words in use such that the constant application of a particular vocabulary comes to be associated with certain messages. This phenomenon, first observed in the discourse analysis of Norman Fairclough and Ian Greener as applied to New Labour policies relating to the National Health Service has since been transferred to the arena of cultural policy-making. Mark Ryan, in his contribution to *Art for All? Their Policies and our Culture* gives an only too familiar example involving the (over-) use of the words 'creativity' and 'understanding':

> Not only are they very complex words, they have also become extremely vague in their meaning in recent years, largely as a result of their use in the culture industry. 'Creativity' could refer to an artistic or intellectual process, but the very definition of such a process has now become so loose and subjective as to be itself meaningless. (Wallinger & Warnock 2000: 16)

The repercussions for the autonomy of dance as an art form are serious when seen in the light of such cleverly constructed, but ultimately commercially oriented discourses. As Mark Ryan tellingly suggests

> Although the precise meaning is unclear, there is never a doubt as to what the new language intends. The artistic director, who is concerned only with the merit of his work, when he hears that he must tackle social exclusion, knows he is being warned. Perhaps he is thinking too much about art and not enough about the People. (ibid.: 17)

In 1996, one year before the Labour Party came into power in the UK, the ACE published a document entitled *The Policy for Dance of the English Arts Funding System*. This document stated a number of principles that were intended to underpin a policy for dance in the UK. None of these principles stated explicitly any role that dance might play in satisfying or helping to achieve other Government policy objectives. Tellingly one even stated that 'artists are the key decision-makers on whether, and how, their work should be categorised by the funding system' (ACE 1996: 7).

By the time the Dance UK Manifesto was published in 2006, a subtle change of emphasis had taken place. Although references and commitments to dance as an art form were still evident, extra 'ambitions' for dance had been introduced. For example, dance was to be:

- An integral part of every young person's education
- Available for everyone to watch and participate in
- A sustainable and healthy profession

In Germany the ambitions are much clearer and much more 'about' dance as a force in cultural politics itself. When the 10 Maxims for Action for dance were announced in 2006 the demand was unequivocal:

> Cultural politics must acknowledge dance as an art form with equal rights.

Such frequent juxtaposing of the words *culture, cultural, politics* and *dance* emphasises the desire to position dance in Germany as an art form as influential and powerful as theatre or opera.

In the UK an equivalent anchoring of dance as, first and foremost, a powerful art form in its own right is missing. The frequent association of commercial and managerial themes with the arts threatens to displace a broad range of competences and dispositions that were previously judged as being part of the knowledge-base required not only to understand and appreciate, but also to participate in the arts themselves. New 'cultural' competences that do not require the previous internalisation or acquisition of knowledge required to appreciate, for example, dance as an art form rarely cite originality or quality as the primary criteria (Bourdieu 1993: 7). In other words, the knowledge that is required to appreciate dance according to its 'new' meanings requires less effort and time to accumulate than previously. Moreover, these new meanings and the competences associated with them are increasingly reified by political consecration; whereby the use of language that is full of emotive metaphors and which elevates the arts to a position where they can fulfil emotional needs and help to address social disengagement distracts from, or even displaces the intellectual, innovative expectations usually made of high art forms (Mirza 2005).

Away from the Aesthetic

As dance becomes less valued for its purely aesthetic appeal there will inevitably be a shift in organisational and individual practices and priorities to ensure that they are aligned in accordance with the 'new' socio-political objectives for the arts. This is likely to be true both in the UK and in Germany especially in the context of the subsidised arts sector that includes contemporary dance. The increasing attention paid to the education programmes of dance companies and the almost obligatory participation by many companies in education work as a means of securing funding and thus ensuring their own survival is an example of this (Castle et al. 2002).

However, whilst companies that are involved in subsidised educational programmes thereby achieve some degree of financial stability, concern has increased amongst dance professionals about the integrity and even independence of the performances undertaken. This can manifest itself, for instance, in a feeling of awkwardness when a dancer performs in front of an audience of physically disabled people (ibid.). The obligation to be 'inclusive' (for financial or other reasons) can thus inhibit performers and make the performance appear artificial and contrived. However, where this compunction to be socially inclusive is not paramount, the role of a disabled person can become an integral part of the performance itself; as illustrated by Wim Vandekeybus's choreography for Saïd Gharbi in *Her Body Doesn't Fit Her Soul*, where the blind Saïd is seen to teach a dance to other dancers by getting them to feel his body as he demonstrates the dance and then imitate his movements (Jans 1999). Hence dance becomes a medium for expression of the artist's physical condition, encouraging able-bodied performers to experience his world on his terms. Instead of simply being a sop to the demands of politically correct observers and policy makers the participation of the disabled performer takes on a much more genuinely artistic and even creative form.

Furthermore, competition for funding may give rise to intense struggles for dominance amongst rival organisations to gain appropriate hierarchical status as a means to ensure survival. This will inevitably have implications for a whole host of dance organisations, including not only dance companies but also festival and event organisers, dance schools and those bodies responsible for the distribution of subsidies. These implications include the need for more commercially oriented individuals who are conversant with environments where funding is dependent on performance measurement and target setting of some kind (HC 587-I, 2004). However, in Germany there is evidence that the competition for high profile funding can result in much greater collaboration amongst applicants when they realise that only through joint efforts can they create more permanent support structures for dance (*Kultur-Kompetenz-Bildung* 2008: 4). This is in stark contrast to the concerns voiced some ten years ago by the Länder when the first attempts were made to harmonise cultural policy at a federal level.

In the UK, dance companies are also being encouraged to tap into the commercial sponsorship market more. However, as some of the contributions in the House of Commons report show, companies find it hard to have 'grown-up conversations' with local businesses, suggesting not only a lack of experience, but also a certain lack of professionalism (HC 587-I, 2004: §35). In fact, the contributions from the dance sector representatives in the report contain several justifications to account for the relative lack of success in tapping commercial organisations for funding, e.g. the transience and small size of many dance companies being seen as a risk factor (HC 587-I, 2004: §34 & §35).

In Germany, private sector involvement is seen in a slightly different light. Michael Naumann, Germany's first Federal Commissioner for Culture and the Media considered foundations as a way of '... open[ing] up new opportunities for Germany's citizens to participate in its cultural life. They [the foundations] are the expression of an active and self-confident civil society' (Burns & van der Will 2003: 145). For dance organisations in Germany several sponsoring bodies can be involved at any one time. For example, *tanzhaus nrw* in Düsseldorf is sponsored by national and regional cultural foundations as well as the cultural foundation of the city's public savings bank. In Frankfurt, William Forsythe, the American choreographer, has established what is effectively a public-private partnership with the German federal states of Saxony, Hesse and the cities of Dresden and Frankfurt; this after nearly two decades of state support for the Frankfurt Ballet.

The competition for funding is an important element in Bourdieu's work on culture and power. Explicit use of economic capital to influence a field of cultural production such as contemporary dance can be interpreted as an attempt to establish alternative value criteria. In a highly subsidised arts sector such as dance, companies and choreographers tend to have the power to determine their own set of criteria for the production and evaluation of their work. This is what Bourdieu termed a 'field of restricted production' and is certainly true of much of the performing arts establishment in Germany. However, when selection criteria other than artistic worth are used to decide on funding applications there is a power shift to intermediary funding bodies and commercial sponsors. Suddenly the rules that govern a 'field of large-scale production' replace those that informed programming and performance choices previously. Moreover, these rules are defined to attract as wide an audience as possible such that the design and content of the performances and other forms of dance events are

> ... obliged to orient [themselves] towards a generalization of the social and cultural composition of the public. This means that the production of goods, even when they are aimed at a specific statistical category [...] must represent a kind of highest social denominator. (Bourdieu 1993: 126)

Increased social capital and healthy living, two popular themes in many UK Government policies, are positioned as important outcomes of the dance sector's involvement at a local level and the sector's ability to contribute to local communities is clearly linked to successful funding. This is amply illustrated by the ACE's own case studies on dance (ACE website 2008). Advice is given on how to apply for funding and examples also show how applications must reflect commercial practices and be justified on social as well as artistic grounds. In contrast, out of the German '10 Maxims for Dance' only the fourth maxim 'Dance as cultural training' references the 'great somatic-physical potential' offered by dance.

Implications for Dance: Measuring Benefits

The growing reliance on measurement and targets in the UK arts sector generally presupposes that the outcomes are measurable in a quantitative manner. Just as in (commercial) industries where outputs and consumption rates are routinely measured to assess the economic productivity of a process or set of processes, so too has the same method been applied to the arts. An extract taken from the 1999 agreement between the DCMS and the ACE refers to developing performance indicators to measure 'consumption' of the arts (Wallinger & Warnock 2000: 20–21).

However, as some commentators have pointed out, there is a difference between outputs and outcomes when evaluating the effect of an artistic activity and the pressure to justify its position often leads an organisation to spend an inordinate amount of effort on collecting data used to underpin grant and sponsorship applications (Chong 2002). Although commendable attempts have been and are being made to evaluate the social impact of the arts, methodological issues have been highlighted by some researchers that give cause for concern when these methodologies unduly influence policy agendas and arts funding debates (Merli 2002, and Belfiore 2006). Fundamental misunderstandings exist with regard to the interpretation of performance indicators such that their value is seriously undermined when assessing the efficacy of an arts initiative. For example, in 2003, Estelle Morris, the then UK Minister for the Arts admitted that there was a mismatch between the way that the 'transformative' effect of culture is articulated and the manner in which it is actually measured (Selwood 2006).

In the UK case the danger for dance lies in moving from vaguely worded notions of intent to immediately specifying the benefits expected from investment in various dance forms without a sound appreciation of the implications for those involved in the delivery of a variety of 'dance-related services'. One example of this is in the complete abandonment of the word 'elite' in favour of 'excellence' in select committee papers on the future of dance in the UK (House of Commons 2004). Whereas elite suggests selection, excellence evokes a picture of broader attempts to promote high standards generally. The subtle difference lies in the inference that the majority no longer need to aspire to become part of a minority, but rather the other way round. Appreciation (and success) of a performance may then no longer stem from a grasp of the technical, emotional and creative talents that generated the dance, but rather be linked to a more mundane awareness of the health, educational or sporting benefits of the activity or to broader access. The ACE's website illustrates this role for dance with the profiling of initiatives that include using dance to rehabilitate offenders, promote healthier attitudes to fitness amongst young people and even to advance the notion of 'active ageing' for older people (ACE website 2008). In Germany, in public discourses at least, no mention is made of targets or benefit measurement, but rather of dance regaining its rightful place alongside the other major art forms: opera, music and art.

For UK-based dance professionals the possibility thus arises that less attention will be paid to inventiveness and technical accomplishment and more to the facilitation and communication of dance as a worthy physical activity. This development is already evident in other cultural sectors such as the commissioning of public artworks where '… it's the "working with" that's key here, not the end result' (Appleton 2006: 67).

Discussion and Conclusion

Much of what we have seen in the UK regarding dance policy in recent times reflects a desire to achieve cost savings through increased operational efficiency or reducing the reliance of dance and other performance forms on public funding. This is being done at the expense of more engaging, collaborative forms of debate and consultation between the government and its citizens (Siddall 2001) on the unique role that dance, as a truly multidisciplinary art form, plays in the performing arts sector. The increasingly market-oriented perspective that arts policy makers have been obliged to adopt in recent years in the UK fails to recognise the basis upon which the different cultural fields of original artistic innovation and more derivative forms of creativity exist.

In Germany, the legacy of aestheticism and artistry as ends in themselves has mitigated the effects of more pronounced commercialism in the arts sector as budget cuts in government funding oblige cultural bureaucrats to find other sources of finance without compromising the range and quality of output that German audiences take for granted. Experimental, ground-breaking work takes place almost exclusively in the field of restricted production, where much less emphasis is placed on entertaining the audience and far more on challenging them with alternative perspectives, interpretations and using a variety of techniques to do so. In contrast, the field of large-scale production is far more limited in its experimental freedom for fear of losing its appeal among its consumers. As Bourdieu asserts

> Original experimentation entering the field of large-scale production almost always comes up against the breakdown in communication liable to arise from the use of codes inaccessible to the 'mass public'. Moreover, middle-brow art cannot renew its techniques and themes without borrowing from high art or, more frequently still, from the 'bourgeois art' of a generation or so earlier. (Bourdieu 1993: 129)

In effect, cultural renewal is a gradual process, initiated by various members of a group of producers whose claim to legitimacy is primarily through an educational system that has endowed them with the means to remain independent of the mass market. That is not, however, to say that these producers cannot move from one field of production to another. For example, in the UK Matthew Bourne, a graduate of the Laban Centre, has had great commercial success in reinterpreting classical dance works in modern settings for non-dance audiences in non-traditional venues (Rowell 2000: 194). However, it can be argued that this 'innovative' form of reinterpretation fails really to extend the boundaries of dance as an art form. Indeed, opinion is divided as to whether Bourne's revision of classical works represents 'true choreographic genius' or is simply 'an alarming signal of the choreographer's lack of inventiveness...' (Poesio 1999: 36). Whilst William Forsythe's approach to dance creation embraces a very intricate, exploratory relationship between the dancers, the choreographer, and the performance, Bourne tends to favour visual metaphors that simply reflect popular tastes and fashions.

From an artistic as well as commercial standpoint the public-private partnership model adopted by the American choreographer Forsythe is innovative in a truer sense of the word. His model allows him to reach audiences beyond Frankfurt and the region around it, and to be financially viable despite reduced public funding whilst at the same time retaining both artistic integrity and autonomy. But in spite of such notable examples of success, we still come up against Bourdieu's assertion that true experimentation is only really feasible when mass audience appeal does not lie at the heart of the production. How then can this apparent truism be reconciled with the need to broaden the appeal of dance and reduce reliance on public funding?

For some, the potential of instrumentalist policies offers a possible lifeline for levelling out the uneven cultural and social capital pools that distinguish cultural producers and consumers, thus possibly rendering the bias in arts policy-making to discriminate against creative works in favour of the 'masses' superfluous. Indeed, the ACE's priorities for dance for the period 2007–2011 make it obvious that dance organisations will need to be 'contemporary in their approach and committed to engaging people in their work in new ways' (ACE 2006b: 10). In short, 'the future will require those working in dance to take risks, yet the traditional model of public funding for the arts provides neither the potential for gain nor a baseline of security' (Siddall 2001: viii).

In the current governmental policy vacuum affecting the dance sector in the UK lies a very real threat to the future and integrity of dance as an autonomous art form. As it is purposefully directed towards organisational models and forms of collaboration by intermediary bodies such as the ACE, the UK policy appears to favour commercially effective rather than purely aesthetic principles. It is this undermining of the 'symbolic power' of the high arts by economic means that underlies much of current government thinking regarding the arts and needs to be critically assessed if the dance sector in the UK is ever to find its true artistic identity. In contrast, Germany with its very institutionalised, but independent (of the federal government) approach to the arts in the realm of cultural policy-making and funding implies that culture, whilst highly political, is less susceptible than in the UK to being governed by just one set of interests, economically or politically.

In the future both policy models should examine more closely how to benefit from each other's positive features. Despite its complexity, the German cultural bureaucratic machine has been able to create a demonstrably co-ordinated approach to furthering the aims of dance in Germany through the *Tanzplan* programme. Several other European countries including Belgium, Switzerland, Austria and the Netherlands have initiated similar programmes. For the UK, which tends to follow the more capitalist-oriented US, the political and cultural structures in place have become more agile in responding to changing circumstances, but have still to confirm the role of dance as a truly authentic art form amongst its peers. Meanwhile the continuing confusion regarding UK dance policy, the associated political objectives and their measurability will hinder a consistent approach to the development of dance. Dance in general is likely to remain dwarfed by the shadows of its theatrical and operatic peers and only with a concerted Europe-wide form of collaboration will dance be able to dictate, rather than be dictated to, in matters of cultural influence and ultimately funding.

Works Cited

Adorno, T. 1991. *The Culture Industry, Selected Essays on Mass Culture*. Edited by J. M. Bernstein. London, New York: Routledge.

Adorno, T., & Horkheimer, M. 1947. *Dialektik der Aufklärung*. Amsterdam: Querido Verlag.

Appleton, J. 2006. Who owns public art? In *Culture Vultures: Is UK Arts Policy Damaging the Arts?* Edited by Munira Mirza. London: Policy Exchange: 53–70.

Arts Council of England. 1996. The Policy for Dance of the English Arts Funding System.

Arts Council of England. 2004. Submission to the Culture, Media and Sport Committee. Inquiry into Dance.

Arts Council of England. 2006a. Arts Policies, Developing arts practice and engagement.

Arts Council of England. 2006b. Combined Arts Policy.

Arts Council of England. 2006c. Dance Policy.

Arts Council of England. 2008. Available: <http://www.artscouncil.org.uk/aboutus/
project_detail.php?sid=24&id=546> [3 November 2008].

BBC News. 2007. Director condemns Games arts cuts. Available: <http://news.bbc.
co.uk/1/hi/entertainment/6583657.stm> [23 April 2007].

Belfiore, E. 2006. The Social Impacts of the Arts – Myth or Reality? In *Culture Vultures: Is UK Arts Policy Damaging the Arts?* Edited by Munira Mirza. London:
Policy Exchange: 20–37.

Bourdieu, P. 1993. *The Field of Cultural Production*. New York: Columbia University
Press/ Polity Press.

Burns, R. & van der Will, W. 2003. *International Journal of Cultural Policy* 2/2:
133–152.

Castle, K., Ashworth, M., & Lord, P. 2002. *Aims in Motion: Dance Companies and
Their Education Programmes*. Slough: National Foundation for Educational
Research.

Caust, J. 2003. Putting the 'Art' Back into Arts Policy Making: How Arts Policy Has
Been 'Captured' by the Economists and the Marketers. *International Journal of
Cultural Policy* 9/1: 51–63.

Chong, D. 2002. *Arts Management*. Abingdon: Routledge.

DCMS. 2004. Government Response to the Culture, Media and Sport Select Committee Report on Arts Development: Dance (Cm 6326). Available: <http://
www.culture.gov.uk/global/publications/archive_2004> [May 2006].

DCMS. 2006. Available: <http://www.culture.gov.uk/arts/policy_for_arts/goals_
for_arts.htm> [May 2006].

Franco, S. & Nordera, M. (eds.). 2007. *Dance Discourses: Keywords in Dance Research*.
Abingdon: Routledge.

Franko, M. 2007. Dance and the Political: States of Exception, in *Dance Discourses:
Keywords in Dance Research*. Edited by Susanne Franco and Marina Nordera.
Abingdon: Routledge.

Gerlach, R. 2006. The Question of Quality in a Comparison of British and German
Theatre, in *Cultural Industries: The British Experience in International Perspec-
tive*. Edited by Christiane Eisenberg, Rita Gerlach and Christian Handke. Berlin:
Humboldt University.

Grau, A. & Jordan, S. 2000. *Europe Dancing: Perspectives on Theatre Dance and Cultural Identity*. Abingdon: Routledge.

Gray, C. 2002. Local Government and the Arts. *Local Government Studies* 28:
77–90.

Greener, I. 2004. The Three Moments of New Labour's Health Policy Discourse.
Policy & Politics 32/3: 303–316.

Hesmondhalgh, D. 2005. Media and Cultural Policy as Public Policy. The Case of the British Labour government. *International Journal of Cultural Policy* 11/1: 95–109.

Hesmondhalgh, D. & Pratt, A. C. 2005. Cultural Industries and Cultural Policy. *International Journal of Cultural Policy* 11/1: 1–13.

Heun, W. 2007. Working to Build an Infrastructure for Contemporary Dance in Germany. Interview in *Performing Arts Network*, Japan, 22 January 2007: 1–7.

House of Commons Culture, Media and Sport Committee. 2004. Arts Development: Dance, Sixth Report of Session 2003–04, Volume 1, HC 587-I. Available: <http://www.publications.parliament.uk/pa/cm200304/cmselect/cmcumeds/cmcumeds.htm> [May 2006].

Jans, E. 1999. Wim Vandekeybus. Kritisch Theater Lexicon II E.

Jasper, L., & Siddall, J. 1999. *Managing Dance: Current Issues and Future Strategies.* Horndon, Devon: Northcote House.

Kultur-Kompetenz-Bildung. 2008. January/February, Issue 14. Supplement to *Politik und Kultur*, sponsored by the Bundesministerium für Bildung and Forschung.

Merli, P. 2002. Evaluating the Social Impact of Participation in Arts Activities: A critical review of François Matarasso's Use or Ornament? *International Journal of Cultural Policy* 8/1: 107–118.

Mirza, M. 2005. The Therapeutic State: Addressing the emotional needs of the citizen through the arts. *International Journal of Cultural Policy* 11/3: 261–273.

Neligan, A. 2006. Public Funding and Repertoire Conventionality in the German Public Theatre Sector: An Econometric Analysis. *Applied Economics* 38/10: 1111–1121.

Poesio, G. 1999. Matthew Bourne, in *Fifty Contemporary Dancers*. Edited by Martha Bremser. Abingdon: Routledge: 34–36.

Reed, S. 1998. The Politics and Poetics of Dance. *Annual Review of Anthropology* 27: 503–532.

Rowell, B. 2000. United Kingdom: An Expanding Map, in *Europe Dancing*. Edited by Andrée Grau & Stephanie Jordan. Abingdon: Routledge: 188–205.

Selwood, S. 2006. Unreliable Evidence – The Rhetorics of Data Collection in the Cultural Sector, in *Culture Vultures: Is UK Arts Policy Damaging the Arts?* Edited by Munira Mirza. London: Policy Exchange.

Siddall, J. 2001. *21st Century Dance: Present Position, Future Vision.* London: Arts Council of England.

Steven, S. 2000. Matters of the Arts... Stewert Steven reviews 'Art matters' by John Tusa. *Art News, The Magazine of the National Campaign for the Arts*, 1 December 2000.

Ständige Konferenz Tanz, 2006. *10 Maxims of Action*. Available: <http://www.dance-germany.org> [28 November 2008].

Traub, S. & Missong, M. 2005. On the public provision of the performing arts. *Regional Science and Urban Economics* 35/6: 862–882.

Wallinger, M., & Warnock, M. (eds.). 2000. *Art for All? Their Policies and our Culture*. London: Peer.

Weber, C. 1991. German Theatre: Between the Past and the Future. *Performing Arts Journal* 13/1: 43–59.

LUKE PURSHOUSE

13 Class and Thatcherism in *Billy Elliot*

The British film industry has achieved unlikely recent success by blend-ing themes of declining industrialism in the 1980s and 1990s with the performing arts. *Billy Elliot* (2000), written by Lee Hall and directed by Stephen Daldry, is set in a fictional colliery town called Everington in County Durham during the most infamous confrontation between Mar-garet Thatcher's Conservative government and the trade union movement: the coalminers' strike of 1984–1985. Its title character is an eleven-year-old boy, the son of a miner, who discovers a prodigious talent for ballet at the time his father and elder brother are embroiled in a campaign against the government's programme of pit closures. The contrast between Billy's artistic passion and the plight of his imperilled community is reminiscent of two slightly earlier films which showed the (later) upshot of deindus-trialisation in the 1990s. Mark Herman's *Brassed Off* (1996) centred on an award-winning brass band comprising members of a colliery on the very point of closure, while Peter Cattaneo's *The Full Monty* (1997) followed the exploits of a group of newly unemployed Sheffield steelworkers who form a striptease troupe. All three screenplays combine elements of comedy and pathos and are largely critical of the impact of Margaret Thatcher's ideology and policies on the working-class neighbourhoods they depict. All three, moreover, present performance practices, whether of dance or music, as individual or collective responses to economic turmoil.

Billy Elliot the Musical opened in 2005 in the West End, again with Daldry as director, and featuring Hall's adaptation of his original screenplay with some changes to the dialogue and the addition of a dozen or so songs for which Elton John – a self-proclaimed fan of the film version – composed the music. The film and musical follow virtually identical plots although the latter is longer and contains more explicitly political commentary, particularly in some of the musical numbers. The discussions in this article draw on both versions, referencing the film's screenplay together with the lyrics in the musical score, alongside various reviews and commentaries. I shall address three themes explored in Hall's work: (a) his portrayal of social class and specifically the class status of ballet, (b) the critique of so-called 'Thatcherism' in the context of a narrative about dance and (c) the treatment of values of community versus individual freedom and their differing ideological implications.

The story of *Billy Elliot* is simple and provides ample opportunity for character development. The determined and independent Billy secretly attends lessons at a local ballet school, initially as the sole boy in a class of girls. His father Jackie – a rough, short-tempered but ultimately decent man, recently widowed and under considerable stress from the strike – at first seeks to forbid his son's unusual hobby. Billy persists, however, and recognising a rare potential his teacher, the straight-talking Mrs Wilkinson, offers him private tuition with the aim of auditioning for the Royal Ballet School in London. Following further conflicts with his father and militant elder brother Tony, they are eventually persuaded of Billy's outstanding talent and agree to support his application. Father and son travel to London where after a nervous audition and fracas with another candidate, Billy convinces a selection panel headed by the school principal of his talent and passion for dance. He receives his acceptance letter on the day the miners' strike ends in failure, creating a bittersweet climax. The musical ends with Billy setting off for school in London, while the film shows him briefly as a 25-year-old professional dancer performing for an audience including his father and brother.

Class, Ballet and Elitism

George Orwell, writing in 1937, noted that

> ... the essential point about the English class-system is that it is not entirely expli-
> cable in terms of money. Roughly speaking it is a money-stratification, but it is also
> interpenetrated by a sort of shadowy caste-system; rather like a jerrybuilt modern
> bungalow haunted by medieval ghosts. (1986: 114)

While there have been numerous categorisations of social class, a tripar-
tite division is most often drawn between the upper, middle and working
classes; sometimes with added borderline categories such as upper-middle
and lower-middle[1] and the inclusion of an underclass populated by unpro-
ductive and criminal elements. An individual's class is primarily determined
not by their level of income so much as by their occupation, or in Marxist
terms their relationship to the means of production: aristocratic landowners
constitute the upper class, professionals and businesspeople (capitalists) the
middle, and skilled and unskilled employees the working class. Employment is not, however, the only determining factor: in departure from a
purely Marxist analysis, historian David Cannadine identifies a range of
class hallmarks including 'ancestry, accent, education, deportment, mode
of dress, patterns of recreation, type of housing...' (2000: 22); in short, he
presents class as a matter of holistic 'lifestyle'. Writing just before the turn
of the millenium, Cannadine also contends that Britain remained a heavily class-conscious society, retaining intact 'an elaborate, formal system of
rank and precedence, culminating in the monarchy itself, which means
that prestige and honour can be transmitted across the generations' (ibid.).
While UK politicians of all parties have professed intentions to reduce class
divides or even establish a classless society, their success has been limited.
As recently as 2009, Will Atkinson's report to the British Sociological
Association's annual conference found that 'the fact that some are better

---

1   Orwell's own categorisation is more complex still: he describes himself, for example,
     as belonging to the 'lower-upper-middle class' (1986: 113).

educated, with more choice in their lives and with more money still persists, and this maintains class differences that are as wide as they were in
the 1970s' (quoted in Gammell 2009).

Class division is a major theme of *Billy Elliot*, with virtually every
character being marked as belonging to a particular class either in the
dialogue or through certain visual or aural clues. The working-class Elliot
family and fellow members of the mining community are contrasted with
the middle-class (albeit Northern) Wilkinsons by marked differences in
their jobs, neighbourhoods, homes and possessions. One notable example
is car ownership: the Wilkinsons have a 'big Ford Granada' parked outside their property (Screenplay, Hall 2008: 37) while Billy and his father
travel to London by coach. Class emerges as a contentious issue between
the families when Mrs Wilkinson is called a 'middle-class cow' by Billy's
brother Tony in the midst of an argument over Billy's dance lessons (ibid.:
63). The London-based characters, encompassing senior staff at the Royal
Ballet School, Billy's fellow interviewee Simon and his smart-suited father
(who appears only in the stage version) belong to the upper-middle class,
signalled through their accents and clothing. The riot police who clash
with the striking miners are also delineated as middle-class, at least in the
musical, through their chorus lyrics in the number 'Solidarity': 'We'll send
our kids to private school and on a private bus' (Score, John et al. 2006:
38); to which the miners respond with repeated chants of 'We're proud to
be working class' (ibid.: 30ff.).

The class associations of ballet itself are explored in several passages,
most explicitly in Tony's argument with Mrs Wilkinson where he pin-
points her middle-class status and insists 'I'm not having any brother of
mine running round [...] for your gratification' (Screenplay, Hall 2008:
62). This implies that he associates the dance form with the entertainment
of the bourgeoisie, and fears that the working-class Billy is in danger of
being 'exploited' to this end. He goes further by suggesting that a career
in dance would actually render Billy a traitor to his own class: 'What you
trying to do, make him a fuckin' scab[2] for the rest of his life?' (ibid.). Mrs
Wilkinson responds in kind by mocking various pursuits associated with

---

2   A derogatory term for a strikebreaker used throughout the screenplay.

working-class identity: 'What are you scared of? That he won't grow up to race whippets or grow leeks or piss his wages up the wall?' (ibid.: 63).

Tony's concerns are perhaps symptomatic of a widespread conception, admittedly challenged in the course of *Billy Elliot*, that ballet is an elitist art form appealing only to the upper-echelons of society and excluding others through a mix of financial, educational and ideological barriers. In 2007, Mario Lopez-Goicoechea wrote in *The Guardian* that 'with its elitist nature, ballet polarises audiences rather than acting as a common denominator. And a quick look at the ticket prices of any ballet will prove to anyone that this dance form cannot be a benchmark for accessibility' (2007: 35). Such concerns have even been shared by members of the classical dance establishment; in 2002 Matz Skoog, director of the English National Ballet, remarked in a public seminar that ballet 'took form in a society that was elitist and portrays a society that is elitist' (quoted in McCarthy, 2002). Looking back to the 1980s, several reasons for the class-based exclusivity of ballet were considered by Richard Dyer in an issue of the journal *Marxism Today*:

> It is elitist in part because it is expensive. Not only are sets on a grand scale and not only do most of the classics require large casts, but behind all that there are the years of investment in training. Even a solo ballerina on a bare stage is the culmination of years of support and tuition. This elitism of money cuts two ways – those who get to be professional ballet dancers are the product of a rigorous process of selection; the high cost of putting on ballet means that there is not much of the live stuff about – to get in you either have to be wealthy or in the know. The symbol of classical ballet's elitism is Covent Garden, with its awe-inspiring entrance and studiedly dressed down clientele, the usual story of the middle and upper classes getting reduced what they had paid full price for before. (1986: 36)

To Dyer's points one might add the symbolism of institutional titles such as the Royal Ballet School and Royal Academy of Dance, which refer directly to the British monarchy as patron of the art form. The subjects of the most famous ballet choreographies, moreover, seem to be class-ridden: works such as *Sleeping Beauty* and *Swan Lake* are based on fairy-tales which depict aristocrats (e.g. princes and princesses) in a virtuous light while presenting those who threaten the hierarchical status quo (magicians etc.) as villainous.

A significant feature of ballet's supposed elitism is the notion that its appreciation requires what journalist Mark Lawson calls 'an off-putting level of technical knowledge from the viewer' (2001), which it is probably difficult for working-class people to acquire. This is explored in Billy Elliot, for example when Jackie is asked at Billy's interview whether he is a 'fan' of ballet. The tone of his answer – 'I wouldn't exactly say I was an expert' (Screenplay, Hall 2008: 87) – suggests that he thinks its enjoyment is dependent on learning that men of his background do not and cannot possess. Billy himself is shown stealing a book on ballet from a library in order to supplement his knowledge; his schooling in Everington, we may assume, has taught him little or nothing about this highbrow pursuit. On the other hand, the musical version does present us with a counterexample of an apparently working-class man who is erudite on matters of dance theory. The pianist at Mrs Wilkinson's classes, the obese and heavy-drinking Mr Braithwaite, surprises everyone and produces a comic moment by suddenly waxing lyrical on the dance philosophies of Serge Diaghilev, saying: 'Well basically, it was all down to Diaghilev who ran the Ballet Russes, who wanted to revolutionise a purely decorative medium and reconnect it to dance's histrionic roots as a primordial means of expression.'[3] His eloquence, we are later told, stems from his having a BTEC[4] from Sunderland Polytechnic.

As for Billy himself, his lack of formal education about ballet does not present an insuperable barrier to his being admitted to its inner circle. When asked at interview about his motivation to dance, his reply refers to his instinctual and emotional faculties rather than anything he has learnt cognitively: 'I feel a change in me whole body – like there's fire in me [...] Like electricity' (ibid.: 88). It is perhaps unclear whether we should see this as evidence of Billy's exceptional 'genius', which his father wonders about

---

3   At the time of writing, the full script of the musical is not available; this line is quoted as remembered by an audience member on an online discussion forum: <http:// billyelliotthemusical.me.uk/forum/viewtopic.php?t=2342&view=next&sid=492 c09a50c44b0b7c5da97d406c65f3> [1 June 2009].

4   A vocational qualification issued by the Business and Technology Education Council.

(ibid.: 78), or rather a potential which others of his background might realise given sufficient encouragement. In any case, while Billy's instinctual route to dance leads to him becoming a top-level professional, the academic approach embodied by Mr Braithwaite is by contrast presented as somewhat laughable, and he remains the piano accompanist at a small provincial school.

Another feature of the class discourse in *Billy Elliot* involves the images of masculinity which are presented in association with the working and middle classes respectively. This again relates to a common preconception of ballet, addressed in scholarly literature on the topic (see for instance Burt 1995), that men who engage in it are 'unmanly', feminised, or homosexual. Jackie unsurprisingly betrays such views. When he first discovers Billy's predilection for ballet, his hostility seems largely based on its perceived effeminacy: he claims it is 'For girls. Not for lads, Billy. Lads do football or boxing or ... wrestling. Not friggin' ballet' (Screenplay, Hall 2008: 35). Though he never verbalises an association with homosexuality, this is heavily implied in an awkward conversation with Billy, when the latter ends by protesting that 'It's not just poofs, Dad' (ibid.: 36). The ideal of working-class manhood held by Jackie and his mining colleagues seems to be characterised by courage, steadfastness, loyalty to one's fellows, physical strength and control of emotions – most of which are directly relevant to their difficult and demanding trade, which is a major source of self-esteem for its practitioners. But the ideal is extended to encompass leisure activities too; Jackie and his own father pursued boxing as boys, a sport with an obvious masculine image, but for which Billy's lack of aptitude is established when he is easily defeated in a practice bout (ibid.: 7). This scene gives an early indication that both his abilities and interests differ from his community's (male) norm.

A more negative aspect of Hall's image of the male working-class is the use of violence – outside of a 'legitimate' sporting context. All three male Elliots have fights at some stage: Jackie punches his elder son Tony, Tony is arrested for clashes with the police, and even Billy physically attacks Simon at the auditions. If these incidents paint a less than romantic picture, they are also in stark contrast with Hall's portrayal of middle-class male characters – many of whom appear as weak, anodyne and emasculated.

Simon's effeminate body-language and excessive tactility towards Billy, for example, prompt the latter to call him a 'bent bastard' (ibid.: 85). He seems to personify a sort of anaemic girlishness which corresponds, perhaps, to Jackie's initial expectations of a male ballet-student, together with a public-school accent which links these attributes firmly to the middle (or upper-middle) class. Likewise Mr Wilkinson, the redundant husband of the ballet mistress and opponent of the miner's strike, is characterised as a somewhat inadequate man who has turned to alcoholism after losing his office job and, according to his daughter Debbie, leaves his wife sexually 'unfulfilled' (ibid.: 40).

Hall thus presents two interwoven preconceptions of class and gender which underpin Billy's family's suspicions of his dancing: first, that ballet is connoted with the middle and upper classes and secondly, that the men of these classes are lacking virility. However, as their opposition dwindles in the course of narrative, so certainly the first of these claims and perhaps the second are called into question. Hall's personal rejection of an essential link between class and ballet (and by extension 'high art' in general) can be seen in an introduction he wrote for his screenplay's publication, where he comments on the increased diversity in the backgrounds of UK arts professionals from the 1970s onwards – of which the fictional Billy is an example: '... the great unwashed were constantly renewing the High Arts and some of the finest practitioners were actually ordinary lads' (ibid.: vii). In the musical, moreover, Billy is not the only 'unwashed' male ballet dancer to appear: an added scene shows Jackie, waiting outside Billy's audition at the Royal Ballet School, meeting a young man in full ballet regalia on a rehearsal-break. It transpires he has a strong Northern accent, and explains that he pursued his career without his (presumably working-class) father's approval, pleading with Jackie to 'get behind your lad'.[5]

5   Hall has spoken in an interview (Mitchell 2000) of a similar encounter when research-
     ing for his film: 'I realised I didn't know much about the specifics of ballet at all, so
     I rang up the Royal Ballet in Covent Garden and to my amazement found this lad
     from Barnsley who is one of their principal dancers whose brother was a miner and
     had grown up during the strike. Since then there are a couple of people who've come
     out of the woodwork with similar stories.'

Another feature of both incarnations of *Billy Elliot* which undermines
the stereotypical picture of ballet as elitist is the blending of the depiction of this so-called 'high' art form with frequent references to 'popular'
culture. Hall describes his film as a whole, with its gritty language, social
realism and no-nonsense narrative style, as 'a popular (read "Low") form'
for a story about 'a kid reaching for High Art' (ibid.: ix). The boundaries
between the two are also blurred in the presentation of ballet itself, notably
in the music that is used in the film to accompany Billy's training. In the
early scenes when he joins in the girls' classes, a conventional piano backing is provided by Mr Braithwaite; but later when Billy has private lessons
he brings along his own music – a taped rendition of *I Love to Boogie* by
the British 1970s glam-rock band *T Rex*, to which he and Mrs Wilkinson
devise a choreography (ibid.: 49). (The corresponding scene in the musical
substitutes a song and dance number called *Born to Boogie*, with a similar
up-tempo, swing-like rhythm.) Subsequently in the film Billy is shown to
enjoy the more traditional ballet music of Tchaikovsky's *Swan Lake* (ibid.:
56); but when he finally appears as an adult performing in Matthew Bourne's
version of this ballet, a close-up shows him imagining dancing to the music
of another *T Rex* hit, the aptly named *Ride a White Swan*. This oscillation between classical and popular music forms implies that ballet is not
exclusively bound to the former. Not only can a rock song be successfully
used to accompany a balletic choreography, but pop music can provide
the inspiration to drive an elite artist. Again, it is suggested that success
in the dance world is achievable by someone who has not been trained in
the high arts from an early age, and who has greater affinity with material
produced for the mass market.

Billy Elliot the Musical does even more than the film to popularise
and demystify ballet. First, it self-consciously embraces the pop-music
scene with the choice of Elton John as songwriter. Secondly, unlike the
movie it combines radically different styles of dance itself: classical and
popular techniques are used side by side in the choreographies, with the
solo and group works combining ballet steps with passages of tap, jazz
and other social dance forms. While this hybridisation of styles is by no
means a new idea on the dance stage it nonetheless seems significant in
the context of *Billy Elliot*'s general take on cultural elitism. The seamless

movement between ballet and what are often viewed as 'lower' styles serves
to challenge any suggestion that the former is privileged or sacrosanct. It is
rather presented as just one species of dance – and indeed brand of theatrical entertainment – among others. The performers, in particular the boy
playing the demanding title role, are required to show versatility rather
than specialising in a classical movement vocabulary. Thus, the notion of
ballet's distinctness or separateness from other dance genres – as befits the
image of an elitist practice – is implicitly deconstructed, and the form is
accessibly packaged for spectators who would more readily identify with
elements of popular (dance) culture. This widens its appeal and further
diminishes class associations.

Perspectives on (Anti-) Thatcherism

Billy Elliot is set in a period of profound economic change and political
polarisation in the UK. The Conservative Government led by Margaret
Thatcher pursued radical free-market policies, including the privatisation
of formerly state-owned industries (such as steel, telecommunications,
gas and water), widespread deregulation of business, tax cuts, and a series
of laws designed to limit the powers of trade unions. These moves came
at a time when much of Britain's manufacturing industry was already in
decline, due to increased competition from low-cost foreign producers.
Thatcher's refusal to protect or subsidise domestic manufacturing infuri-
ated her opponents who highlighted the consequences in terms of rising
blue-collar unemployment and damage to traditional working communities and ways of life; towns and cities in the industrial North of England
(such as the fictional Everington) being particularly hard hit. The miners'
strike at the centre of *Billy Elliot* was the direct consequence of the government announcing in 1984 the intended closure of twenty mines which had
become unprofitable, with twenty thousand workers in the then nationalised coal industry due to be made redundant (see Milne 2004: 16).

First elected in 1979, Thatcher dominated the 1980s British political landscape, winning three general elections before losing the support of much of her Cabinet and the parliamentary Conservative Party in 1990. The doctrine of 'Thatcherism' expounded during her period of office had several defining characteristics. As outlined above, it was economically liberal; favouring free and flexible markets over state intervention, with particularly virulent opposition to socialism and trade unionism. As historian David Marquand puts it, 'It rejects the whole idea of "planning", [...] the quasi-corporatism of the 1960s, and the 1970s. It does all this in the belief that only the market can allocate resources efficiently...' (1988: 162). At the same time, Thatcherism was socially conservative; demanding strong police and national defences and promoting the traditional family in preference to alternative or experimental lifestyles. In Marquand's words, 'Thatcherism also stresses patriotism, pride in being British, the need to re-assert British traditions. Victorian values, and the rhetoric of Victorian values, are clearly central to it' (ibid.: 164). Finally, Thatcherism was strongly individualist, placing responsibility on each citizen to provide for their own (and their family's) needs, rather than relying on state support. In an infamous interview for *Woman's Own* magazine, attacking a perceived culture of dependency on social benefits, the Prime Minister claimed that 'there is no such thing' as society, but only 'individual men and women and [...] families' (Thatcher, 1987).

Various elements of Thatcherism are echoed in the events and characters of *Billy Elliot*; with a largely (if not entirely) negative picture being portrayed thereof. This hostility is perhaps predictable given the context: a coalmining industry over whose decline Thatcher presided, and a strike which saw a bitter standoff between the government and the National Union of Mineworkers (NUM), of which Jackie and Tony are members. *Billy Elliot the Musical* devotes an entire song, entitled 'Merry Christmas Maggie Thatcher', to a savage personal critique of the Prime Minister and her then Defence Secretary Michael Heseltine, who is crudely insulted as a 'Tory swine' (Score, John et al. 2006: 65) by a chorus of ballet girls (perhaps alluding to the government's alleged lack of concern for children in families affected by rising unemployment). The song's verses also lampoon the Thatcherite policy of selling off nationalised industries as tantamount to 'privatising Santa' (ibid.: 63), and cynically dismiss the Government's failure to halt the decline of British manufacturing: 'The economic infrastructure must be swept away / To make way for business parks and lower rates of pay' (ibid.).

This strongly satirical number is given considerable visual impact on stage as a number of chorus members don Margaret Thatcher facemasks and/or carry puppets of the Prime Minister, while a large, somewhat sinister model of Thatcher is inflated behind them. Reviewer Peter Brown (2005) describes the scene thus:

> A vision of hell appeared to me last night at the Victoria Palace! A huge effigy of Margaret Thatcher, maybe 20 or 30 feet tall, stood glowering at me from the darkness. And if that wasn't enough, dozens of smaller Margaret Thatchers gleefully pranced around the larger version like crazed goblin apprentices.

There are no such explicit references to Thatcher in *Billy Elliot* the film, but it portrays a family and community suffering considerable hardship, both economic and emotional, as a result of her government's industrial policies and determination to 'fight' the trade union movement. This is most evident when Jackie is shown chopping up the family piano for Christmas firewood (a scene which, incidentally, also again emphasises his unappreciative attitude to the performing arts). The political backdrop is a direct cause of personal tension within the Elliot household: Jackie fights with his elder son in an unsuccessful attempt to prevent him attending a violent protest (Screenplay, Hall 2008: 52), while Tony justifies his invective against Billy's clandestine dance lessons by asking Mrs Wilkinson if she has 'any idea what we're going through' (ibid.: 62).

For Billy, dance is presented as an escape, both from his family's problems and the broader disintegration facing his local community. He is quite literally able to 'get away' by moving to London in the more prosperous South and pursuing a career which we suspect (and with hindsight know) will not be available in mining by the time he grows up. He also finds a psychological refuge through ballet, out of the stresses of his surrounding environment and into his own inner-world; as he himself puts it 'once I get going [dancing] then I like forget everything, and sort of disappear' (ibid.: 88). A similar idea of performance serving a consolatory function for the victims of Thatcherism is explored in the other films mentioned above. In *Brassed Off* the residents of a dying mining town seek solace in the excellence of their brass-band playing, whilst in *The Full Monty* the laid-off steelworkers throw themselves wholeheartedly into their male-striptease project. Performance thus figures in all three films as a utopian activity pursued by those seeking a better life than is available to them in Thatcher's Britain or its immediate aftermath. *Billy Elliot* also alludes to a different therapeutic function of dance: the expression of anger with the status quo. In the film, following an argument with his family Billy is shown letting off steam with a frantic series of movements closely resembling dance steps, described in the screen directions as a 'cathartic fit' (ibid.: 64). The equivalent scene in the musical is set to an instrumental backing entitled 'Angry Dance'.

The historical miners' strike was characterised by several bloody clashes between the police and strikers picketing colliery entrances. The most serious was the 'Battle of Orgreave' in South Yorkshire in June 1984, which resulted in half a million pounds' compensation later being paid to miners for injury and unlawful arrest during their demonstration (Milne 2004: 21–22). Criticism of the police was extended by many left-wing critics to Thatcher and her government, who were seen as exploiting the force for political ends in a battle of wills with the NUM (see Scraton 1985). This issue is given significant coverage in both the film and stage productions of *Billy Elliot*. The former contains scenes of violence between strikers and riot police, as a result of which Tony is prosecuted. In the musical, the conflict is transformed into a major choreographic scene in which choruses of hard-hatted miners and helmeted policemen mutually hurl insults from either side of the stage while a troupe of ballet girls dances between them; the three groups later combining in a routine which blends balletic steps with belligerent gestures. The words of the accompanying chorus 'Solidarity' are replete with foulmouthed taunts and threats of reprisals: the miners address the police as 'cockney[6] shite' (Score, John et al. 2006: 29) and the

---

6   Nickname for a Londoner: note that the police are not local men but residents of
     the capital city. This emphasises the view that they are national Government agents

latter respond with 'fucking Geordie[7] shits' (ibid.: 31). In 'Merry Christmas Maggie Thatcher', police forces are even described as 'fascist boot boys' (ibid.: 62), a reference both to their strong-arm tactics and their purported co-option by a right-wing administration.

Exposition of the Thatcherite position in Hall's work is certainly limited. The only defence in the film is mounted by the rather unsympathetic Mr Wilkinson, who sees the pit closures as a logical consequence of market forces combined with the workers' unrealistic pay demands: 'Some pits are just uneconomical. If it costs more money to pay everybody to dig the coal out than you get for the coal when you sell it, what does that tell you?' (Screenplay, Hall 2008: 38). He is also sceptical of the degree of grassroots support for the strike, claiming that 'If they had a ballot they'd be back tomorrow. It's just a few bloody commies stirring it up' (ibid.). While it is historical fact that the strike was called without a national vote of union members, Wilkinson's speech also rehearses a common Thatcherite allegation that the radical socialist leaders of the union – notably Arthur Scargill, an avowed Marxist who was friendly with communist Cuban president Fidel Castro (cf. Milne 2004: 23) – did not reflect the views of the majority of miners and had imposed their own militant agenda.[8] In *Billy Elliot*, however, most of the Everington community is shown as supporting the strike action. There is just a handful of vilified 'scabs', one of whom is so overcome with guilt (in the musical) that he offers the money he has earned from strikebreaking towards Billy's interview expenses.

Mr Wilkinson (and the police) aside, it is notable that even the representatives of the middle-class in *Billy Elliot* are often sympathetic to the miners' cause. Most interestingly, at the end of Billy's interview, the

---

    with little understanding of, or sympathy for, the problems of the industrial region they are policing.

7   Nickname for someone from the Tyneside area, or more generally North-East England.

8   Thatcher herself, for example, claimed at a conference during the strike that it 'would have finished long ago had it not been kept going by violence and intimidation. We have witnessed an ugly chapter in trade union history. And the majority of trade unionists know it and are sickened by it' (Thatcher 1985).

Principal of the Royal Ballet School wishes Jackie 'good luck with the strike' (Screenplay, Hall 2008: 68). He might be seen to represent another species of opponent (and arguably victim) of Thatcher: the highly educated arts professional. Publicly-funded cultural institutions such as the Arts Council suffered in the 1980s from a tightening of government spending, intended to finance tax cuts while controlling inflation and balancing the budget. Cultural historian Keith Peacock suggests that the Thatcherite attitude to the arts was founded on the idea that, much like the mining industry, they should be forced to compete in a market environment rather than being subsidised by the state on grounds that they provide a social benefit:

> ... the Thatcher government's unwillingness to continue to increase funding and its begrudging, but loudly trumpeted, occasional allocation of additional money late in the financial year, were intended to convey the impression that theatre was not an agency of the cultural, spiritual, social or psychological welfare, but an entertainment industry that was otherwise irrelevant to the workings of society. (1999: 215)

This is supported by Peter Aspden's account of the Barbican Theatre's opening in 1982, posted on their website, which describes a time when 'the newly elected Thatcher government came to power with a heavy agenda, which regarded public subsidy as an unnecessary evil and sought to expose all its recipients to the bracing wind of freemarket Economics'. *Guardian* journalist Hanif Kureishi (2009) goes even further in a retrospective of 1980s cultural policy, alleging that Thatcher 'had no understanding of what a central place the arts have in British life' and even 'actively hated culture, as she recognised that it was a form of dissent'.

One might hypothesise, then, that the Principal's remark to Jackie is born partly of empathy, as his own sector is under a similar threat to the mining industry from Thatcherite policies. He is moreover part of a cultural intelligentsia whose views often tend to be socially progressive and to whom Thatcher's right-wing populism was therefore anathema. This is evidenced by the fact that in 1985, Oxford University denied the Prime Minister an honorary doctorate – making her the first Oxford-educated PM since World War II to be refused this honour – in protest against her attitude to education funding. *Times* writer Richard Morrison also testifies to an anti-Thatcher consensus among the intellectual elite; writing in

2007 he recalled: 'In the 13 years that followed [her election] I never met a single academic who didn't hate Thatcher. Nor an actor, writer, musician, artist or anyone else who worked in culture.'

Lee Hall himself gives a clear indication that in his view the arts industry had – and perhaps still has – more allies on the left than the right of politics. He chooses to conclude his introduction to the *Billy Elliot* screenplay by quoting none other than the National Union of Mineworkers' leader Arthur Scargill, as an (unlikely?) advocate of a more culturally enlightened Britain:

> I know that we can produce a society where man [...] will release his latent talent and begin to produce music, poetry, writing, sculpture, whole works of art that at the moment are literally lying dormant because as a society we are unable to tap it. (Screenplay, Hall 2008: x) [9]

Hence, just as Hall portrays a (fictional) ballet-school director as supporting the miners, he quotes the miners' (real-life) chief representative as a crusader for the arts. A picture is thus painted of a potential coalition between industrial workers and cultural professionals, who notwithstanding their class and educational differences can find common ground in opposition to Thatcher's free-market dogma.

Communal Values versus Individual Expression

Taken at face value, *Billy Elliot* asserts the virtues of community, solidarity and mutual support as an antidote to the individualistic pursuit of self-interest allegedly propagated by Thatcher. Her creed of self-reliance, culminating in the suggestion that there is 'no such thing as society', has been seized on by left-wing critics as showing her indifference to the value

---

9   This quotation is from an interview with Scargill on the BBC's *Person to Person* in 1979, though Hall for some reason dates it 1984.

of community and failure to acknowledge the fact of human interdepend-ence. *Billy Elliot* appears to promote the merits of collective action, for instance in the striking miners' willingness to club together for the money needed for Billy's interview rather than have Jackie cross the picket line and betray his fellow workers. In the musical, several lyrics speak of the Everington people's shared pride in their community and lifestyle in the face of perceived hostility (largely, one assumes, that of the government); in the opening number *The Stars Look Down*, the chorus sings: 'And although they try to break you and although you'll feel alone / We will always stand together in the dark, right through the storm' (Score, John et al. 2006: 6). Towards the end of the story when the strike folds and the miners reluc-tantly return to work, they describe their struggle in even more romantic terms, as striving for an egalitarian utopia: 'Once we built visions on ground we hewed / We dreamt of justice and of men renewed / All people equal in all things' (ibid.: 82). Sentiments such as these, expressing a reverence for class solidarity and desire for equality, have led commentators such as Alastair Macaulay of the *New York Times* (2008) to term Billy Elliot a 'socialist musical', albeit one 'about a failure of socialist action' (i.e. the unsuccessful strike).

This interpretation may be questioned, however, as Hall's account of Billy's surrounding community is at times critical of its prevailing collectiv-ist ethos. Moreover, one of the narrative's foremost themes is an individual striving for self-realisation, often in the face of community peer-pressure. The doctrinal implications of such a message seem primarily liberal rather than socialist. In the early stages of the story, Billy is shown in an antago-nistic relationship with his family, particularly with his father. Pursuing his self-determined ambition by autonomous means, he defies not only Jackie's wishes and expectations but ultimately his explicit orders. Recognis-ing that he differs from the bulk of his peers, Billy goes about his dancing in a largely solitary fashion: practising in private, initially being the only boy in the ballet school and later actually attending lessons alone. Thus, both his decision to dance and the manner of his training appear strongly individualist. We might furthermore see him as responding to the logic of the free labour market so beloved of Thatcherites: the industry of his hometown is dying, therefore he seeks to develop a skill which will offer him very different employment prospects elsewhere. In the musical this idea is captured by his deceased mother appearing to advise him robustly from beyond the grave: 'Piss off out of here; start everything afresh, and don't look back. There is sod all left for you here' (Score, John et al. 2006: 81).

Thatcherites deemed it each individual's responsibility to show energy and initiative in tailoring to the needs of the labour market, rather than 'blaming' society or the state for failing to provide them with work. Norman Tebbit, a populist right-winger who was Trade and Industry Minister during the miners' strike and a key opponent of the union, contrasted their angry protests with his own father's calmly constructive response to being unemployed in the 1930s: 'He didn't riot. He got on his bike and looked for work' (see Reitan 2003: 108). In *Billy Elliot*, while Jackie and Tony (and their fellow workers) rail against the decline of their dead-end industry, Billy alone makes the effort to forge an alternative career – 'getting on his bike' as Tebbit recommended. He enshrines mobility not only occupationally but geographically, being willing to leave his home town and head for London at a young age. The contrast with his father's attitude is emphasised in the musical when Jackie sings a nostalgic solo about his implacable commitment to coalmining and Everington whatever the cost: 'I'll love these dark, dark hills forever / And I won't leave them until I die' (Score, John et al. 2006: 79).

Billy can thus be seen as instantiating many of the virtues lauded by Thatcherite free-marketeers. They include enterprise, self-reliance, and we can also assume a willingness to compete; for while competition within the professional ballet scene may be less fierce for male than for female practitioners, it is still renowned for its cutthroat environment. This does not mean, of course, that *Billy Elliot* is fully supportive of Thatcher's individualist agenda. Whether or not Billy is the 'genius' his father speculates about (Screenplay, Hall 2008: 78), he clearly has an exceptional talent which enables him to succeed despite his difficult background. For those without such ability, the threatened loss of the local industry together with the government's laissez-faire approach leaves them without secure employment prospects. In the musical Tony specifically points out that Billy's highly individual route to success is not available to most of his working-class peers. As reviewer Natasha Tripney describes:

The show thankfully dispenses with the film's schmaltzy epilogue and rounds things up in a subtler manner. 'We can't all be dancers,' Billy's brother reminds him and it's a point that resonates stronger on the stage than it did on celluloid; as Billy's star rises the mining community he grew up in is in permanent decline. There's change in the air for all concerned and, with the exception of Billy, it's unlikely to be for the better.

The implication is that while people with Billy's outstanding talent and drive can flourish in a Thatcherite environment, the rest are lost. Such a view is by no means unfamiliar: among the most widespread criticisms of Thatcher's policies have been the resultant inequality between 'winners' and 'losers' from the market system, and more specifically the failure to manage the decline of blue-collar industries by providing assistance or retraining for those left without work. As economic historian Rick Garside concluded:

> The largely unregulated market failed to trigger any reskilling of the labour force, or to lead to the growth of new sectors, or to encourage substantial internal investment in either industry or education as a means of improving productivity further. (1998: 59)

While it is Tony who makes this point in *Billy Elliot the Musical*, his position is actually less serious than that of his father, whose age makes a career change much more difficult. Hall's account of the free labour-market is therefore double-edged: for Billy, it opens a novel path to fulfil his aspirations and potential, but for those with more limited ambitions or attributes there are few choices in practice and little societal support on offer.

The theme of individual freedom within a community is played out in *Billy Elliot* in the social, as well as the economic, sphere. While Hall's portrayal of the miners' collective spirit is generally positive, it is tempered with a warning that strong communal structures can be intolerant of those who differ from the norm. The verbal and physical abuse of miners who chose not to strike was a serious issue at the time and something of a public relations disaster for the union. This is tackled in the film with scenes of angry chanting outside mine entrances and Tony's aggressive confrontation of a 'scab' in a local supermarket: 'First rule of the union, [...] you never cross a picket line' (Screenplay, Hall 2008: 33). The family's disapproval of Billy's dancing might be seen to manifest a similar demand (or assumption) that everyone should adhere to similar social behaviour: the boy's unconventional tastes bewilder, disorientate and even anger these 'ordinary' working men. Again, it is Billy's mother who is used to advocate the contrary view, writing him a letter before her death with the advice to 'Always be yourself' (ibid.: 49). The issue of unorthodox lifestyles is further developed through the introduction of Michael, Billy's school friend who is a transvestite and, it later emerges, homosexual. While he is not actively victimised for these tendencies in the course of the narrative, one suspects they would not be widely approved of in the strongly masculine culture of the mining town, and even the relatively tolerant Billy addresses him with the derogatory term 'poof' (ibid.: 70).[10]

There is some evidence that Hall intends the Michael sub-plot to raise issues of freedom and diversity which are also relevant to Billy's own case. While – perhaps in deliberate defiance of stereotypical views of the male ballet dancer – Billy is not presented as gay[11], he does experiment with unconventional male behaviour by joining in Michael's dressing-up sessions and affectionate displays such as kissing him on the cheek (ibid.: 94). In the musical, the two boys perform a duet called *Expressing Yourself* in which they protest against societal limitations whilst trying on women's clothes and make-up: 'Start a new fashion, buck all the trends / Emphasise integrity / 'Cause what the hell is wrong with expressing yourself / For wanting to be me?' (Score, John et al. 2006: 38–39). Interestingly, this number is chosen for a reprise by the full cast at the end of the show, suggesting that its liberal sentiments are regarded as pivotal to the whole work.

The social conservatism of the Everington mining community, with its suspicion of abnormal behaviour or interests, would in fact have largely cohered with the attitudes of the Thatcher government. Although economically libertarian, Thatcher's social agenda was based on 'authoritarian populism'; as Ivor Crewe argues, this was in part designed to appeal

10   Michael does allege that his father is also a transvestite – but almost certainly a closet one.

11   He rejects Michael's advances and insists that 'just 'cos I like ballet, doesn't mean I'm a poof' (Screenplay, Hall 2008: 68).

to the traditionalist outlook of working-class voters who felt threatened in other respects: 'In the eyes of the Right, the unavoidable deprivation of economic security in the working class made it all the more essential to satisfy their moral and cultural prejudices, to avoid adding moral insult to material injury' (1988: 33). The conventional model of the family, with its heterosexual norms and stable gender identities, belonged to these prejudices which are flouted by Michael and to a lesser extent Billy himself. The 1980s actually witnessed open criticism of homosexuality by some prominent Conservative MPs and the controversial Section 28 of the Local Government Act (1988) – later repealed under Labour – which prevented councils and state schools from 'promoting' homosexuality or teaching its 'acceptability [...] as a pretended family relationship'.[12] Arch-Thatcherite minister Norman Tebbit was and remains in the vanguard of attacks on the 'permissive society', writing in the right-wing *Spectator* magazine that 'the advocates of [...] sexual licence, which undermines the family, are advocates not of tolerance or freedom but of perpetual instability and disorder' (2000).

Like Billy, however, Michael is shown in the film as ultimately succeeding in his quest for 'self-expression': we see him in the final scene as an adult attending Billy's performance of *Swan Lake*, camply attired and with an apparent male partner. In seeming to vindicate Michael's emergent homosexuality as well as Billy's unusual choice of career and associated 'alternative' identity, Hall questions both the orthodox attitudes of a communally-orientated working-class town – stuck in its ways and sceptical of non-conformity – and by implication the contemporary Thatcherite effort to defend traditional mores. Neither readily offers sufficient freedom in the personal sphere or adequately accounts for individual difference; significantly, the very last sung lines of the musical are: 'Everyone is different, it's a natural state / it's a fact, it's plain to see / The world's grey enough without making it worse / we need individuality / 'Cause what the hell is wrong with expressing yourself? / What we need is individuality' (Score, John et al. 2006: 101–102). If this encapsulates Hall's main political message, it is self-evidently a liberal one.

---

12   For a critical account see Hari (2008).

Conclusion

Billy Elliot challenges a commonly held view of ballet as an elitist or class-specific art form. The title-character achieves success in the field without compromising his working-class identity; a point strongly reiterated by Hall in an interview for *Socialist Review* magazine:

> The most horrifying conclusion for me is that the film is Blairite – i.e., that by being cultured you transcend your class. [...] It makes me furious to think people really believe you can't articulate yourself in an artistic way and remain working class. It shows such an ignorance of the whole tradition of the working class, where art is an absolutely fundamental thing. (quoted in Mitchell 2000)

A similar message can be taken from the 'redemption' of Billy's family, from their initial knee-jerk scepticism to an apparently wholehearted support for his endeavours, culminating (in the film) in their proud attendance of his premiere – suggesting that Billy has remained in contact with his roots despite his idiosyncratic journey. In particular, Jackie's intellectual and emotional progress from a stereotypical male working-class prejudice against ballet, to its acceptance as a worthy career for his son is perhaps the work's most interesting psychological study.

As for Thatcherism, there can be no escaping its overwhelmingly negative portrayal; on grounds ranging from poverty and (the fear of) unemployment, through politicisation of the police force, to the alienation of cultural industries. However, while Hall in some respects embraces the collectivism of the trade union movement, through the character of Billy he also recognises individualist virtues and plays on a liberal theme of respect for personal difference. On this last point, we might reflect that the positive and relatively gentle nature of Billy's individualism distinguishes him from some other working-class heroes; in particular 'Angry Young Men' such as Jimmy Porter in John Osbourne's *Look Back in Anger*, or Colin Smith in Alan Sillitoe's *The Loneliness of the Long-Distance Runner*. The latter, as an outstanding athlete, shares much of Billy's talent and passion for his chosen pursuit, but he is unable – or unwilling – to realise it as fully because he ultimately prioritises class-based rebellion over individual achievement, opting for an anti-establishment gesture rather than sporting success.[13] Billy also partly functions as a rebel against his family background and circumstances, but his revolt is more a means to the end of artistic expression than an attack on authority *per se*. He thus presents an almost unqualifiedly constructive working-class role-model, enshrining qualities of enterprise and self-reliance that are (paradoxically) not completely divorced from Thatcherite principles.

Works Cited

Aspden, P. (undated). Out of Adversity. *Barbican* [Online]. The Barbican Theatre. Available: <http://www.barbican.org.uk/media/upload/Barbican%20at%20 25/291OutOfAdversityByPeterAspden.pdf> [30 May 2009].

Brown, P. 2005. Billy Elliot – The Musical. *London Theatre Guide Online*. [Online]. Available: <http://www.londontheatre.co.uk/londontheatre/reviews/billyel­liot05.htm> [30 May 2009].

Burt, R. 1995. *The Male Dancer: Bodies, Spectacle, Sexualities*. New York/London: Routledge.

Cannadine, D. 2000. *Class in Britain* (1998). London: Penguin Books.

Crewe, I. 1988. Has the Electorate become Thatcherite? in *Thatcherism*. Edited by Robert Skidelsky. London: Chatto & Windus: 25–49.

Dyer, R. 1986. A Bit of Uplift: Tutus and Tights. *Marxism Today*, January: 36–37.

Gammell, C. 2009. Britain's Class System 'Alive and Well', Claims Research. *Telegraph. co.uk*. [Online]. Telegraph Media Group Limited. Available: <http://www. telegraph.co.uk/news/uknews/5165594/Britains-class-system-alive-and-well-claims-research.html> [1 June 2009].

Garside, W. R. 1998. Industrial Policy and the Developmental State: British Responses to the Competitive Environment before and after the 1970s. *Business and Economic History* 27/1: 47–60.

---

13   Entered for an inter-school cross-country event by the borstal where he is imprisoned, Smith pulls up shortly before the finish line when leading as a deliberate act of defiance. For detailed discussion of this work see Hughson (2005).

Hall, L. 2008. *Billy Elliot* (Screenplay). London: Faber and Faber. (First published in 2000. Special edition by The Times Film School.)

Hari, J. 2008. Section 28: An Obituary. *JohannHari.com*. [Online]. Johann Hari. Available: <http://www.johannhari.com/archive/article.php?id=1324> [30 May 2009].

Hughson, J. 2005. The 'Loneliness' of the Angry Young Sportman. *Film & History* 35/2: 41–48.

John, E., Hall, L., & Daldry, S. 2006. *Billy Elliot the Musical* (Score). London: Wise Publications.

Kureishi, H. 2009. The Thatcher Years: The Arts. *The Guardian*, 11 April: 16.

Lawson, M. 2001. What's the Point of Ballet? *The Guardian* (Features and Reviews Section), 8 September: 5.

Local Government Act. 1988. Section 28. [Online]. Available: <http://www.opsi.gov.uk/acts/acts1988/ukpga_19880009_en_5> [3 February 2010].

Lopez-Goicoechea, M. 2007. Ballet Is Elitist and Won't Enthuse Children to Take Part. *The Guardian*, 12 June: 35.

Macaulay, A. 2008. Gotta Dance, Gotta Transcend. *NYTimes.com* [Online]. The New York Times. Available: <http://query.nytimes.com/gst/fullpage.html?res=980 4E6DC163BF933A05752C1A96E9C8B63> [30 May 2009].

Marquand, D. 1988. The Paradoxes of Thatcherism, in *Thatcherism*. Edited by Robert Skidelsky. London: Chatto & Windus: 159–172.

McCarthy, B. 2002. State of the Art Discussion. *ballet.co.uk* [Online]. Ballet Magazine (December). Available: <http://www.ballet.co.uk/magazines/yr_02/dec02/bmc_big_state_of_the_art.htm> [6 February 2010].

Milne, S. 2004. *The Enemy Within: The Secret War Against the Miners*. London: Verso.

Mitchell, I. 2000. Northern Soul. *socialistreviewindex.org.uk* [Online]. Socialist Review. Available: <http://pubs.socialistreviewindex.org.uk/sr247/mitchell.htm> [4 August 2009].

Morrison, R. 2007. Things Can only Get Worse.... *timesonline.co.uk* [Online]. The Times. Available: <http://www.timesonline.co.uk/tol/comment/columnists/richard_morrison/article1955406.ece> [30 May 2009].

Orwell, G. 1986. *The Road to Wigan Pier* (1937). London: Penguin Books.

Peacock, D. K. 1999. *Thatcher's Theatre: British Theatre and Drama in the Eighties*. Westport: Greenwood Press.

Reitan, E. A. 2003. *The Thatcher Revolution: Margaret Thatcher, John Major, Tony Blair, and the Transformation of Modern Britain, 1979–2001*. Lanham: Rowman & Littlefield.

Scraton, P. 1985. *The State of the Police*. London: Pluto.

Tebbit, N. 2000. There is Such a Thing as Society. *BNET United Kingdom*. [Online].
The Spectator. Available: <http://findarticles.com/p/articles/mi_qa3724/is_/
ai_n8906595> [30 May 2009].

Tripney, N. (undated) Billy Elliot – The Musical. *MusicOMH* [Online] Available:
<http://www.musicomh.com/theatre/billy-elliot.htm> [30 May 2009].

Thatcher, M. 1987. Interview for Woman's Own ('no such thing as society'). *Margaret
Thatcher Foundation*. [Online]. Available: <http://www.margaretthatcher.org/
speeches/displaydocument.asp?docid=106689> [30 May 2009].

Thatcher, M. 1985. Speech to Young Conservative Conference. *Margaret Thatcher
Foundation*. [Online]. Available: <http://www.margaretthatcher.org/speeches/
displaydocument.asp?docid=105960> [30 May 2009].

Notes on Contributors

RAMSAY BURT is Professor of Dance History at De Montfort University. His publications include *The Male Dancer* (1995, revised 2007), *Alien Bodies* (1997), *Judson Dance Theater* (2006) and, with Valerie Briginshaw, *Writing Dancing Together* (2009). In 1999 he was Visiting Professor at the Department of Performance Studies, New York University. With Susan Foster, he is founder editor of *Discourses in Dance*.

TATJANA E. BYRNE is a PhD student in the Department of Management, Birkbeck College, University of London, undertaking studies into the impact of governmental policy on contemporary dance organisations in the UK and Germany. Her research interests include 'competing logics' of institutional change and power relationships in professional practice and the influence of digital technology on the arts with particular reference to power, trust and identity in the creative process. She has presented on these themes at the European Group for Organization Studies conference in 2007 and 2008.

ROGER COPELAND is Professor of Theater and Dance at Oberlin College in the US. His books include the widely used anthology, *What Is Dance?*, and *Merce Cunningham: The Modernizing of Modern Dance*. His essays about dance, theater and film have appeared in *The New York Times*, *The New Republic*, *The Village Voice*, *Dance Theatre Journal*, *Partisan Review*, *Dance Chronicle* and many other publications. Copeland has also contributed chapters to numerous books and anthologies including *Conversations with Susan Sontag*, *Dance History: An Introduction*, *The Routledge Dance Studies Reader*, *Dance, Gender, and Culture*, *The American Theater Reader* and *The Encyclopedia of Dance and Ballet*. 'The Unrecovered', his feature-length fictional narrative film about the psychological aftermath of 9/11, was screened as part of the New Filmmakers Series in New York City at Anthology Film Archives in 2007.

NAOMI M. JACKSON holds an MA from the University of Surrey and a PhD from New York University. She is an Associate Professor in the School of Dance at Arizona State University. Her reviews and articles appear in such publications as *Dance Research Journal, Dance Chronicle* and *Dance Research.* She has served as a board member of the Society of Dance History Scholars and Congress on Research in Dance and has helped to organise various conferences, including the International CORD Dance and Human Rights Conference in 2005. Her books include *Converging Movements: Modern Dance and Jewish Culture at the 92nd Street Y* (Wesleyan University Press, 2002), *Right to Dance: Dancing for Rights* (Banff Centre Press, 2004) and, co-edited with Toni Shapiro-Phim, *Dance, Human Rights, and Social Justice: Dignity in Motion* (Scarecrow Press, 2008).

MARION KANT is a musicologist and dance historian. She received her PhD in 1986 from Humboldt University, Berlin. She has taught in Germany and Great Britain and presently teaches dance/theatre history, performance criticism, cultural theory and creative writing at the University of Pennsylvania, Philadelphia. Her publications include *Hitler's Dancers: German Modern Dance and the Third Reich* (Berghahn Books: New York/ Oxford, 2003) and, as editor, *The Cambridge Companion to Ballet* (Cambridge: CUP 2007). Together with musicians Marshall Taylor and Samuel Hsu, she has presented concerts commemorating Entartete Musik, music forbidden by the Nazis.

ALEXANDRA KOLB is Senior Lecturer and Chair of Dance Studies at Otago University in New Zealand, having received her doctorate from Cambridge. She trained professionally in dance in Düsseldorf and at John Neumeier's Academy of the Hamburg Ballet. Prior to her time at Otago, she was in charge of the Academic Studies department at the Northern School of Contemporary Dance in Leeds (UK). She is the author of *Performing Femininity: Dance and Literature in German Modernism* (2009) and has contributed to a range of international journals, including *Discourses in Dance, Journal of European Studies* and *About Performance.* Her dance reviews have appeared in *Theatreview.*

SOO HEE LEE is News International Lecturer and Director of Research at the Department of Management, Birkbeck College, University of London. He is a Visiting Professor at the Graduate School of Culture Technology, KAIST, Korea and the Director of the Creative City Forum. His research focuses on comparative political economy, science and technology policy, cultural policy and knowledge-based exchange. More recently he has explored the socio-cultural implications of digital convergence with reference to artistic innovation, collective creativity, and design futures. In 2009 he gave a keynote speech on creative cities and dance festivals at the Fifth Busan international Dance Festival.

SUZANNE LITTLE is a lecturer in Theatre Studies and co-ordinator of the interdisciplinary Performing Arts Studies Programme at the University of Otago in New Zealand. She has worked in visual arts and film alongside completing a doctorate in Theatre Studies at The Queensland University of Technology. Her doctoral thesis, *Framing Dialogues – Towards an Understanding of the Parergon in Theatre*, was an exploration and development of framing theory specific to theatre. Other research interests include political and documentary theatre, reflective practice, the ethics of representation in performance, the politics of place and interdisciplinary and globalised performance.

VICTORIA MARKS creates dances for the stage, for film, and in community settings. Her recent work has addressed citizenship, as well as the representation of both virtuosity and disability. Marks is a Professor of Choreography in the Department of World Arts and Cultures at UCLA, where she has been teaching since 1995. Recent awards include first prize in the 2008 'Festival of Video Dance' Barcelona for *Veterans*, and a 2010 CHIME award for mentoring in her field. Marks is a 2005 Guggenheim Fellow and has received numerous other grants and fellowships. In 1997, she was honored with the Alpert Award for Outstanding Achievement in Choreography. She has received a Fulbright Fellowship in Choreography and numerous awards for her dance films co-created with Margaret Williams.

GUNHILD OBERZAUCHER-SCHÜLLER studied theatre studies and art history at Vienna University and earned a PhD for her work on Bronislava Nijinska. She taught dance history at the universities of Vienna, Bayreuth, and Salzburg. From 1982 to 2002 she worked for the Forschungsinstituts für Musiktheater at Bayreuth University, where she was responsible for the ballet section of the *Pipers Enzyklopädie des Musiktheaters*. She is the editor of books on *Rosalia Chladek. Klassikerin des bewegten Ausdrucks* (2002), *Ausdruckstanz* (second edition 2004), and *Viva la danza! Festschrift für Sibylle Dahms* (2004). In 2007 she published *Taglioni-Materialien der Derra de Moroda Dance Archives* and *Souvenirs de Taglioni* and in 2009, together with Gabriele Brandstetter, *Mundart der Wiener Moderne: Der Tanz der Grete Wiesenthal*. From 2003 to 2009, she was the director of the *Derra de Moroda Dance Archives* at Salzburg University.

STACEY PRICKETT is Principal Lecturer in Dance Studies at Roehampton University, London, where sociological methodologies inform her teaching and research. Her conference presentations and articles have appeared in journals such as *Studies in Dance History, Dance Chronicle* and *Dance Research*, on topics ranging from the left-wing dance of the 1930s to the San Francisco Bay Area dance scene and South Asian dance. She was a Senior Researcher in the Arts and Humanities Research Council funded Centre for Cross-Cultural Music and Dance Performance. She has also contributed to the edited collections *Dance in the City* and *50 Contemporary Choreographers*.

LUKE PURSHOUSE studied PPE at Balliol College, Oxford and then completed a PhD in philosophy at St. John's, Cambridge, where he also lectured for several years. He now teaches Politics at Eton College. His academic interests have ranged from political and economic theory to ethics and the philosophy of mind, having published several journal articles and *Plato's Republic: A Reader's Guide* (Continuum, 2006).

Index

Milton Keynes UK
Ingram Content Group UK Ltd.
UKHW020638140923
428670UK00014B/583